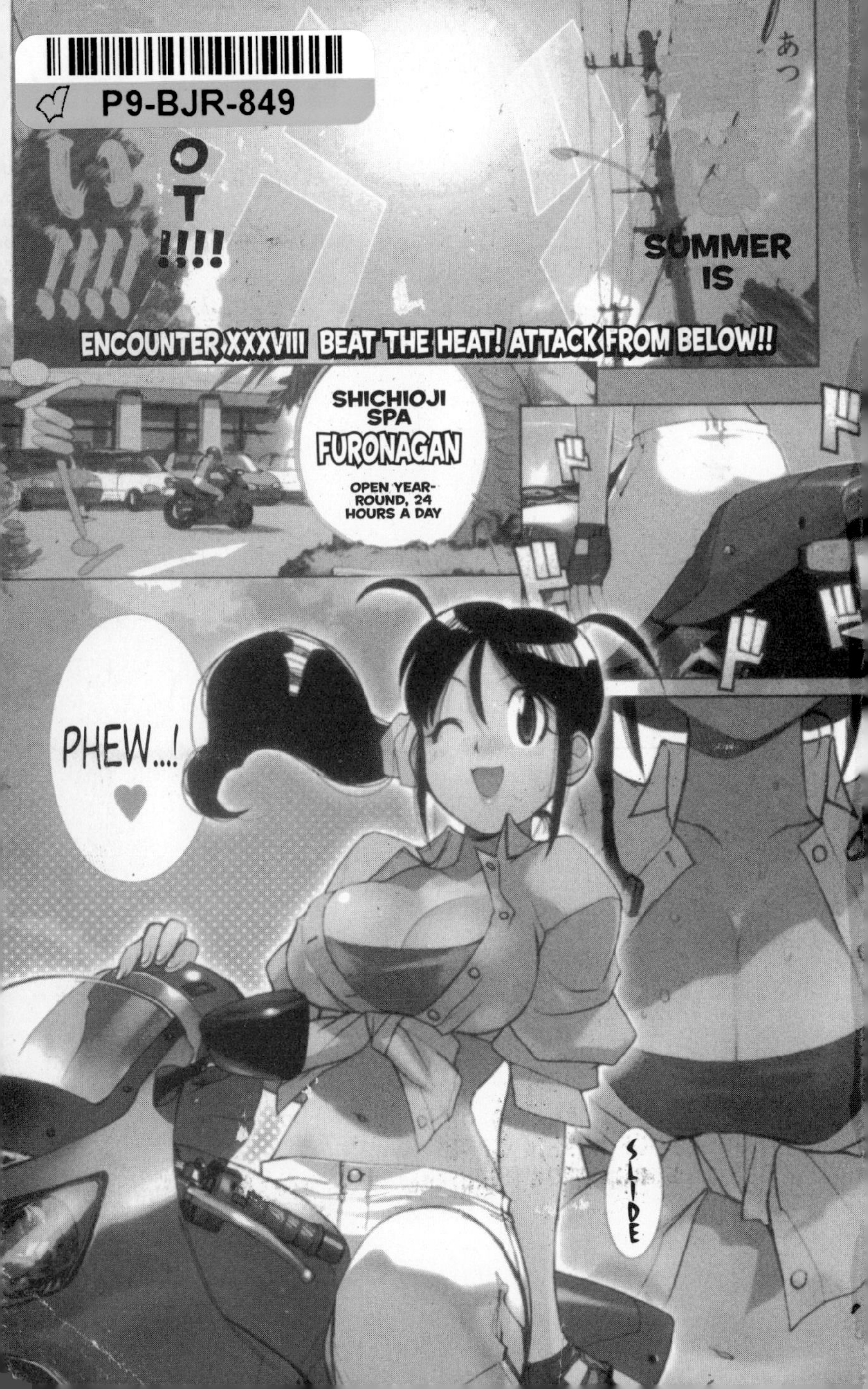

あっ
SUMMER IS
OT
!!!!
ENCOUNTER XXXVIII BEAT THE HEAT! ATTACK FROM BELOW!!
ド
ド
ド
ド
ド
SHICHIOJI SPA
FURONAGAN
OPEN YEAR-ROUND, 24 HOURS A DAY
SLIDE
PHEW...! ♥

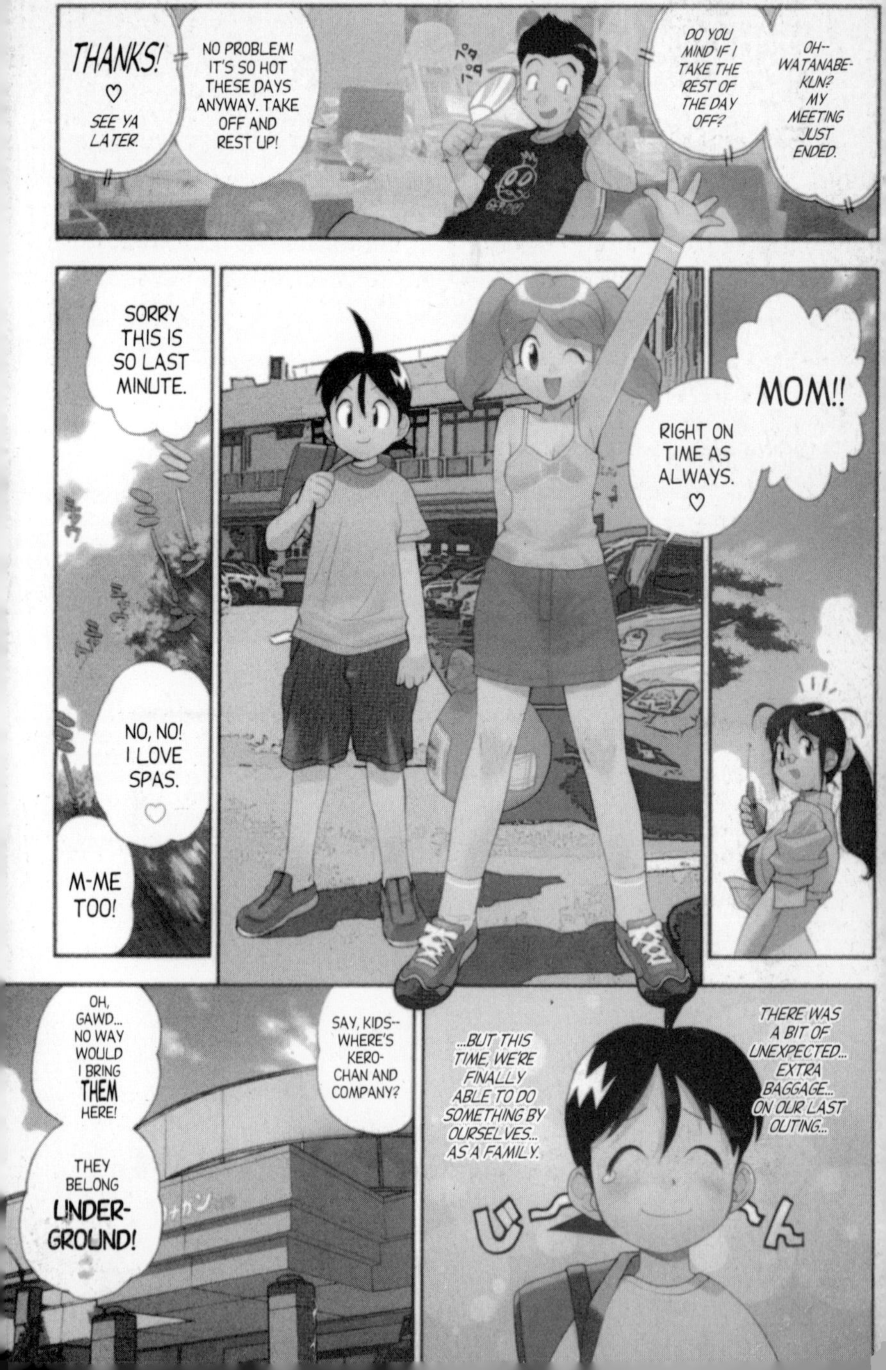
OH-- WATANABE-KUN? MY MEETING JUST ENDED.
DO YOU MIND IF I TAKE THE REST OF THE DAY OFF?
NO PROBLEM! IT'S SO HOT THESE DAYS ANYWAY. TAKE OFF AND REST UP!
THANKS! ♡ SEE YA LATER.
MOM!!
RIGHT ON TIME AS ALWAYS. ♡
SORRY THIS IS SO LAST MINUTE.
NO, NO! I LOVE SPAS. ♡
M-ME TOO!
THERE WAS A BIT OF UNEXPECTED... EXTRA BAGGAGE... ON OUR LAST OUTING...
...BUT THIS TIME, WE'RE FINALLY ABLE TO DO SOMETHING BY OURSELVES... AS A FAMILY.
SAY, KIDS-- WHERE'S KERO-CHAN AND COMPANY?
OH, GAWD... NO WAY WOULD I BRING THEM HERE!
THEY BELONG UNDER-GROUND!

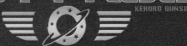

SGT FROG

KERORO GUNSOU

VOL # 5 BY MINE YOSHIZAKI

ENCOUNTER XXXVIII BEAT THE HEAT! ATTACK FROM BELOW!!

very venture in the midsummer.

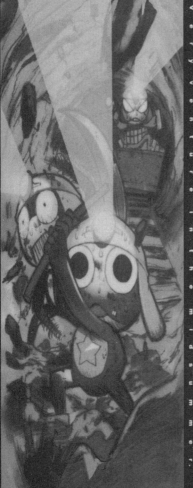

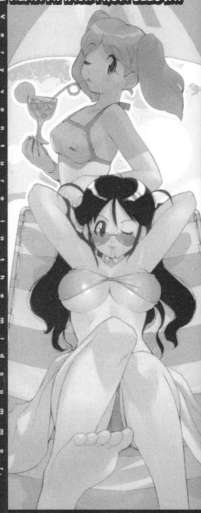

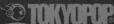

TOKYOPOP®

HAMBURG // LONDON // LOS ANGELES // TOKYO

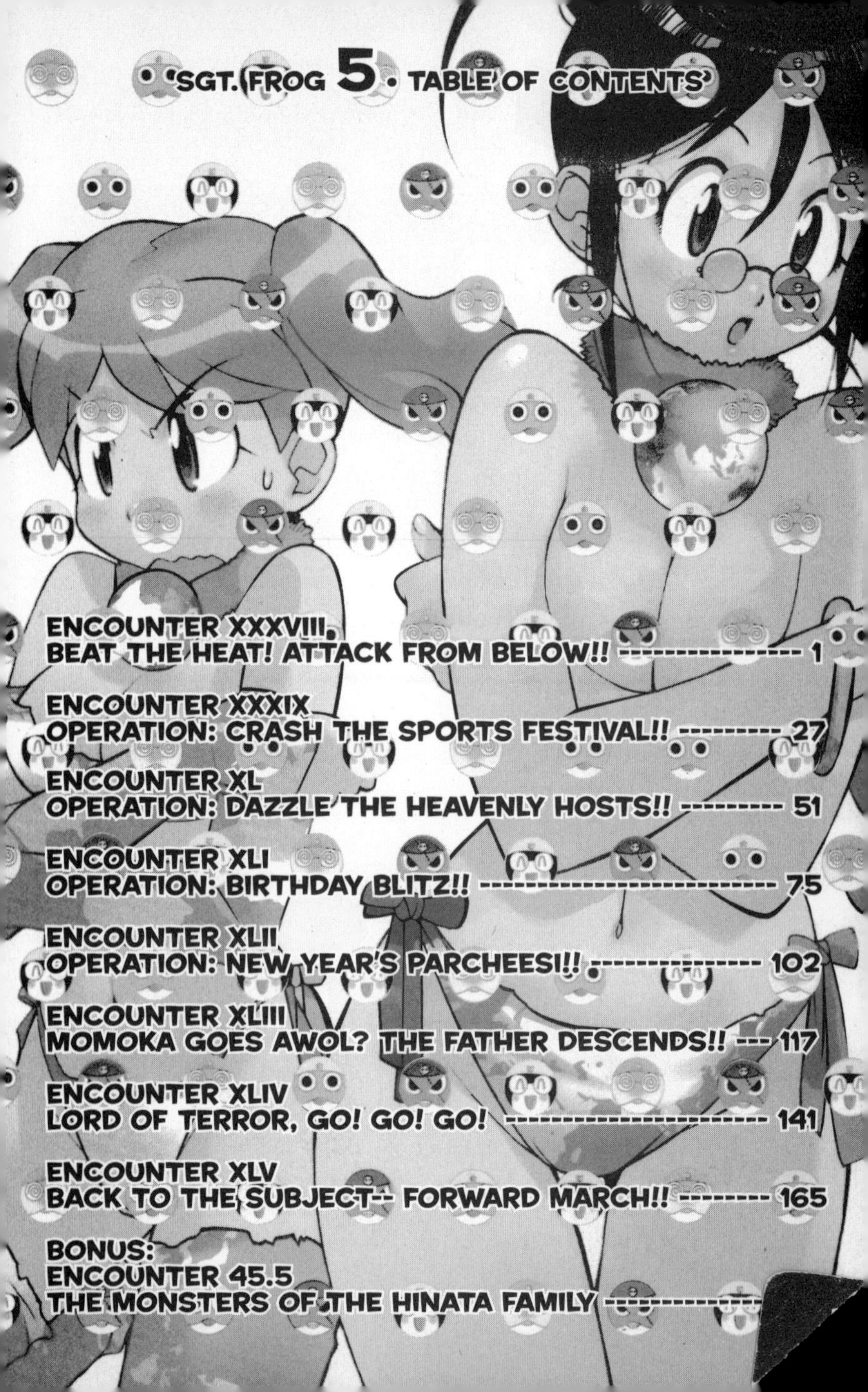

SGT. FROG 5 • TABLE OF CONTENTS

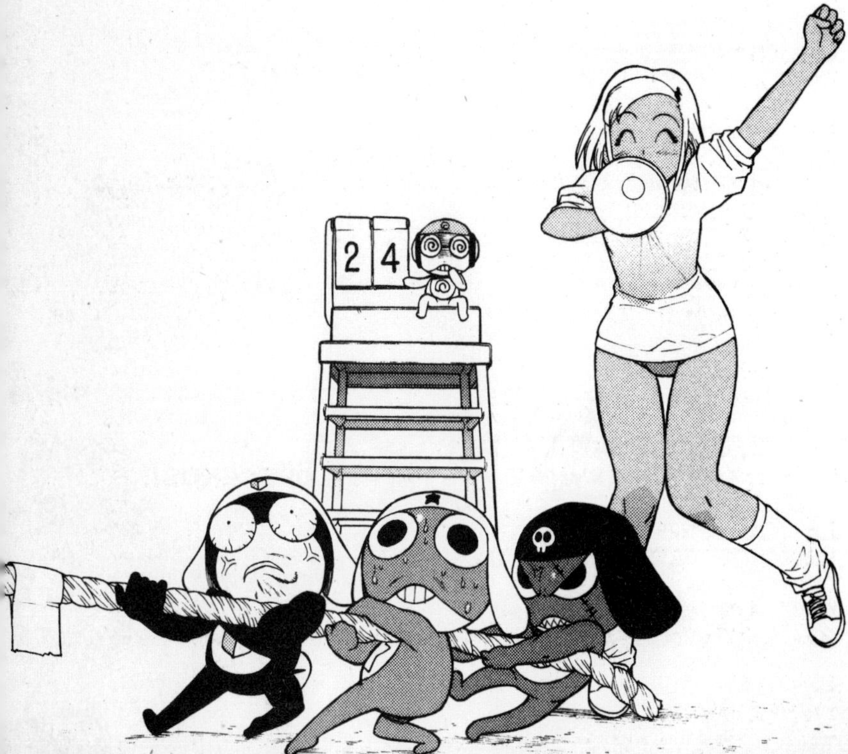
24

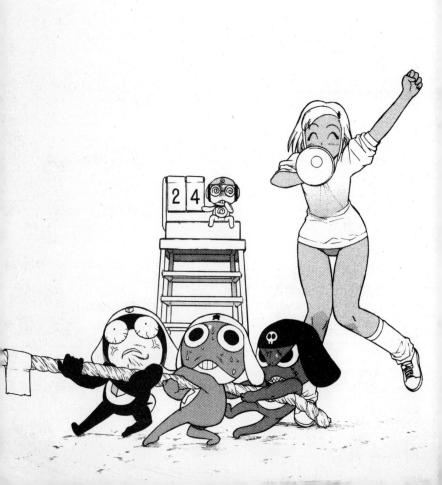

SGT FROG
KERORO GUNSOU

VOLUME #5
BY
MINE YOSHIZAKI

TOKYOPOP®

HAMBURG // LONDON // LOS ANGELES // TOKYO

SGT. Frog Vol. 5
Created by Mine Yoshizaki

Translation - Yuko Fukami
English Adaptation - Carol Fox
Copy Editor - Peter Ahlstrom
Retouch and Lettering - Jose Macasocol, Jr.
Production Artist - John Lo
Cover Design - Raymond Makowski

Editor - Paul Morrissey
Digital Imaging Manager - Chris Buford
Pre-Press Manager - Antonio DePietro
Production Managers - Jennifer Miller and Mutsumi Miyazaki
Art Director - Matt Alford
Managing Editor - Jill Freshney
VP of Production - Ron Klamert
President and C.O.O. - John Parker
Publisher and C.E.O. - Stuart Levy

A  Manga

TOKYOPOP Inc.
5900 Wilshire Blvd. Suite 2000
Los Angeles, CA 90036

E-mail: info@TOKYOPOP.com
Come visit us online at www.TOKYOPOP.com

ISBN: 1-59182-707-8

First TOKYOPOP printing: November 2004
10 9 8 7 6 5 4 3 2
Printed in the USA

SGT FROG

KERORO GUNSOU

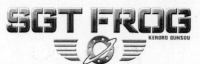

CHARACTER RELATIONSHIPS AND THE STORY SO FAR

(FACT-CHECKING PERFORMED BY SHONEN ACE MAGAZINE)

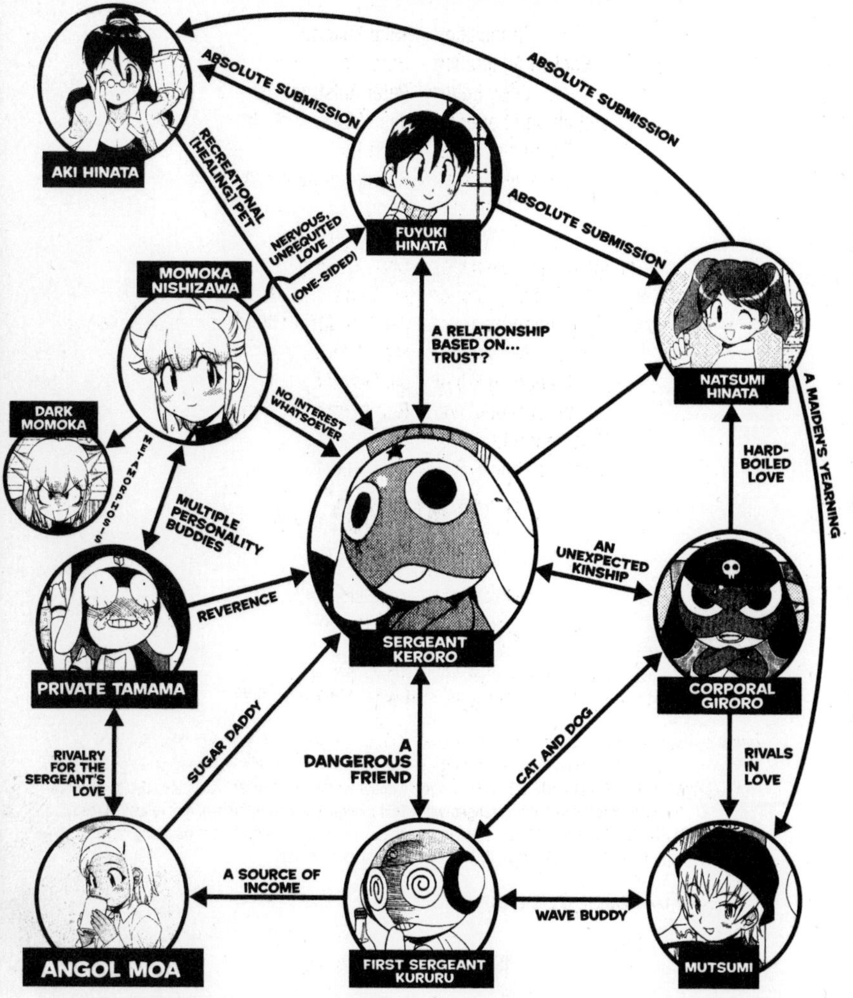

AKI HINATA
ABSOLUTE SUBMISSION
ABSOLUTE SUBMISSION
RECREATIONAL [HEALING] PET
FUYUKI HINATA
ABSOLUTE SUBMISSION
NERVOUS, UNREQUITED LOVE
(ONE-SIDED)
MOMOKA NISHIZAWA
A RELATIONSHIP BASED ON... TRUST?
NATSUMI HINATA
A MAIDEN'S YEARNING
DARK MOMOKA
METAMORPHOSIS
NO INTEREST WHATSOEVER
MULTIPLE PERSONALITY BUDDIES
HARD-BOILED LOVE
AN UNEXPECTED KINSHIP
REVERENCE
SERGEANT KERORO
PRIVATE TAMAMA
CORPORAL GIRORO
SUGAR DADDY
CAT AND DOG
RIVALRY FOR THE SERGEANT'S LOVE
A DANGEROUS FRIEND
RIVALS IN LOVE
A SOURCE OF INCOME
WAVE BUDDY
ANGOL MOA
FIRST SERGEANT KURURU
MUTSUMI

SERGEANT KERORO, CAPTAIN OF THE SPACE INVASION FORCE'S SPECIAL ADVANCE TEAM OF THE 58TH PLANET OF THE GAMMA STORM CLOUD SYSTEM, CAME TO THE HINATA HOUSEHOLD AS A PRE-ATTACK PREPARATION FOR THE INVASION OF EARTH... UNFORTUNATELY, HE WAS EASILY CAPTURED BY THE HINATA CHILDREN, FUYUKI AND NATSUMI. THANKS TO FUYUKI'S KINDNESS, OR AT LEAST HIS CURIOSITY, SGT. KERORO QUICKLY BECAME A BONA FIDE MEMBER OF THE HINATA FAMILY... IN OTHER WORDS, A TOTAL FREELOADER. THE SERGEANT'S SUBORDINATES--"DUAL PERSONALITY" PRIVATE TAMAMA; "BLAZING MILITARY MAN" CORPORATE GIRORO; THE "WAVISH" FIRST SERGEANT KURURU; AND THE MUCH-HERALDED "LORD OF TERROR," ANGOL MOA--SOON JOINED HIM TO REFORM THE KERORO PLATOON, WHICH DOES AS IT PLEASES IN A TOP-SECRET BASE BENEATH THE HINATA HOME. A LOT OF GUEST CHARACTERS APPEAR IN THIS VOLUME, TOO...

BUT HOW'S ABOUT THAT INVASION OF POKOPEN, GUYS?

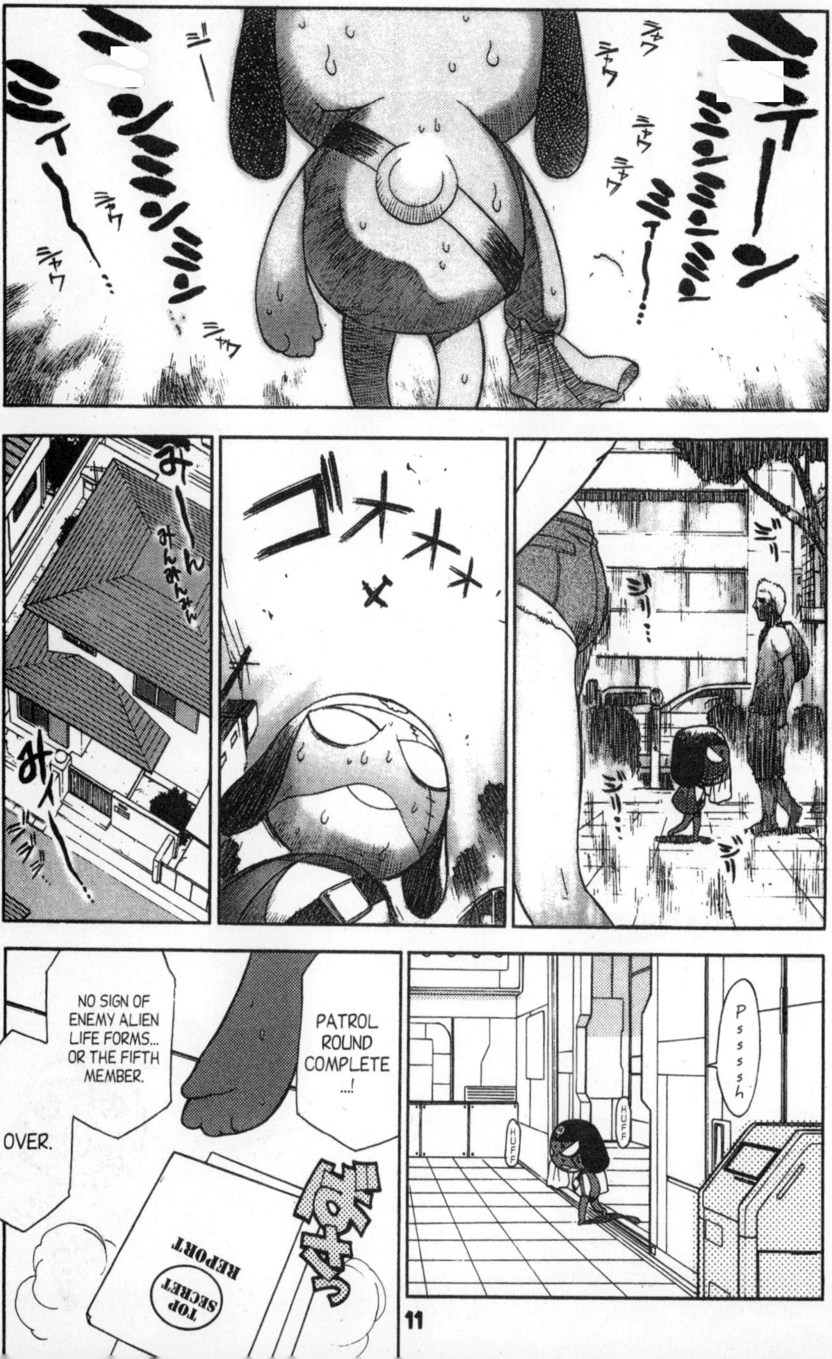
Psssssh
HUFF
HUFF
PATROL ROUND COMPLETE ...!
NO SIGN OF ENEMY ALIEN LIFE FORMS... OR THE FIFTH MEMBER.
OVER.
TOP SECRET REPORT

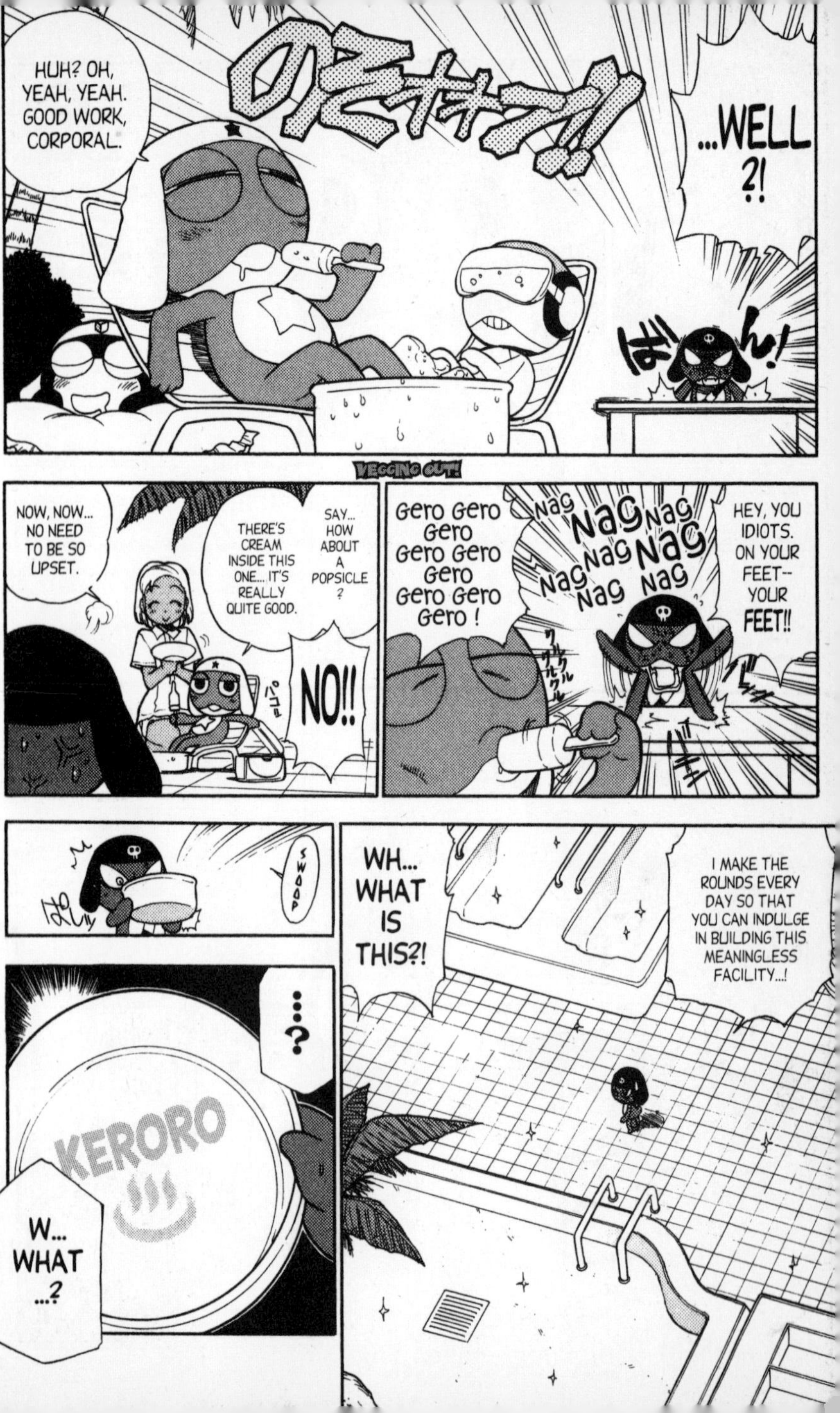
...WELL ?!
HUH? OH, YEAH, YEAH. GOOD WORK, CORPORAL.
VEGGING OUT!
HEY, YOU IDIOTS. ON YOUR FEET-- YOUR FEET!!
Nag Nag Nag Nag Nag Nag Nag Nag Nag
Gero Gero Gero Gero Gero Gero Gero Gero Gero!
NO!!
SAY... HOW ABOUT A POPSICLE?
THERE'S CREAM INSIDE THIS ONE... IT'S REALLY QUITE GOOD.
NOW, NOW... NO NEED TO BE SO UPSET.
I MAKE THE ROUNDS EVERY DAY SO THAT YOU CAN INDULGE IN BUILDING THIS MEANINGLESS FACILITY...!
WH... WHAT IS THIS?!
SWOOP
...?
KERORO
W... WHAT ...?

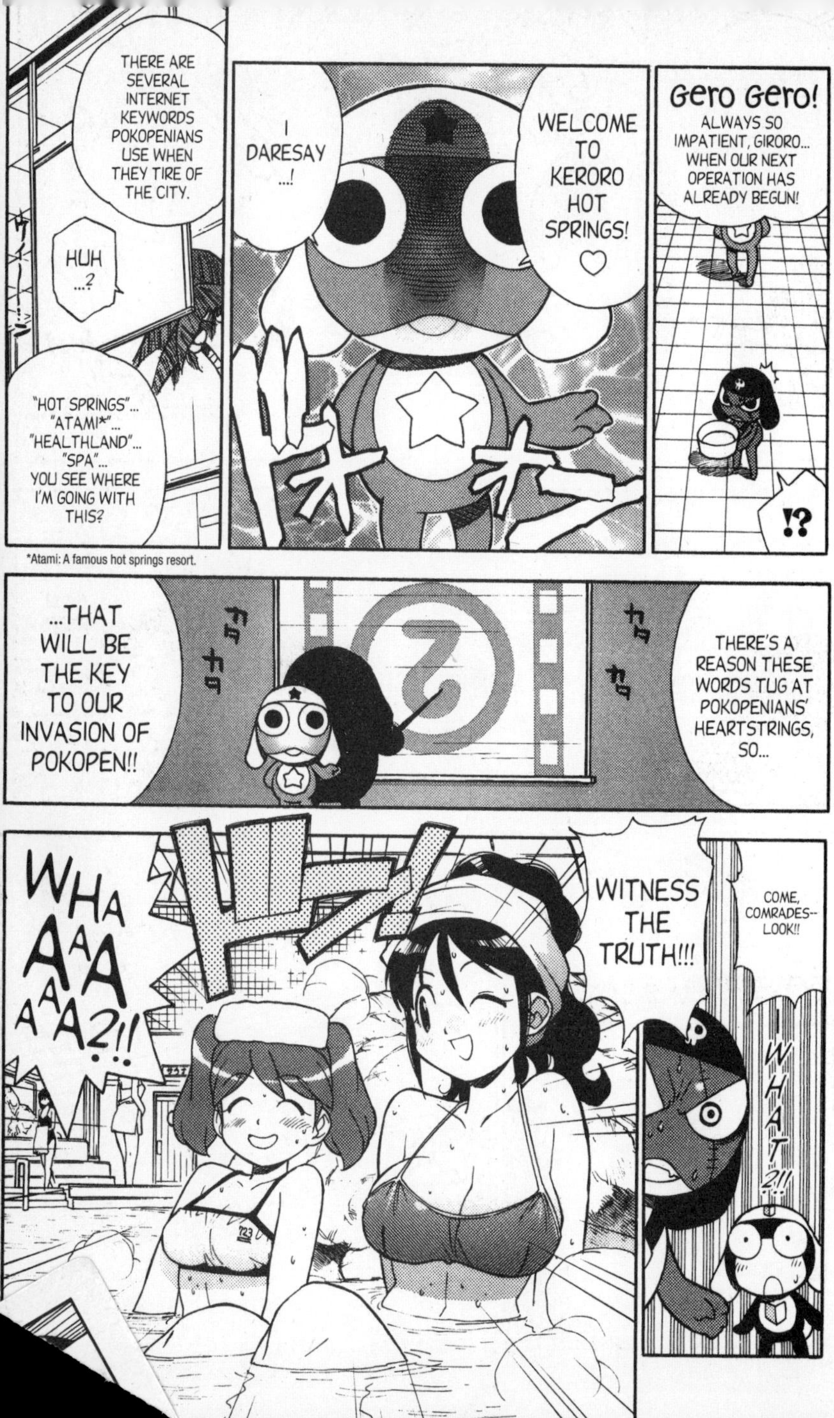
Gero Gero!
ALWAYS SO IMPATIENT, GIRORO... WHEN OUR NEXT OPERATION HAS ALREADY BEGUN!
!?
WELCOME TO KERORO HOT SPRINGS! ♡
I DARESAY ...!
THERE ARE SEVERAL INTERNET KEYWORDS POKOPENIANS USE WHEN THEY TIRE OF THE CITY.
HUH ...?
"HOT SPRINGS"... "ATAMI*"... "HEALTHLAND"... "SPA"... YOU SEE WHERE I'M GOING WITH THIS?
THERE'S A REASON THESE WORDS TUG AT POKOPENIANS' HEARTSTRINGS, SO...
...THAT WILL BE THE KEY TO OUR INVASION OF POKOPEN!!
COME, COMRADES--LOOK!!
WITNESS THE TRUTH!!!
WHAT?!!
WHAAAAAA?!!
*Atami: A famous hot springs resort.

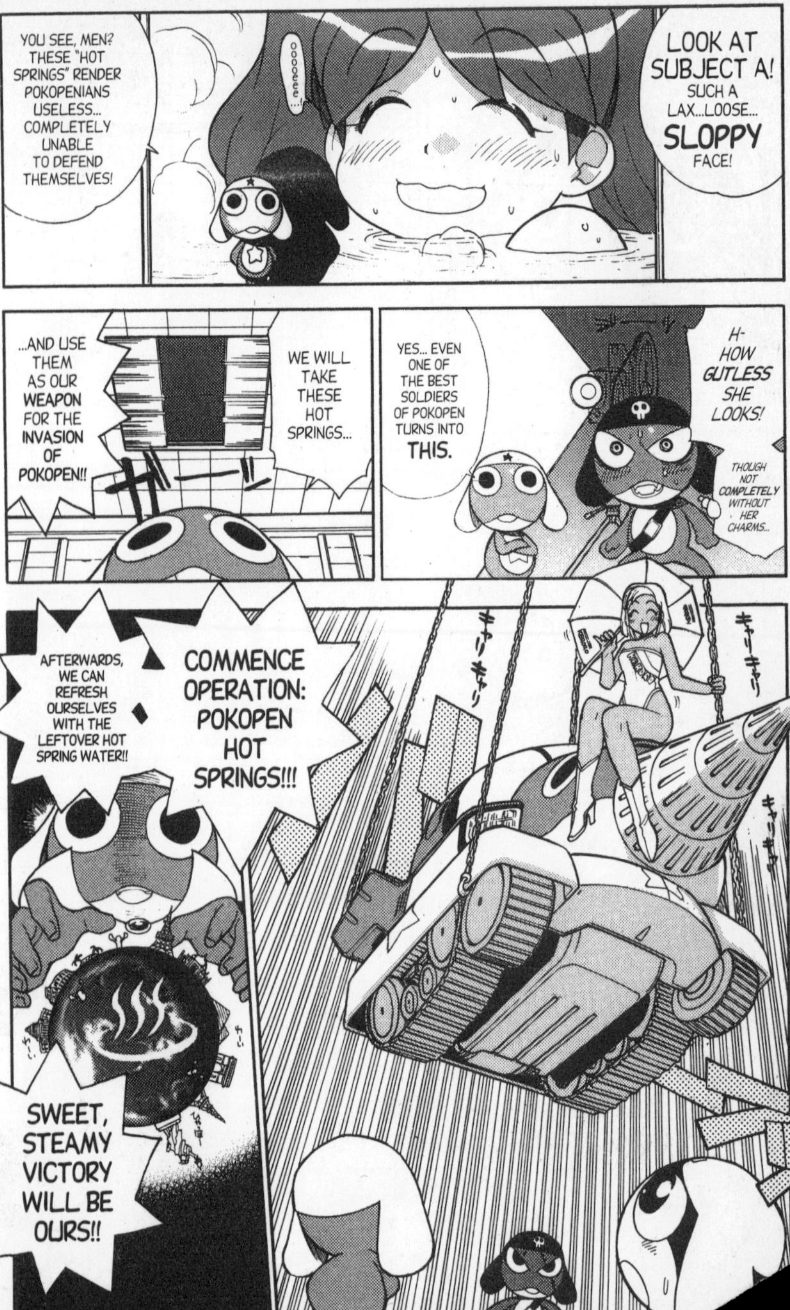
LOOK AT SUBJECT A! SUCH A LAX...LOOSE... SLOPPY FACE!
Oooooeee...!
YOU SEE, MEN? THESE "HOT SPRINGS" RENDER POKOPENIANS USELESS... COMPLETELY UNABLE TO DEFEND THEMSELVES!
H-HOW GUTLESS SHE LOOKS!
YES... EVEN ONE OF THE BEST SOLDIERS OF POKOPEN TURNS INTO THIS.
THOUGH NOT COMPLETELY WITHOUT HER CHARMS...
WE WILL TAKE THESE HOT SPRINGS...
...AND USE THEM AS OUR WEAPON FOR THE INVASION OF POKOPEN!!
COMMENCE OPERATION: POKOPEN HOT SPRINGS!!!
AFTERWARDS, WE CAN REFRESH OURSELVES WITH THE LEFTOVER HOT SPRING WATER!!
SWEET, STEAMY VICTORY WILL BE OURS!!

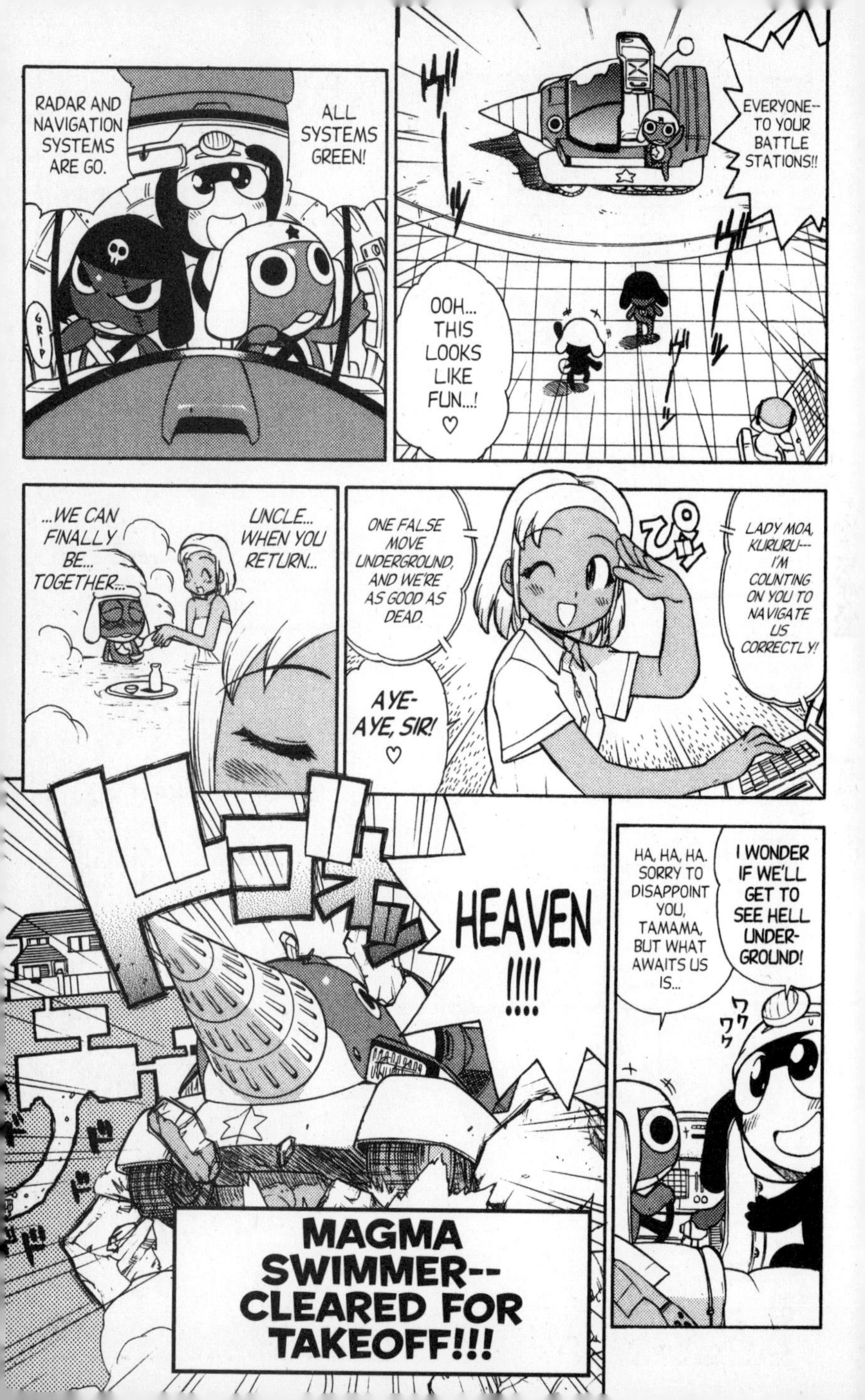
EVERYONE-- TO YOUR BATTLE STATIONS!!
OOH... THIS LOOKS LIKE FUN...! ♡
ALL SYSTEMS GREEN!
RADAR AND NAVIGATION SYSTEMS ARE GO.
GRIP
LADY MOA, KURURU--- I'M COUNTING ON YOU TO NAVIGATE US CORRECTLY!
ONE FALSE MOVE UNDERGROUND, AND WE'RE AS GOOD AS DEAD.
AYE-AYE, SIR! ♡
UNCLE... WHEN YOU RETURN...
...WE CAN FINALLY BE... TOGETHER...
I WONDER IF WE'LL GET TO SEE HELL UNDERGROUND!
HA, HA, HA. SORRY TO DISAPPOINT YOU, TAMAMA, BUT WHAT AWAITS US IS...
HEAVEN !!!!
MAGMA SWIMMER-- CLEARED FOR TAKEOFF!!!

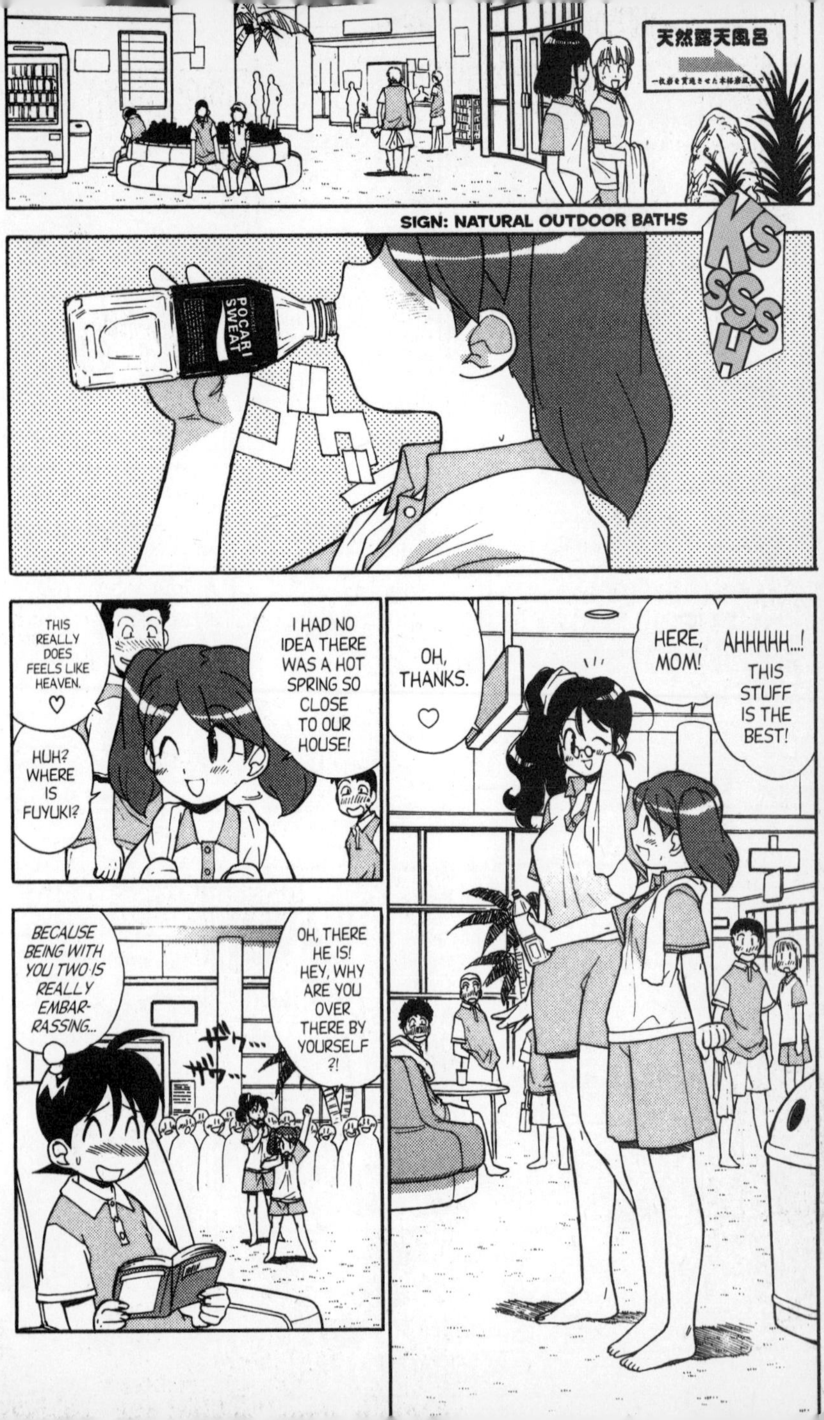
天然露天風呂
SIGN: NATURAL OUTDOOR BATHS
KSSSSH
POCARI SWEAT
HERE, MOM!
AHHHHH...! THIS STUFF IS THE BEST!
OH, THANKS. ♡
I HAD NO IDEA THERE WAS A HOT SPRING SO CLOSE TO OUR HOUSE!
THIS REALLY DOES FEELS LIKE HEAVEN. ♡
HUH? WHERE IS FUYUKI?
OH, THERE HE IS! HEY, WHY ARE YOU OVER THERE BY YOURSELF?!
ザワ…
ザワ…
BECAUSE BEING WITH YOU TWO IS REALLY EMBARRASSING...

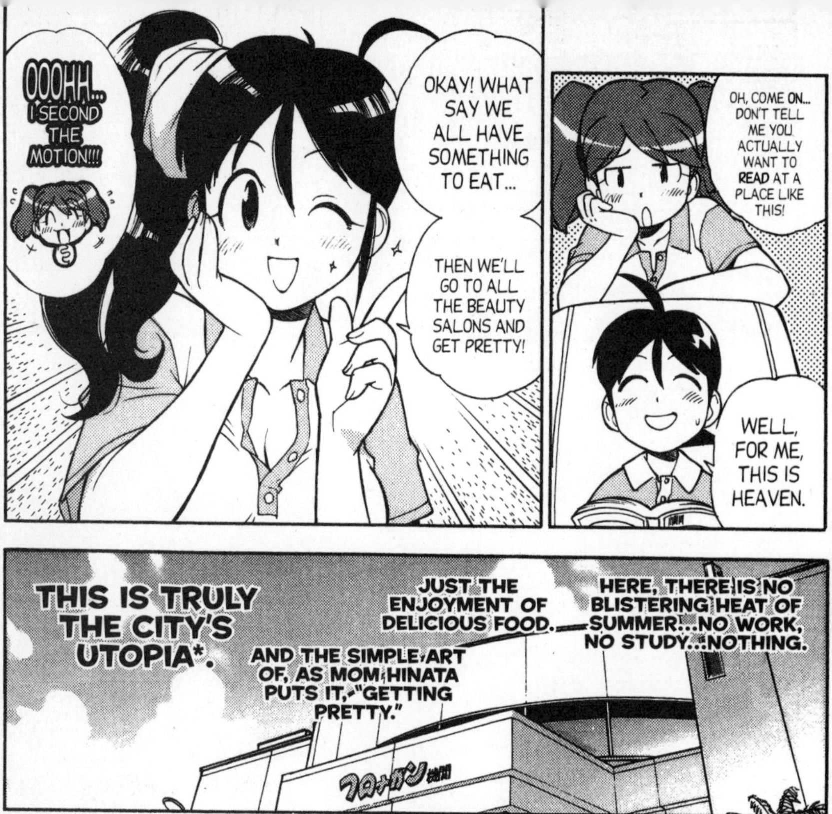
OH, COME ON... DON'T TELL ME YOU ACTUALLY WANT TO READ AT A PLACE LIKE THIS!
WELL, FOR ME, THIS IS HEAVEN.
OKAY! WHAT SAY WE ALL HAVE SOMETHING TO EAT...
THEN WE'LL GO TO ALL THE BEAUTY SALONS AND GET PRETTY!
OOOHH... I SECOND THE MOTION!!!
HERE, THERE IS NO BLISTERING HEAT OF SUMMER...NO WORK, NO STUDY...NOTHING.
JUST THE ENJOYMENT OF DELICIOUS FOOD.
AND THE SIMPLE ART OF, AS MOM HINATA PUTS IT, "GETTING PRETTY."
THIS IS TRULY THE CITY'S UTOPIA*.

*Pun in Japanese--the word "yu" means bath/hot water.

SIGN: FURONAGAN

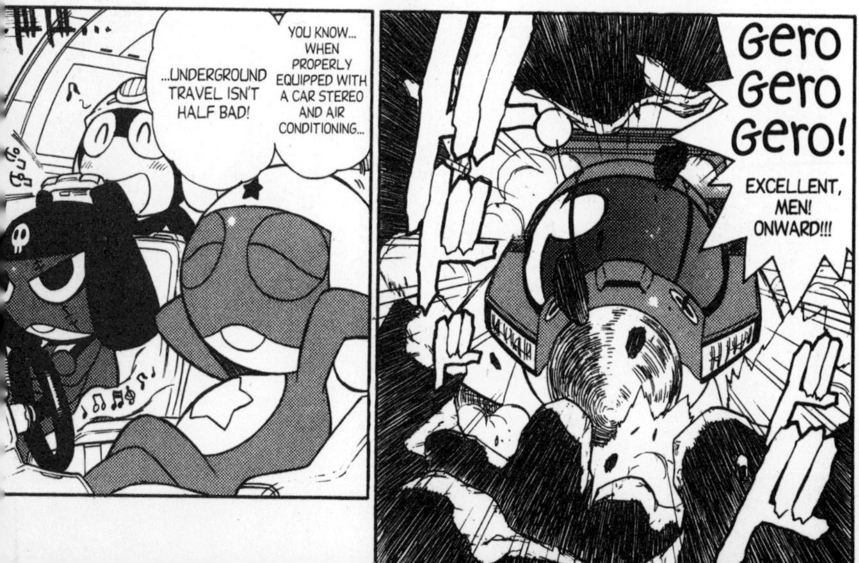
Gero Gero Gero!
EXCELLENT, MEN! ONWARD!!!
YOU KNOW... WHEN PROPERLY EQUIPPED WITH A CAR STEREO AND AIR CONDITIONING...
...UNDERGROUND TRAVEL ISN'T HALF BAD!

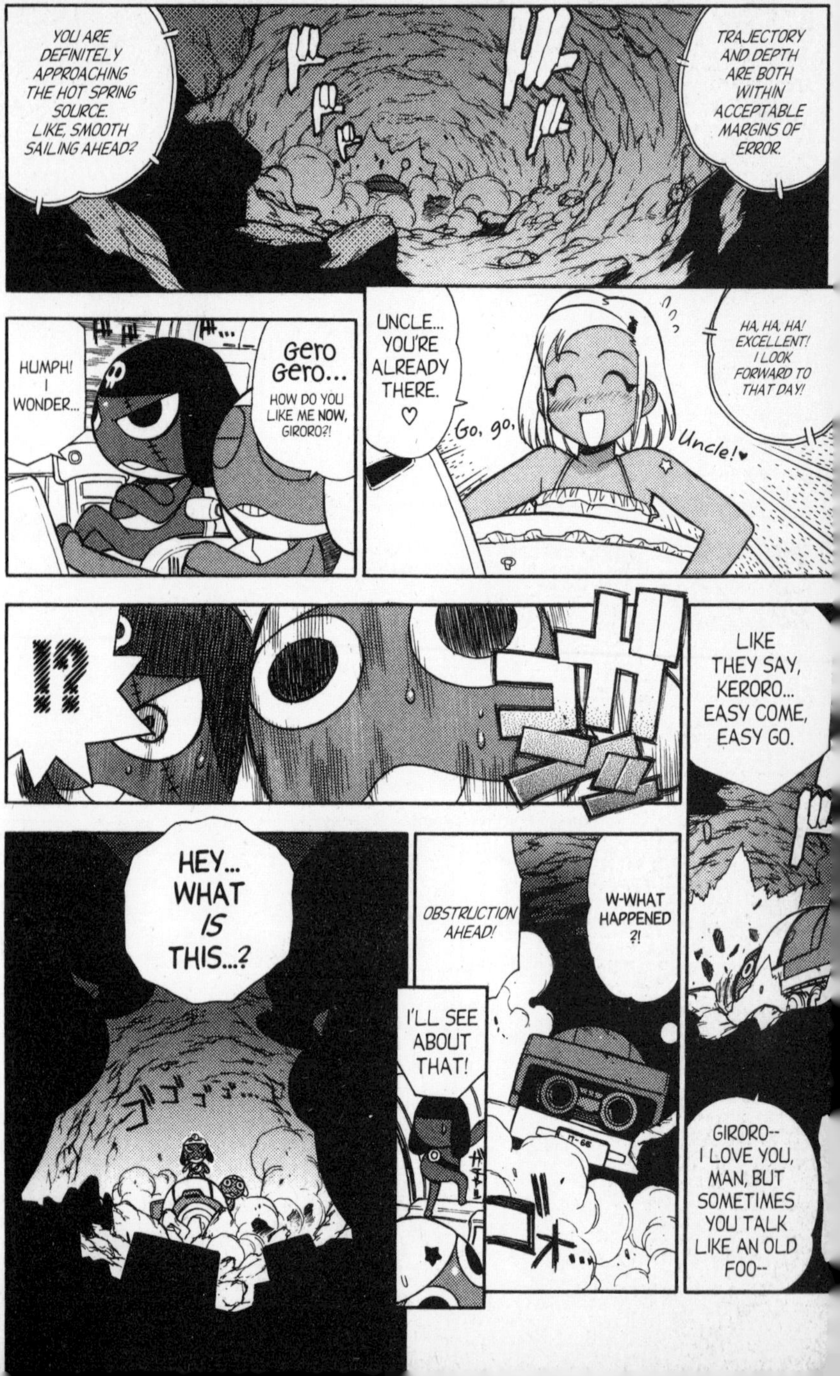
TRAJECTORY AND DEPTH ARE BOTH WITHIN ACCEPTABLE MARGINS OF ERROR.
YOU ARE DEFINITELY APPROACHING THE HOT SPRING SOURCE. LIKE, SMOOTH SAILING AHEAD?
HA, HA, HA! EXCELLENT! I LOOK FORWARD TO THAT DAY!
UNCLE... YOU'RE ALREADY THERE. ♡
Go, go, Uncle!♥
Gero Gero... HOW DO YOU LIKE ME NOW, GIRORO?!
HUMPH! I WONDER...
LIKE THEY SAY, KERORO... EASY COME, EASY GO.
GIRORO-- I LOVE YOU, MAN, BUT SOMETIMES YOU TALK LIKE AN OLD FOO--
!?
W-WHAT HAPPENED ?!
OBSTRUCTION AHEAD!
I'LL SEE ABOUT THAT!
HEY... WHAT IS THIS...?

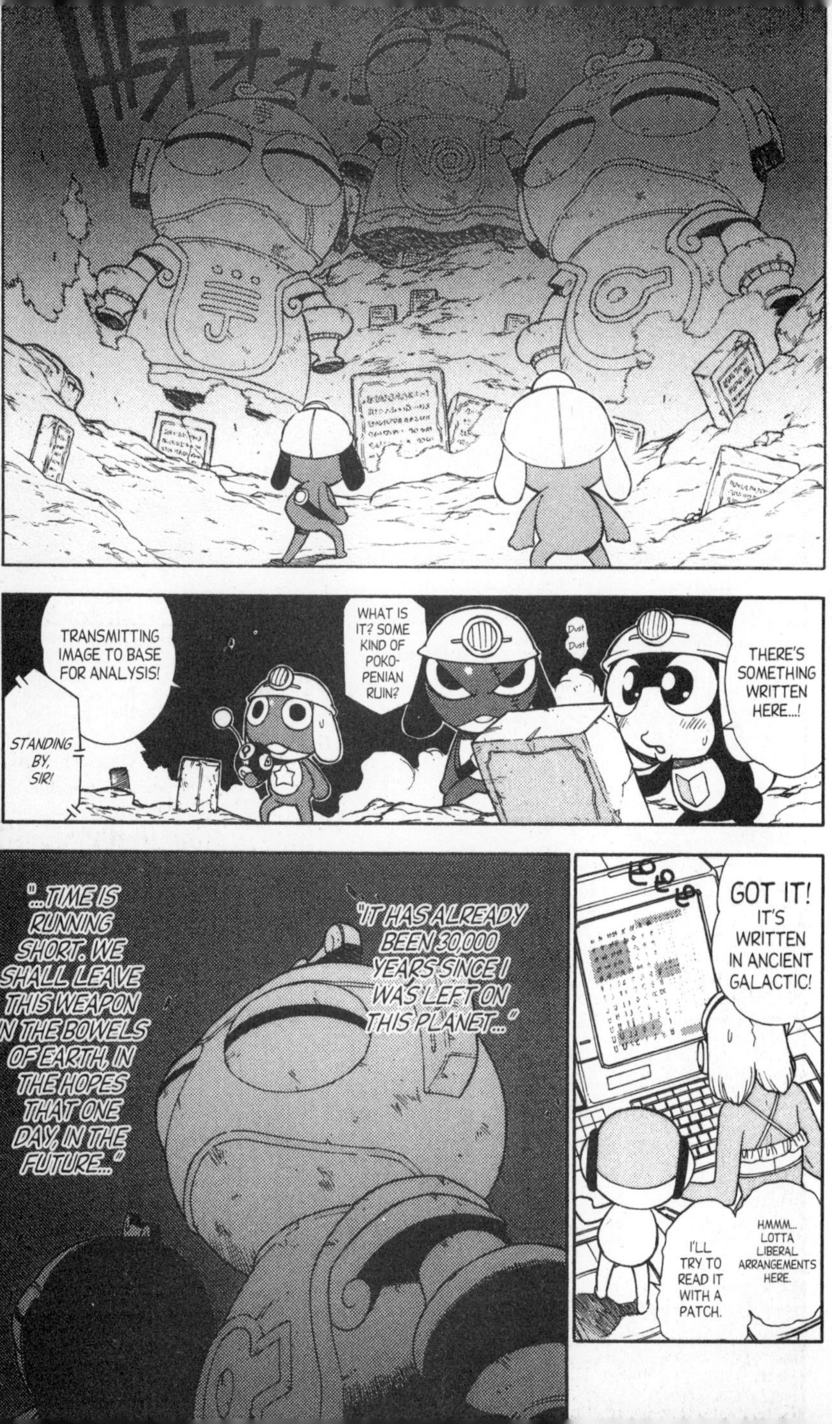
THERE'S SOMETHING WRITTEN HERE...!
Dust
Dust
WHAT IS IT? SOME KIND OF POKO-PENIAN RUIN?
TRANSMITTING IMAGE TO BASE FOR ANALYSIS!
STANDING BY, SIR!
GOT IT! IT'S WRITTEN IN ANCIENT GALACTIC!
HMMM... LOTTA LIBERAL ARRANGEMENTS HERE.
I'LL TRY TO READ IT WITH A PATCH.
"IT HAS ALREADY BEEN 30,000 YEARS SINCE I WAS LEFT ON THIS PLANET..."
"...TIME IS RUNNING SHORT. WE SHALL LEAVE THIS WEAPON IN THE BOWELS OF EARTH, IN THE HOPES THAT ONE DAY, IN THE FUTURE..."

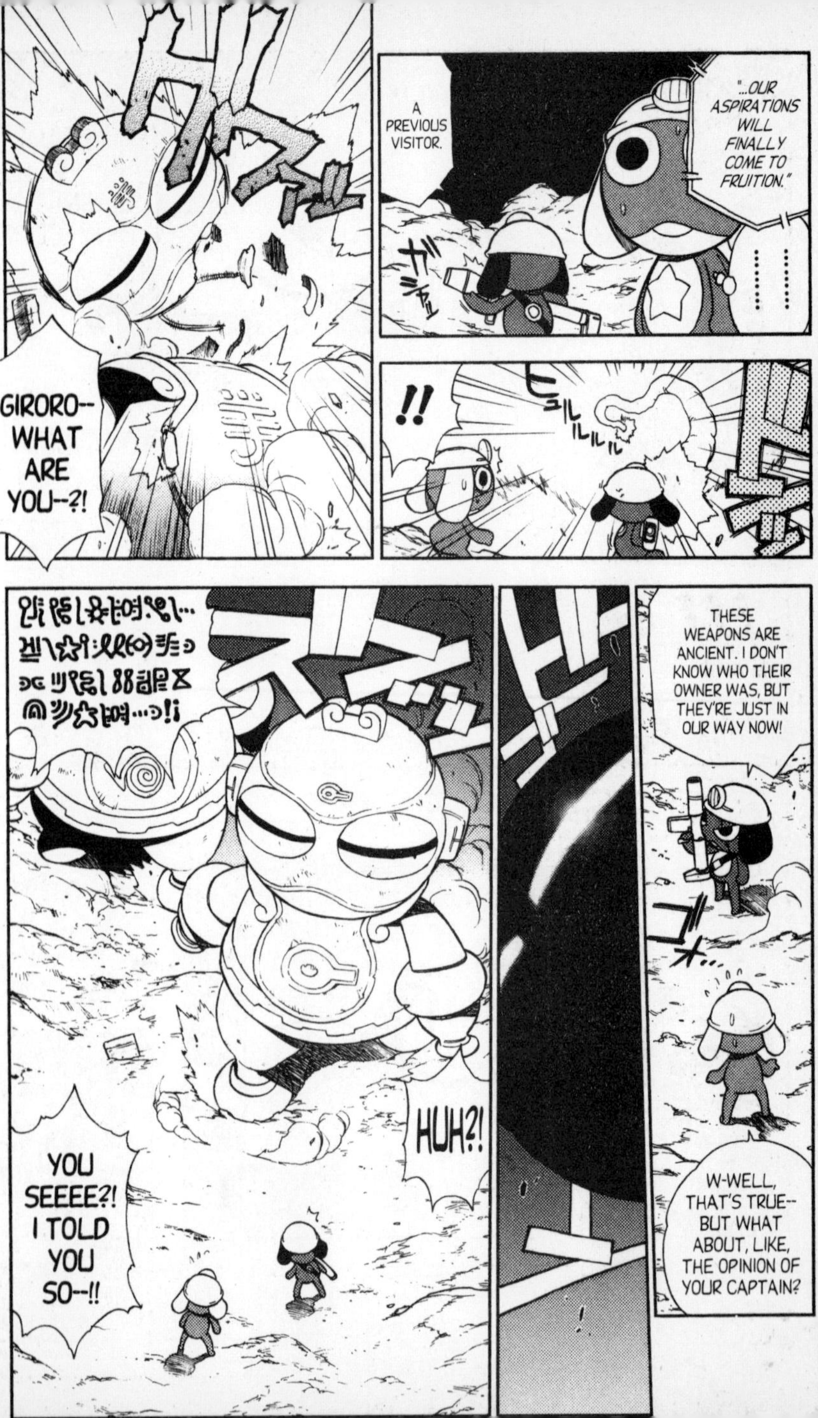
"...OUR ASPIRATIONS WILL FINALLY COME TO FRUITION."
......
A PREVIOUS VISITOR.
!!
GIRORO-- WHAT ARE YOU--?!
THESE WEAPONS ARE ANCIENT. I DON'T KNOW WHO THEIR OWNER WAS, BUT THEY'RE JUST IN OUR WAY NOW!
W-WELL, THAT'S TRUE-- BUT WHAT ABOUT, LIKE, THE OPINION OF YOUR CAPTAIN?
HUH?!
YOU SEEEE?! I TOLD YOU SO--!!

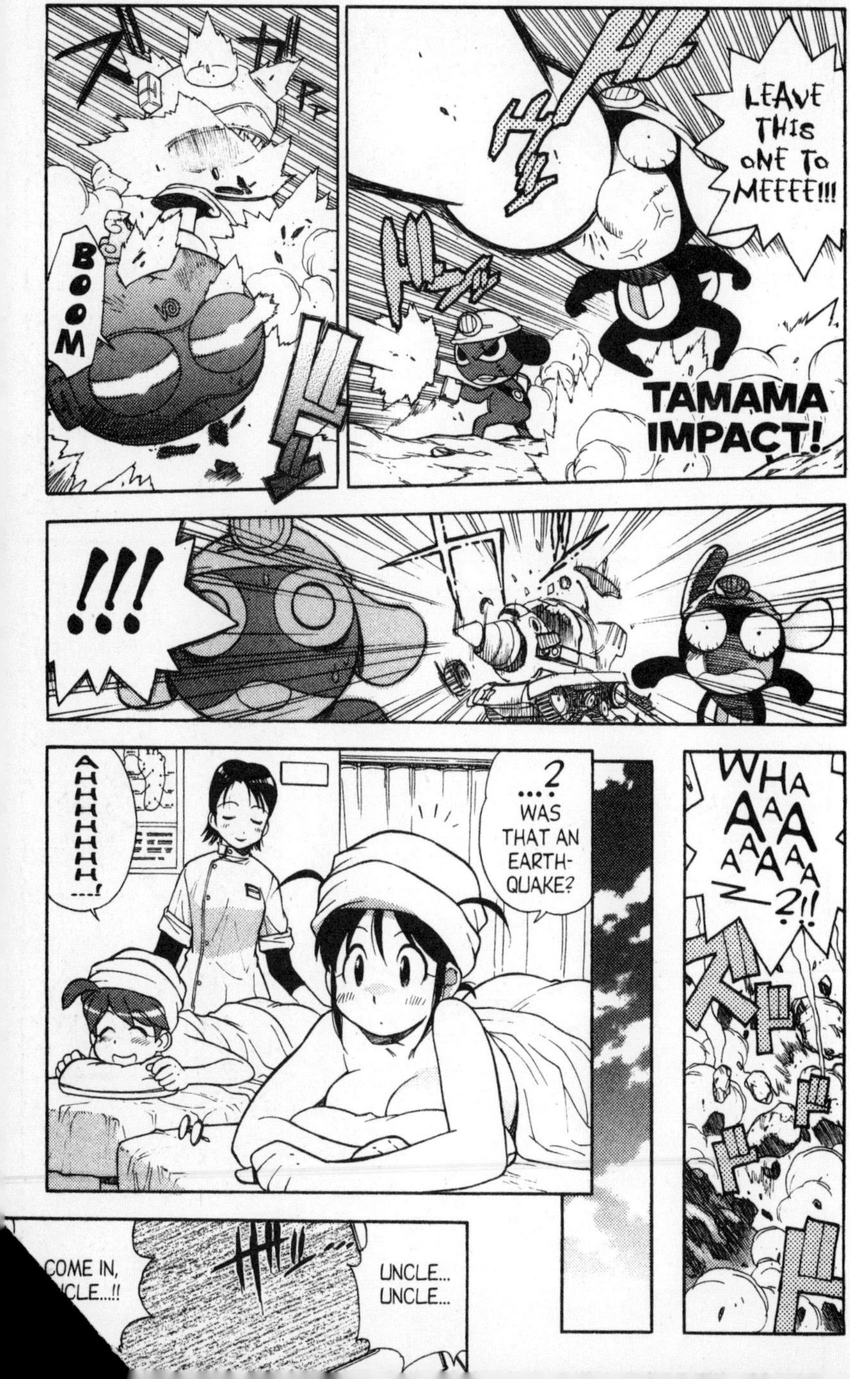
LEAVE THIS ONE TO MEEEE!!!
TAMAMA IMPACT!
BOOM
!!!
WHAAAAAAAAAZ?!!
...? WAS THAT AN EARTH-QUAKE?
AHHHHHHH...!
UNCLE... UNCLE...
COME IN, NCLE...!!

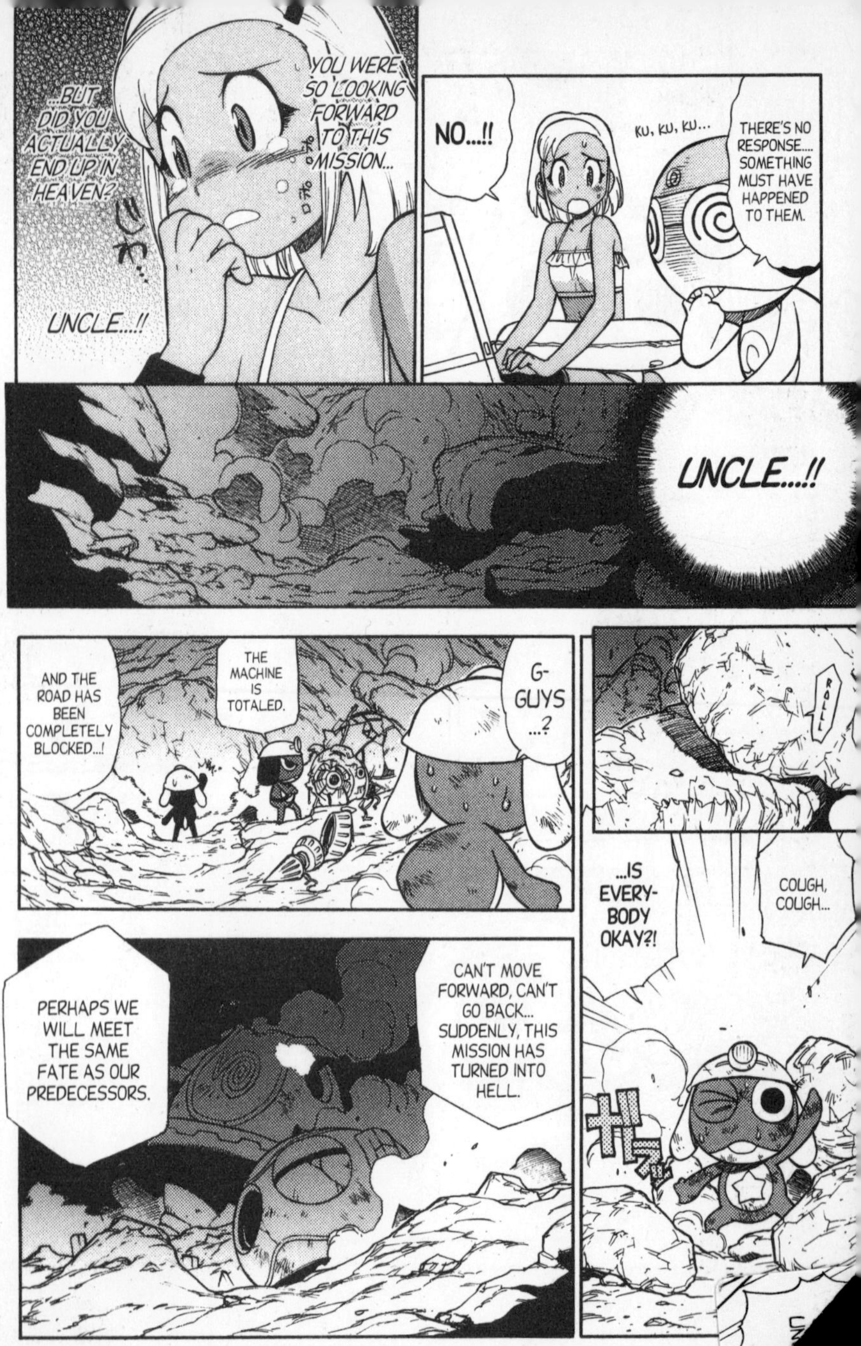
THERE'S NO RESPONSE.... SOMETHING MUST HAVE HAPPENED TO THEM.
KU, KU, KU...
NO...!!
YOU WERE SO LOOKING FORWARD TO THIS MISSION...
...BUT DID YOU ACTUALLY END UP IN HEAVEN?
UNCLE...!!
UNCLE...!!
ROLL
COUGH, COUGH...
...IS EVERY-BODY OKAY?!
G-GUYS ...?
THE MACHINE IS TOTALED.
AND THE ROAD HAS BEEN COMPLETELY BLOCKED...!
CAN'T MOVE FORWARD, CAN'T GO BACK... SUDDENLY, THIS MISSION HAS TURNED INTO HELL.
PERHAPS WE WILL MEET THE SAME FATE AS OUR PREDECESSORS.

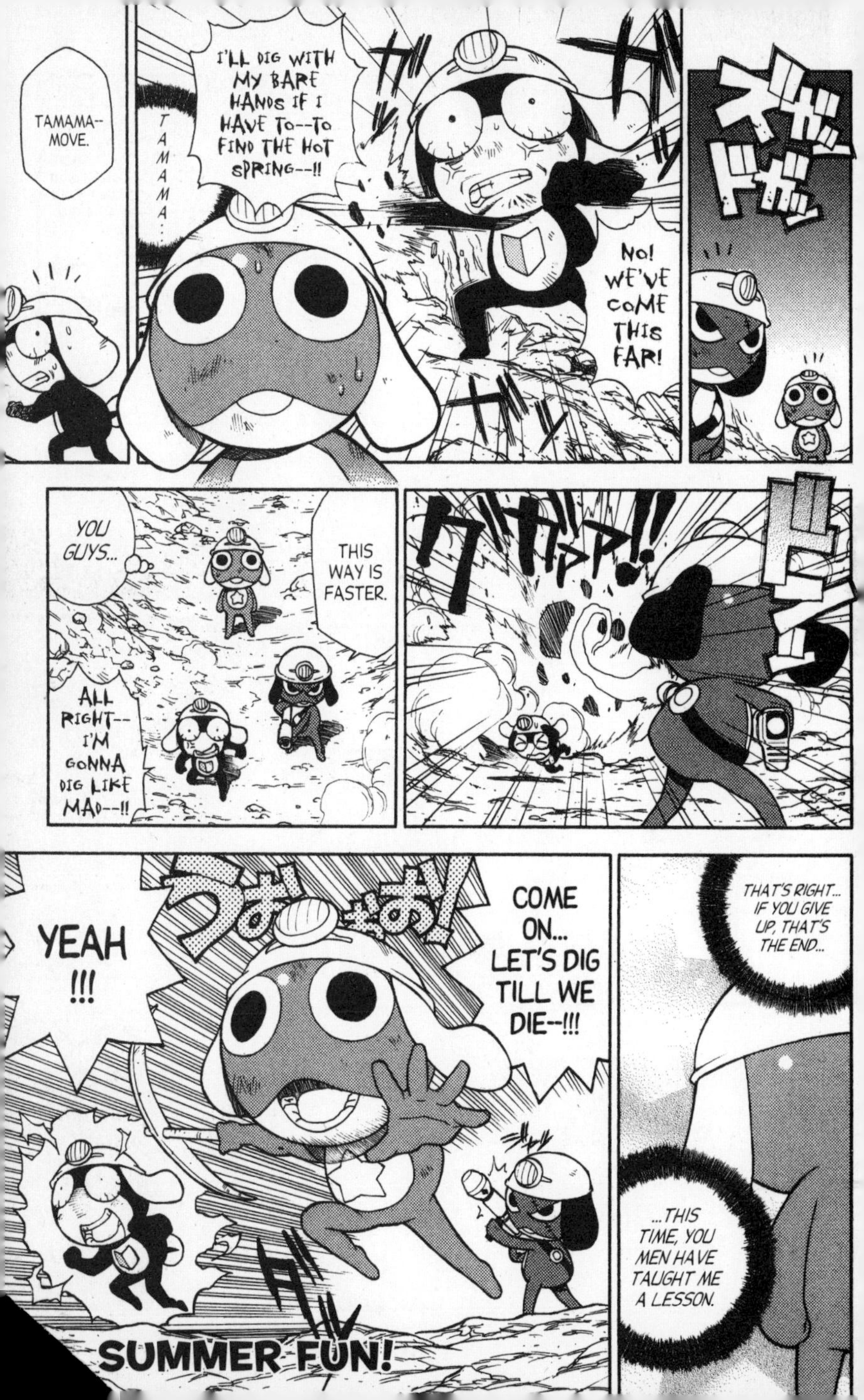
I'LL DIG WITH MY BARE HANDS IF I HAVE TO--TO FIND THE HOT SPRING--!!
No! WE'VE COME THIS FAR!
TAMAMA...
TAMAMA--MOVE.
KAPPP!!
THIS WAY IS FASTER.
YOU GUYS...
ALL RIGHT--I'M GONNA DIG LIKE MAD--!!
THAT'S RIGHT... IF YOU GIVE UP, THAT'S THE END...
...THIS TIME, YOU MEN HAVE TAUGHT ME A LESSON.
COME ON... LET'S DIG TILL WE DIE--!!!
YEAH !!!
SUMMER FUN!

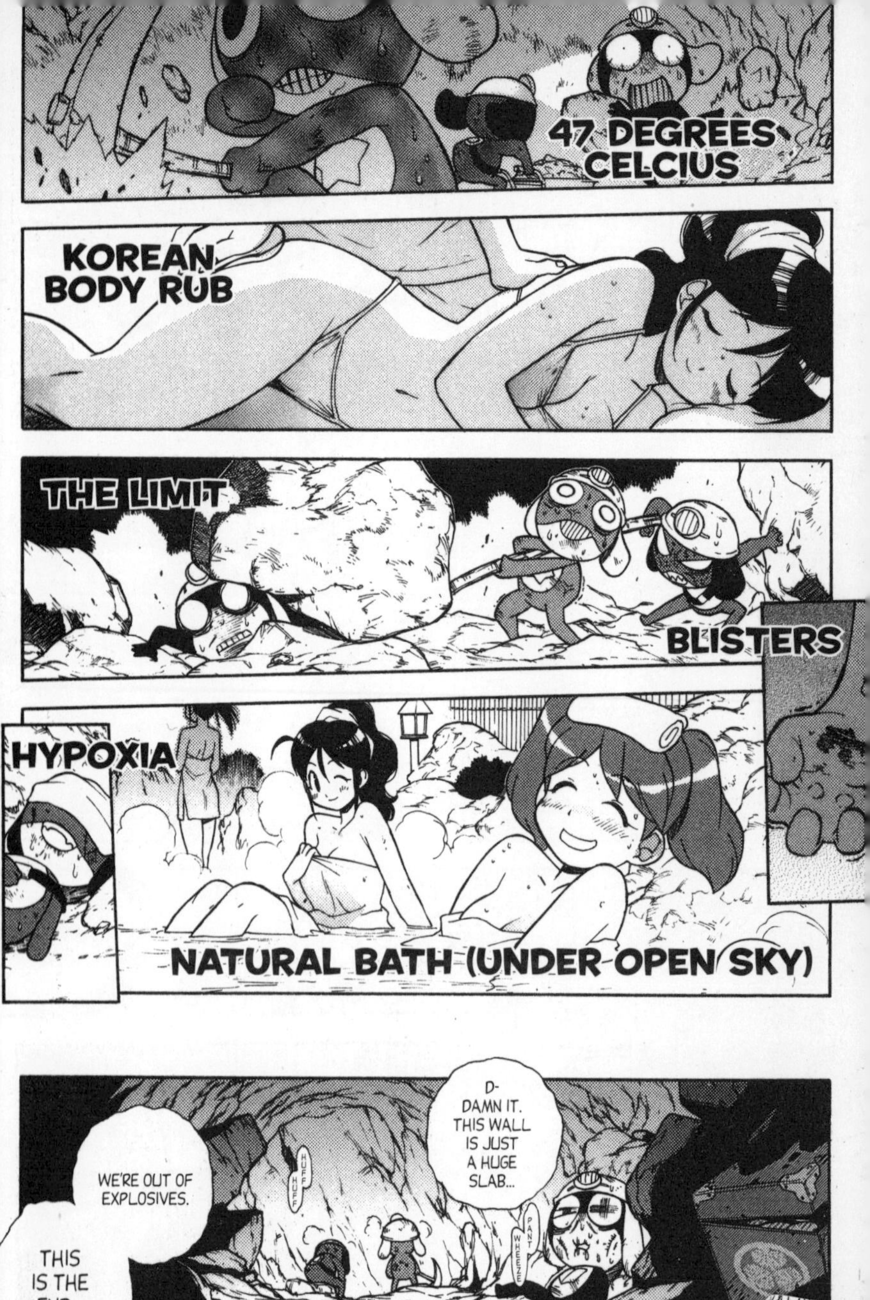

47 DEGREES CELCIUS
KOREAN BODY RUB
BLISTERS
THE LIMIT
NATURAL BATH (UNDER OPEN SKY)
HYPOXIA
D- DAMN IT. THIS WALL IS JUST A HUGE SLAB...
PANT WHEEZE
HUFF HUFF
WE'RE OUT OF EXPLOSIVES.
THIS IS THE END...

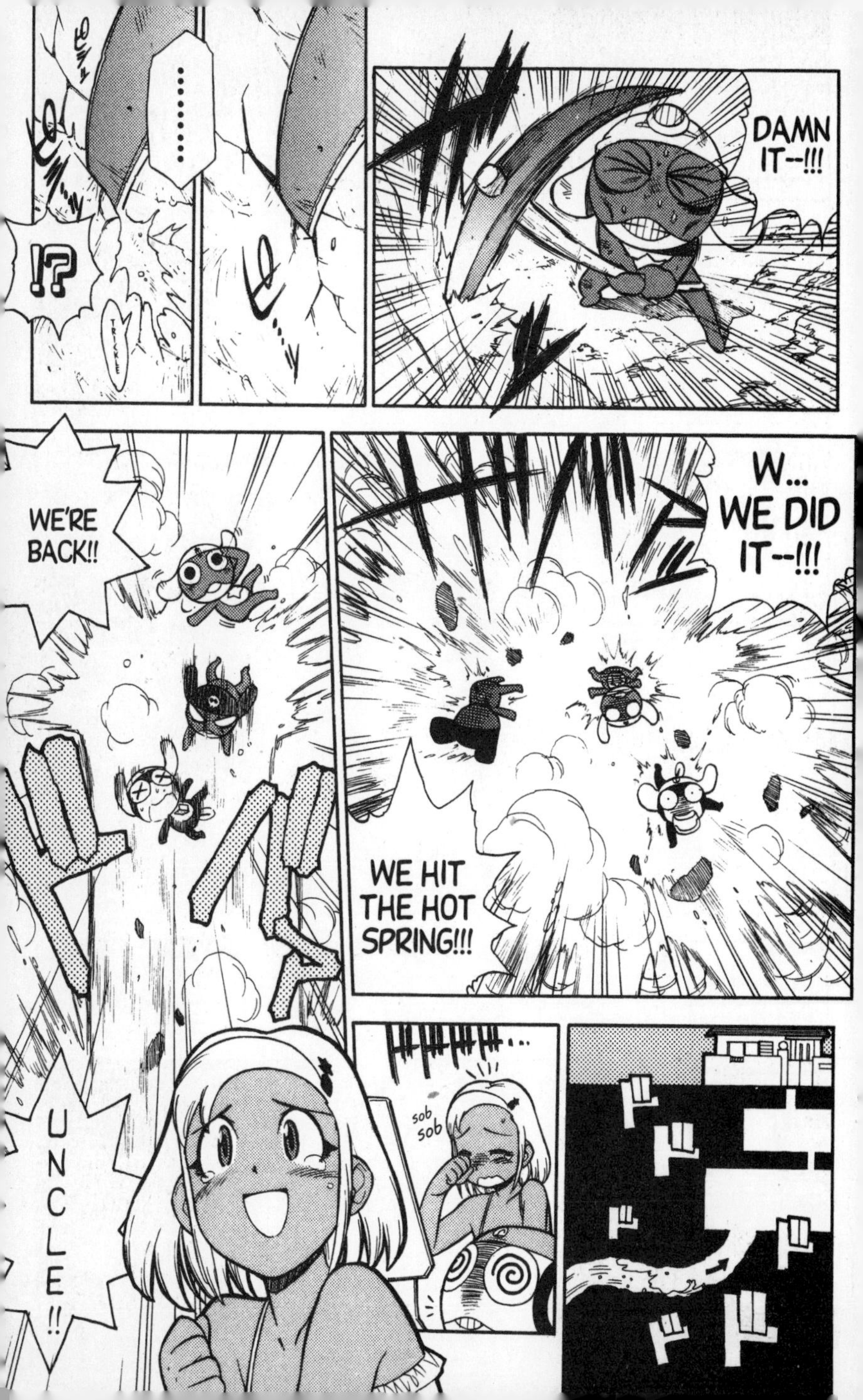
DAMN IT--!!!
......
!?
TRICKLE
W... WE DID IT--!!!
WE HIT THE HOT SPRING!!!
WE'RE BACK!!
sob sob
UNCLE!!

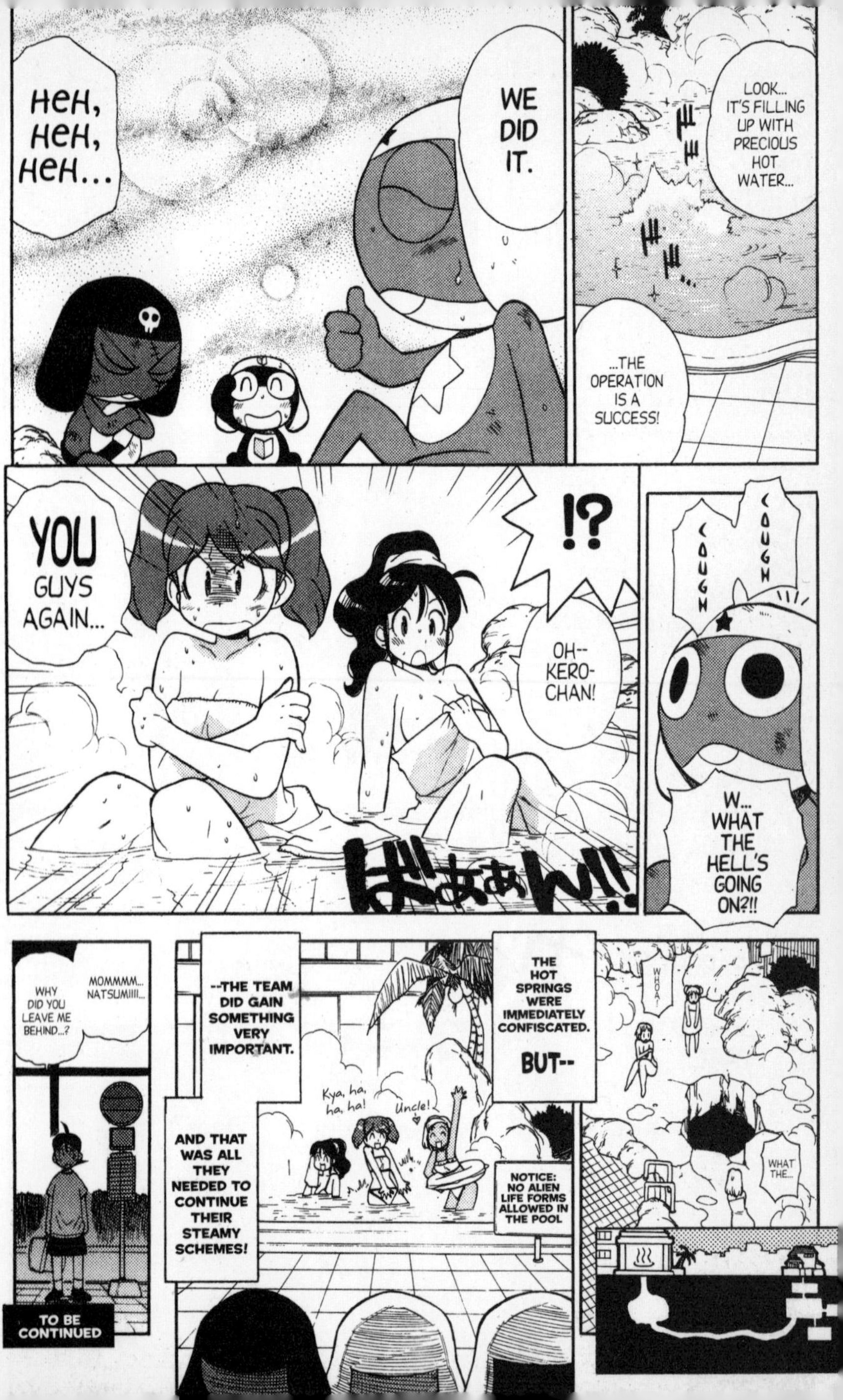
LOOK... IT'S FILLING UP WITH PRECIOUS HOT WATER...
...THE OPERATION IS A SUCCESS!
WE DID IT.
HEH, HEH, HEH...
COUGH
COUGH
W... WHAT THE HELL'S GOING ON?!!
!?
OH-- KERO-CHAN!
YOU GUYS AGAIN...
ばぁあん!!
WHOA!
WHAT THE...
THE HOT SPRINGS WERE IMMEDIATELY CONFISCATED.
BUT--
--THE TEAM DID GAIN SOMETHING VERY IMPORTANT.
Uncle!
Kya, ha, ha, ha!
NOTICE: NO ALIEN LIFE FORMS ALLOWED IN THE POOL
AND THAT WAS ALL THEY NEEDED TO CONTINUE THEIR STEAMY SCHEMES!
MOMMMM... NATSUMIIII...
WHY DID YOU LEAVE ME BEHIND...?
TO BE CONTINUED

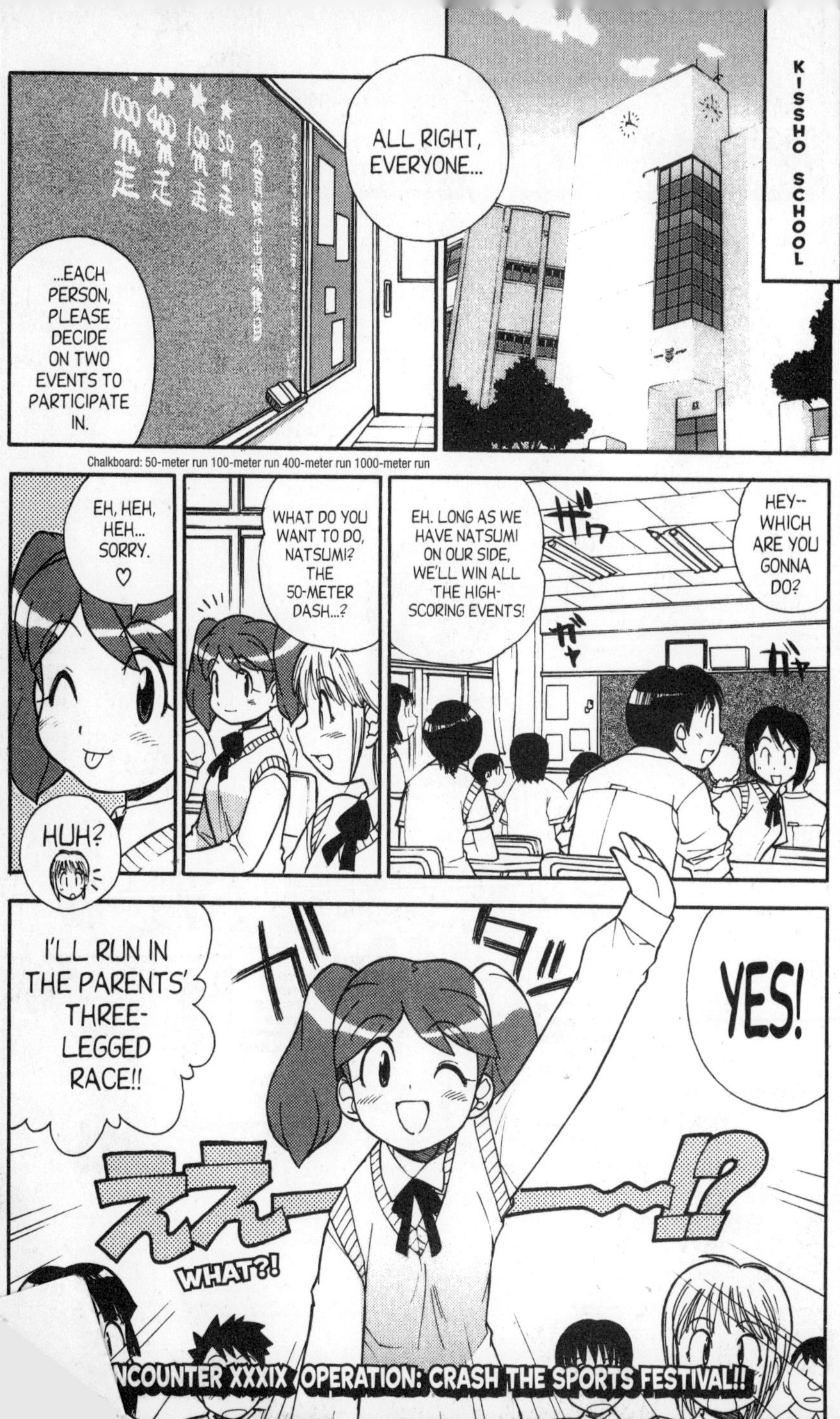
KISSHO SCHOOL
ALL RIGHT, EVERYONE...
...EACH PERSON, PLEASE DECIDE ON TWO EVENTS TO PARTICIPATE IN.
Chalkboard: 50-meter run 100-meter run 400-meter run 1000-meter run
HEY-- WHICH ARE YOU GONNA DO?
EH. LONG AS WE HAVE NATSUMI ON OUR SIDE, WE'LL WIN ALL THE HIGH-SCORING EVENTS!
WHAT DO YOU WANT TO DO, NATSUMI? THE 50-METER DASH...?
EH, HEH, HEH... SORRY. ♡
HUH?
YES!
I'LL RUN IN THE PARENTS' THREE-LEGGED RACE!!
WHAT?!
NCOUNTER XXXIX OPERATION: CRASH THE SPORTS FESTIVAL!!

ENCOUNTER XXXIX
OPERATION: CRASH THE SPORTS FESTIVAL!!

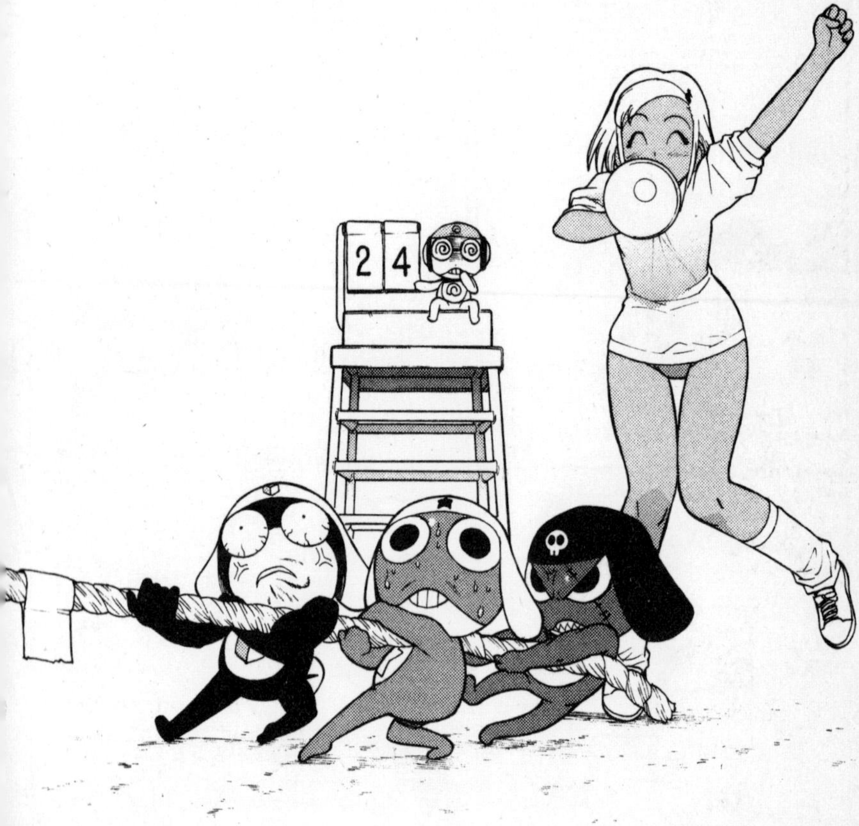
24

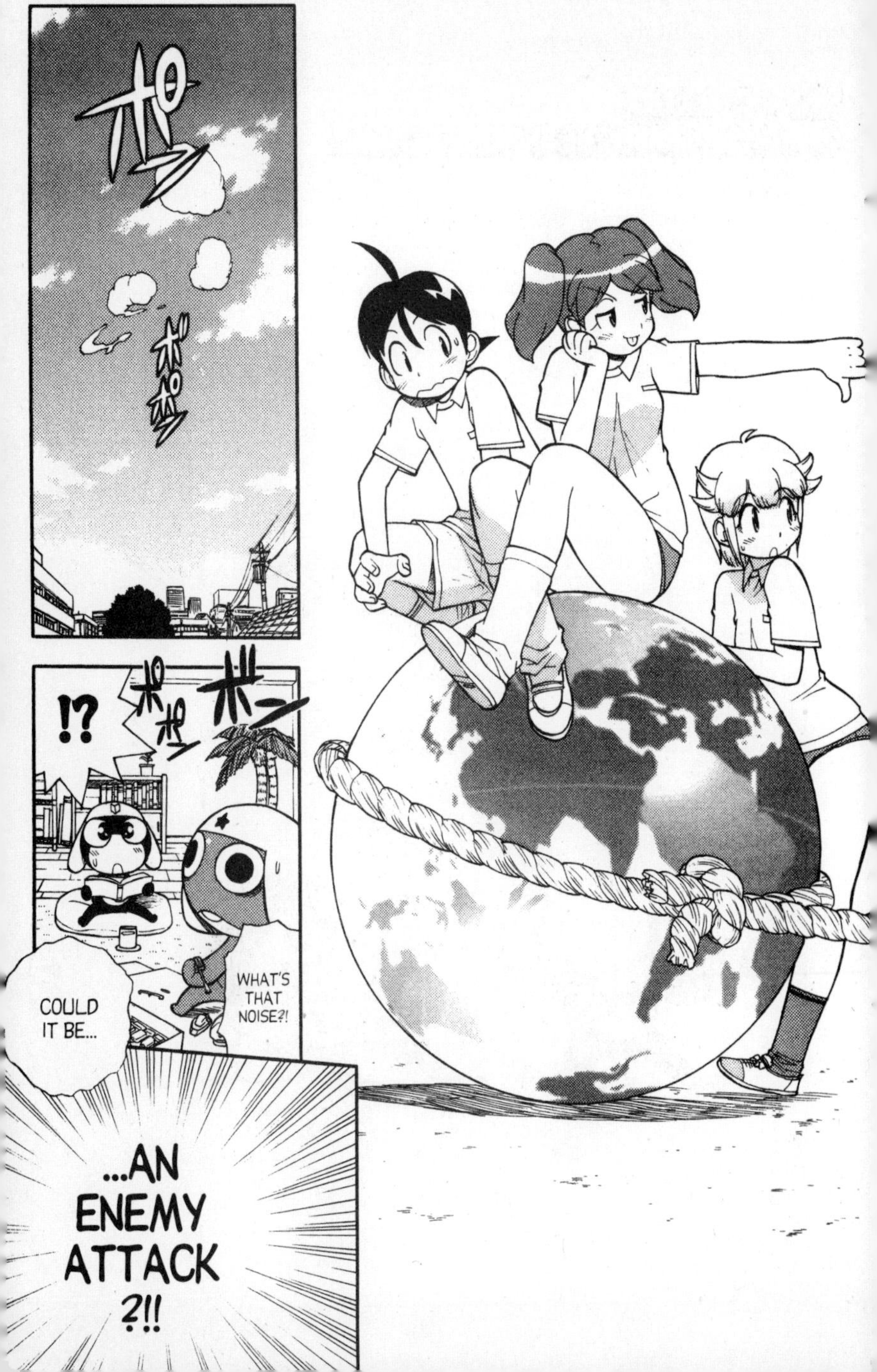
!?
WHAT'S THAT NOISE?!
COULD IT BE...
...AN ENEMY ATTACK ?!!

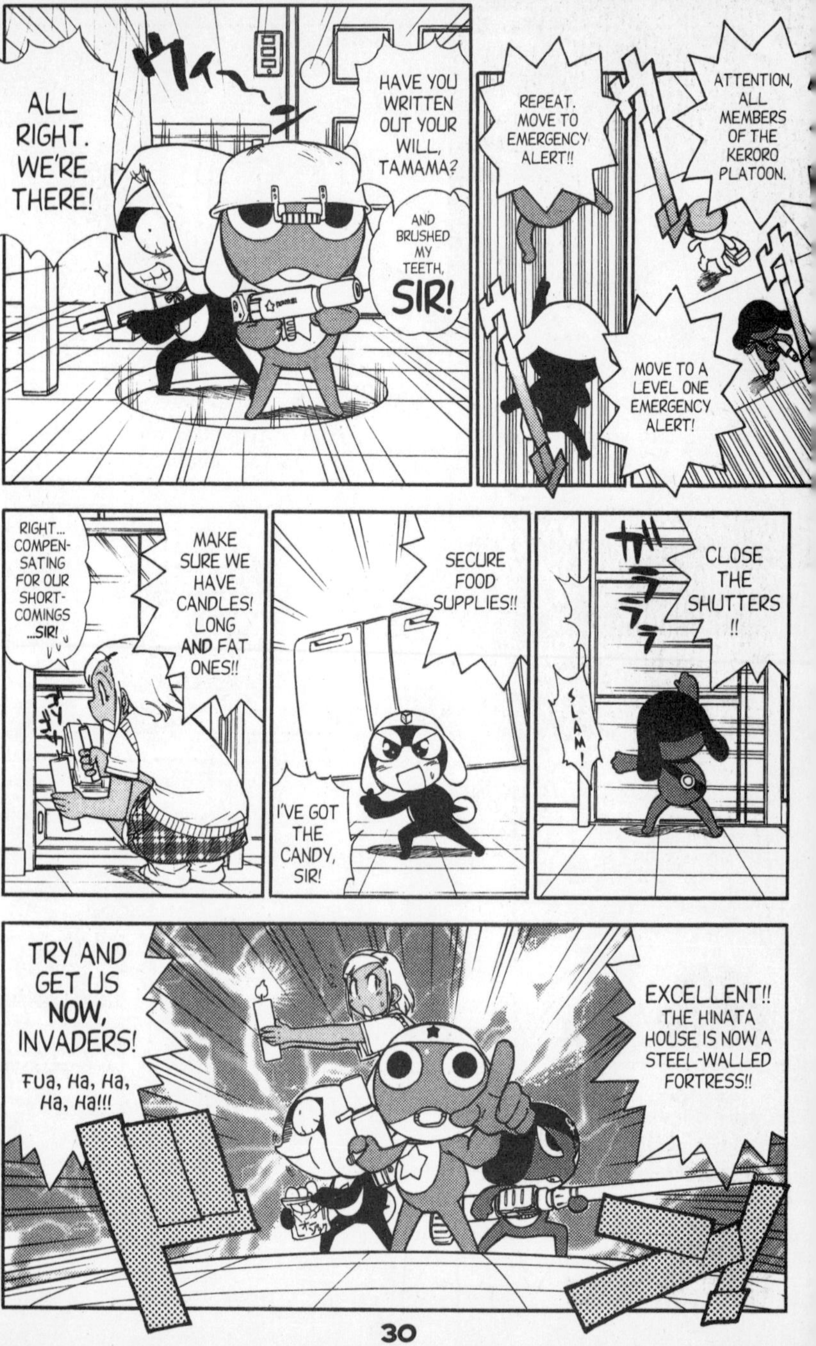
ATTENTION, ALL MEMBERS OF THE KERORO PLATOON.
MOVE TO A LEVEL ONE EMERGENCY ALERT!
REPEAT. MOVE TO EMERGENCY ALERT!!
HAVE YOU WRITTEN OUT YOUR WILL, TAMAMA?
AND BRUSHED MY TEETH, SIR!
ALL RIGHT. WE'RE THERE!
CLOSE THE SHUTTERS!!
SLAM!
SECURE FOOD SUPPLIES!!
I'VE GOT THE CANDY, SIR!
MAKE SURE WE HAVE CANDLES! LONG AND FAT ONES!!
RIGHT... COMPEN-SATING FOR OUR SHORT-COMINGS ...SIR!
EXCELLENT!! THE HINATA HOUSE IS NOW A STEEL-WALLED FORTRESS!!
TRY AND GET US NOW, INVADERS!
Fua, Ha, Ha, Ha, Ha!!!

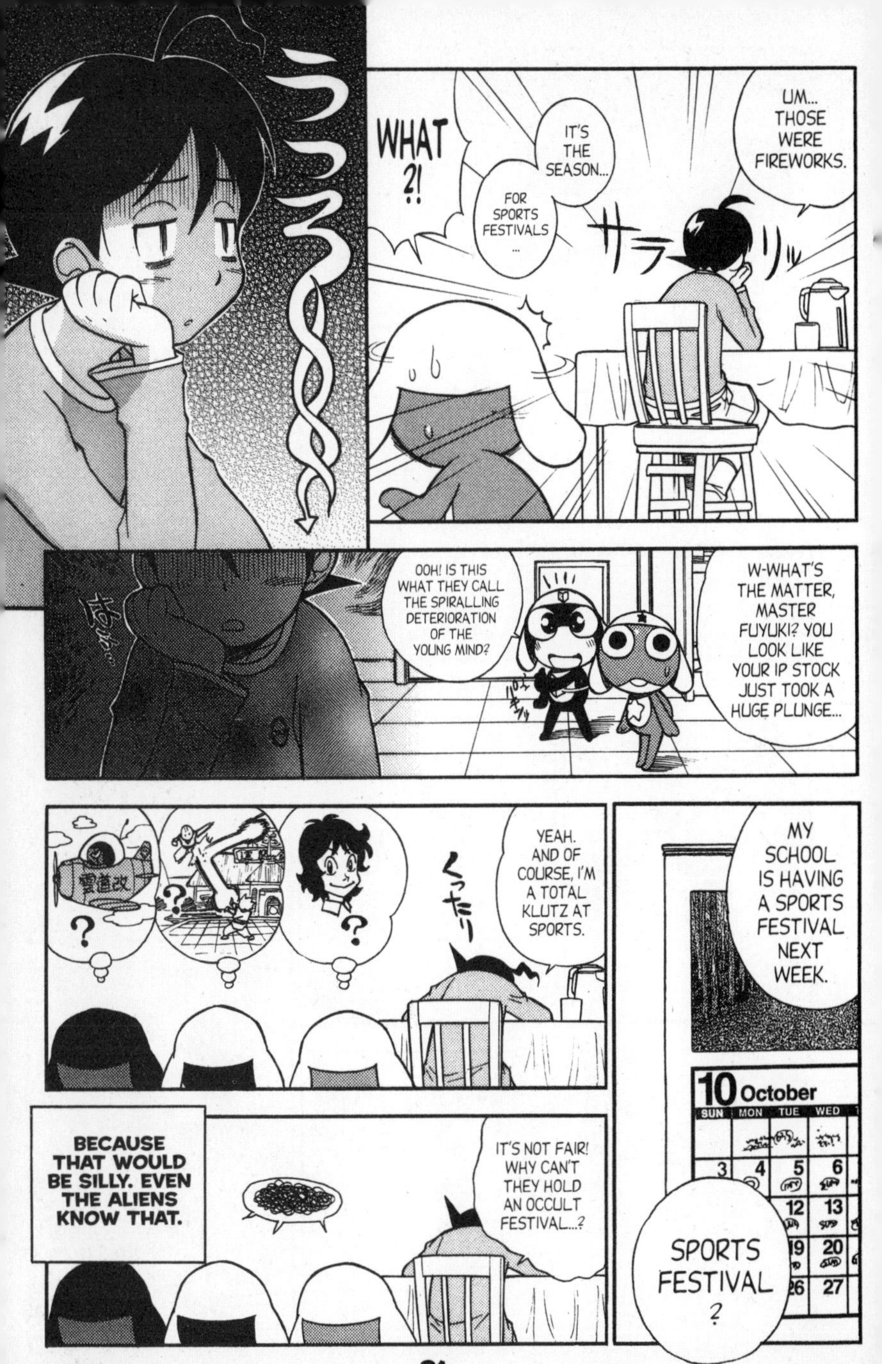
UM... THOSE WERE FIREWORKS.
サラリッ
IT'S THE SEASON...
FOR SPORTS FESTIVALS ...
WHAT ?!
W-WHAT'S THE MATTER, MASTER FUYUKI? YOU LOOK LIKE YOUR IP STOCK JUST TOOK A HUGE PLUNGE...
OOH! IS THIS WHAT THEY CALL THE SPIRALLING DETERIORATION OF THE YOUNG MIND?
MY SCHOOL IS HAVING A SPORTS FESTIVAL NEXT WEEK.
10 October
SUN MON TUE WED
3 4 5 6
12 13
19 20
26 27
SPORTS FESTIVAL ?
YEAH. AND OF COURSE, I'M A TOTAL KLUTZ AT SPORTS.
くったり
?
?
?
IT'S NOT FAIR! WHY CAN'T THEY HOLD AN OCCULT FESTIVAL...?
BECAUSE THAT WOULD BE SILLY. EVEN THE ALIENS KNOW THAT.

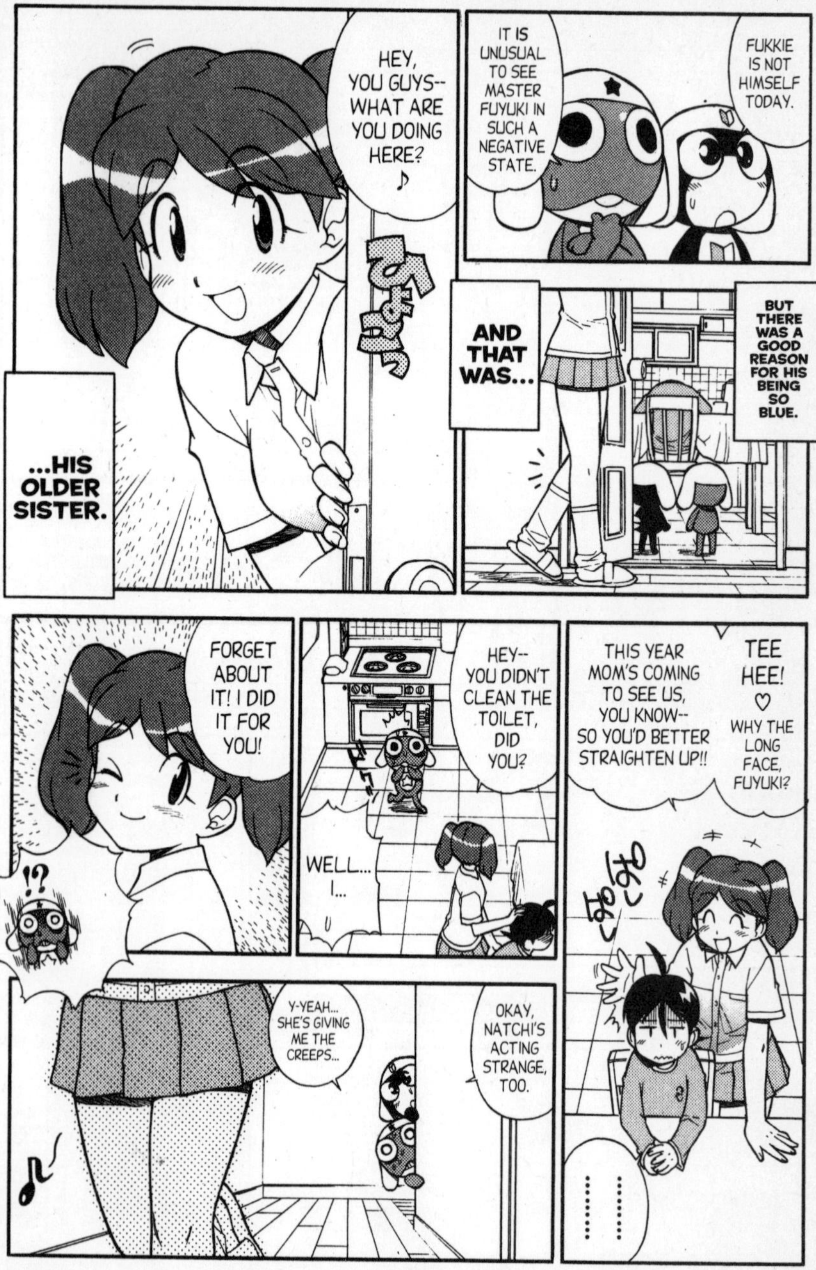
FUKKIE IS NOT HIMSELF TODAY.
IT IS UNUSUAL TO SEE MASTER FUYUKI IN SUCH A NEGATIVE STATE.
BUT THERE WAS A GOOD REASON FOR HIS BEING SO BLUE.
AND THAT WAS...
HEY, YOU GUYS-- WHAT ARE YOU DOING HERE? ♪
...HIS OLDER SISTER.
TEE HEE! ♡ WHY THE LONG FACE, FUYUKI?
THIS YEAR MOM'S COMING TO SEE US, YOU KNOW-- SO YOU'D BETTER STRAIGHTEN UP!!
......
HEY-- YOU DIDN'T CLEAN THE TOILET, DID YOU?
WELL... I...
FORGET ABOUT IT! I DID IT FOR YOU!
!?
OKAY, NATCHI'S ACTING STRANGE, TOO.
Y-YEAH... SHE'S GIVING ME THE CREEPS...

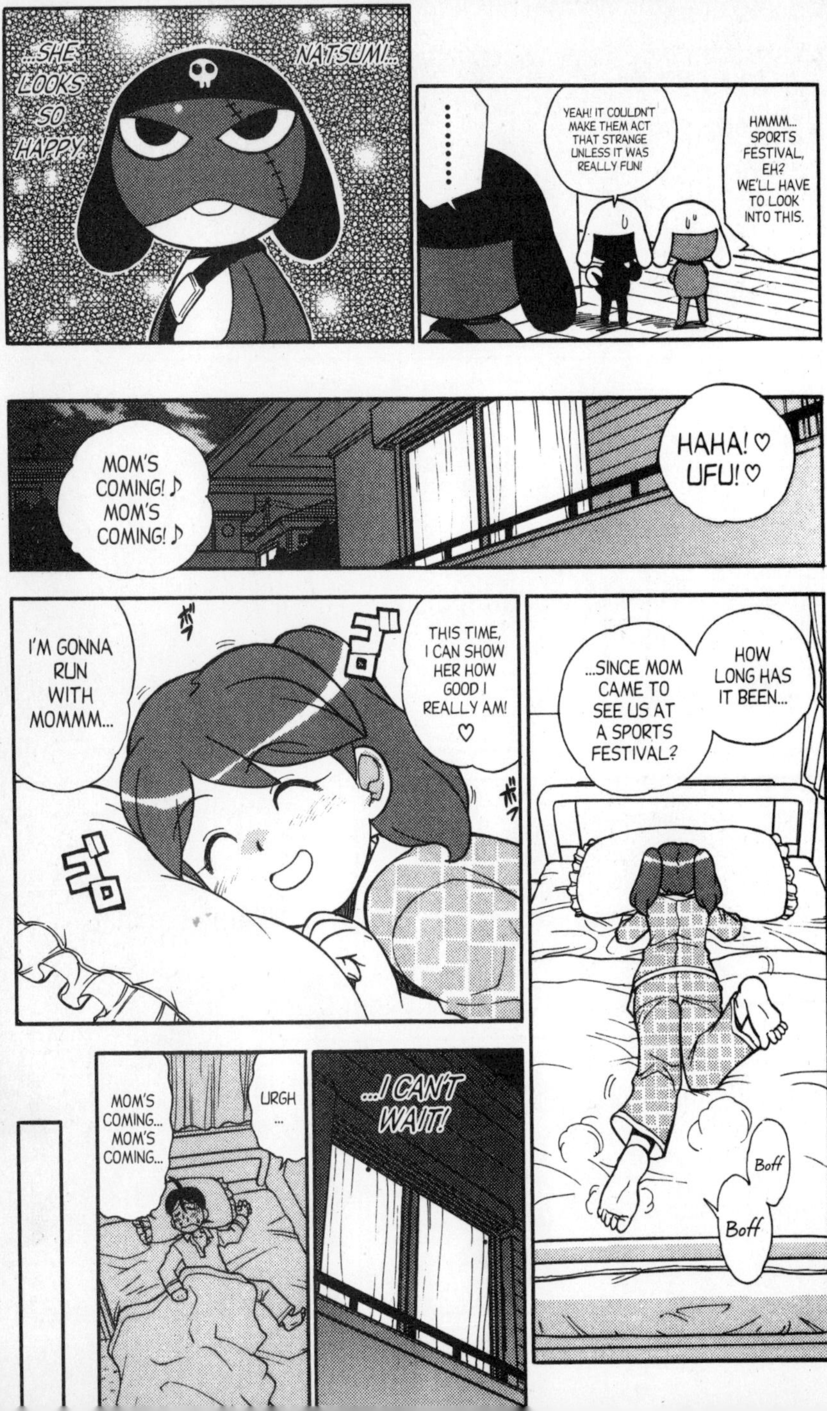
HMMM... SPORTS FESTIVAL, EH? WE'LL HAVE TO LOOK INTO THIS.
YEAH! IT COULDN'T MAKE THEM ACT THAT STRANGE UNLESS IT WAS REALLY FUN!
......
NATSUMI...
...SHE LOOKS SO HAPPY.
HAHA! ♡ UFU! ♡
MOM'S COMING! ♪ MOM'S COMING! ♪
HOW LONG HAS IT BEEN...
...SINCE MOM CAME TO SEE US AT A SPORTS FESTIVAL?
Boff
Boff
THIS TIME, I CAN SHOW HER HOW GOOD I REALLY AM! ♡
I'M GONNA RUN WITH MOMMM...
...I CAN'T WAIT!
URGH ...
MOM'S COMING... MOM'S COMING...

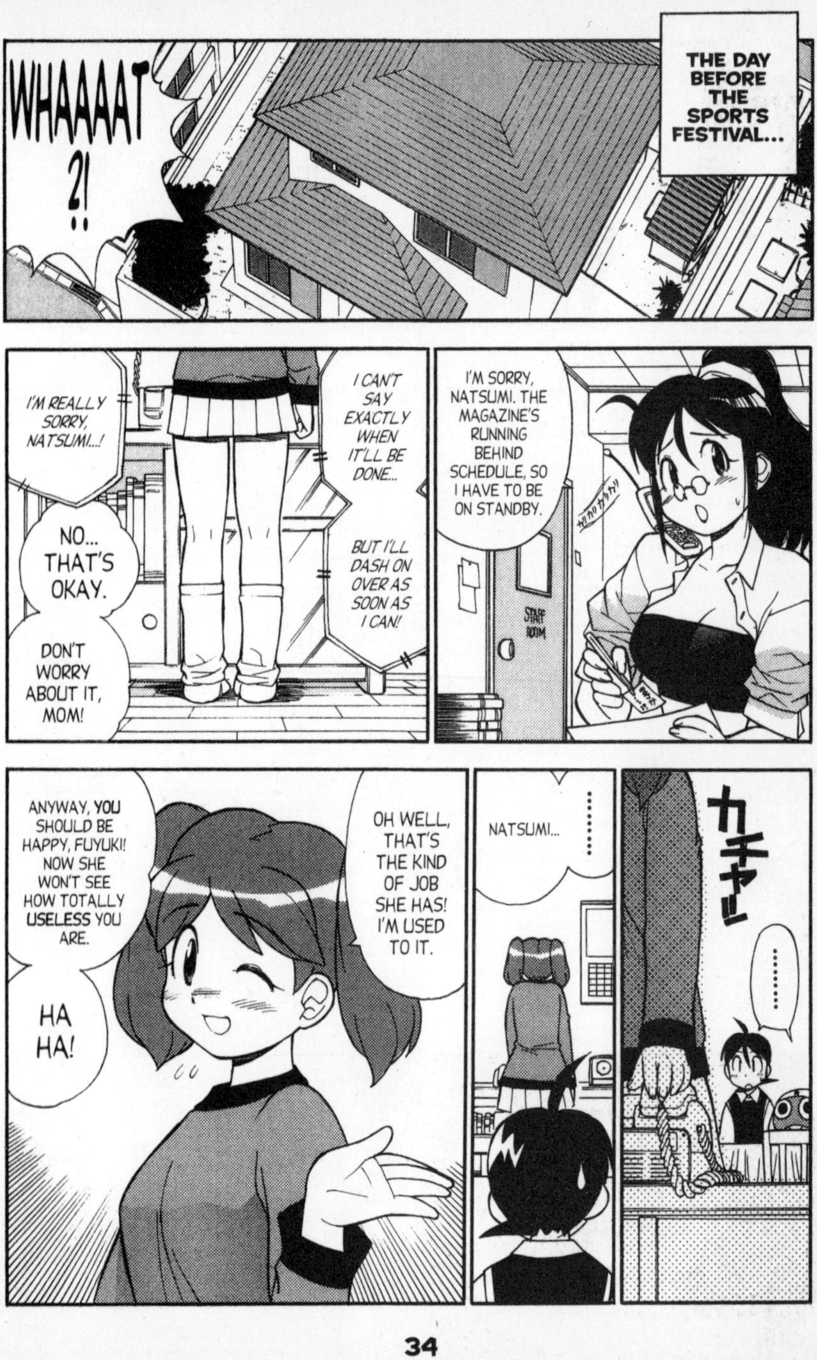
THE DAY BEFORE THE SPORTS FESTIVAL...
WHAAAAT ?!
I'M SORRY, NATSUMI. THE MAGAZINE'S RUNNING BEHIND SCHEDULE, SO I HAVE TO BE ON STANDBY.
I CAN'T SAY EXACTLY WHEN IT'LL BE DONE...
BUT I'LL DASH ON OVER AS SOON AS I CAN!
I'M REALLY SORRY, NATSUMI...!
NO... THAT'S OKAY.
DON'T WORRY ABOUT IT, MOM!
カチャ
......
......
NATSUMI...
OH WELL, THAT'S THE KIND OF JOB SHE HAS! I'M USED TO IT.
ANYWAY, YOU SHOULD BE HAPPY, FUYUKI! NOW SHE WON'T SEE HOW TOTALLY USELESS YOU ARE.
HA HA!

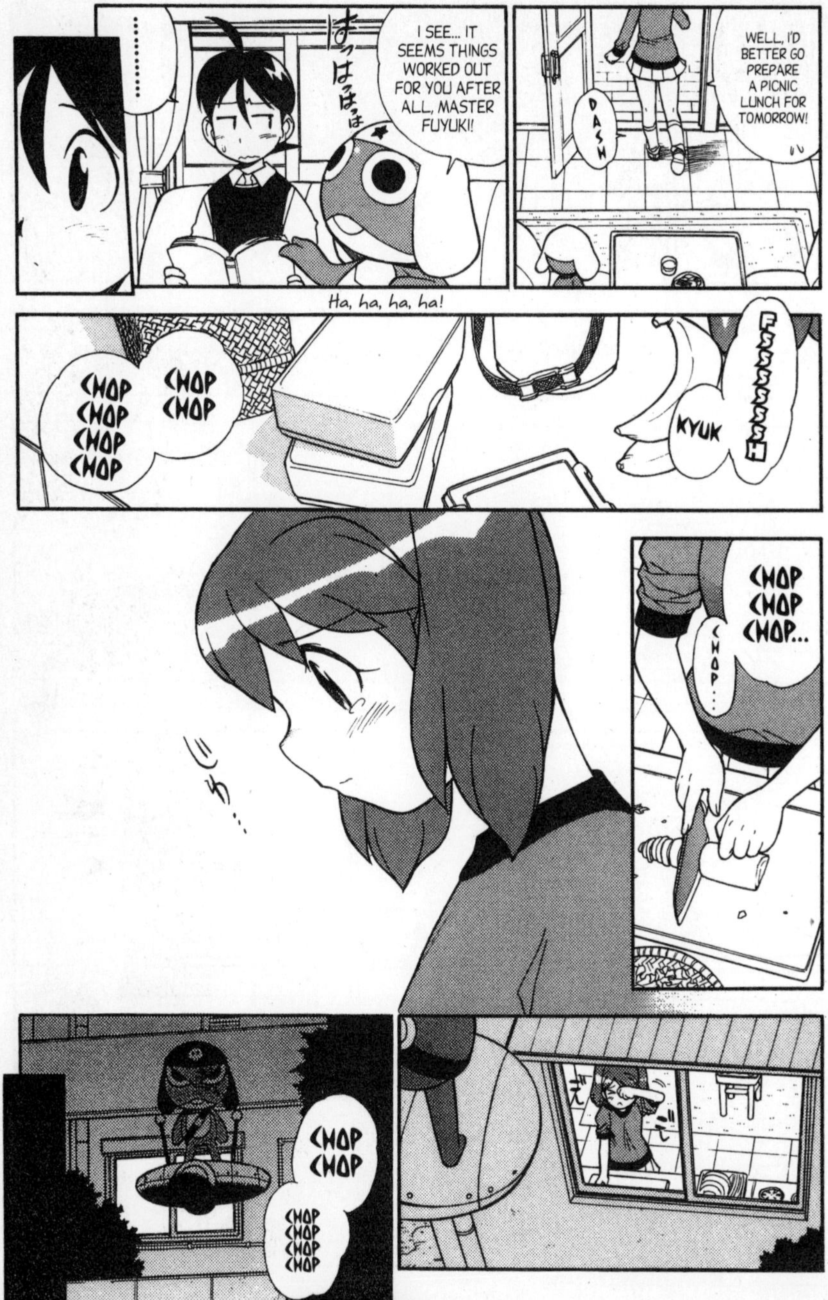
WELL, I'D BETTER GO PREPARE A PICNIC LUNCH FOR TOMORROW!
DASH
I SEE... IT SEEMS THINGS WORKED OUT FOR YOU AFTER ALL, MASTER FUYUKI!!
はっはっはっは
Ha, ha, ha, ha!
......
FSSSSSSSH
KYUK
CHOP CHOP
CHOP CHOP CHOP CHOP
CHOP CHOP CHOP...
CHOP...
じわ...
CHOP CHOP
CHOP CHOP CHOP CHOP

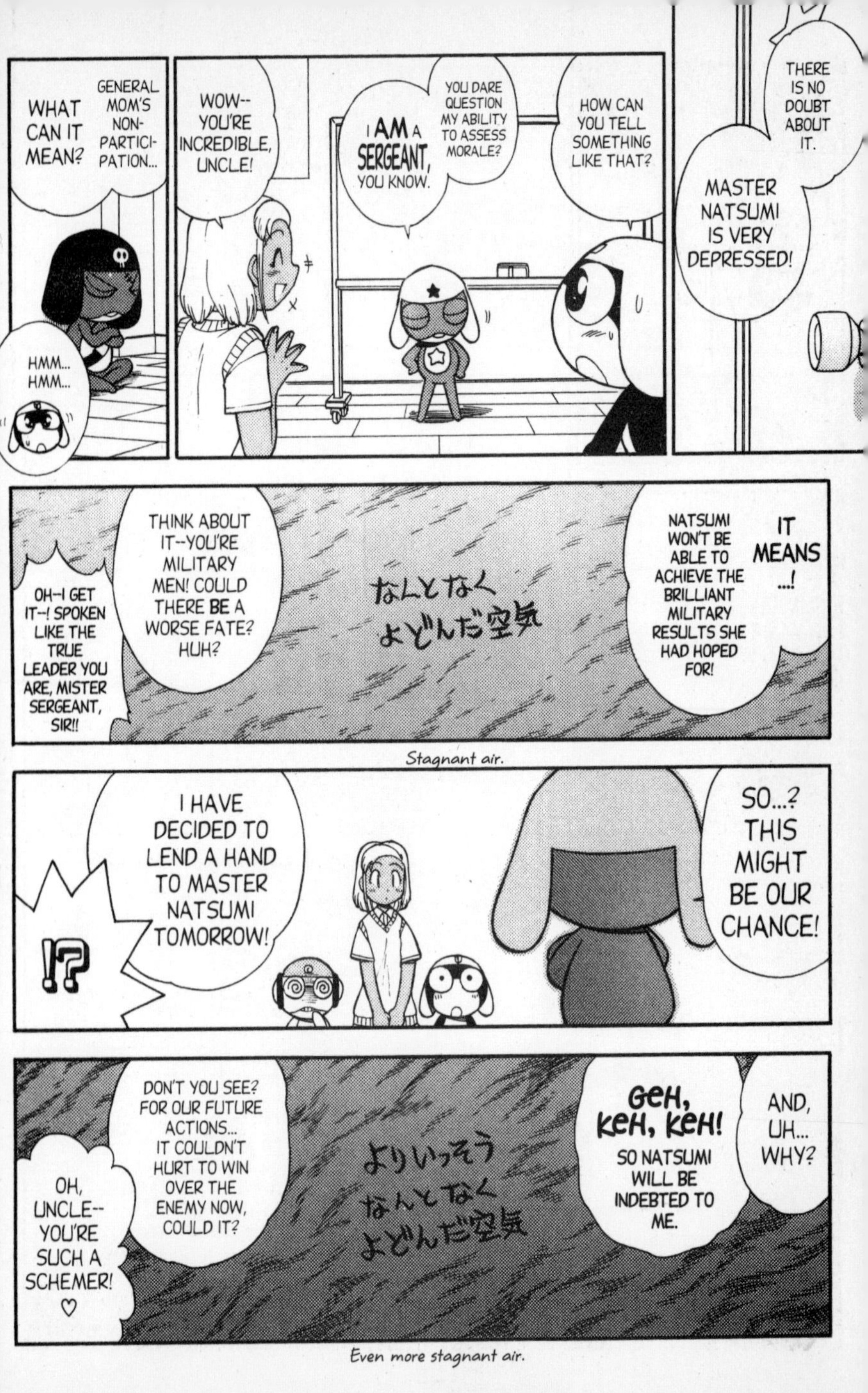
THERE IS NO DOUBT ABOUT IT.
MASTER NATSUMI IS VERY DEPRESSED!
HOW CAN YOU TELL SOMETHING LIKE THAT?
YOU DARE QUESTION MY ABILITY TO ASSESS MORALE?
I **AM** A SERGEANT, YOU KNOW.
WOW-- YOU'RE INCREDIBLE, UNCLE!
GENERAL MOM'S NON-PARTICIPATION...
WHAT CAN IT MEAN?
HMM... HMM...
IT MEANS ...!
NATSUMI WON'T BE ABLE TO ACHIEVE THE BRILLIANT MILITARY RESULTS SHE HAD HOPED FOR!
なんとなくよどんだ空気
THINK ABOUT IT--YOU'RE MILITARY MEN! COULD THERE **BE** A WORSE FATE? HUH?
OH--I GET IT--! SPOKEN LIKE THE TRUE LEADER YOU ARE, MISTER SERGEANT, SIR!!
Stagnant air.
SO...? THIS MIGHT BE OUR CHANCE!
I HAVE DECIDED TO LEND A HAND TO MASTER NATSUMI TOMORROW!
!?
AND, UH... WHY?
GEH, KEH, KEH! SO NATSUMI WILL BE INDEBTED TO ME.
よりいっそうなんとなくよどんだ空気
DON'T YOU SEE? FOR OUR FUTURE ACTIONS... IT COULDN'T HURT TO WIN OVER THE ENEMY NOW, COULD IT?
OH, UNCLE-- YOU'RE SUCH A SCHEMER! ♡
Even more stagnant air.

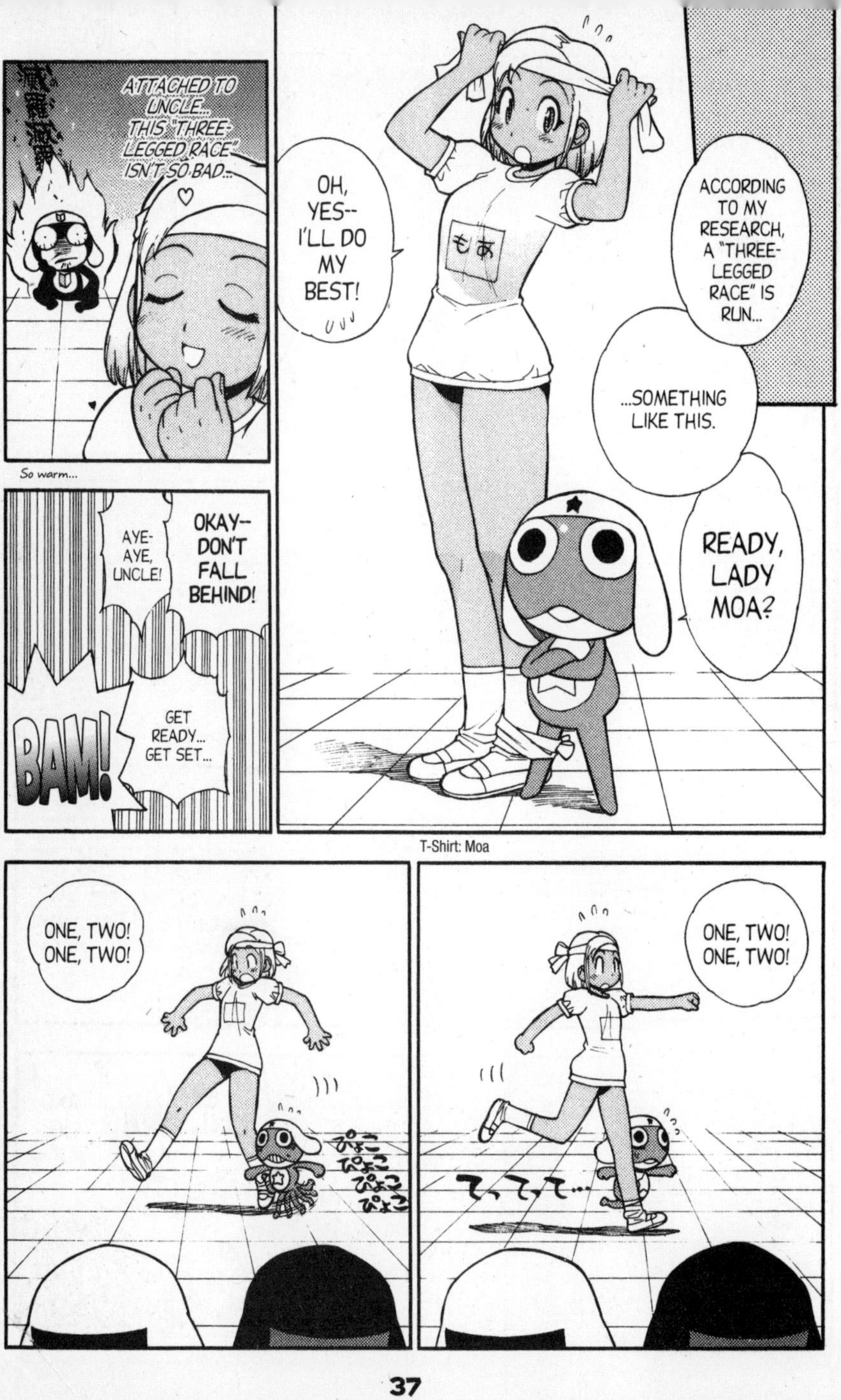
ACCORDING TO MY RESEARCH, A "THREE-LEGGED RACE" IS RUN...
...SOMETHING LIKE THIS.
READY, LADY MOA?
OH, YES-- I'LL DO MY BEST!
もあ
ATTACHED TO UNCLE... THIS "THREE-LEGGED RACE" ISN'T SO BAD...
OKAY-- DON'T FALL BEHIND!
AYE-AYE, UNCLE!
GET READY... GET SET...
BAM!
ONE, TWO! ONE, TWO!
てってって…
ONE, TWO! ONE, TWO!
ぴょこ ぴょこ ぴょこ ぴょこ

T-Shirt: Moa

So warm...

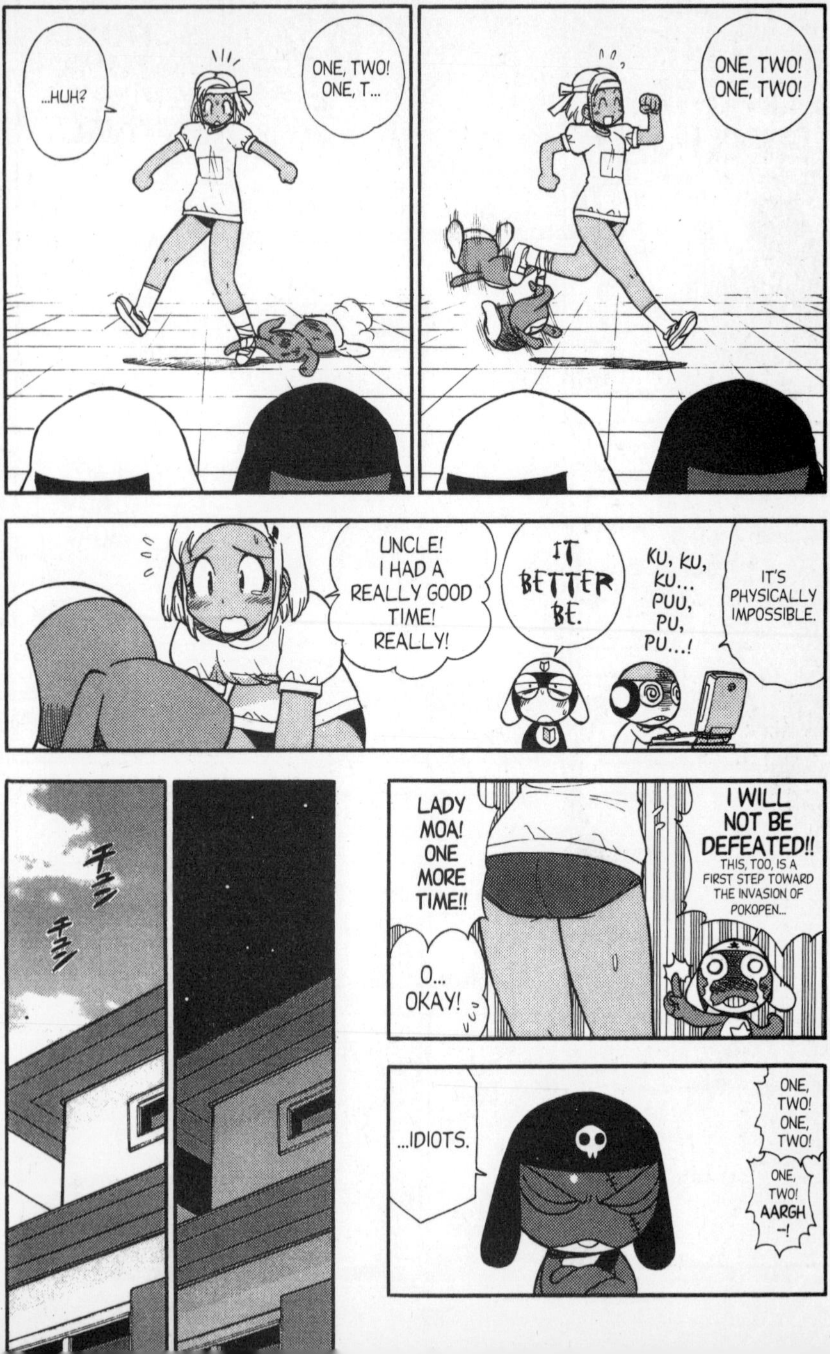
ONE, TWO! ONE, TWO!
ONE, TWO! ONE, T...
...HUH?
IT'S PHYSICALLY IMPOSSIBLE.
KU, KU, KU... PUU, PU, PU...!
IT BETTER BE.
UNCLE! I HAD A REALLY GOOD TIME! REALLY!
I WILL NOT BE DEFEATED!!
THIS, TOO, IS A FIRST STEP TOWARD THE INVASION OF POKOPEN...
LADY MOA! ONE MORE TIME!!
O... OKAY!
ONE, TWO! ONE, TWO!
ONE, TWO! AARGH—!
...IDIOTS.
チュン
チュン

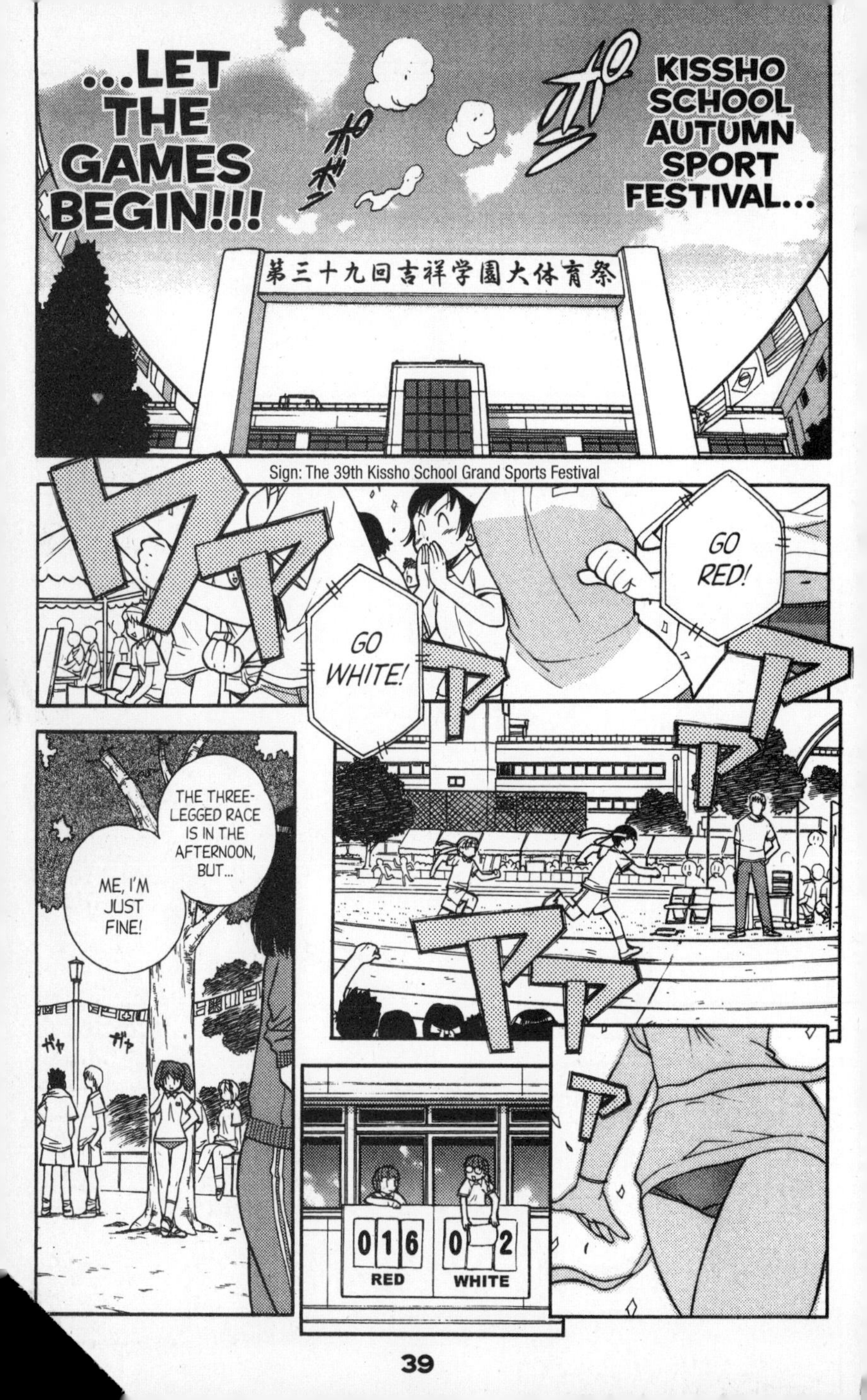
KISSHO SCHOOL AUTUMN SPORT FESTIVAL...
...LET THE GAMES BEGIN!!!
Sign: The 39th Kissho School Grand Sports Festival
GO RED!
GO WHITE!
THE THREE-LEGGED RACE IS IN THE AFTERNOON, BUT...
ME, I'M JUST FINE!
016
RED
0 2
WHITE

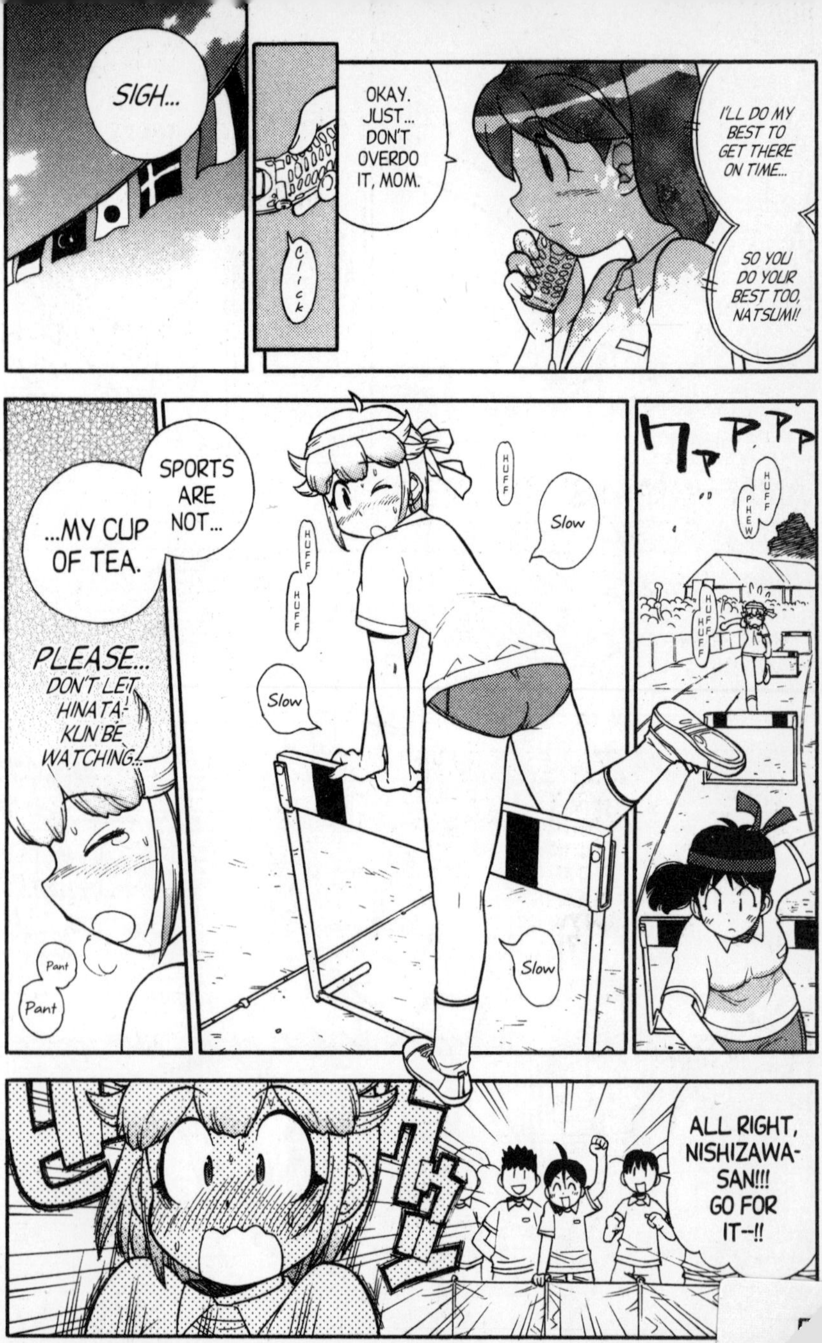
I'LL DO MY BEST TO GET THERE ON TIME...
SO YOU DO YOUR BEST TOO, NATSUMI!
OKAY. JUST... DON'T OVERDO IT, MOM.
Click
SIGH...
HUFF PHEW HUFF
HUFF HUFF
HUFF
Slow
HUFF HUFF
Slow
Slow
SPORTS ARE NOT...
...MY CUP OF TEA.
PLEASE... DON'T LET HINATA-KUN BE WATCHING...
Pant
Pant
ALL RIGHT, NISHIZAWA-SAN!!! GO FOR IT--!!

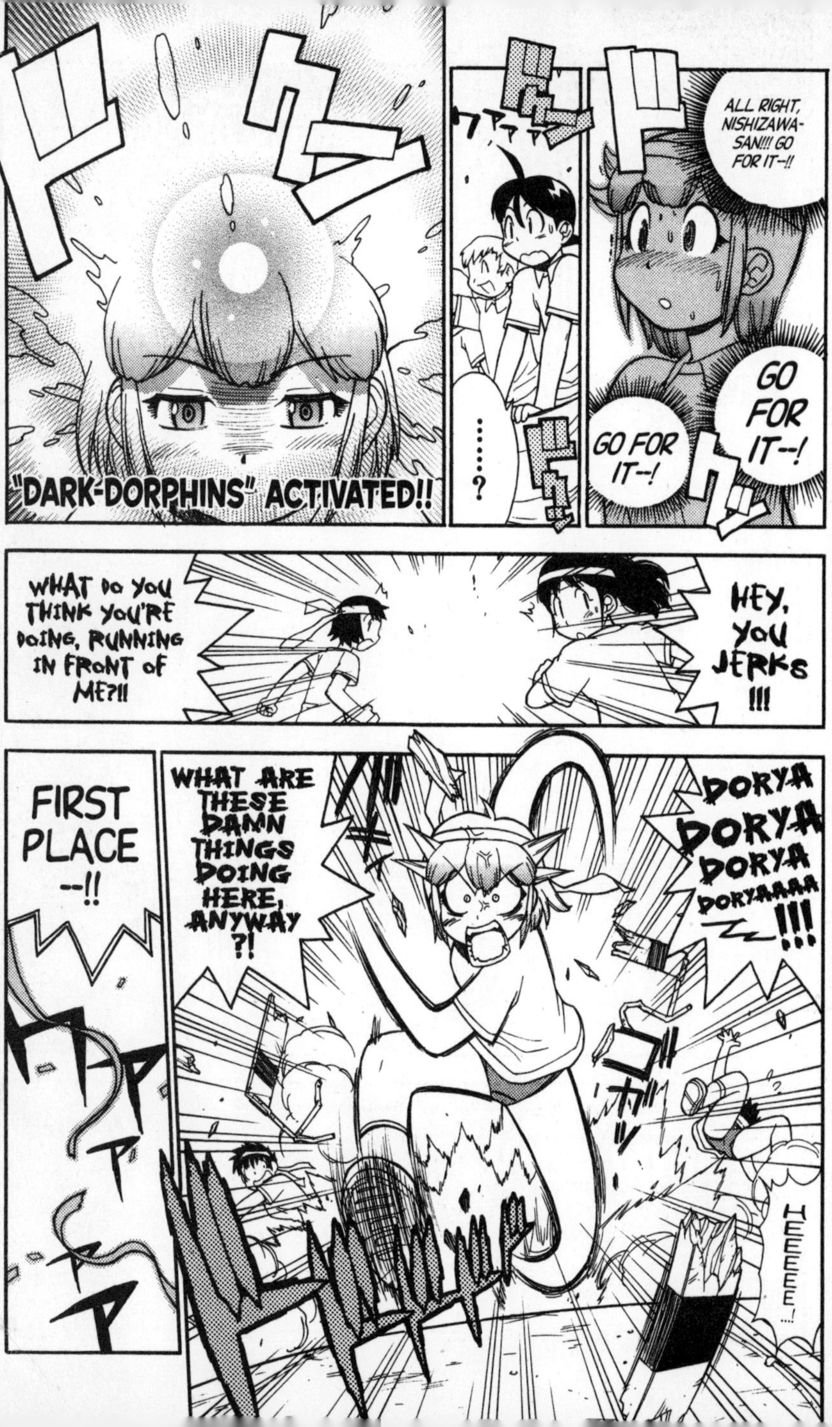
ALL RIGHT, NISHIZAWA-SAN!!! GO FOR IT--!!
GO FOR IT--!
GO FOR IT--!
......?
"DARK-DORPHINS" ACTIVATED!!
HEY, YOU JERKS!!!
WHAT DO YOU THINK YOU'RE DOING, RUNNING IN FRONT OF ME?!!
DORYA DORYA DORYA DORYAAAA---!!!
WHAT ARE THESE DAMN THINGS DOING HERE, ANYWAY?!
HEEEEEE...!
FIRST PLACE--!!

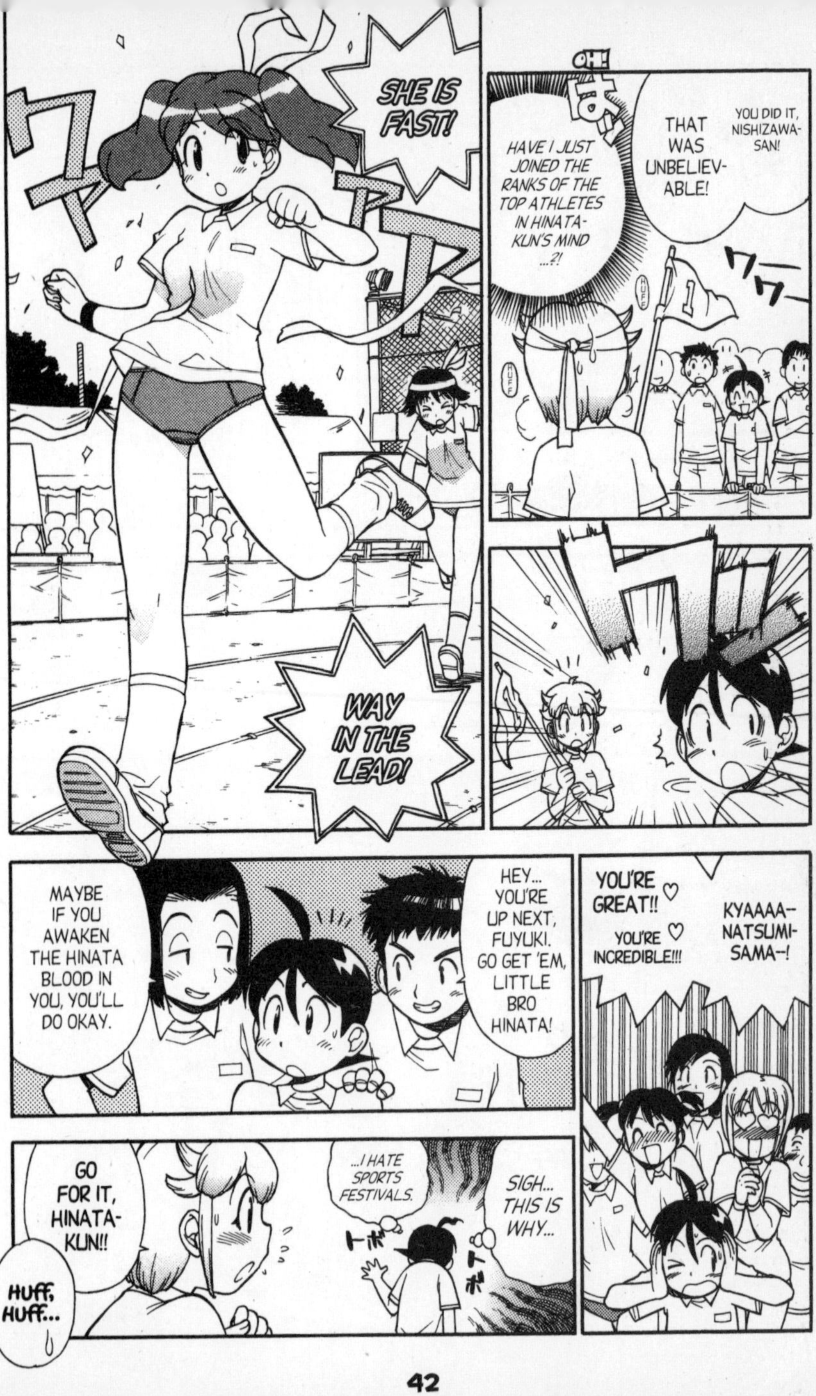
YOU DID IT, NISHIZAWA-SAN!
THAT WAS UNBELIEVABLE!
OH!
HAVE I JUST JOINED THE RANKS OF THE TOP ATHLETES IN HINATA-KUN'S MIND ...?!
HUFF
HUFF
SHE IS FAST!
WAY IN THE LEAD!
KYAAAA-NATSUMI-SAMA--!
YOU'RE GREAT!! ♡
YOU'RE ♡ INCREDIBLE!!!
HEY... YOU'RE UP NEXT, FUYUKI. GO GET 'EM, LITTLE BRO HINATA!
MAYBE IF YOU AWAKEN THE HINATA BLOOD IN YOU, YOU'LL DO OKAY.
SIGH... THIS IS WHY...
...I HATE SPORTS FESTIVALS.
GO FOR IT, HINATA-KUN!!
HUFF, HUFF...

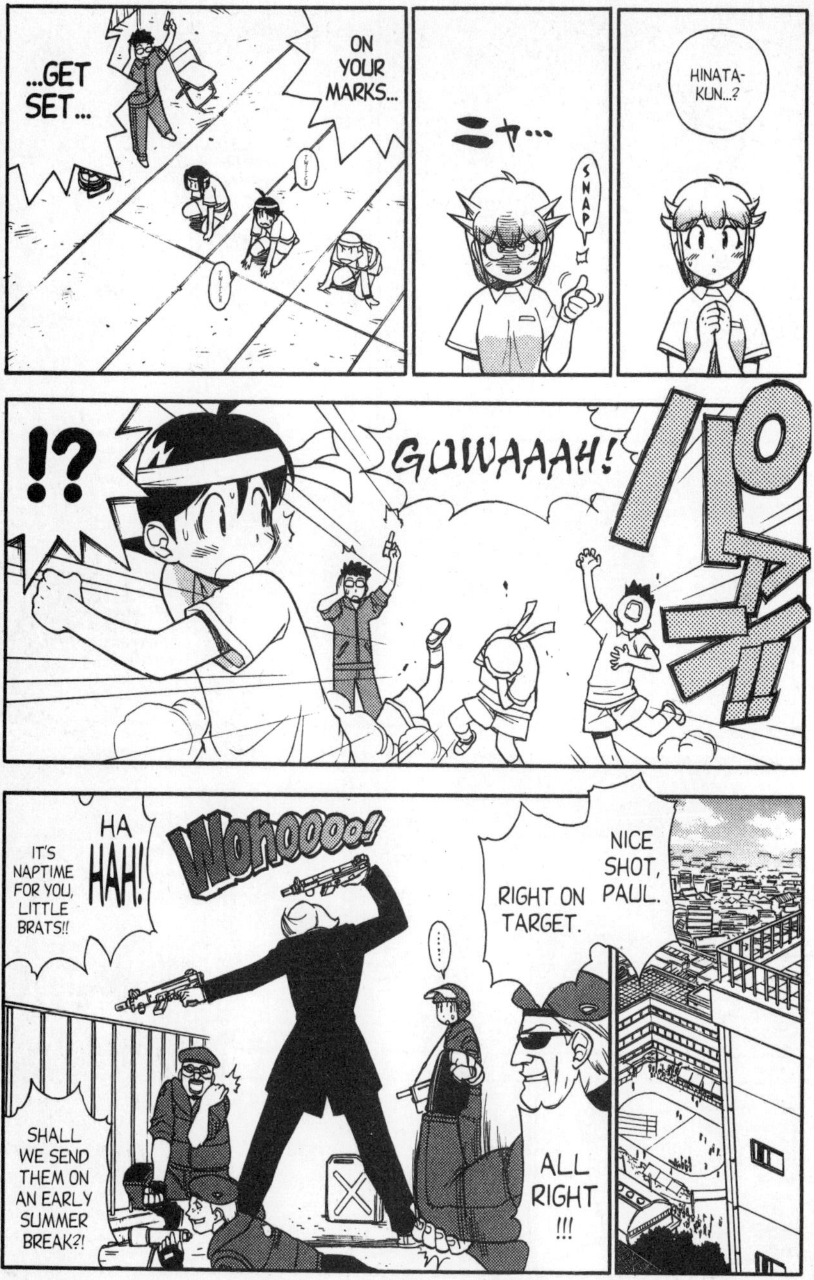
HINATA-KUN...?
ニヤ…
SNAP
ON YOUR MARKS...
...GET SET...
TWITCH
TWITCH
GUWAAAH!
!?
NICE SHOT, PAUL.
RIGHT ON TARGET.
Wohoooo!
HA HAH!
IT'S NAPTIME FOR YOU, LITTLE BRATS!!
......
ALL RIGHT!!!
SHALL WE SEND THEM ON AN EARLY SUMMER BREAK?!

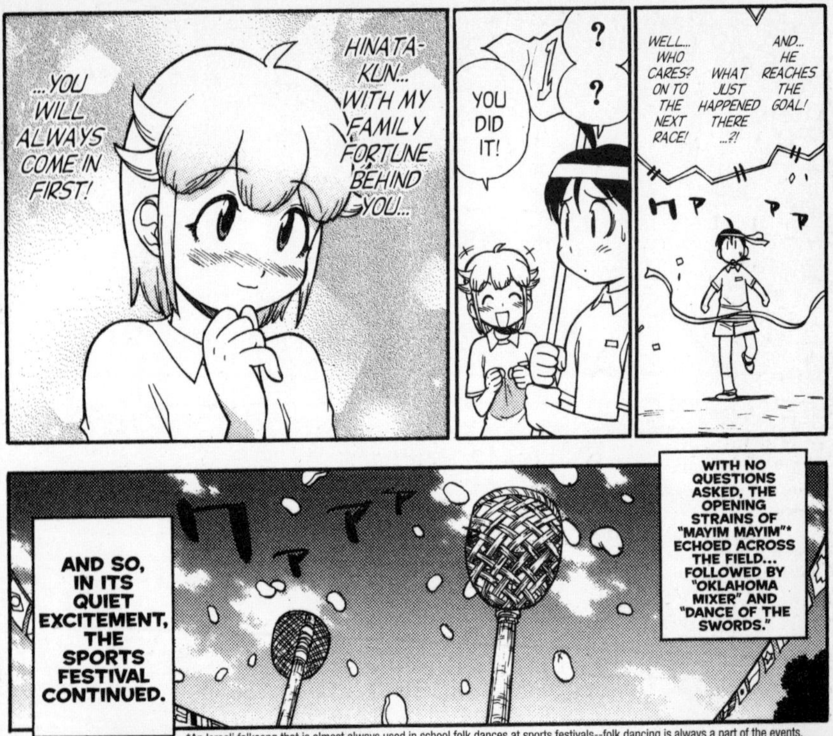
AND... HE REACHES THE GOAL!
WHAT JUST HAPPENED THERE ...?!
WELL... WHO CARES? ON TO THE NEXT RACE!
?
?
YOU DID IT!
HINATA-KUN... WITH MY FAMILY FORTUNE BEHIND YOU...
...YOU WILL ALWAYS COME IN FIRST!
WITH NO QUESTIONS ASKED, THE OPENING STRAINS OF "MAYIM MAYIM"* ECHOED ACROSS THE FIELD... FOLLOWED BY "OKLAHOMA MIXER" AND "DANCE OF THE SWORDS."
AND SO, IN ITS QUIET EXCITEMENT, THE SPORTS FESTIVAL CONTINUED.

*An Israeli folksong that is almost always used in school folk dances at sports festivals--folk dancing is always a part of the events.

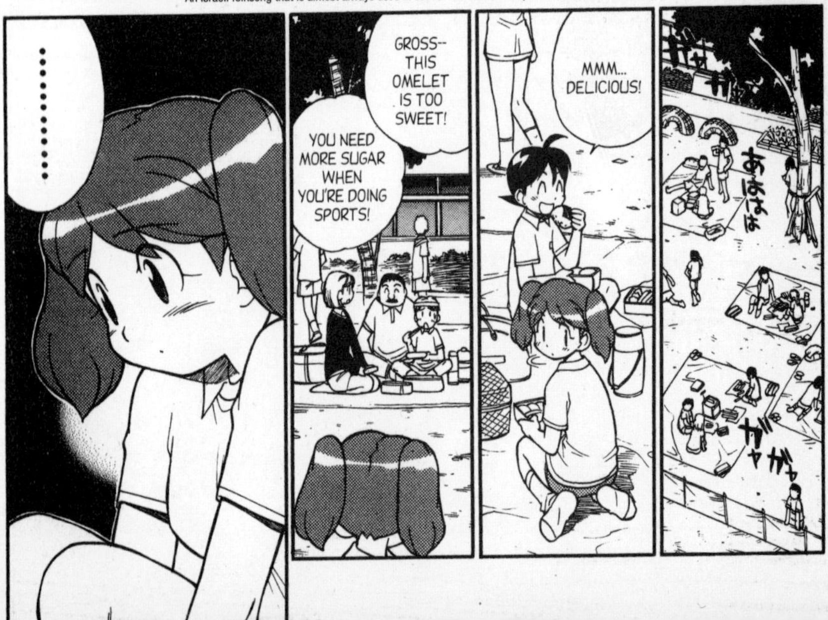
あははは
MMM... DELICIOUS!
GROSS-- THIS OMELET IS TOO SWEET!
YOU NEED MORE SUGAR WHEN YOU'RE DOING SPORTS!
....

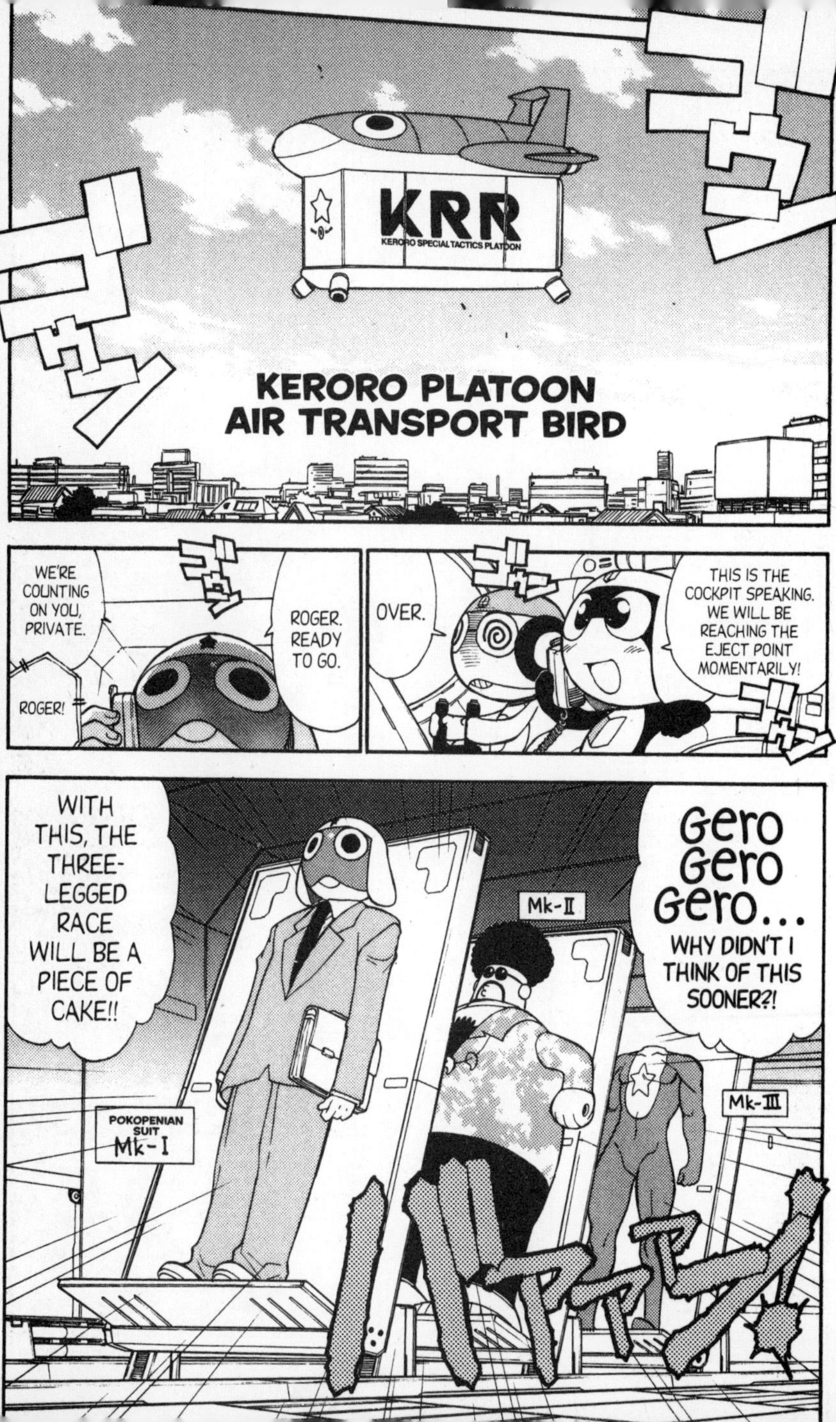
KRR
KERORO SPECIAL TACTICS PLATOON
KERORO PLATOON AIR TRANSPORT BIRD
THIS IS THE COCKPIT SPEAKING. WE WILL BE REACHING THE EJECT POINT MOMENTARILY!
OVER.
ROGER. READY TO GO.
WE'RE COUNTING ON YOU, PRIVATE.
ROGER!
Gero Gero Gero... WHY DIDN'T I THINK OF THIS SOONER?!
Mk-II
Mk-III
WITH THIS, THE THREE-LEGGED RACE WILL BE A PIECE OF CAKE!!
POKOPENIAN SUIT Mk-I

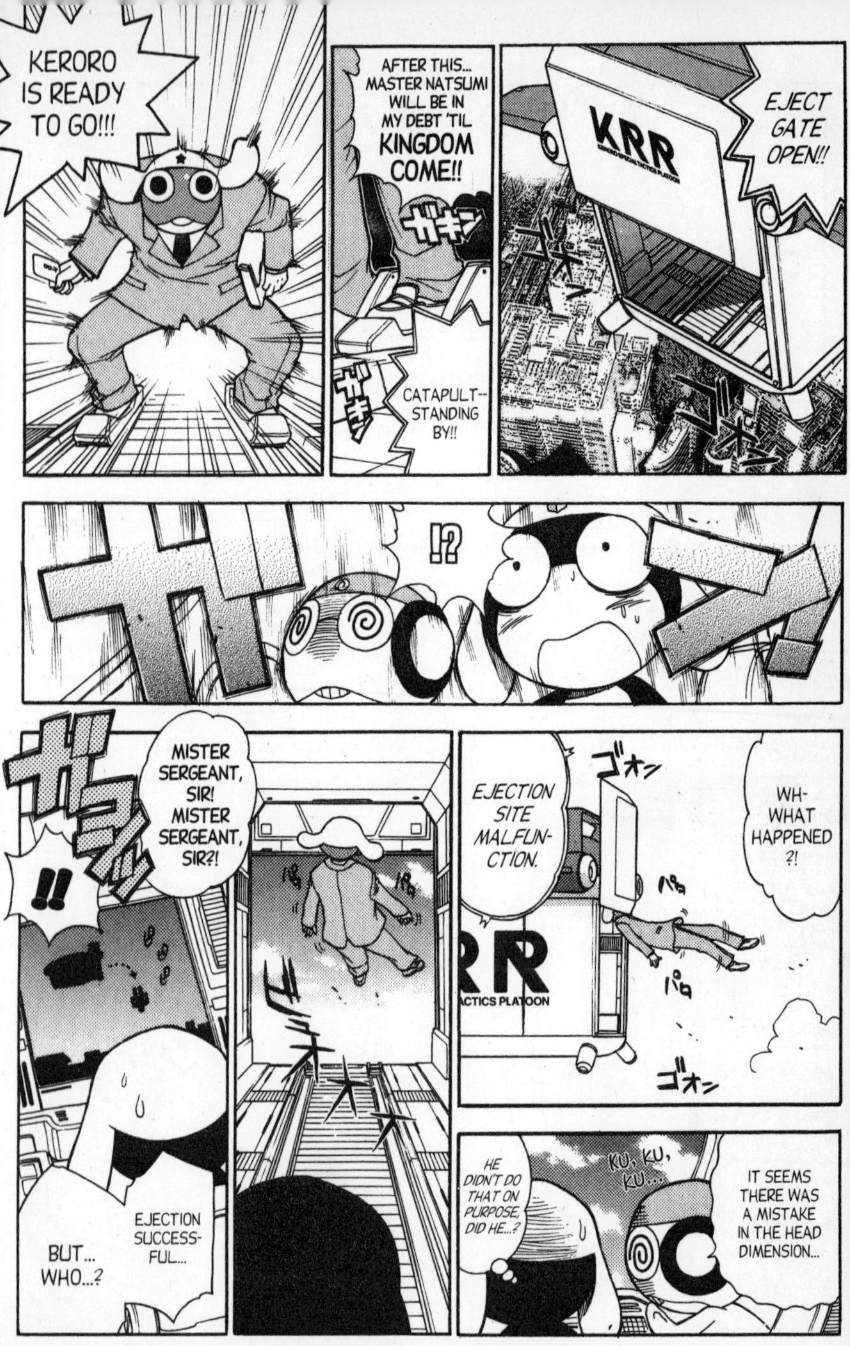
EJECT GATE OPEN!!
AFTER THIS... MASTER NATSUMI WILL BE IN MY DEBT 'TIL KINGDOM COME!!
CATAPULT-- STANDING BY!!
KERORO IS READY TO GO!!!
KRR
!?
WH- WHAT HAPPENED?!
EJECTION SITE MALFUNCTION.
IT SEEMS THERE WAS A MISTAKE IN THE HEAD DIMENSION...
KU, KU, KU...
HE DIDN'T DO THAT ON PURPOSE, DID HE...?
MISTER SERGEANT, SIR! MISTER SERGEANT, SIR?!
!!
EJECTION SUCCESSFUL...
BUT... WHO...?

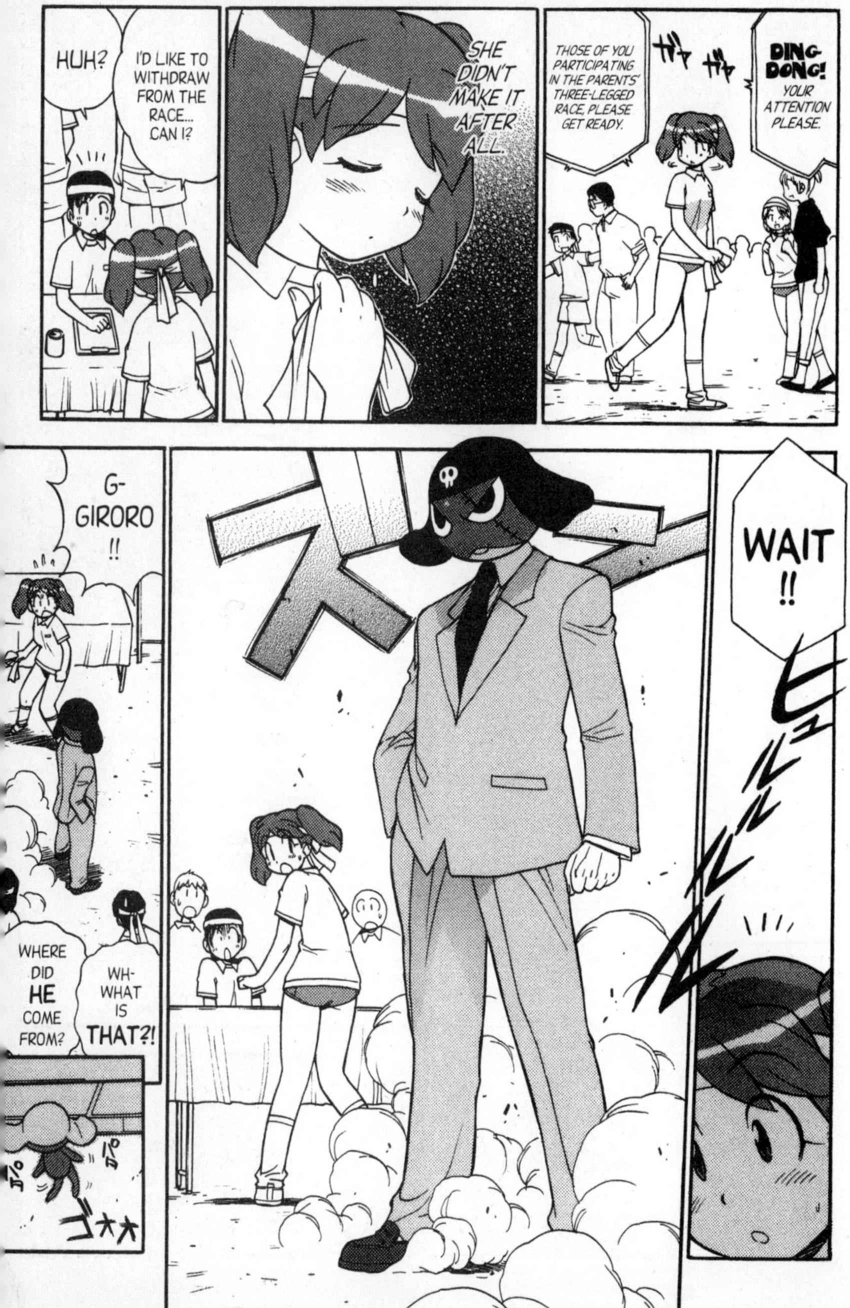

DING-DONG! YOUR ATTENTION PLEASE.
THOSE OF YOU PARTICIPATING IN THE PARENTS' THREE-LEGGED RACE, PLEASE GET READY.
SHE DIDN'T MAKE IT AFTER ALL.
I'D LIKE TO WITHDRAW FROM THE RACE... CAN I?
HUH?
WAIT!!
WH-WHAT IS THAT?!
WHERE DID HE COME FROM?
G-GIRORO!!

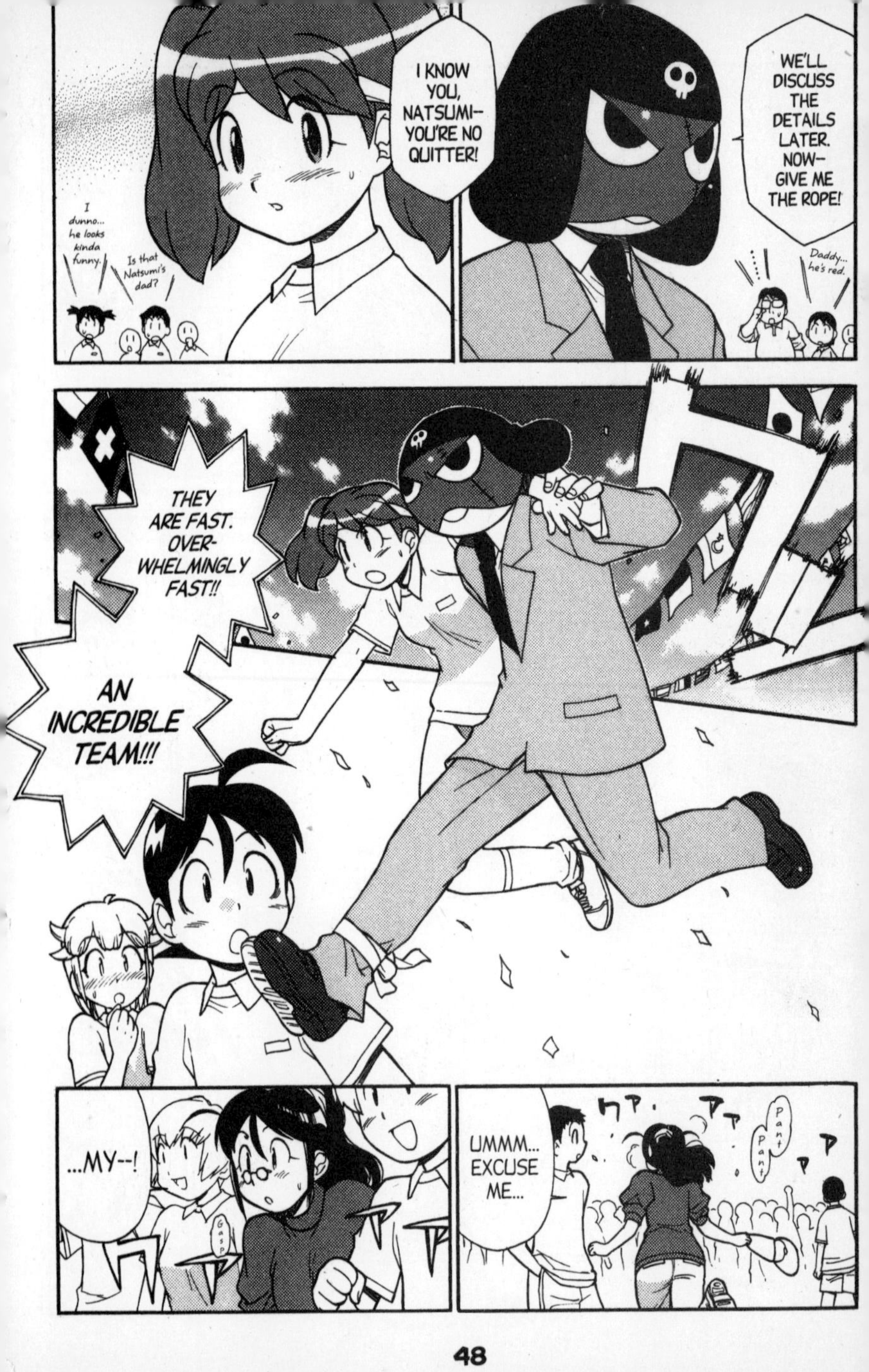
WE'LL DISCUSS THE DETAILS LATER. NOW— GIVE ME THE ROPE!
Daddy... he's red.
I KNOW YOU, NATSUMI— YOU'RE NO QUITTER!
Is that Natsumi's dad?
I dunno... he looks kinda funny.
THEY ARE FAST. OVER-WHELMINGLY FAST!!
AN INCREDIBLE TEAM!!!
Pant Pant
UMMM... EXCUSE ME...
...MY--!
Gasp

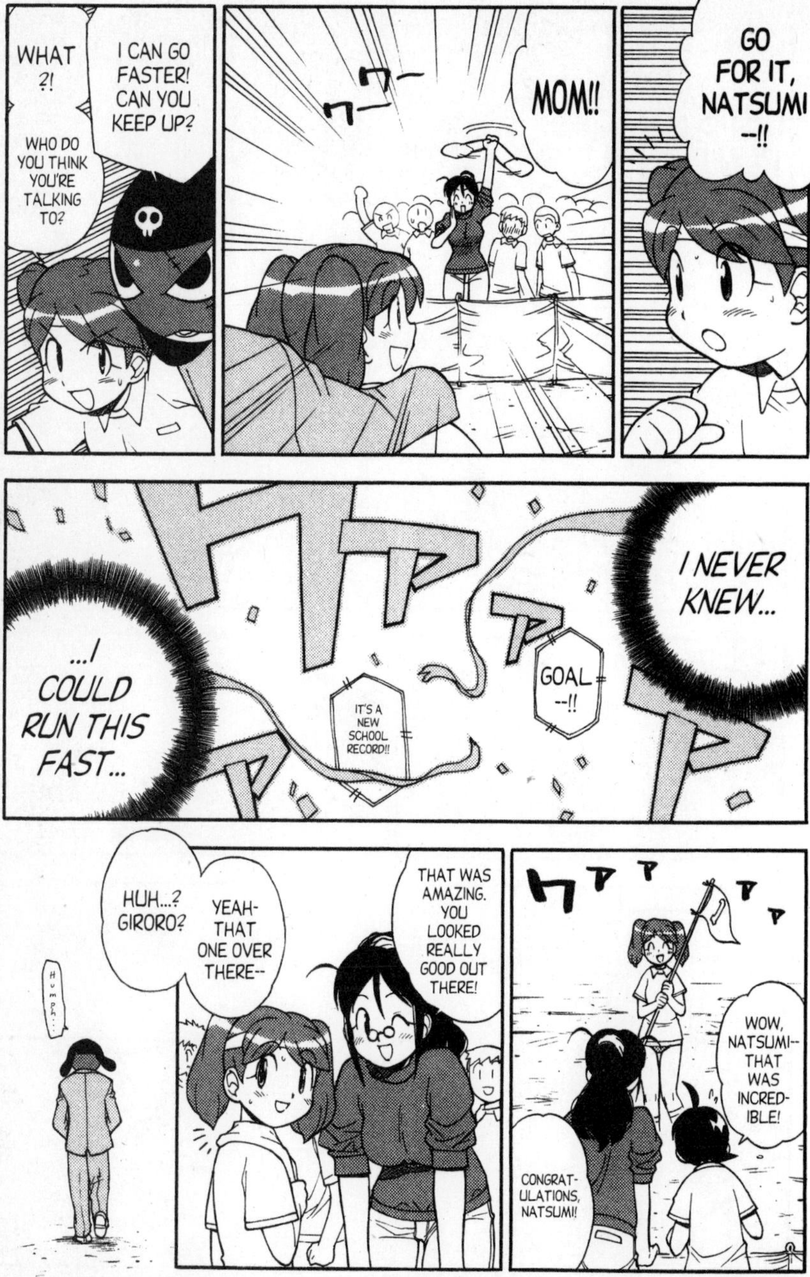
GO FOR IT, NATSUMI--!!
MOM!!
ワー ワー
I CAN GO FASTER! CAN YOU KEEP UP?
WHAT ?!
WHO DO YOU THINK YOU'RE TALKING TO?
I NEVER KNEW...
GOAL--!!
IT'S A NEW SCHOOL RECORD!!
...I COULD RUN THIS FAST...
WOW, NATSUMI--THAT WAS INCREDIBLE!
CONGRATULATIONS, NATSUMI!
THAT WAS AMAZING. YOU LOOKED REALLY GOOD OUT THERE!
YEAH-THAT ONE OVER THERE--
HUH...? GIRORO?
Humph...

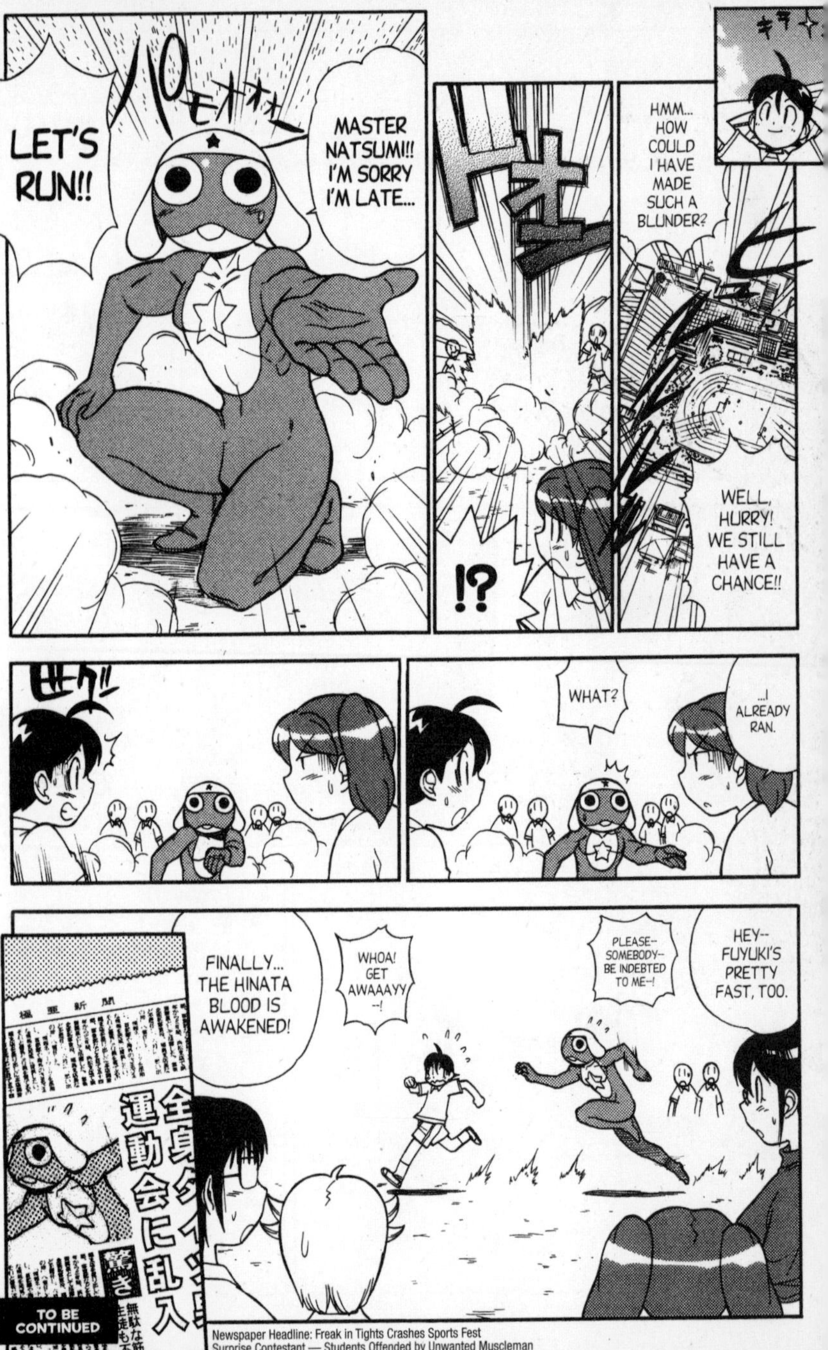
HMM... HOW COULD I HAVE MADE SUCH A BLUNDER?
WELL, HURRY! WE STILL HAVE A CHANCE!!
!?
MASTER NATSUMI!! I'M SORRY I'M LATE...
LET'S RUN!!
WHAT?
...I ALREADY RAN.
HEY-- FUYUKI'S PRETTY FAST, TOO.
PLEASE-- SOMEBODY-- BE INDEBTED TO ME--!
WHOA! GET AWAAAYY --!
FINALLY... THE HINATA BLOOD IS AWAKENED!
運動会に乱入
驚き
TO BE CONTINUED

Newspaper Headline: Freak in Tights Crashes Sports Fest
Surprise Contestant — Students Offended by Unwanted Muscleman

ENCOUNTER XL
OPERATION: DAZZLE THE HEAVENLY HOSTS!!

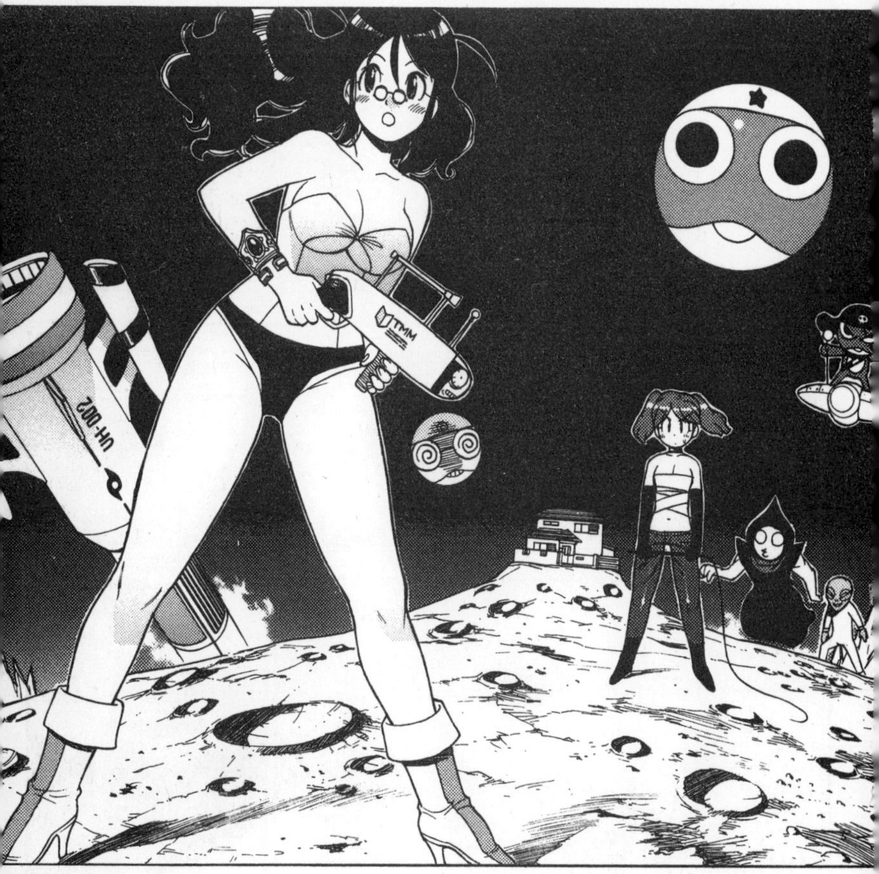
TMM

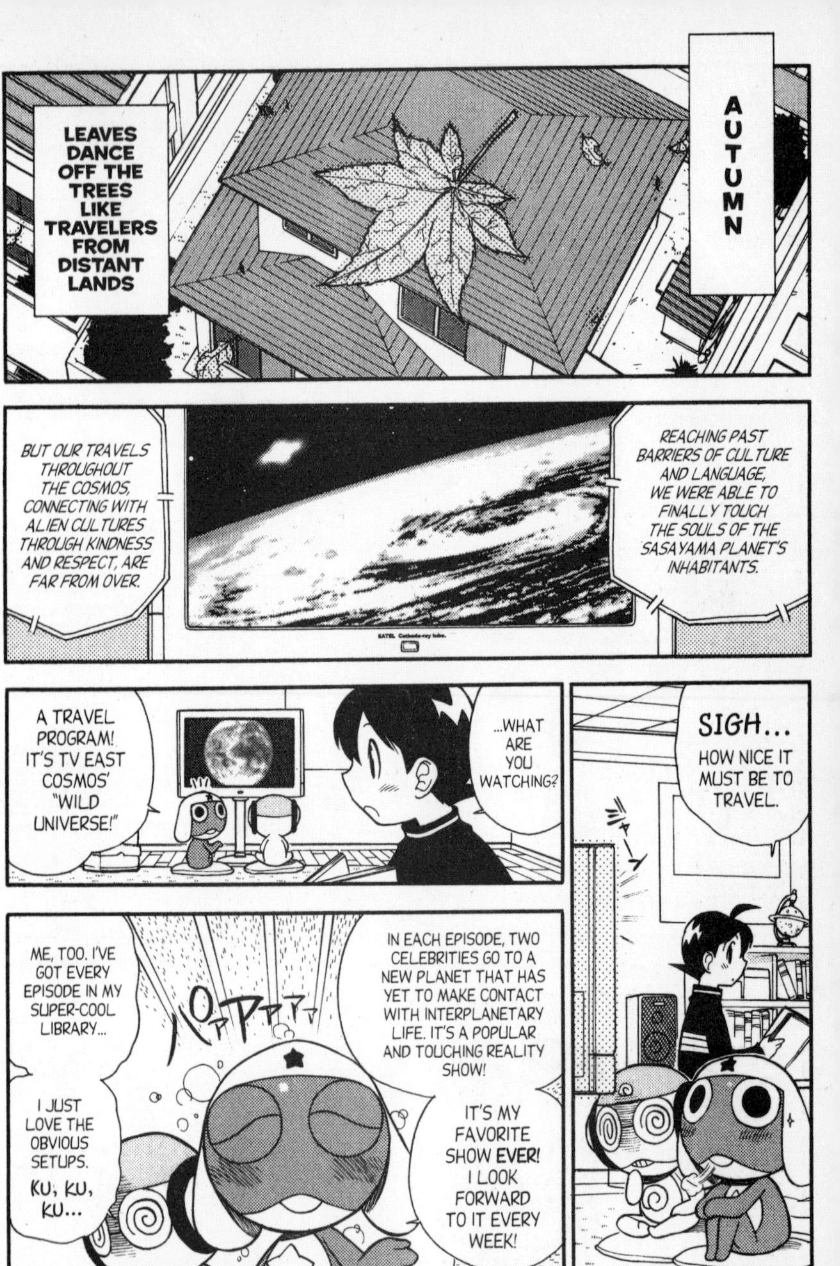
AUTUMN
LEAVES DANCE OFF THE TREES LIKE TRAVELERS FROM DISTANT LANDS
REACHING PAST BARRIERS OF CULTURE AND LANGUAGE, WE WERE ABLE TO FINALLY TOUCH THE SOULS OF THE SASAYAMA PLANET'S INHABITANTS.
BUT OUR TRAVELS THROUGHOUT THE COSMOS, CONNECTING WITH ALIEN CULTURES THROUGH KINDNESS AND RESPECT, ARE FAR FROM OVER.
SIGH... HOW NICE IT MUST BE TO TRAVEL.
...WHAT ARE YOU WATCHING?
A TRAVEL PROGRAM! IT'S TV EAST COSMOS' "WILD UNIVERSE!"
IN EACH EPISODE, TWO CELEBRITIES GO TO A NEW PLANET THAT HAS YET TO MAKE CONTACT WITH INTERPLANETARY LIFE. IT'S A POPULAR AND TOUCHING REALITY SHOW!
IT'S MY FAVORITE SHOW EVER! I LOOK FORWARD TO IT EVERY WEEK!
ME, TOO. I'VE GOT EVERY EPISODE IN MY SUPER-COOL LIBRARY...
I JUST LOVE THE OBVIOUS SETUPS.
KU, KU, KU...

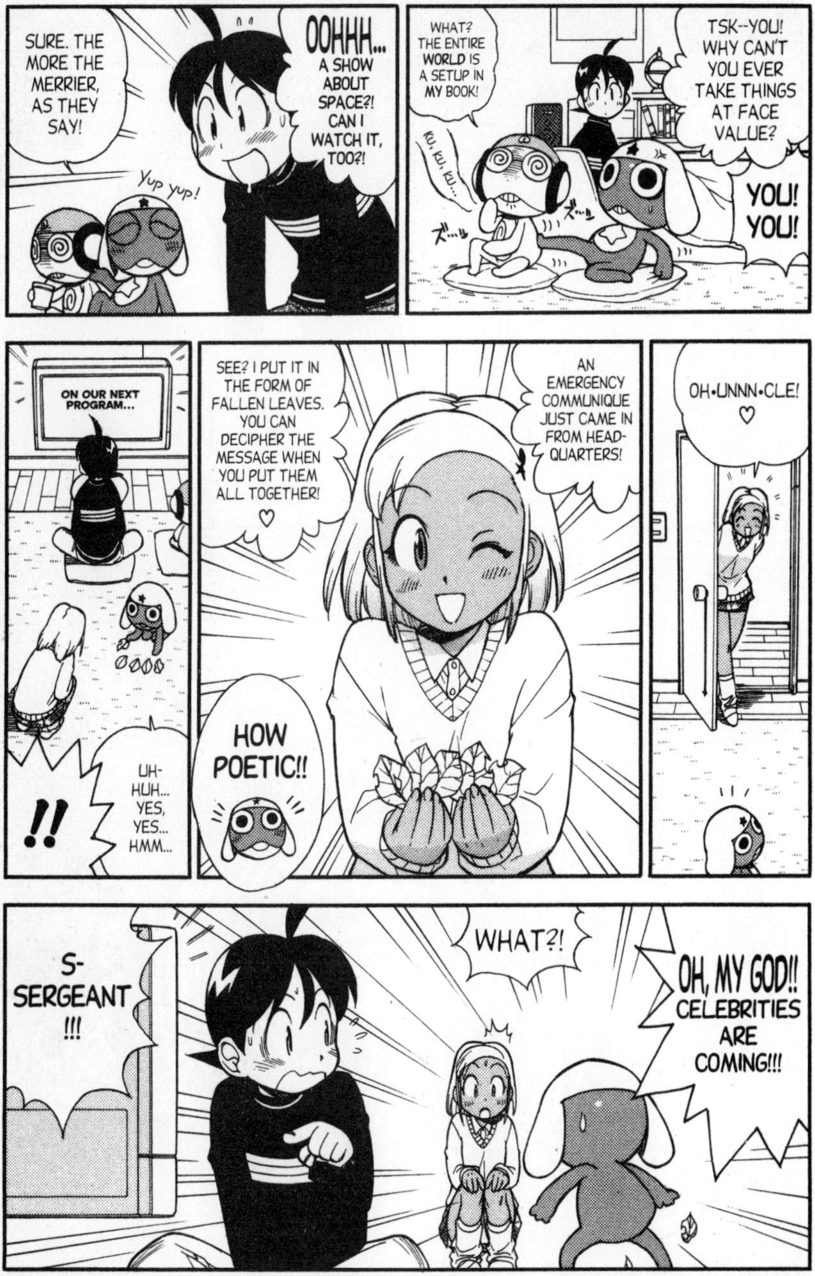
TSK--YOU! WHY CAN'T YOU EVER TAKE THINGS AT FACE VALUE?
WHAT? THE ENTIRE WORLD IS A SETUP IN MY BOOK!
KU, KU, KU...
YOU! YOU!
OOHHH... A SHOW ABOUT SPACE?! CAN I WATCH IT, TOO?!
SURE. THE MORE THE MERRIER, AS THEY SAY!
Yup yup!
OH•UNNN•CLE! ♡
AN EMERGENCY COMMUNIQUE JUST CAME IN FROM HEAD-QUARTERS!
SEE? I PUT IT IN THE FORM OF FALLEN LEAVES. YOU CAN DECIPHER THE MESSAGE WHEN YOU PUT THEM ALL TOGETHER! ♡
HOW POETIC!!
ON OUR NEXT PROGRAM...
UH-HUH... YES, YES... HMM...
!!
OH, MY GOD!! CELEBRITIES ARE COMING!!!
WHAT?!
S-SERGEANT!!!

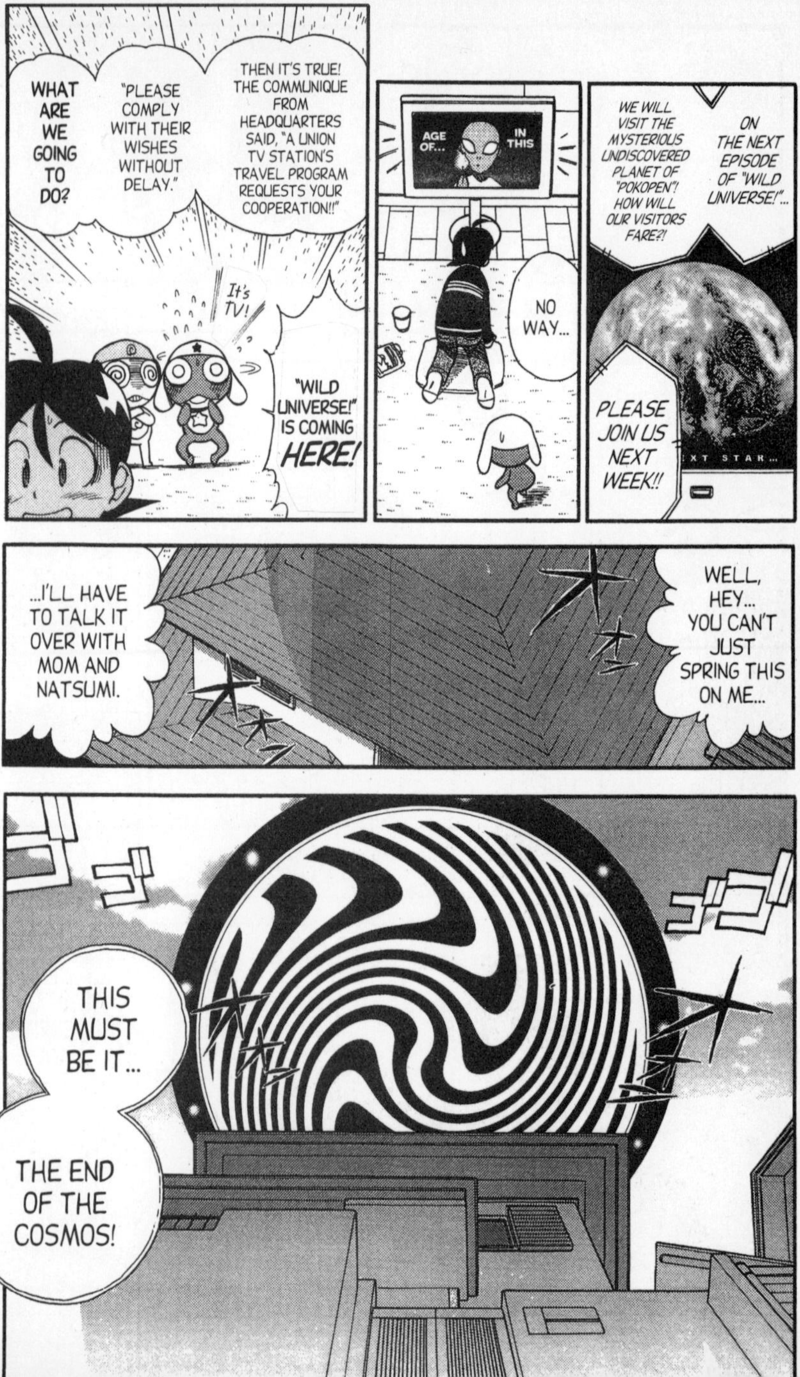
ON THE NEXT EPISODE OF "WILD UNIVERSE!"...
WE WILL VISIT THE MYSTERIOUS UNDISCOVERED PLANET OF "POKOPEN"! HOW WILL OUR VISITORS FARE?!
PLEASE JOIN US NEXT WEEK!!
AGE OF...
IN THIS
NO WAY...
THEN IT'S TRUE! THE COMMUNIQUE FROM HEADQUARTERS SAID, "A UNION TV STATION'S TRAVEL PROGRAM REQUESTS YOUR COOPERATION!!"
"PLEASE COMPLY WITH THEIR WISHES WITHOUT DELAY."
WHAT ARE WE GOING TO DO?
It's TV!
"WILD UNIVERSE!" IS COMING HERE!
WELL, HEY... YOU CAN'T JUST SPRING THIS ON ME...
...I'LL HAVE TO TALK IT OVER WITH MOM AND NATSUMI.
THIS MUST BE IT...
THE END OF THE COSMOS!

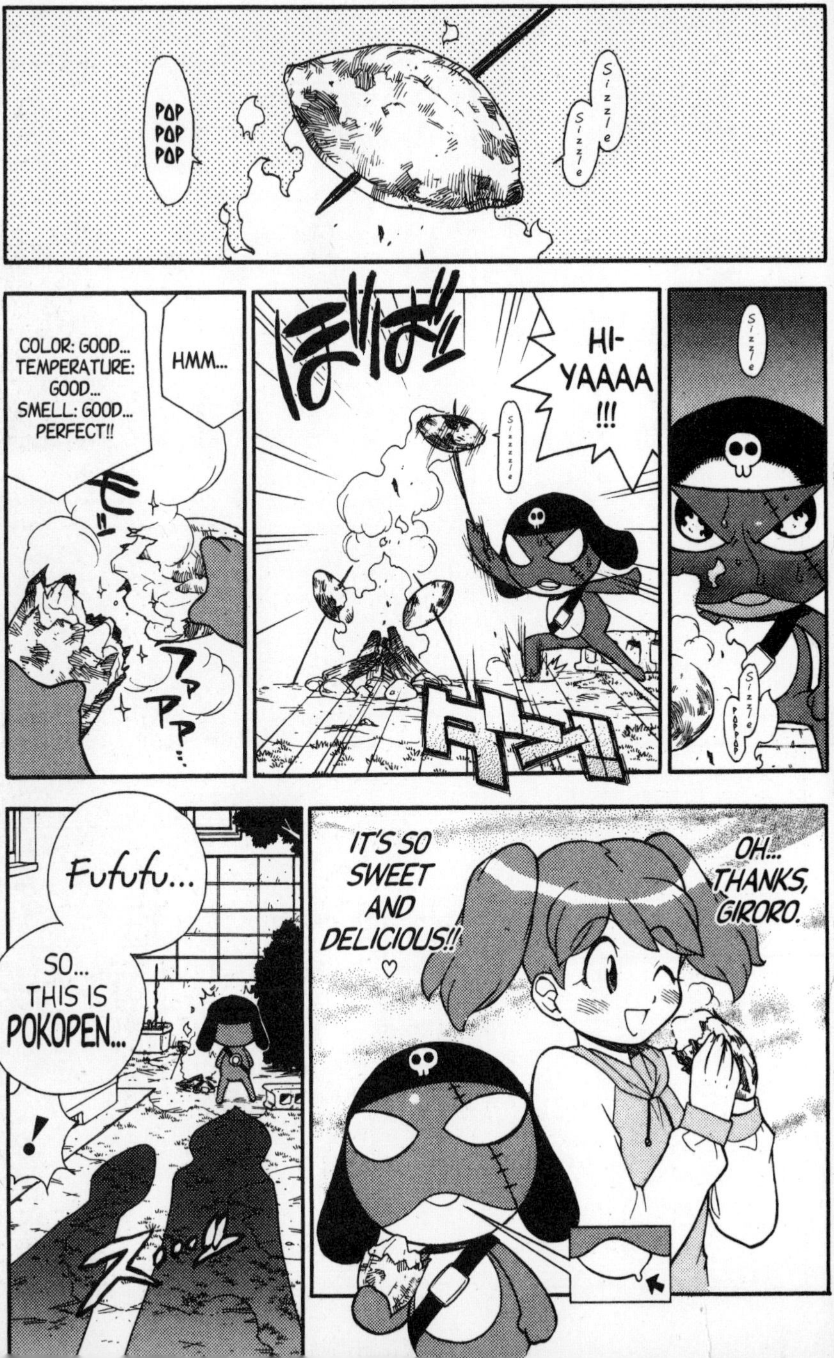
Sizzle
Sizzle
POP
POP
POP
Sizzle
Sizzle
HI-YAAAA!!!
Sizzzzle
HMM...
COLOR: GOOD... TEMPERATURE: GOOD... SMELL: GOOD... PERFECT!!
OH... THANKS, GIRORO.
IT'S SO SWEET AND DELICIOUS!! ♡
Fufufu...
SO... THIS IS POKOPEN...
!

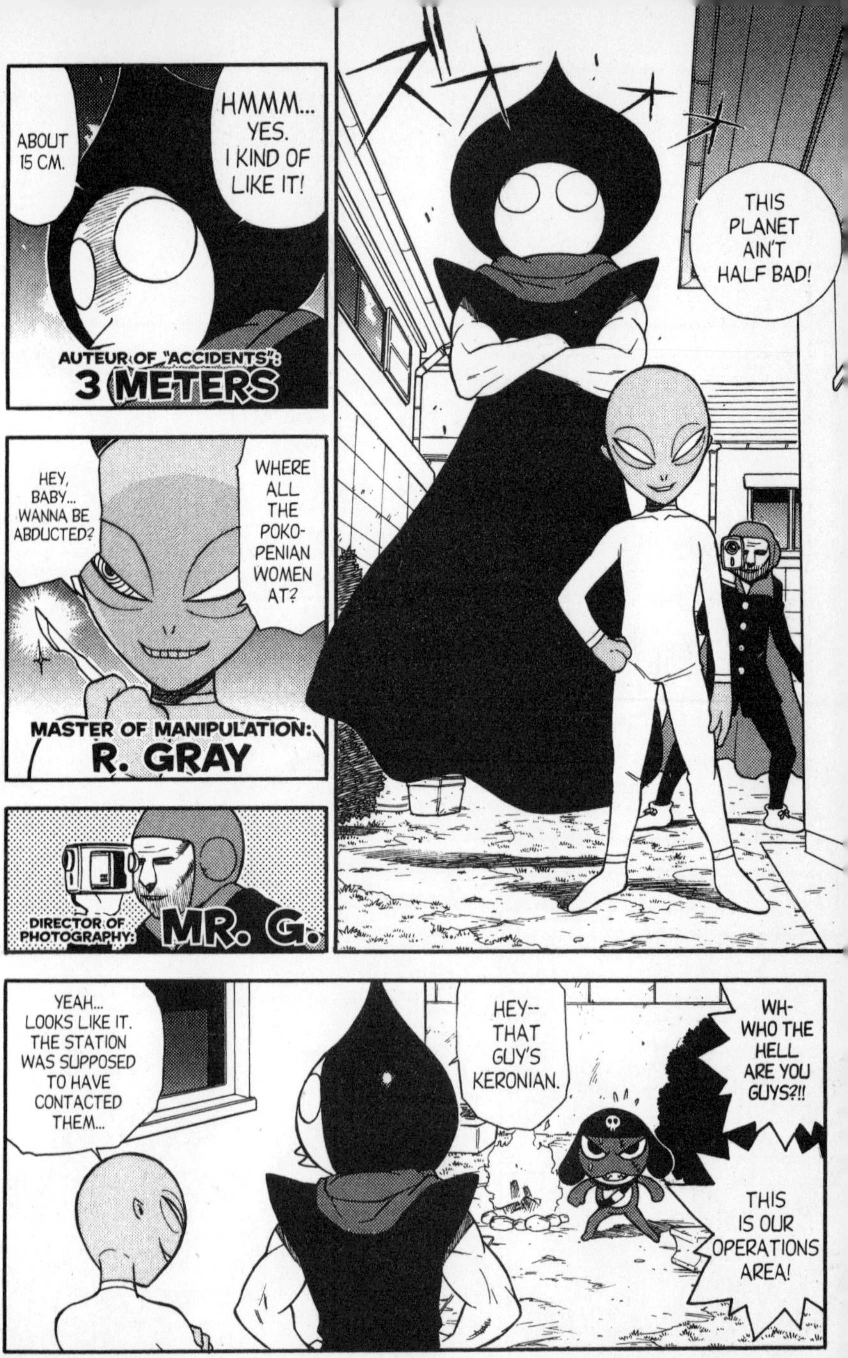
THIS PLANET AIN'T HALF BAD!
HMMM... YES. I KIND OF LIKE IT!
ABOUT 15 CM.
AUTEUR OF "ACCIDENTS": 3 METERS
WHERE ALL THE POKO-PENIAN WOMEN AT?
HEY, BABY... WANNA BE ABDUCTED?
MASTER OF MANIPULATION: R. GRAY
DIRECTOR OF PHOTOGRAPHY: MR. G.
WH-WHO THE HELL ARE YOU GUYS?!!
THIS IS OUR OPERATIONS AREA!
HEY--THAT GUY'S KERONIAN.
YEAH... LOOKS LIKE IT. THE STATION WAS SUPPOSED TO HAVE CONTACTED THEM...

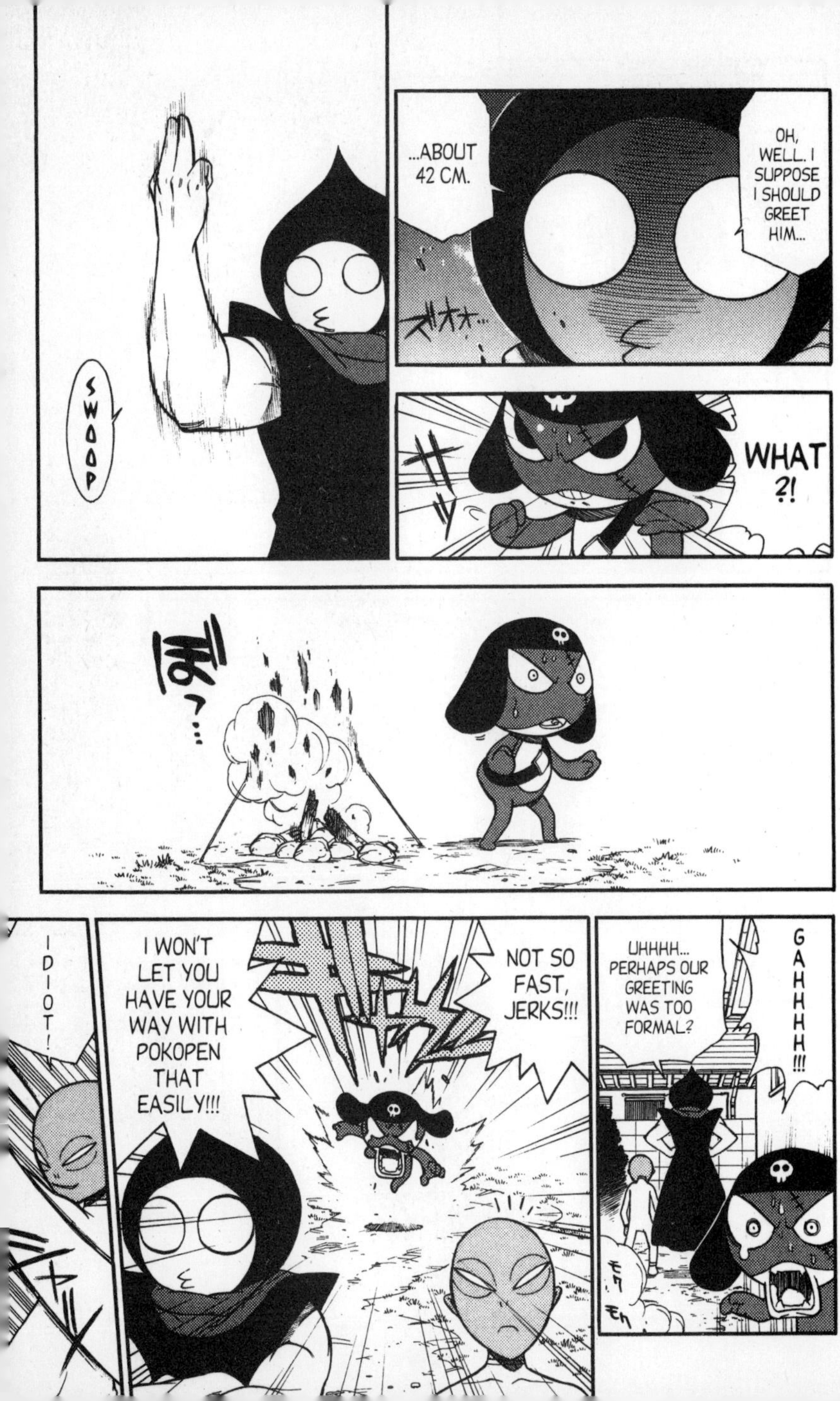
OH, WELL. I SUPPOSE I SHOULD GREET HIM...
...ABOUT 42 CM.
WHAT?!
SWOOP
GAHHHH!!!
UHHHH... PERHAPS OUR GREETING WAS TOO FORMAL?
NOT SO FAST, JERKS!!!
I WON'T LET YOU HAVE YOUR WAY WITH POKOPEN THAT EASILY!!!
IDIOT!

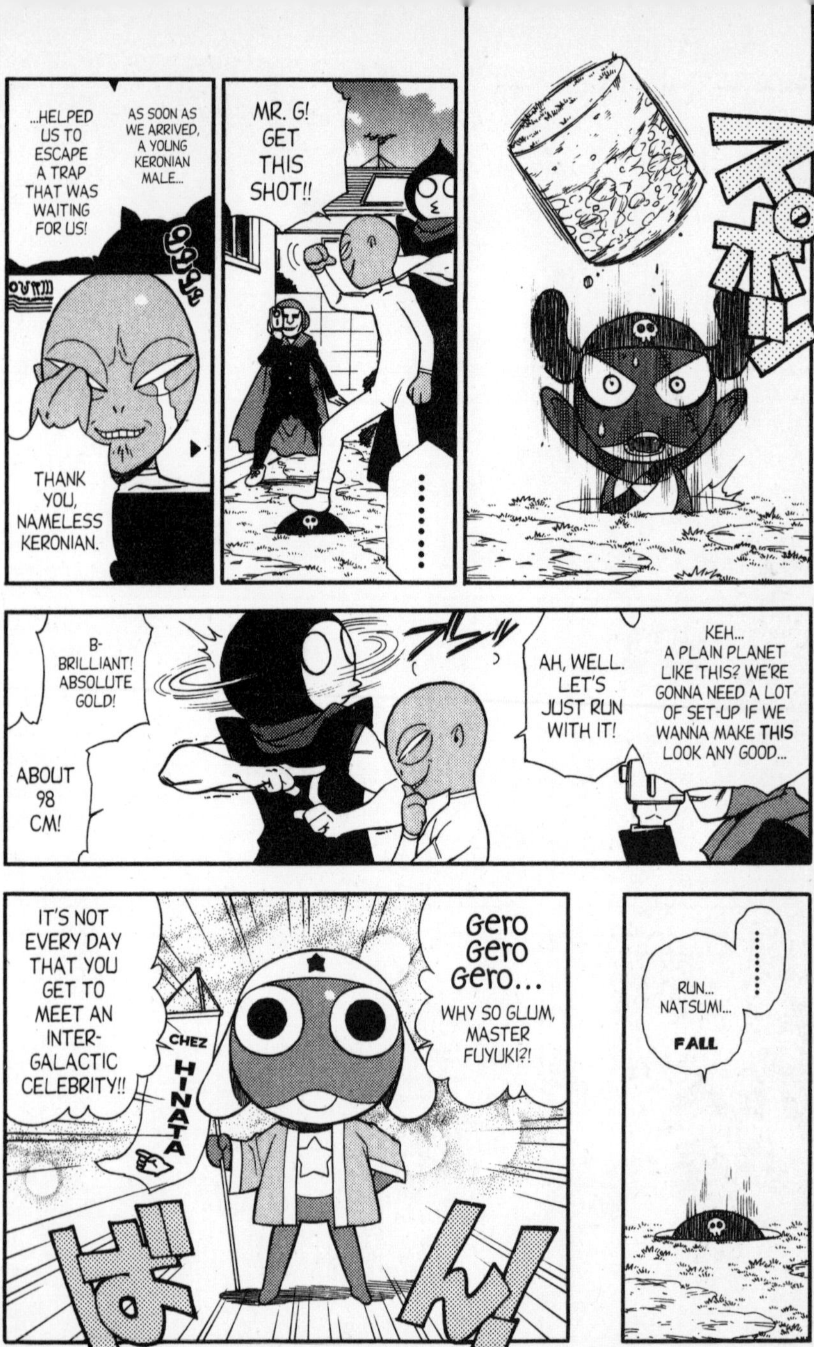

MR. G! GET THIS SHOT!!
......
AS SOON AS WE ARRIVED, A YOUNG KERONIAN MALE...
...HELPED US TO ESCAPE A TRAP THAT WAS WAITING FOR US!
THANK YOU, NAMELESS KERONIAN.
KEH... A PLAIN PLANET LIKE THIS? WE'RE GONNA NEED A LOT OF SET-UP IF WE WANNA MAKE THIS LOOK ANY GOOD...
AH, WELL. LET'S JUST RUN WITH IT!
B-BRILLIANT! ABSOLUTE GOLD!
ABOUT 98 CM!
......
RUN... NATSUMI...
FALL
Gero Gero Gero...
WHY SO GLUM, MASTER FUYUKI?!
IT'S NOT EVERY DAY THAT YOU GET TO MEET AN INTER-GALACTIC CELEBRITY!!
CHEZ HINATA

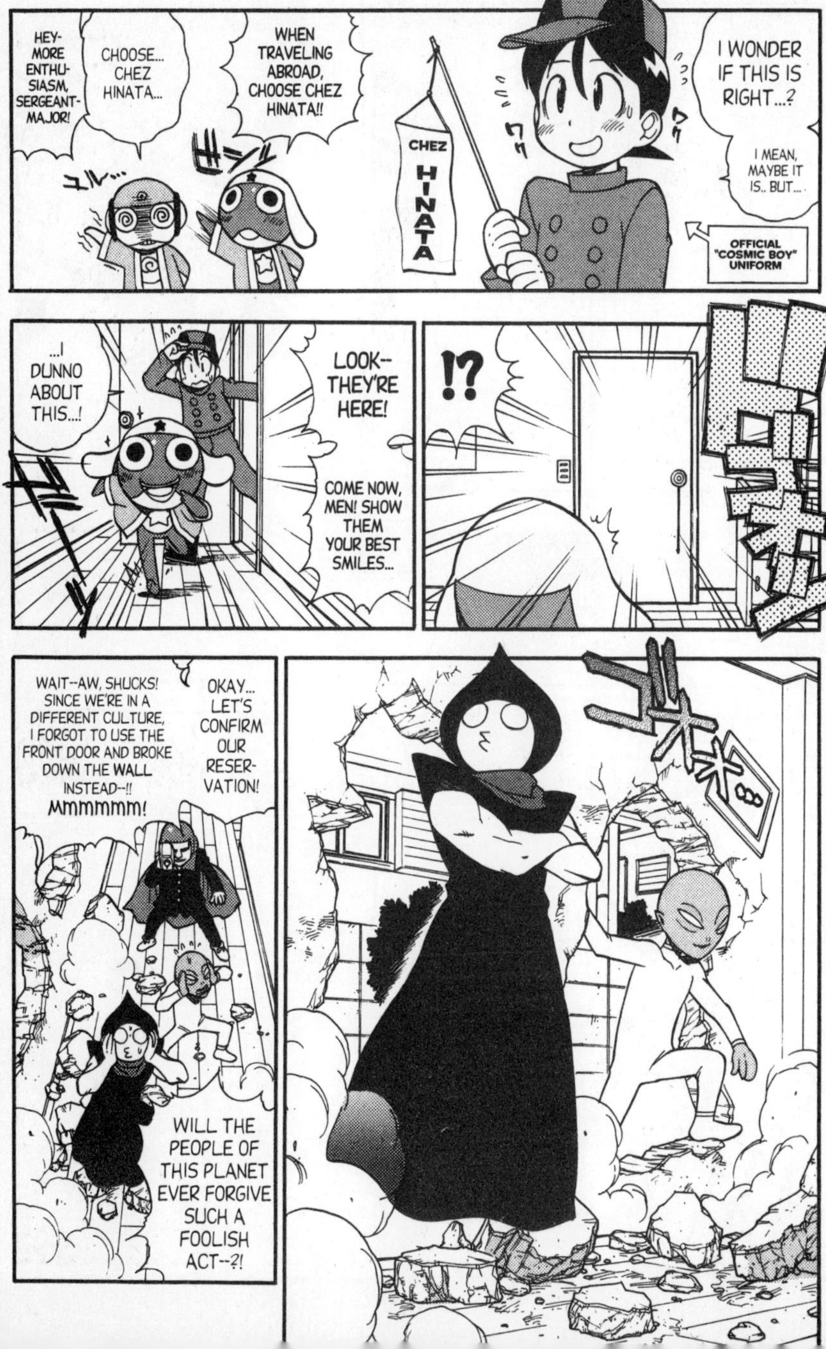
I WONDER IF THIS IS RIGHT...?
I MEAN, MAYBE IT IS.. BUT...
OFFICIAL "COSMIC BOY" UNIFORM
CHEZ HINATA
WHEN TRAVELING ABROAD, CHOOSE CHEZ HINATA!!
CHOOSE... CHEZ HINATA...
HEY- MORE ENTHUSIASM, SERGEANT-MAJOR!
!?
LOOK--THEY'RE HERE!
COME NOW, MEN! SHOW THEM YOUR BEST SMILES...
...I DUNNO ABOUT THIS...!
OKAY... LET'S CONFIRM OUR RESERVATION!
WAIT--AW, SHUCKS! SINCE WE'RE IN A DIFFERENT CULTURE, I FORGOT TO USE THE FRONT DOOR AND BROKE DOWN THE WALL INSTEAD--!! Mmmmmm!
WILL THE PEOPLE OF THIS PLANET EVER FORGIVE SUCH A FOOLISH ACT--?!

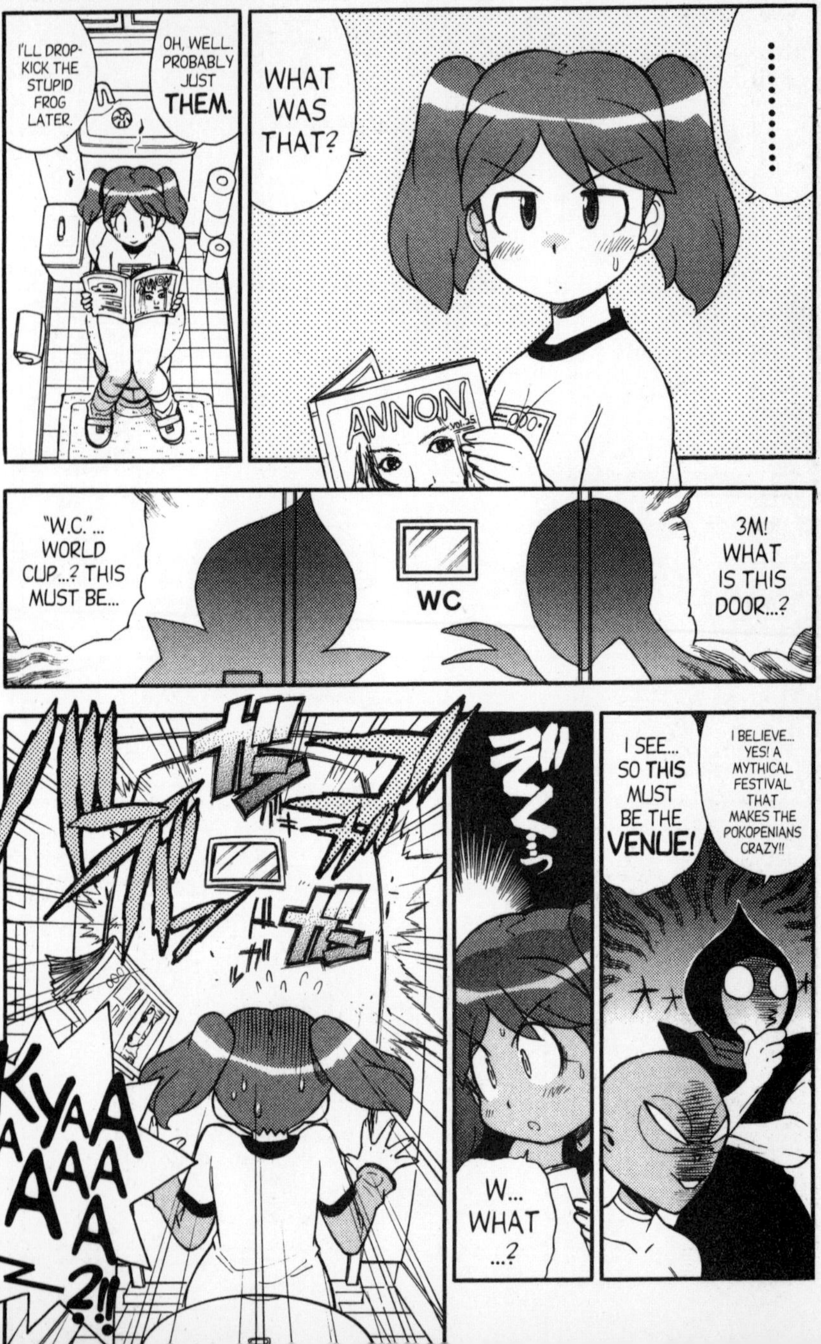
……
WHAT WAS THAT?
OH, WELL. PROBABLY JUST THEM.
I'LL DROP-KICK THE STUPID FROG LATER.
3M! WHAT IS THIS DOOR...?
WC
"W.C."... WORLD CUP...? THIS MUST BE...
I BELIEVE... YES! A MYTHICAL FESTIVAL THAT MAKES THE POKOPENIANS CRAZY!!
I SEE... SO THIS MUST BE THE VENUE!
W... WHAT ...?
KYAAAAAAAAA—?!!

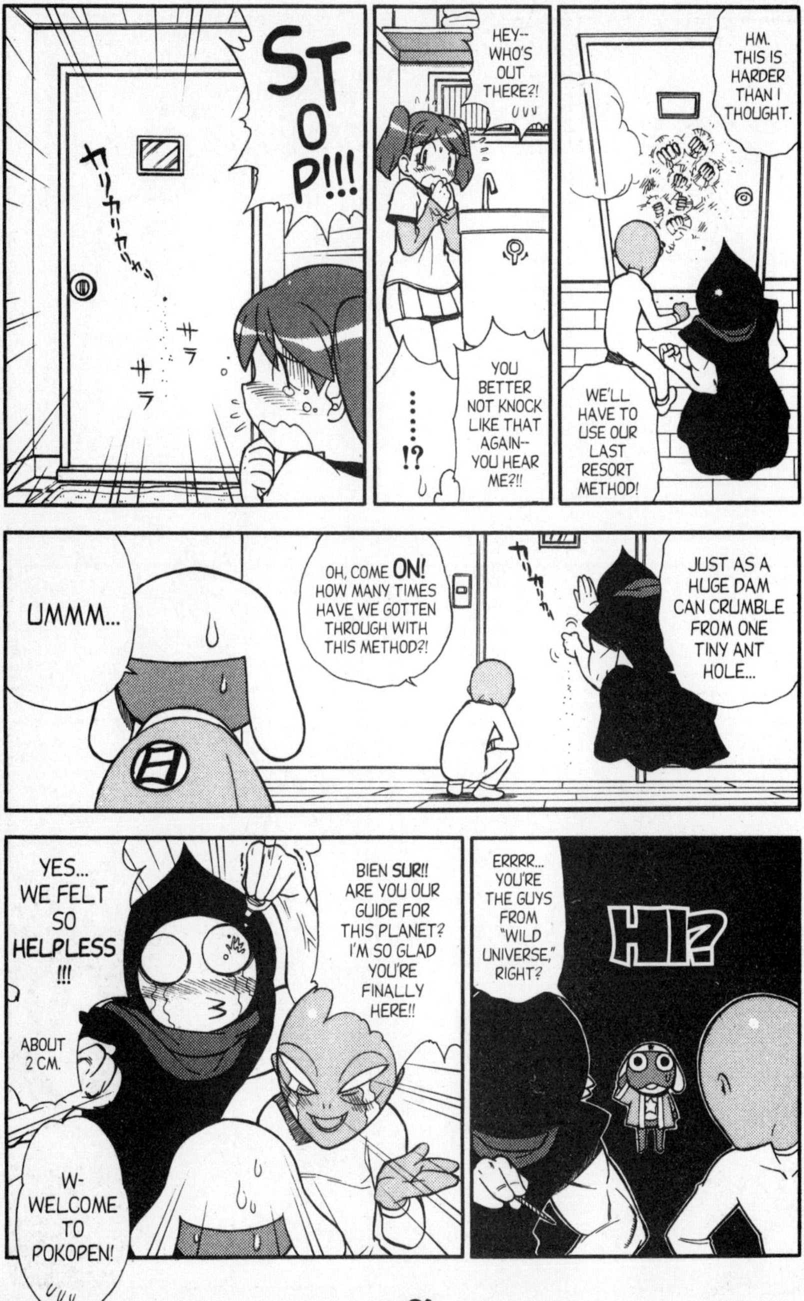
HM. THIS IS HARDER THAN I THOUGHT.
WE'LL HAVE TO USE OUR LAST RESORT METHOD!
HEY-- WHO'S OUT THERE?!
YOU BETTER NOT KNOCK LIKE THAT AGAIN-- YOU HEAR ME?!!
......!?
STOP!!!
JUST AS A HUGE DAM CAN CRUMBLE FROM ONE TINY ANT HOLE...
OH, COME ON! HOW MANY TIMES HAVE WE GOTTEN THROUGH WITH THIS METHOD?!
UMMM...
HI?
ERRRR... YOU'RE THE GUYS FROM "WILD UNIVERSE," RIGHT?
BIEN SUR!! ARE YOU OUR GUIDE FOR THIS PLANET? I'M SO GLAD YOU'RE FINALLY HERE!!
YES... WE FELT SO HELPLESS!!!
ABOUT 2 CM.
W- WELCOME TO POKOPEN!

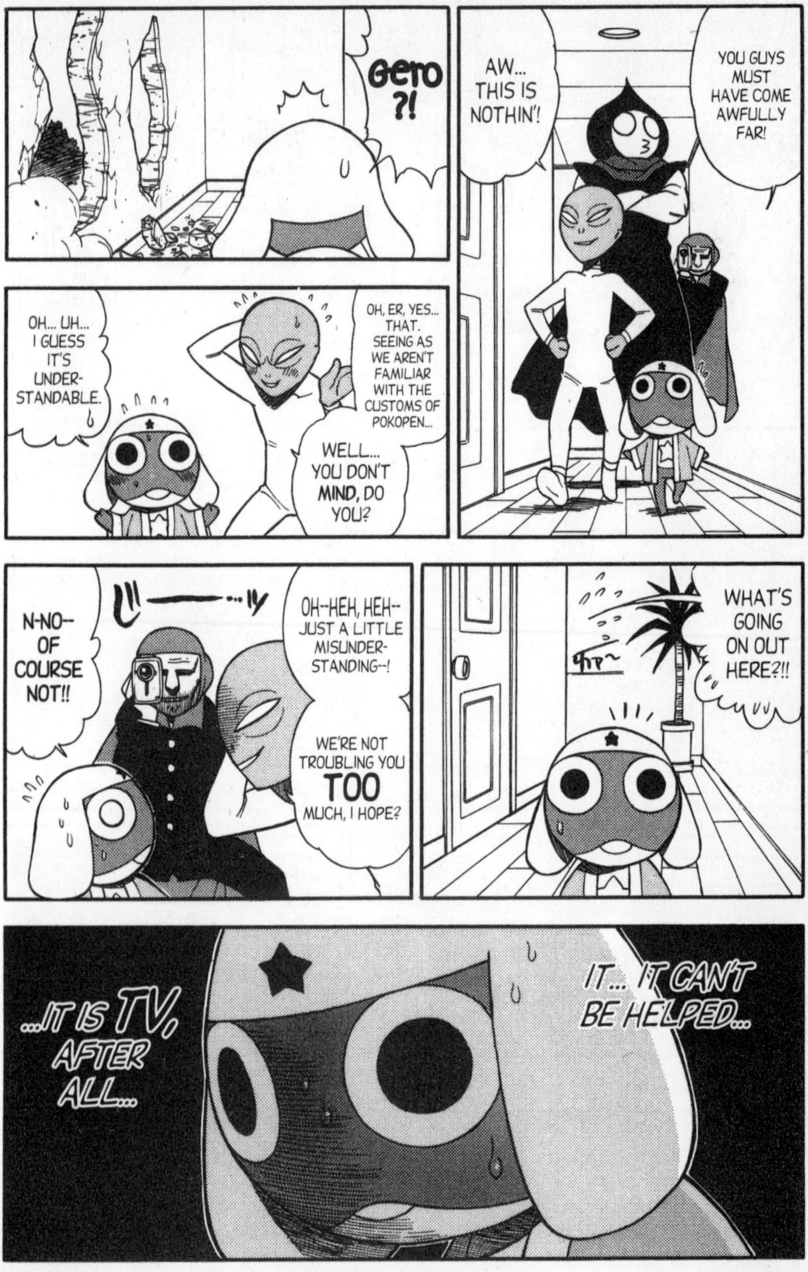
YOU GUYS MUST HAVE COME AWFULLY FAR!
AW... THIS IS NOTHIN'!
GETO ?!
OH, ER, YES... THAT. SEEING AS WE AREN'T FAMILIAR WITH THE CUSTOMS OF POKOPEN...
WELL... YOU DON'T MIND, DO YOU?
OH... UH... I GUESS IT'S UNDER-STANDABLE.
WHAT'S GOING ON OUT HERE?!!
OH--HEH, HEH-- JUST A LITTLE MISUNDER-STANDING--!
WE'RE NOT TROUBLING YOU TOO MUCH, I HOPE?
N-NO-- OF COURSE NOT!!
IT... IT CAN'T BE HELPED...
...IT IS TV, AFTER ALL...

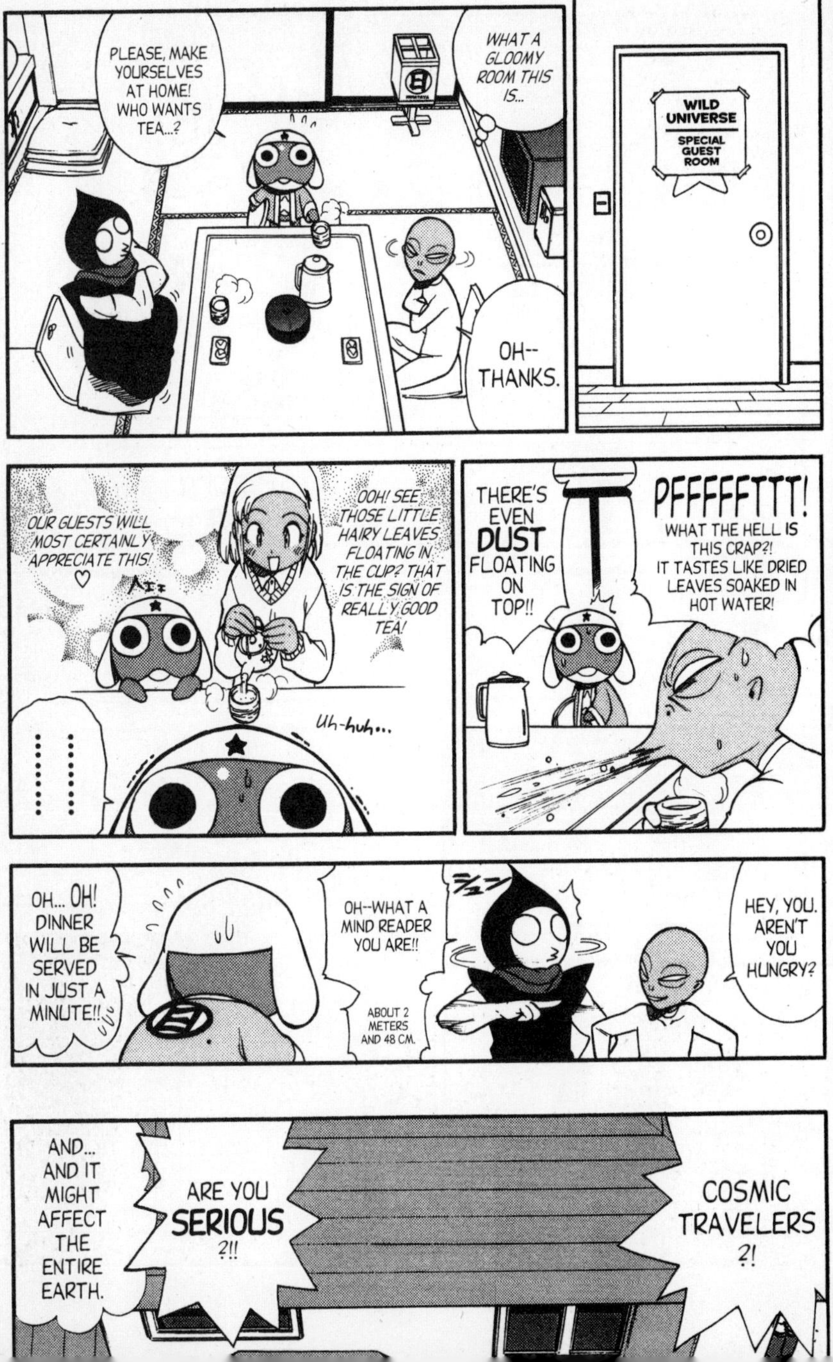
WILD UNIVERSE
SPECIAL GUEST ROOM
WHAT A GLOOMY ROOM THIS IS...
PLEASE, MAKE YOURSELVES AT HOME! WHO WANTS TEA...?
OH-- THANKS.
PFFFFFTTT!
WHAT THE HELL IS THIS CRAP?! IT TASTES LIKE DRIED LEAVES SOAKED IN HOT WATER!
THERE'S EVEN DUST FLOATING ON TOP!!
OOH! SEE THOSE LITTLE HAIRY LEAVES FLOATING IN THE CUP? THAT IS THE SIGN OF REALLY GOOD TEA!
OUR GUESTS WILL MOST CERTAINLY APPRECIATE THIS! ♡
Uh-huh...
....
HEY, YOU. AREN'T YOU HUNGRY?
OH--WHAT A MIND READER YOU ARE!!
ABOUT 2 METERS AND 48 CM.
OH... OH! DINNER WILL BE SERVED IN JUST A MINUTE!!
COSMIC TRAVELERS ?!
ARE YOU SERIOUS ?!!
AND... AND IT MIGHT AFFECT THE ENTIRE EARTH.

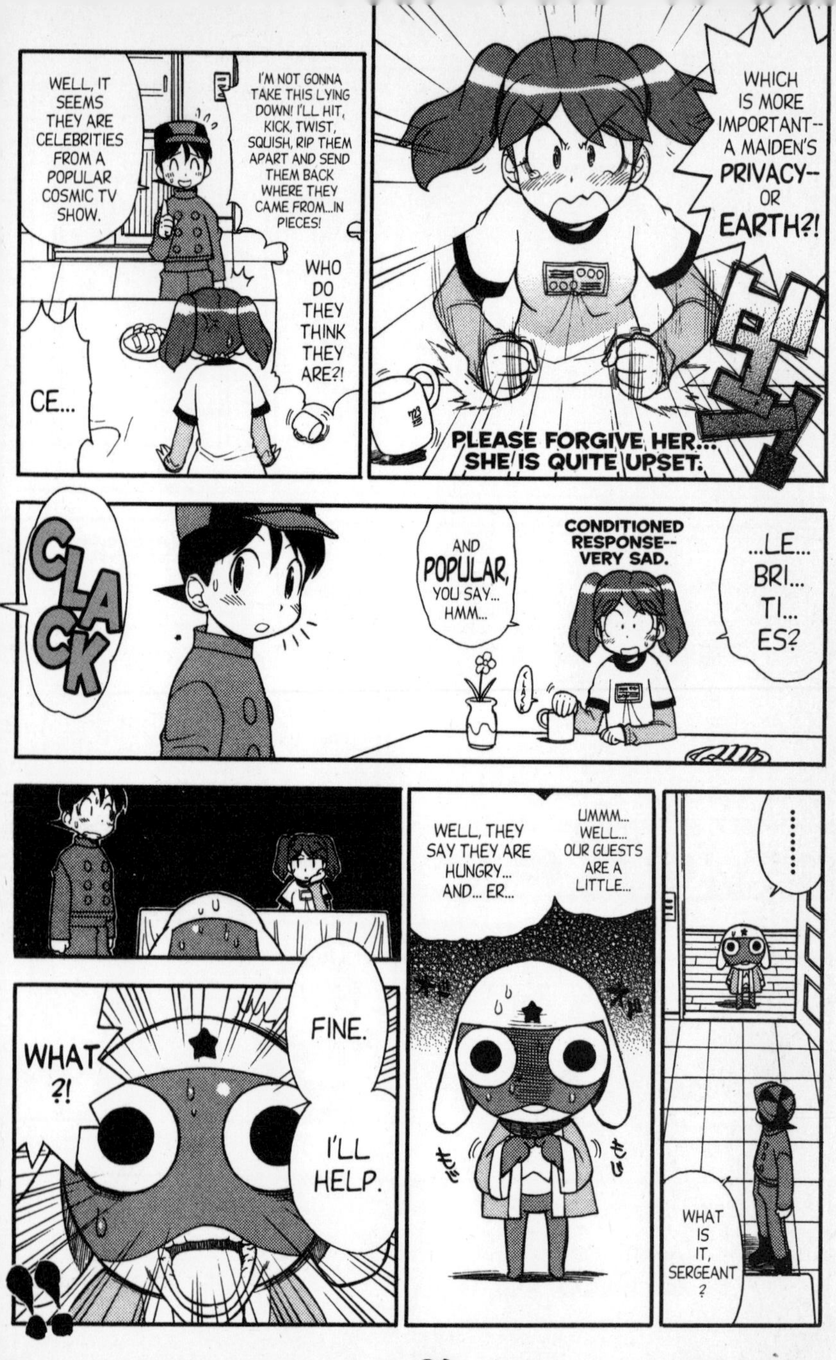
WHICH IS MORE IMPORTANT-- A MAIDEN'S PRIVACY-- OR EARTH?!
PLEASE FORGIVE HER... SHE IS QUITE UPSET.
I'M NOT GONNA TAKE THIS LYING DOWN! I'LL HIT, KICK, TWIST, SQUISH, RIP THEM APART AND SEND THEM BACK WHERE THEY CAME FROM...IN PIECES!
WELL, IT SEEMS THEY ARE CELEBRITIES FROM A POPULAR COSMIC TV SHOW.
WHO DO THEY THINK THEY ARE?!
CE...
...LE... BRI... TI... ES?
CONDITIONED RESPONSE-- VERY SAD.
AND POPULAR, YOU SAY... HMM...
CLACK
CLACK
....
WHAT IS IT, SERGEANT?
UMMM... WELL... OUR GUESTS ARE A LITTLE...
WELL, THEY SAY THEY ARE HUNGRY... AND... ER...
FINE.
I'LL HELP.
WHAT?!

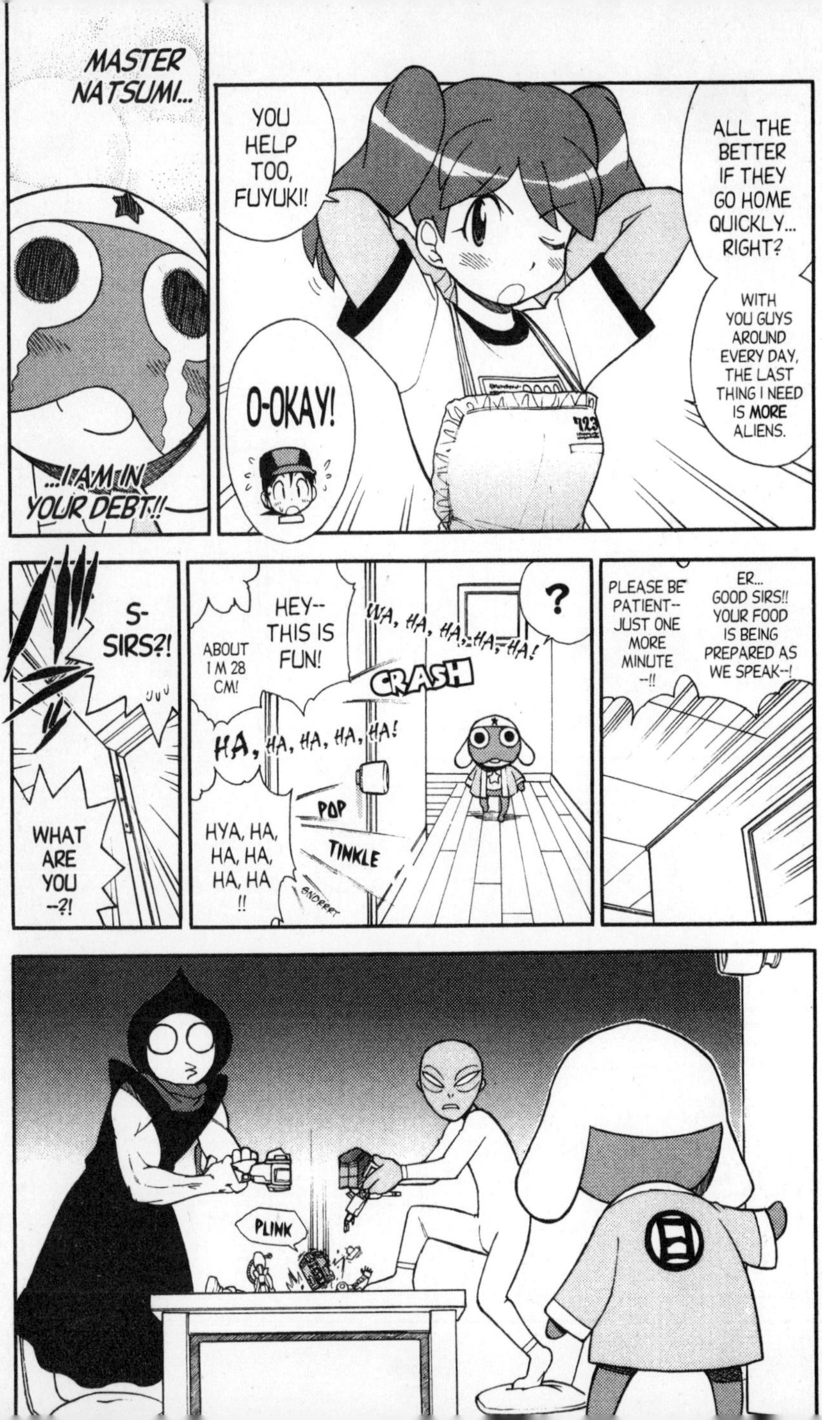
ALL THE BETTER IF THEY GO HOME QUICKLY... RIGHT?
WITH YOU GUYS AROUND EVERY DAY, THE LAST THING I NEED IS MORE ALIENS.
YOU HELP TOO, FUYUKI!
O-OKAY!
MASTER NATSUMI...
...I AM IN YOUR DEBT!!
ER... GOOD SIRS!! YOUR FOOD IS BEING PREPARED AS WE SPEAK--!
PLEASE BE PATIENT-- JUST ONE MORE MINUTE --!!
?
WA, HA, HA, HA, HA!
CRASH
HEY-- THIS IS FUN!
ABOUT 1 M 28 CM!
HA, HA, HA, HA, HA!
POP
TINKLE
HYA, HA, HA, HA, HA, HA !!
SNORRRT
S-SIRS?!
WHAT ARE YOU --?!
PLINK

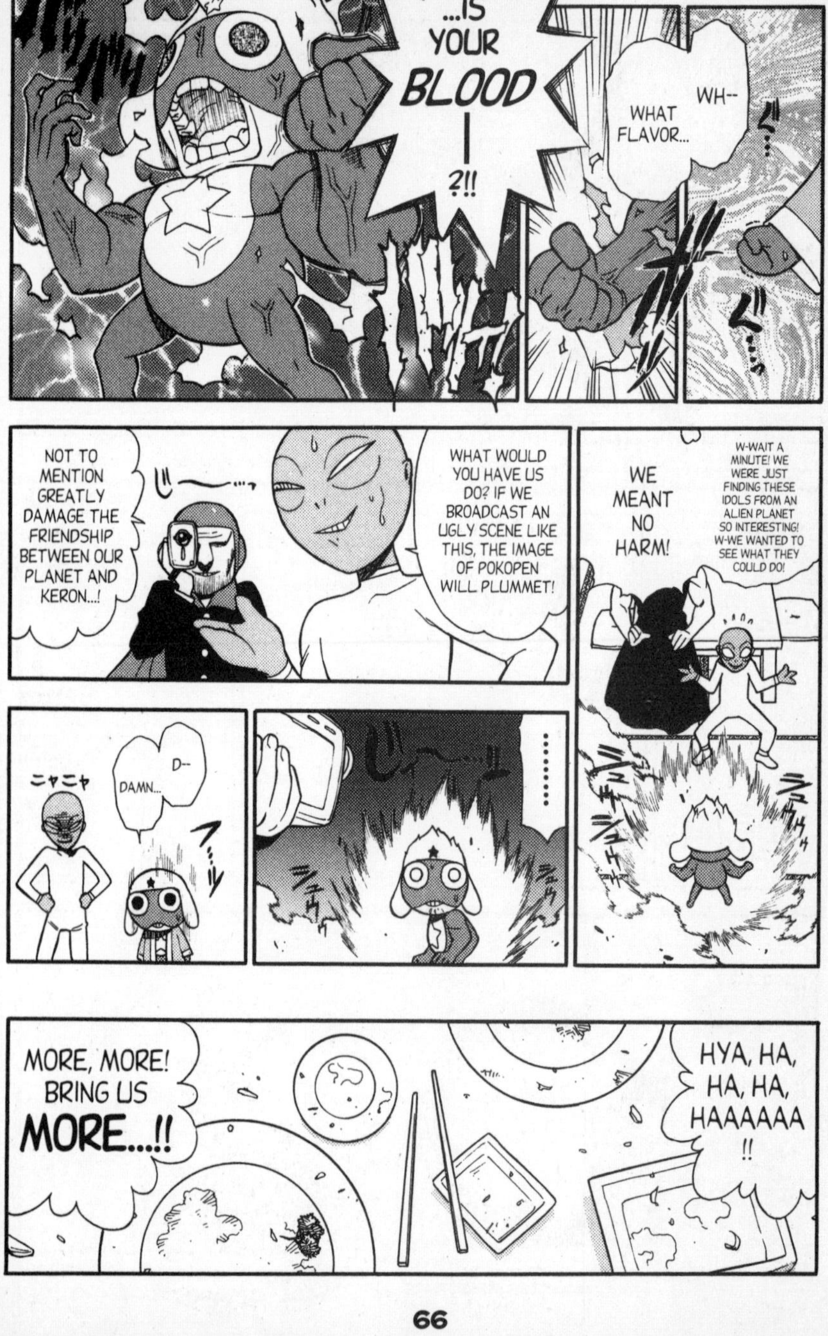
WH-- WHAT FLAVOR...
...IS YOUR BLOOD!?!!
W-WAIT A MINUTE! WE WERE JUST FINDING THESE IDOLS FROM AN ALIEN PLANET SO INTERESTING! W-WE WANTED TO SEE WHAT THEY COULD DO!
WE MEANT NO HARM!
WHAT WOULD YOU HAVE US DO? IF WE BROADCAST AN UGLY SCENE LIKE THIS, THE IMAGE OF POKOPEN WILL PLUMMET!
NOT TO MENTION GREATLY DAMAGE THE FRIENDSHIP BETWEEN OUR PLANET AND KERON...!
....
D-- DAMN...
ニヤニヤ
HYA, HA, HA, HA, HAAAAAA!!
MORE, MORE! BRING US MORE...!!

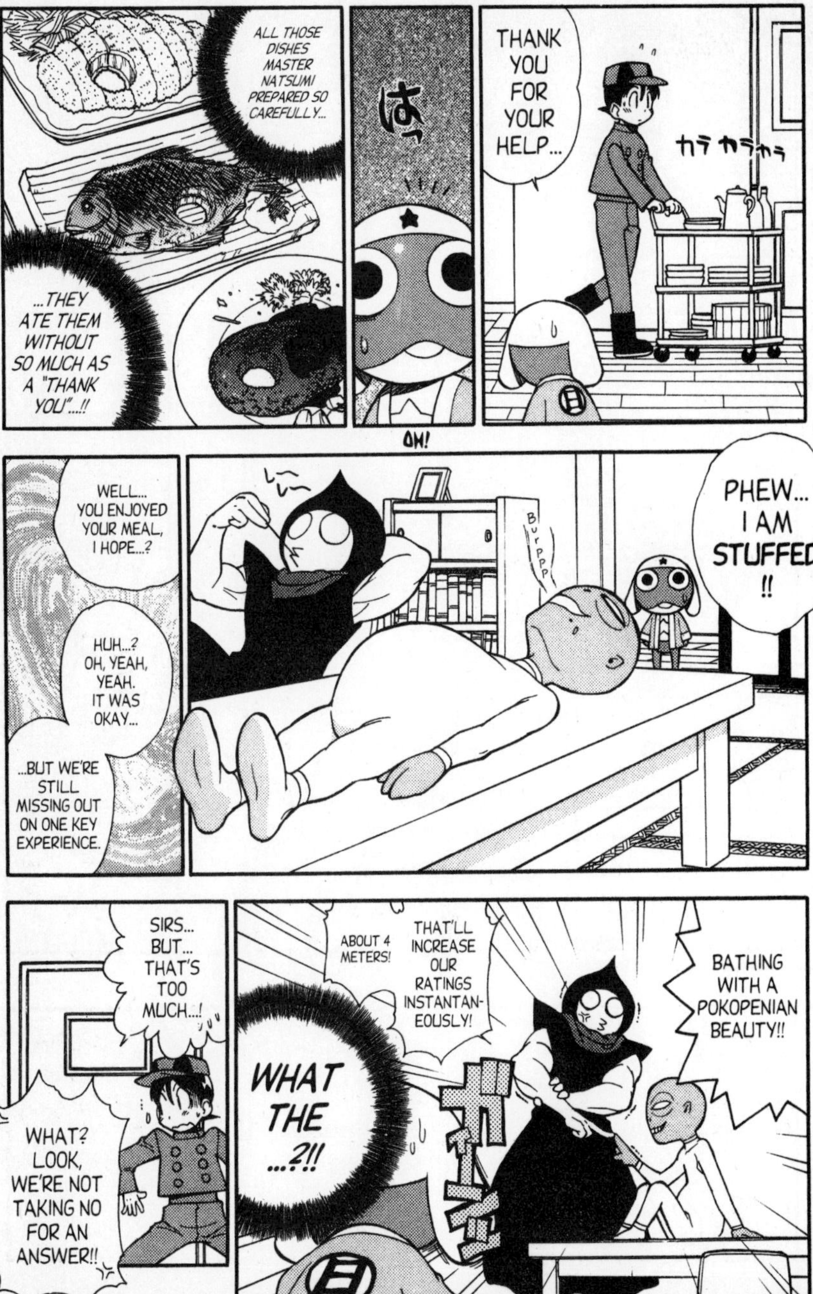
THANK YOU FOR YOUR HELP...
カラ カラカラ
はっ
OH!
ALL THOSE DISHES MASTER NATSUMI PREPARED SO CAREFULLY...
...THEY ATE THEM WITHOUT SO MUCH AS A "THANK YOU"...!!
PHEW... I AM STUFFED!!
Burppp
しー しー
WELL... YOU ENJOYED YOUR MEAL, I HOPE...?
HUH...? OH, YEAH, YEAH. IT WAS OKAY...
...BUT WE'RE STILL MISSING OUT ON ONE KEY EXPERIENCE.
BATHING WITH A POKOPENIAN BEAUTY!!
THAT'LL INCREASE OUR RATINGS INSTANTANEOUSLY!
ABOUT 4 METERS!
WHAT THE ...?!!
SIRS... BUT... THAT'S TOO MUCH...!
WHAT? LOOK, WE'RE NOT TAKING NO FOR AN ANSWER!!

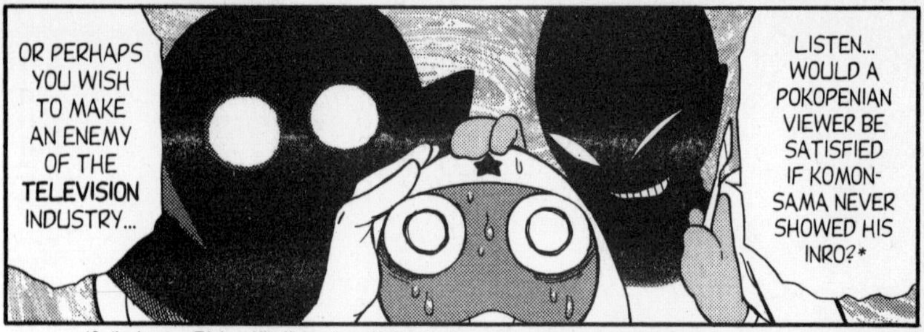
LISTEN... WOULD A POKOPENIAN VIEWER BE SATISFIED IF KOMON-SAMA NEVER SHOWED HIS INRO?*
OR PERHAPS YOU WISH TO MAKE AN ENEMY OF THE TELEVISION INDUSTRY...

*On the Japanese TV show *Mito-Komon*, the main character, Komon-sama, goes around serving justice and showing his inro (imperial seal).

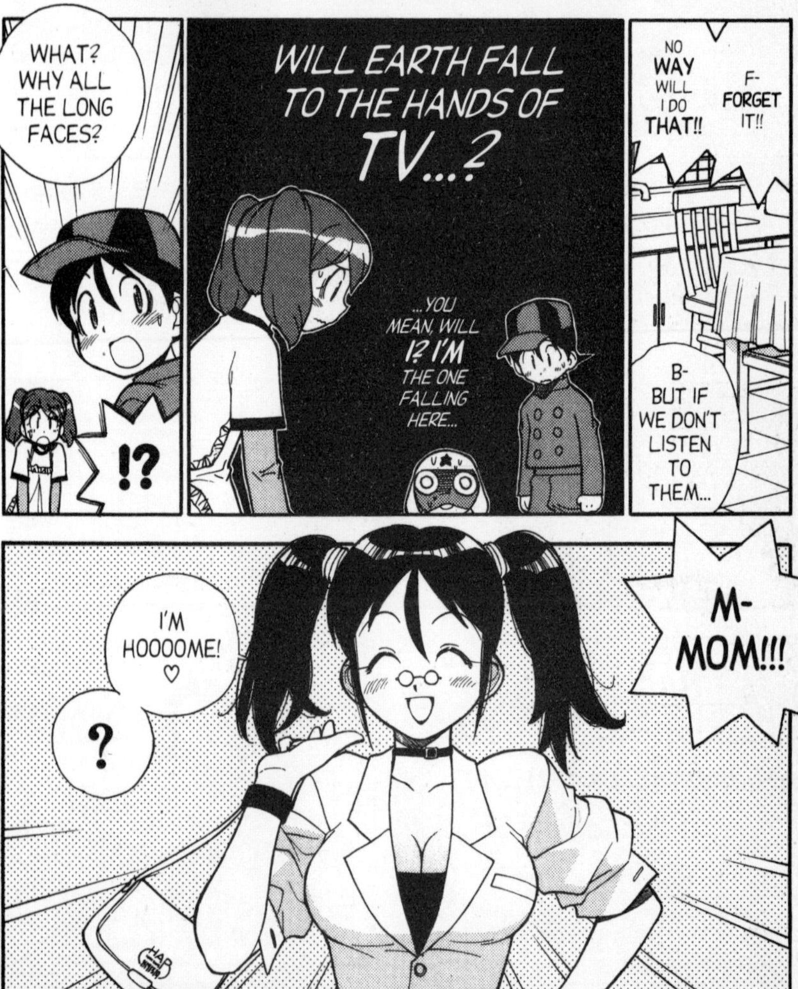
NO WAY WILL I DO THAT!!
F-FORGET IT!!
B-BUT IF WE DON'T LISTEN TO THEM...
WILL EARTH FALL TO THE HANDS OF TV...?
...YOU MEAN, WILL I? I'M THE ONE FALLING HERE...
WHAT? WHY ALL THE LONG FACES?
!?
M-MOM!!!
I'M HOOOOME! ♡
?

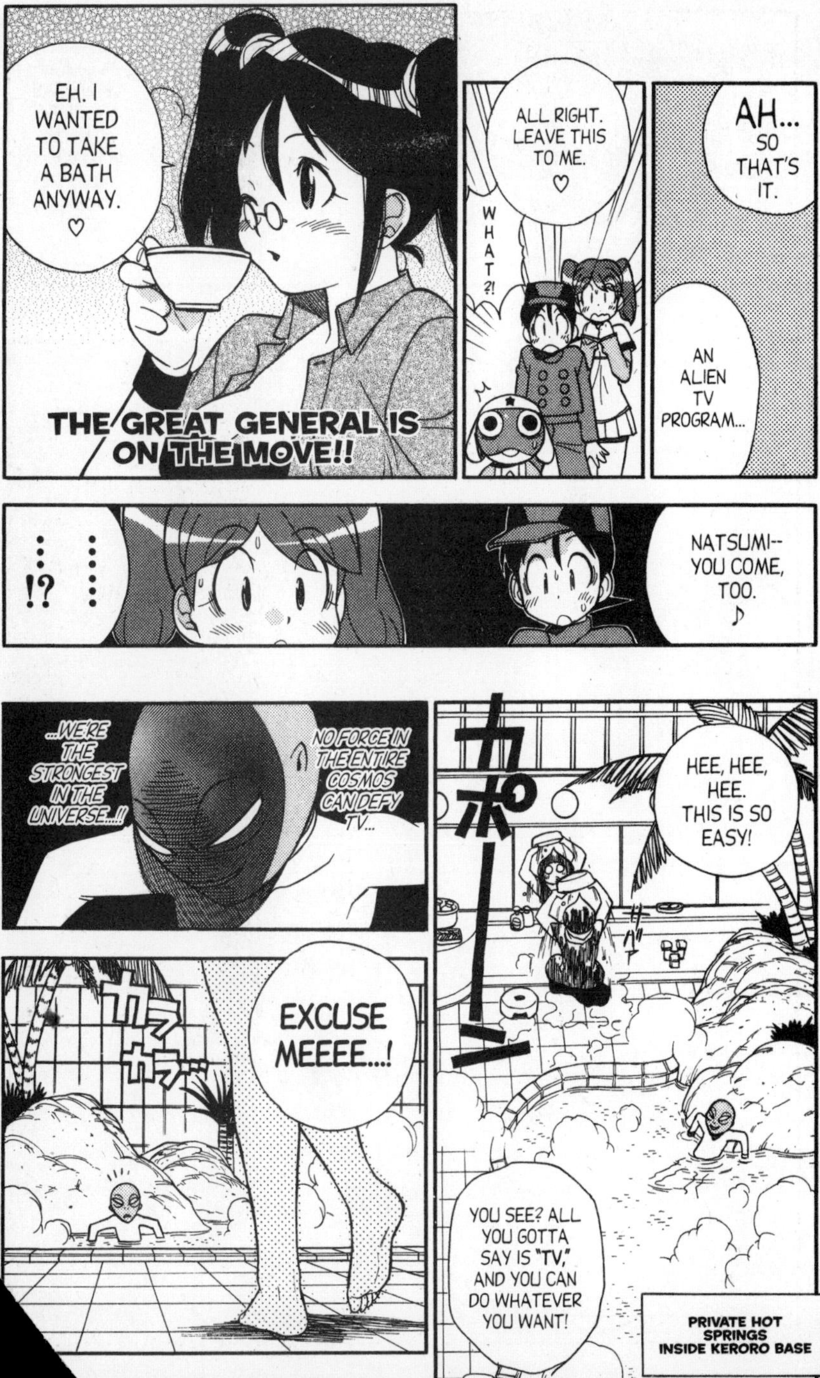
AH... SO THAT'S IT.
AN ALIEN TV PROGRAM...
ALL RIGHT. LEAVE THIS TO ME. ♡
WHAT?!
EH. I WANTED TO TAKE A BATH ANYWAY. ♡
THE GREAT GENERAL IS ON THE MOVE!!
NATSUMI-- YOU COME, TOO. ♪
......
...!?
PRIVATE HOT SPRINGS INSIDE KERORO BASE
カポーン
HEE, HEE, HEE. THIS IS SO EASY!
YOU SEE? ALL YOU GOTTA SAY IS "TV," AND YOU CAN DO WHATEVER YOU WANT!
NO FORCE IN THE ENTIRE COSMOS CAN DEFY TV...
...WE'RE THE STRONGEST IN THE UNIVERSE...!!
EXCUSE MEEEE...!
カラカラッ

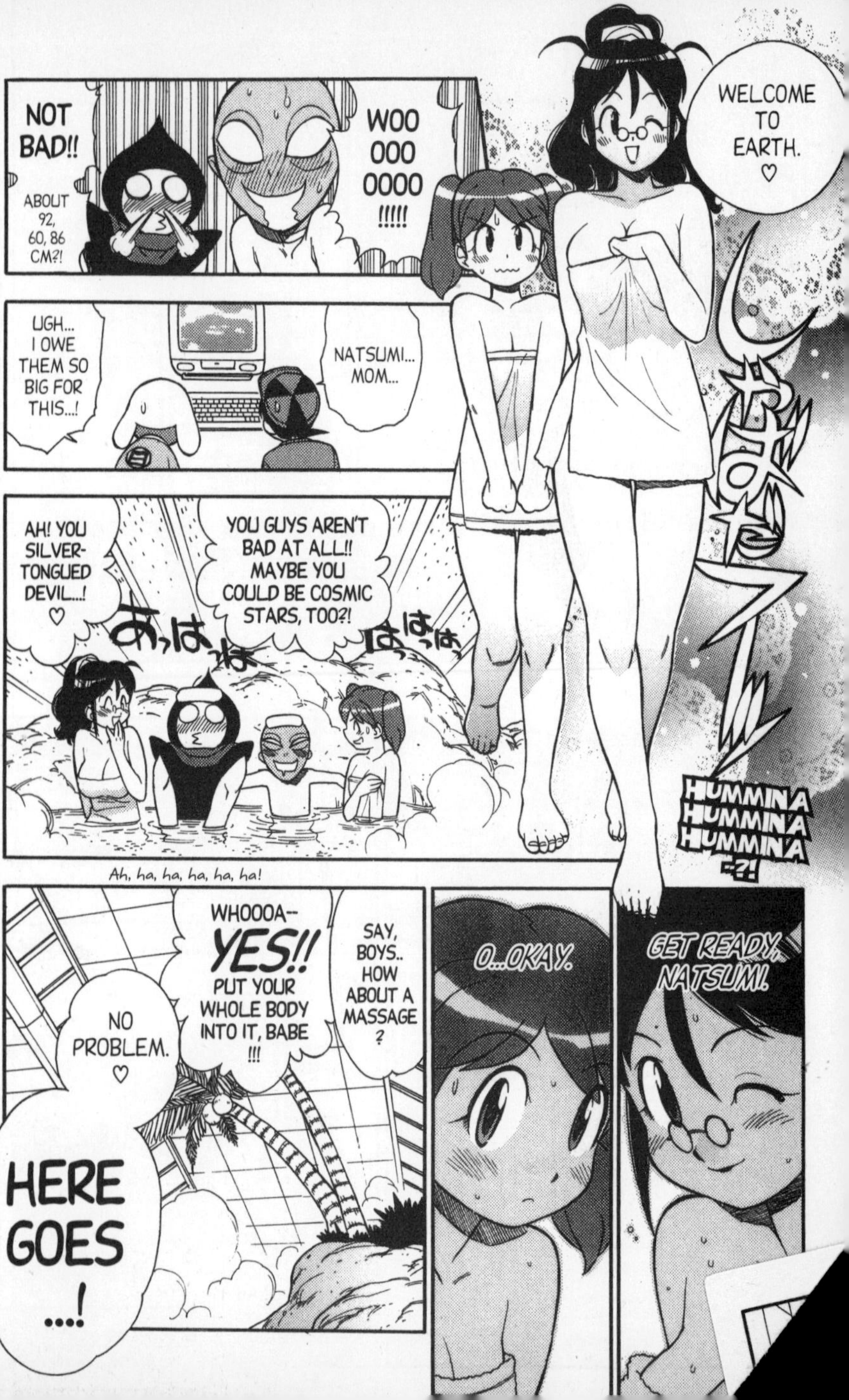
WELCOME TO EARTH. ♡
HUMMINA HUMMINA HUMMINA--?!
WOO OOO OOOO !!!!!
NOT BAD!!
ABOUT 92, 60, 86 CM?!
NATSUMI... MOM...
UGH... I OWE THEM SO BIG FOR THIS...!
YOU GUYS AREN'T BAD AT ALL!! MAYBE YOU COULD BE COSMIC STARS, TOO?!
AH! YOU SILVER-TONGUED DEVIL...! ♡
はっはっ
あっはっは
Ah, ha, ha, ha, ha, ha!
GET READY, NATSUMI.
O...OKAY.
SAY, BOYS.. HOW ABOUT A MASSAGE ?
WHOOOA-- YES!! PUT YOUR WHOLE BODY INTO IT, BABE !!!
NO PROBLEM. ♡
HERE GOES ....!

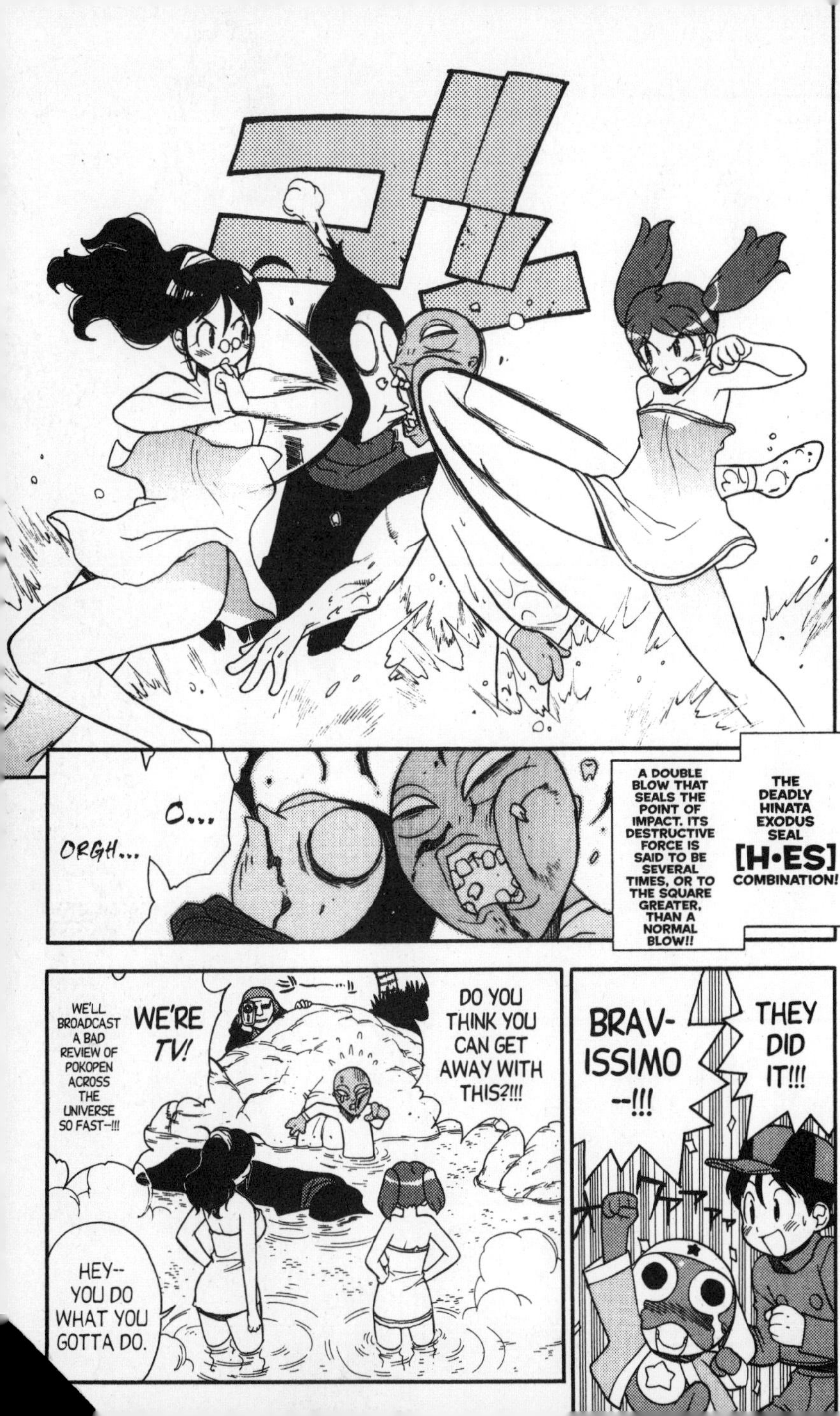
THE DEADLY HINATA EXODUS SEAL [H•ES] COMBINATION!
A DOUBLE BLOW THAT SEALS THE POINT OF IMPACT. ITS DESTRUCTIVE FORCE IS SAID TO BE SEVERAL TIMES, OR TO THE SQUARE GREATER, THAN A NORMAL BLOW!!
O...
ORGH...
THEY DID IT!!!
BRAV-ISSIMO--!!!
DO YOU THINK YOU CAN GET AWAY WITH THIS?!!!
WE'RE TV!
WE'LL BROADCAST A BAD REVIEW OF POKOPEN ACROSS THE UNIVERSE SO FAST--!!!
HEY-- YOU DO WHAT YOU GOTTA DO.

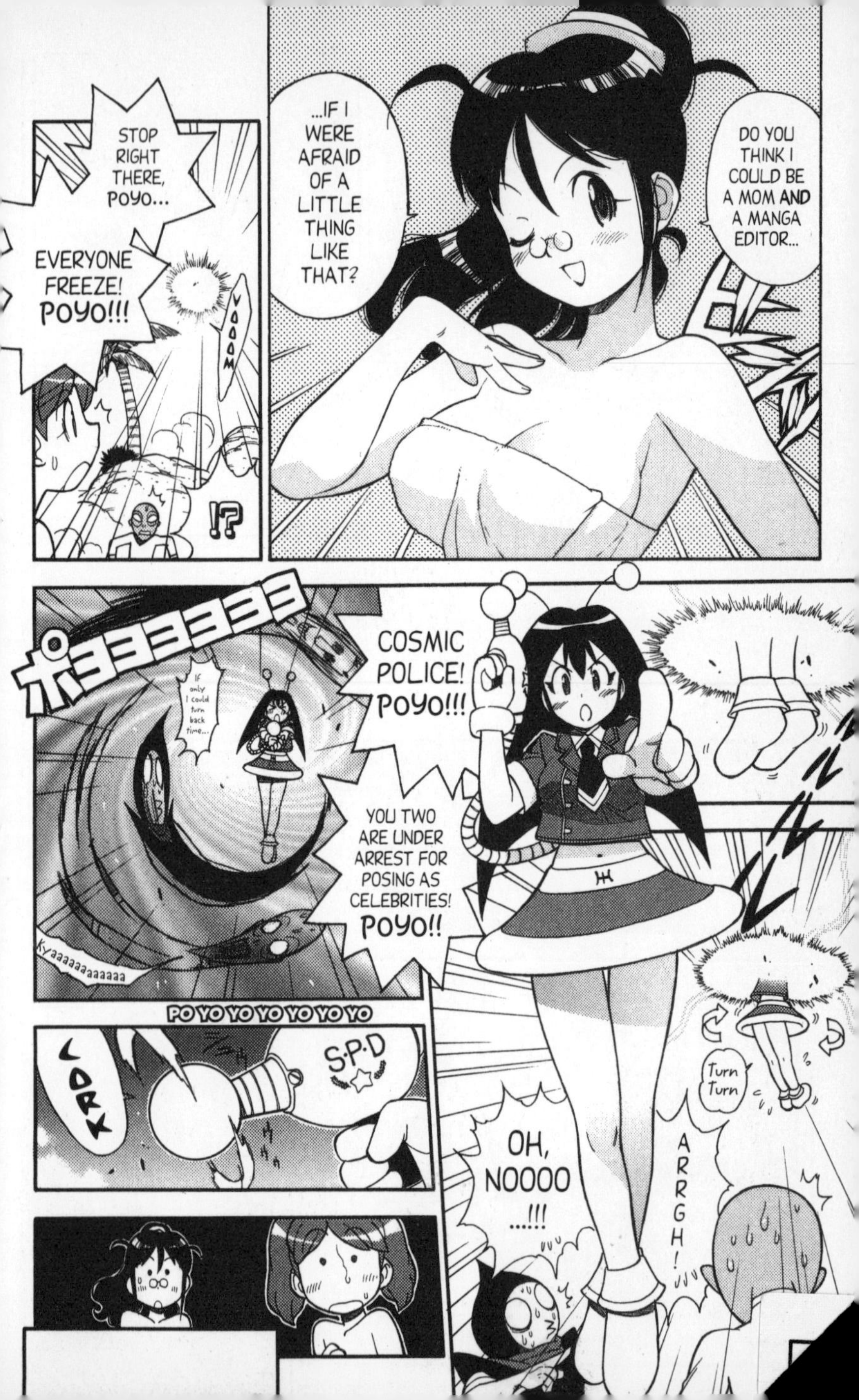
DO YOU THINK I COULD BE A MOM AND A MANGA EDITOR...
...IF I WERE AFRAID OF A LITTLE THING LIKE THAT?
STOP RIGHT THERE, POYO...
EVERYONE FREEZE! POYO!!!
VOOOM
!?
COSMIC POLICE! POYO!!!
YOU TWO ARE UNDER ARREST FOR POSING AS CELEBRITIES! POYO!!
Turn Turn
OH, NOOOO ...!!!
ARRGH!
ポヨヨヨヨヨヨ
If only I could turn back time...
Kyaaaaaaaaaaaa
PO YO YO YO YO YO YO YO
CORK
S·P·D

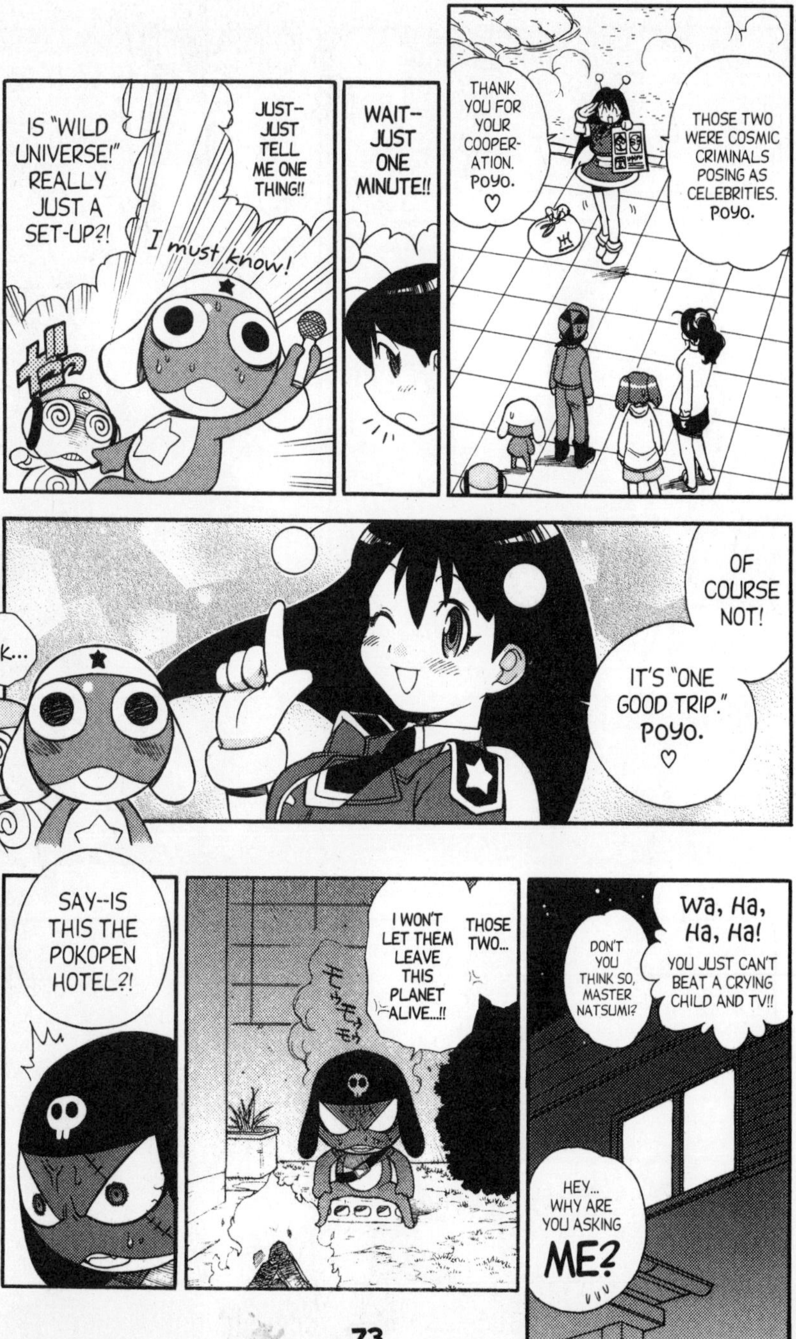
THOSE TWO WERE COSMIC CRIMINALS POSING AS CELEBRITIES. POYO.
THANK YOU FOR YOUR COOPER-ATION. POYO. ♡
WAIT-- JUST ONE MINUTE!!
JUST-- JUST TELL ME ONE THING!!
I must know!
IS "WILD UNIVERSE!" REALLY JUST A SET-UP?!
OF COURSE NOT!
IT'S "ONE GOOD TRIP." POYO. ♡
TSK...
Wa, Ha, Ha, Ha!
YOU JUST CAN'T BEAT A CRYING CHILD AND TV!!
DON'T YOU THINK SO, MASTER NATSUMI?
HEY... WHY ARE YOU ASKING ME?
THOSE TWO...
I WON'T LET THEM LEAVE THIS PLANET ALIVE...!!
SAY--IS THIS THE POKOPEN HOTEL?!

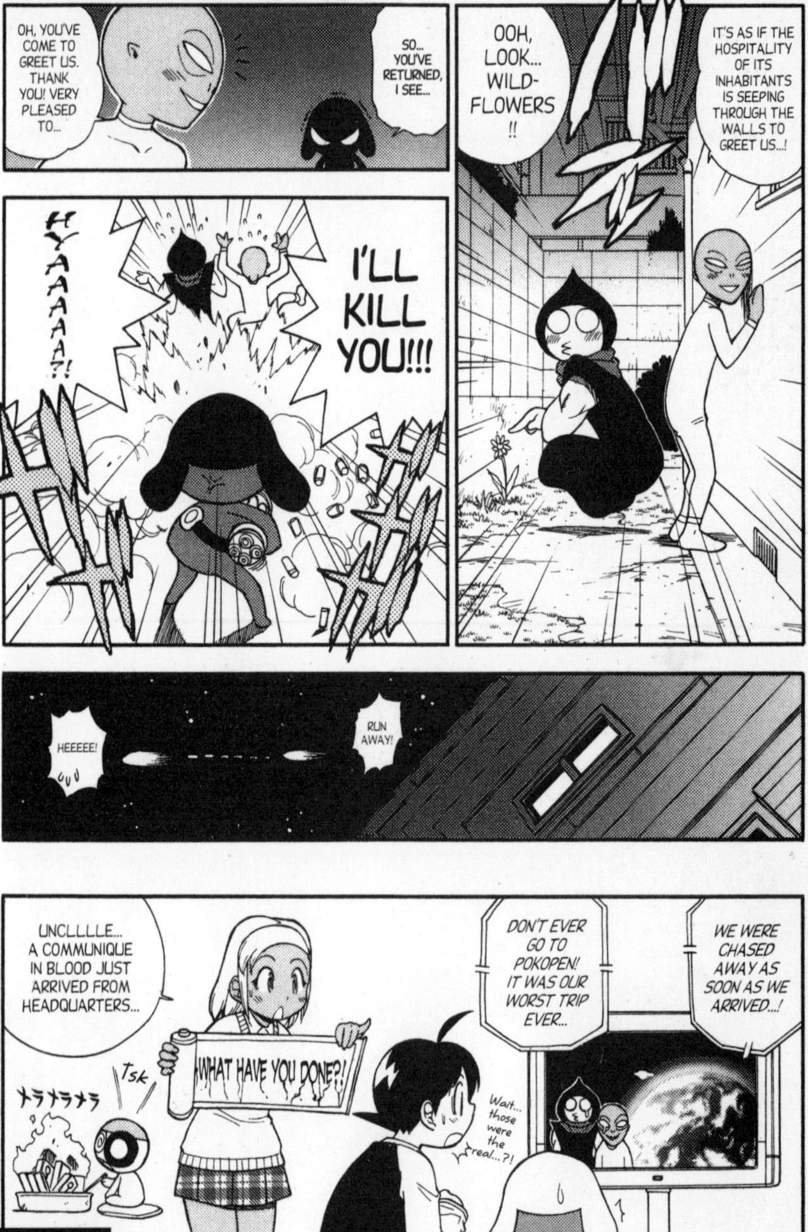
IT'S AS IF THE HOSPITALITY OF ITS INHABITANTS IS SEEPING THROUGH THE WALLS TO GREET US...!
OOH, LOOK... WILD-FLOWERS !!
SO... YOU'VE RETURNED, I SEE...
OH, YOU'VE COME TO GREET US. THANK YOU! VERY PLEASED TO...
I'LL KILL YOU!!!
HYAAAAAAA?!
RUN AWAY!
HEEEEE!
WE WERE CHASED AWAY AS SOON AS WE ARRIVED...!
DON'T EVER GO TO POKOPEN! IT WAS OUR WORST TRIP EVER...
Wait... those were the real...?!
WHAT HAVE YOU DONE?!
UNCLLLLE... A COMMUNIQUE IN BLOOD JUST ARRIVED FROM HEADQUARTERS...
Tsk
メラメラメラ
TO BE CONTINUED

ENCOUNTER XLI
OPERATION: BIRTHDAY BLITZ!!

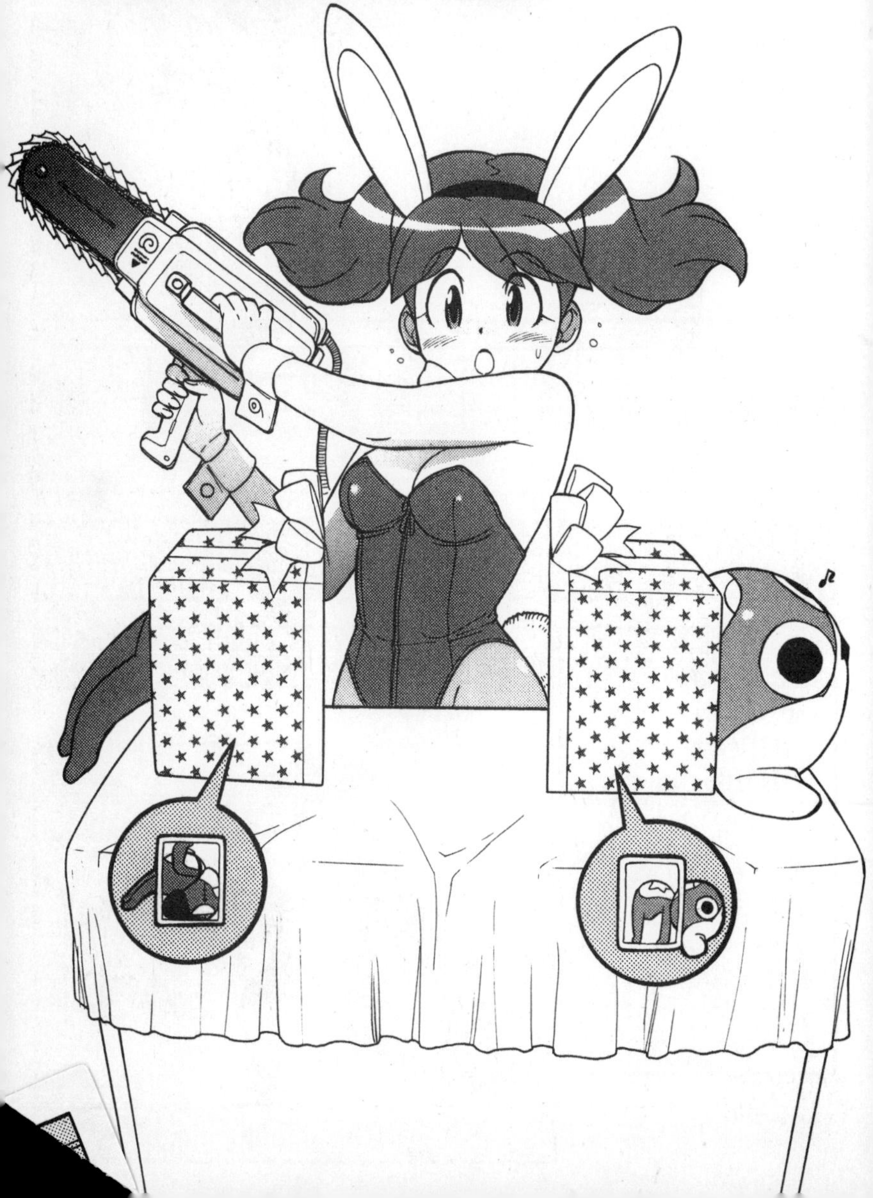

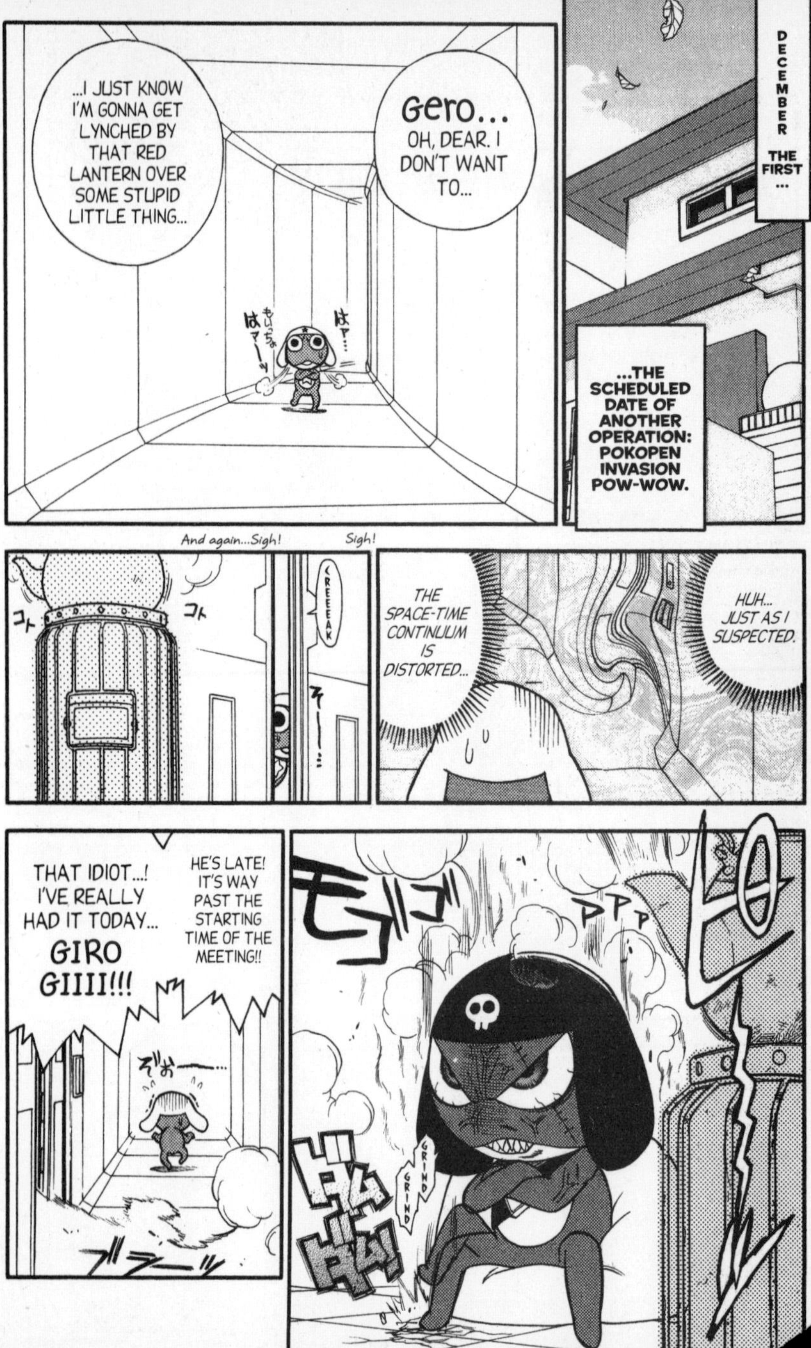
DECEMBER THE FIRST...
...THE SCHEDULED DATE OF ANOTHER OPERATION: POKOPEN INVASION POW-WOW.
Gero... OH, DEAR. I DON'T WANT TO...
...I JUST KNOW I'M GONNA GET LYNCHED BY THAT RED LANTERN OVER SOME STUPID LITTLE THING...
はァ…
Sigh!
And again...Sigh!
HUH... JUST AS I SUSPECTED.
THE SPACE-TIME CONTINUUM IS DISTORTED...
CREEEAK
コト
コト
GRIND GRIND
HE'S LATE! IT'S WAY PAST THE STARTING TIME OF THE MEETING!!
THAT IDIOT...! I'VE REALLY HAD IT TODAY... GIRO GIIII!!!

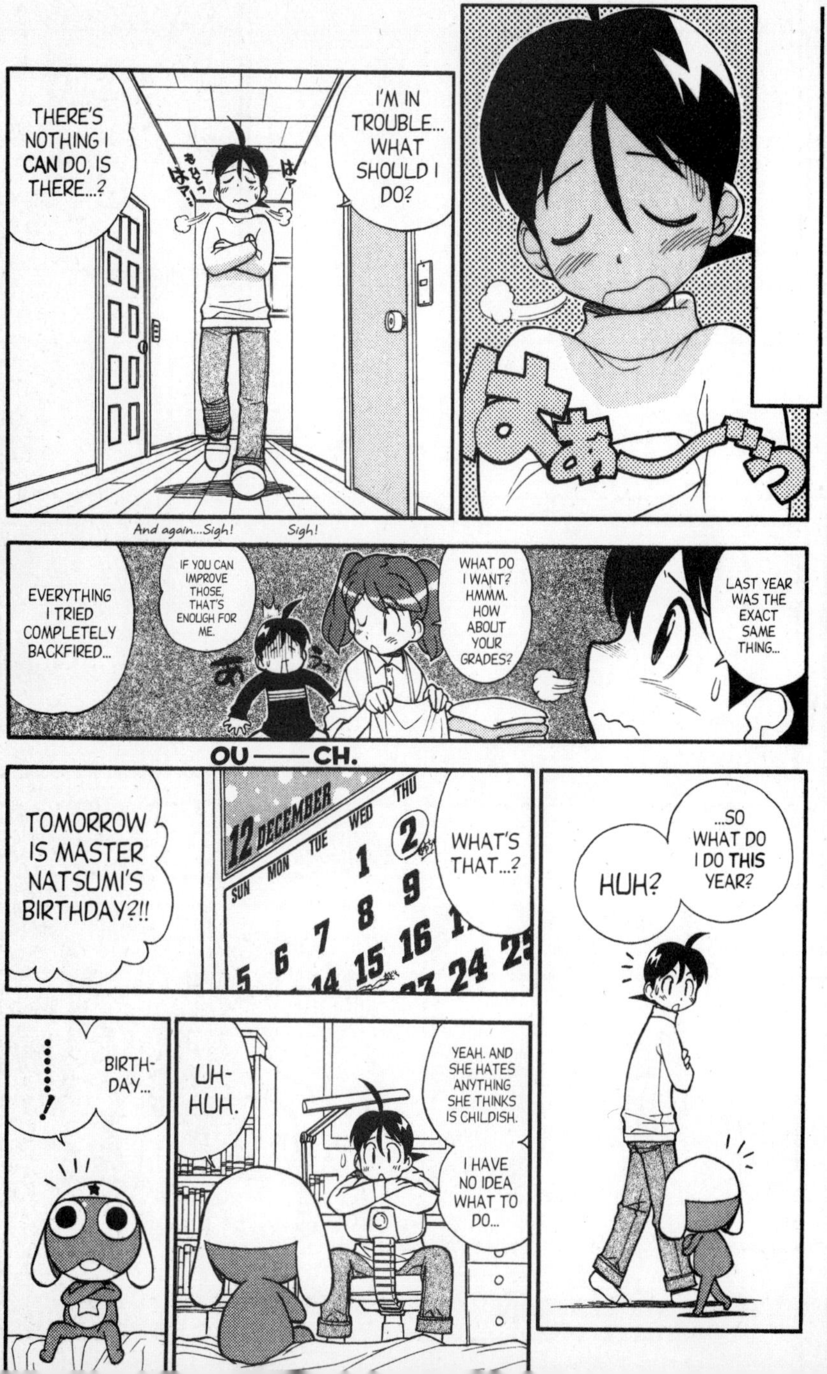

I'M IN TROUBLE... WHAT SHOULD I DO?
THERE'S NOTHING I CAN DO, IS THERE...?
Sigh!
And again...Sigh!
LAST YEAR WAS THE EXACT SAME THING...
WHAT DO I WANT? HMMM. HOW ABOUT YOUR GRADES?
IF YOU CAN IMPROVE THOSE, THAT'S ENOUGH FOR ME.
EVERYTHING I TRIED COMPLETELY BACKFIRED...
OU——CH.
...SO WHAT DO I DO THIS YEAR?
HUH?
WHAT'S THAT...?
TOMORROW IS MASTER NATSUMI'S BIRTHDAY?!!
YEAH. AND SHE HATES ANYTHING SHE THINKS IS CHILDISH.
I HAVE NO IDEA WHAT TO DO...
UH-HUH.
BIRTH-DAY...
......!

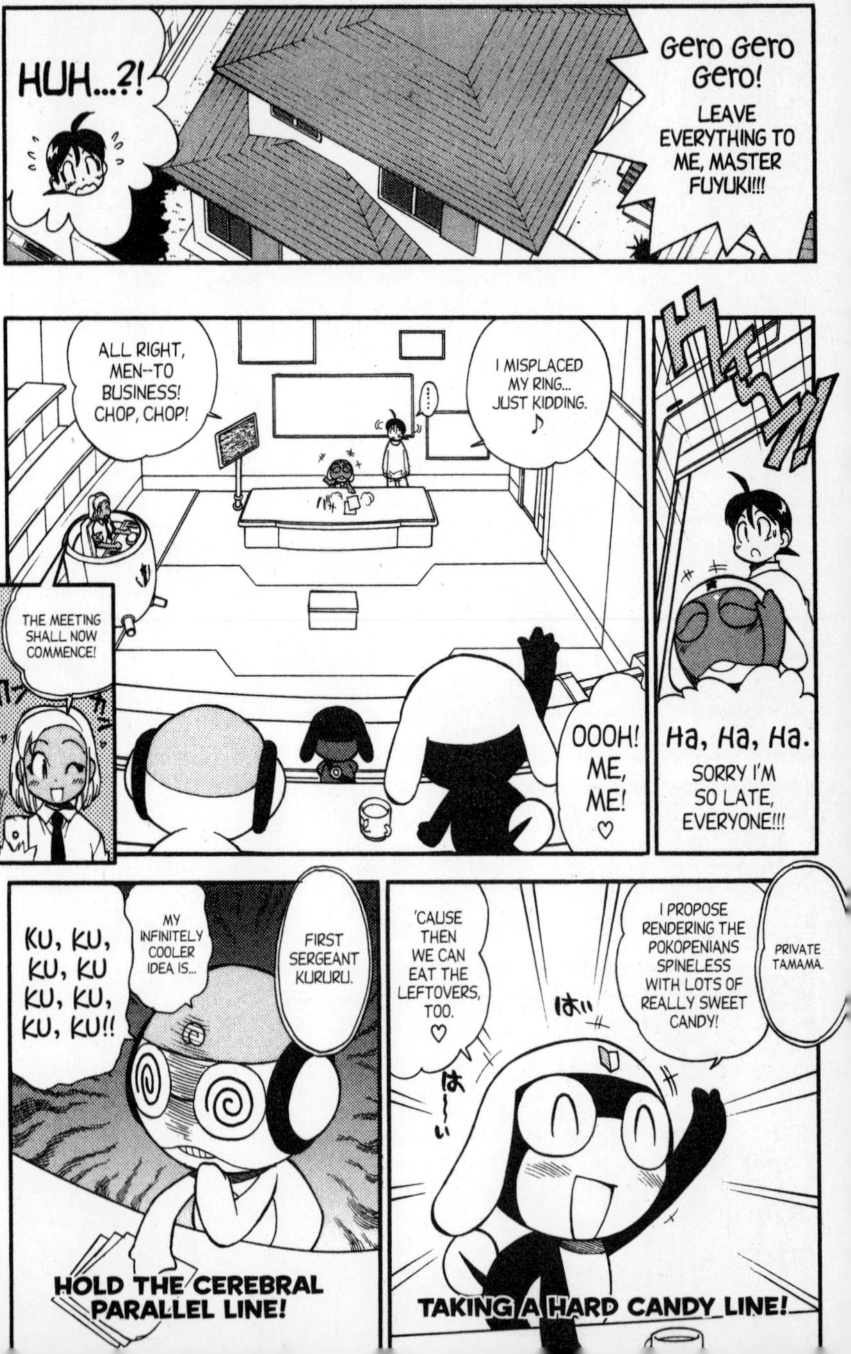
Gero Gero Gero!
LEAVE EVERYTHING TO ME, MASTER FUYUKI!!!
HUH...?!
Ha, Ha, Ha.
SORRY I'M SO LATE, EVERYONE!!!
I MISPLACED MY RING... JUST KIDDING. ♪
....
ALL RIGHT, MEN--TO BUSINESS! CHOP, CHOP!
OOOH! ME, ME! ♡
THE MEETING SHALL NOW COMMENCE!
PRIVATE TAMAMA.
I PROPOSE RENDERING THE POKOPENIANS SPINELESS WITH LOTS OF REALLY SWEET CANDY!
'CAUSE THEN WE CAN EAT THE LEFTOVERS, TOO. ♡
はい
は〜い
TAKING A HARD CANDY LINE!
FIRST SERGEANT KURURU.
MY INFINITELY COOLER IDEA IS...
KU, KU, KU, KU KU, KU, KU, KU!!
HOLD THE CEREBRAL PARALLEL LINE!

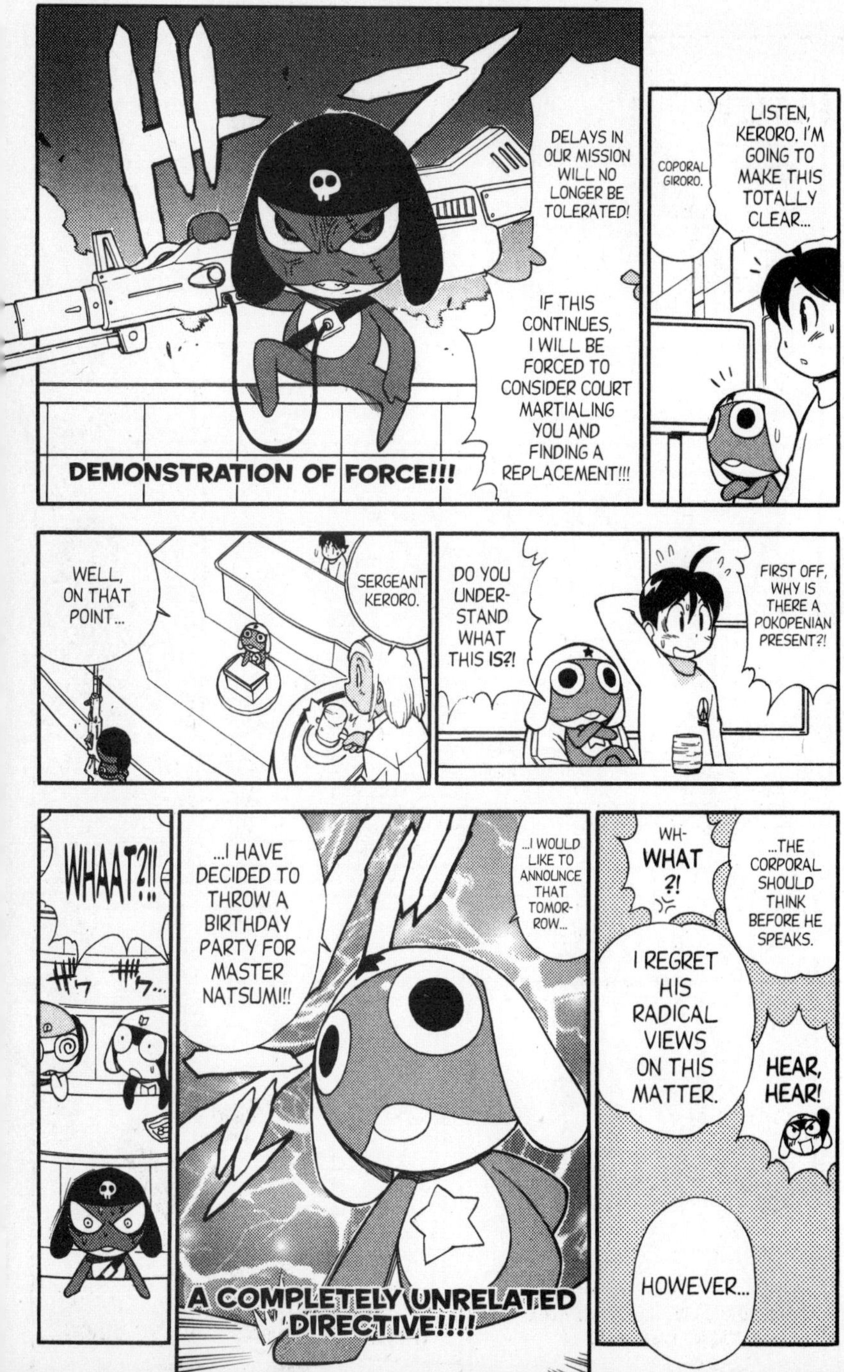
LISTEN, KERORO. I'M GOING TO MAKE THIS TOTALLY CLEAR...
CORPORAL GIRORO.
DELAYS IN OUR MISSION WILL NO LONGER BE TOLERATED!
IF THIS CONTINUES, I WILL BE FORCED TO CONSIDER COURT MARTIALING YOU AND FINDING A REPLACEMENT!!!
DEMONSTRATION OF FORCE!!!
FIRST OFF, WHY IS THERE A POKOPENIAN PRESENT?!
DO YOU UNDER-STAND WHAT THIS IS?!
SERGEANT KERORO.
WELL, ON THAT POINT...
...THE CORPORAL SHOULD THINK BEFORE HE SPEAKS.
WH- WHAT ?!
I REGRET HIS RADICAL VIEWS ON THIS MATTER.
HEAR, HEAR!
HOWEVER...
...I WOULD LIKE TO ANNOUNCE THAT TOMOR-ROW...
...I HAVE DECIDED TO THROW A BIRTHDAY PARTY FOR MASTER NATSUMI!!
A COMPLETELY UNRELATED DIRECTIVE!!!!
WHAAT?!!

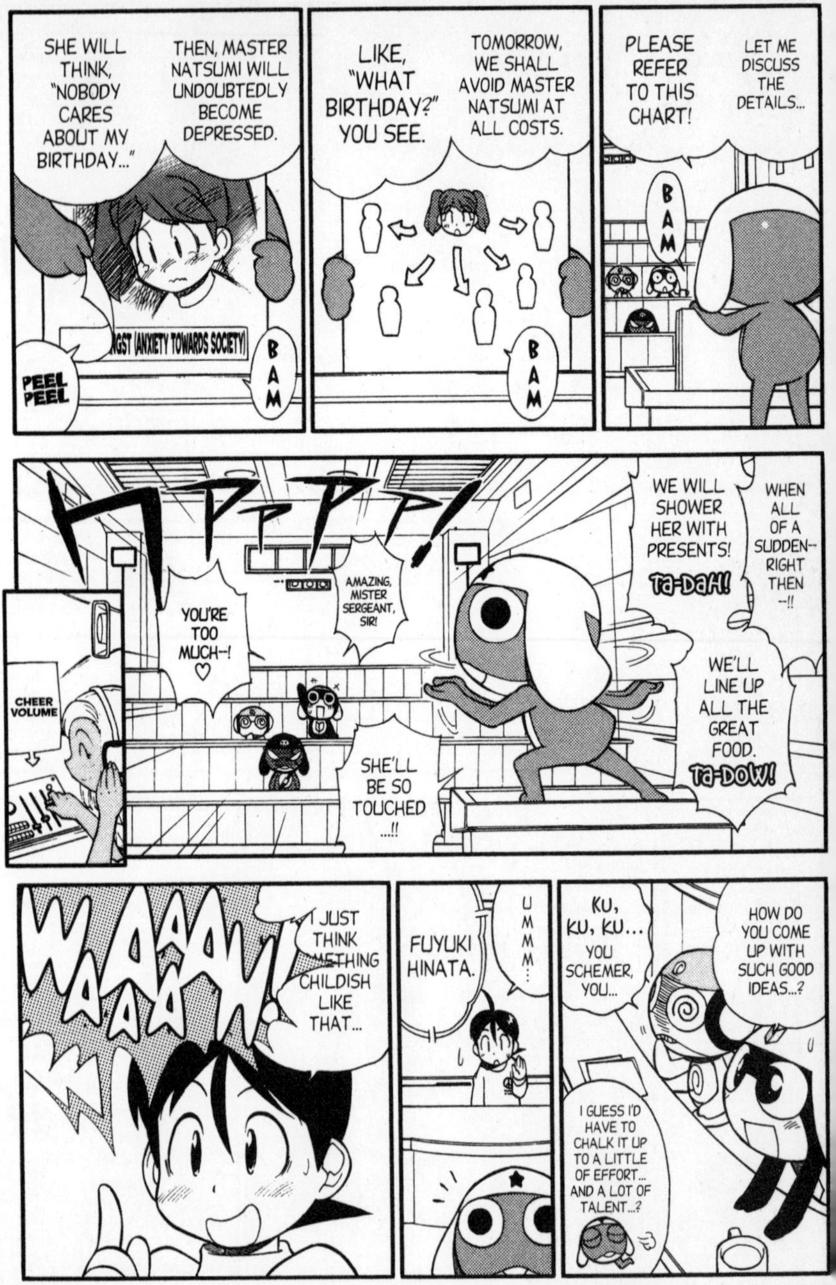
LET ME DISCUSS THE DETAILS...
PLEASE REFER TO THIS CHART!
BAM
TOMORROW, WE SHALL AVOID MASTER NATSUMI AT ALL COSTS.
LIKE, "WHAT BIRTHDAY?" YOU SEE.
BAM
THEN, MASTER NATSUMI WILL UNDOUBTEDLY BECOME DEPRESSED.
SHE WILL THINK, "NOBODY CARES ABOUT MY BIRTHDAY..."
NGST (ANXIETY TOWARDS SOCIETY)
BAM
PEEL PEEL
WHEN ALL OF A SUDDEN--RIGHT THEN--!!
WE WILL SHOWER HER WITH PRESENTS!
TA-DAH!
WE'LL LINE UP ALL THE GREAT FOOD.
TA-DOW!
HPPPP!
AMAZING, MISTER SERGEANT, SIR!
YOU'RE TOO MUCH--! ♡
SHE'LL BE SO TOUCHED ...!!
CHEER VOLUME
HOW DO YOU COME UP WITH SUCH GOOD IDEAS...?
KU, KU, KU...
YOU SCHEMER, YOU...
I GUESS I'D HAVE TO CHALK IT UP TO A LITTLE OF EFFORT... AND A LOT OF TALENT...?
UMMM...
FUYUKI HINATA.
I JUST THINK METHING CHILDISH LIKE THAT...
WAAAAAAH

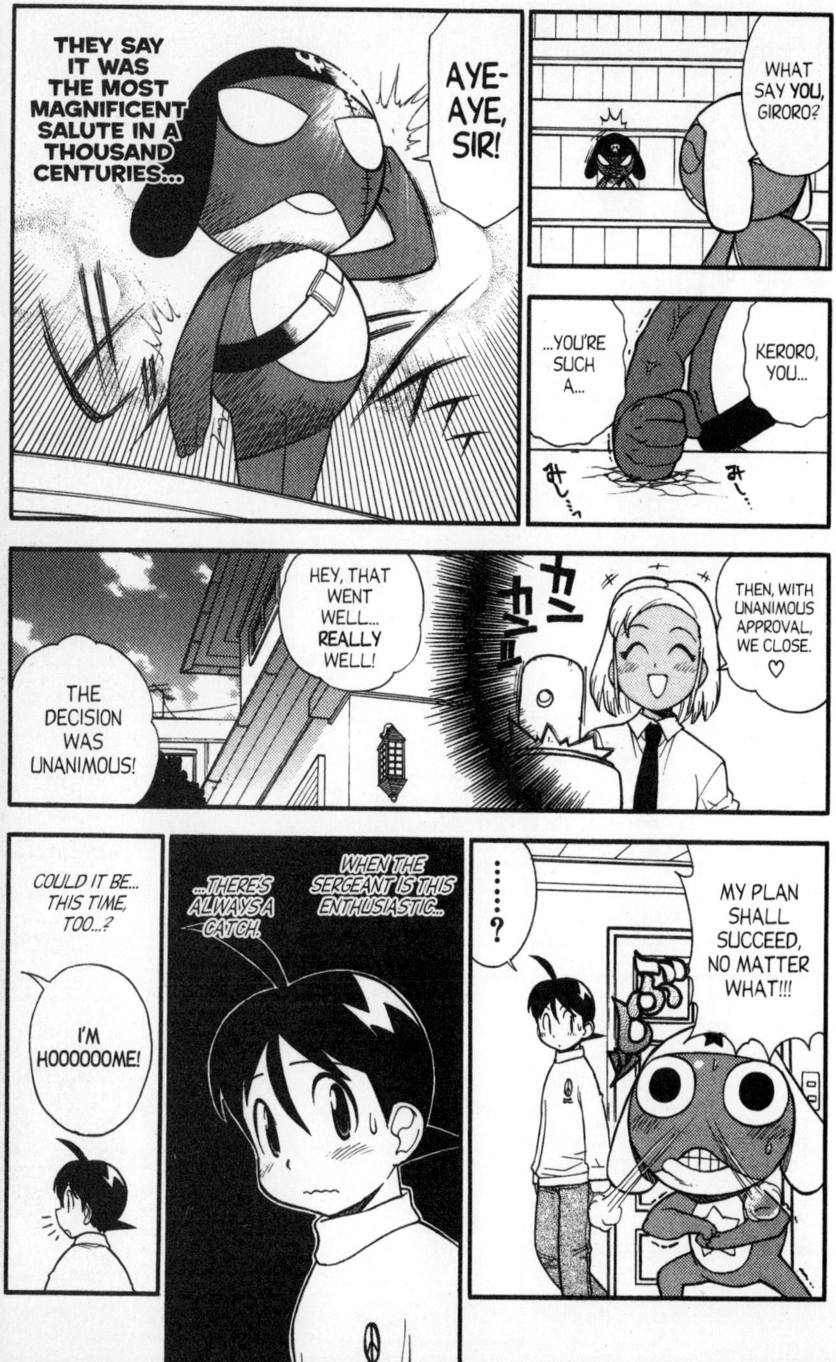
WHAT SAY YOU, GIRORO?
KERORO, YOU...
...YOU'RE SUCH A...
AYE-AYE, SIR!
THEY SAY IT WAS THE MOST MAGNIFICENT SALUTE IN A THOUSAND CENTURIES...
THEN, WITH UNANIMOUS APPROVAL, WE CLOSE. ♡
HEY, THAT WENT WELL... REALLY WELL!
THE DECISION WAS UNANIMOUS!
MY PLAN SHALL SUCCEED, NO MATTER WHAT!!!
......?
WHEN THE SERGEANT IS THIS ENTHUSIASTIC...
...THERE'S ALWAYS A CATCH.
COULD IT BE... THIS TIME, TOO...?
I'M HOOOOOOME!

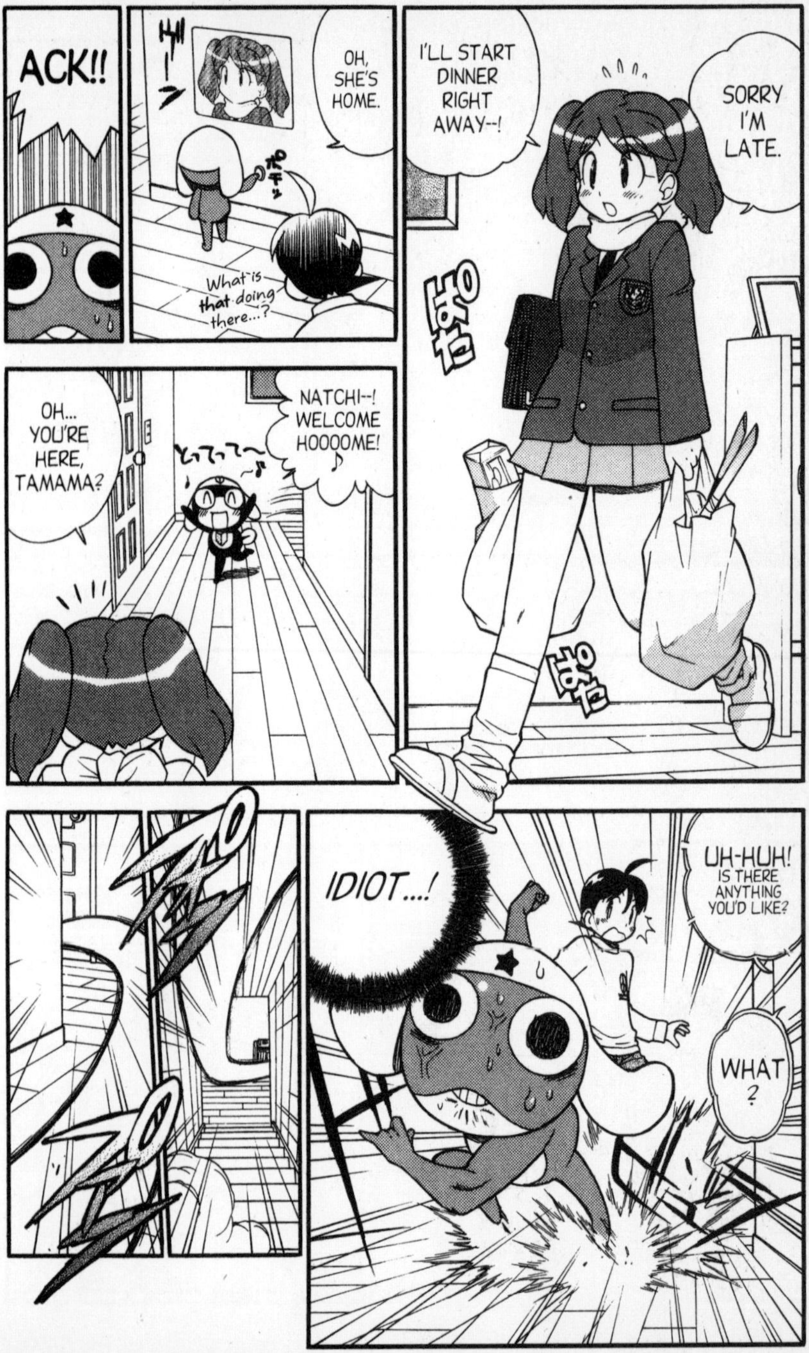
SORRY I'M LATE.
I'LL START DINNER RIGHT AWAY--!
ぱた
ぱた
OH, SHE'S HOME.
What is that doing there...?
ACK!!
NATCHI--! WELCOME HOOOOME! ♪
OH... YOU'RE HERE, TAMAMA?
UH-HUH! IS THERE ANYTHING YOU'D LIKE?
WHAT?
IDIOT...!

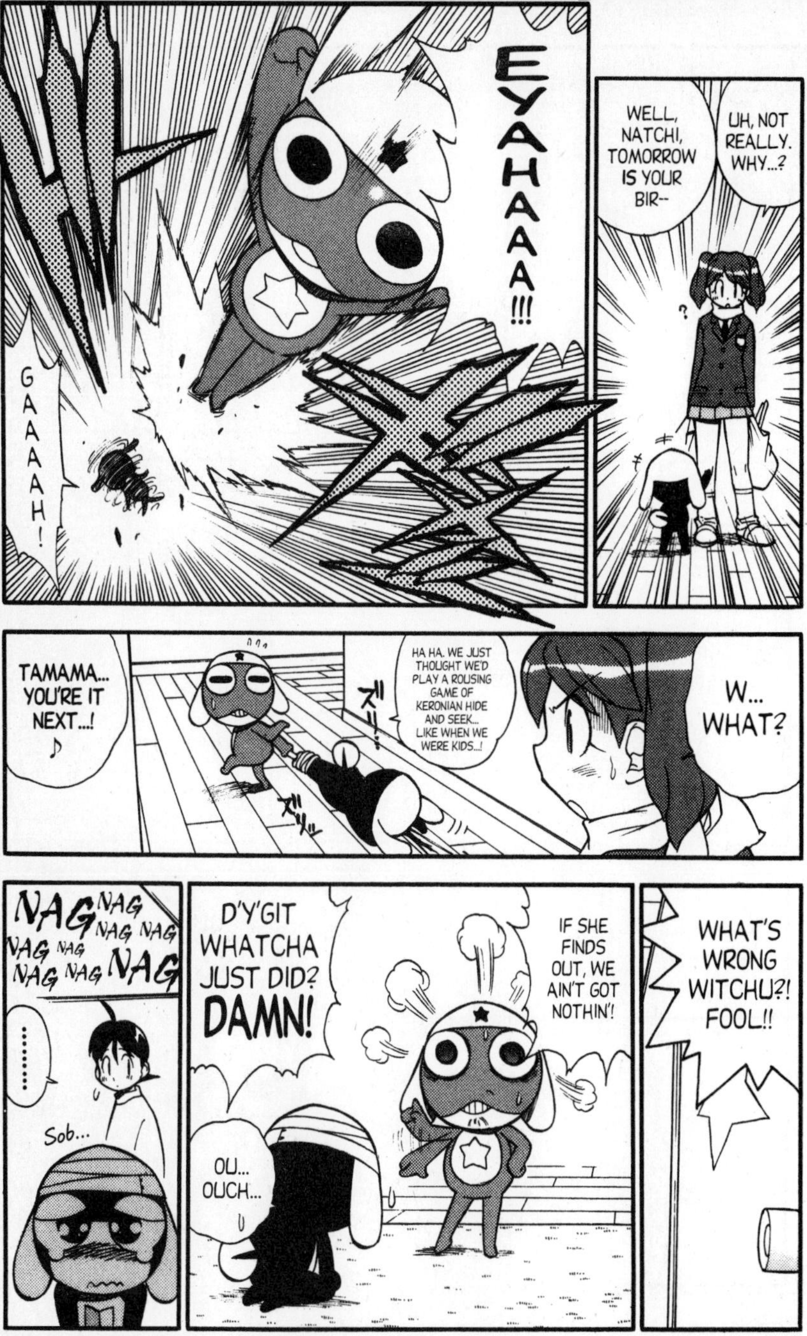
UH, NOT REALLY. WHY...?
WELL, NATCHI, TOMORROW IS YOUR BIR--
EYAHAAAA!!!
GAAAAAH!
W... WHAT?
HA HA. WE JUST THOUGHT WE'D PLAY A ROUSING GAME OF KERONIAN HIDE AND SEEK... LIKE WHEN WE WERE KIDS...!
TAMAMA... YOU'RE IT NEXT...! ♪
WHAT'S WRONG WITCHU?! FOOL!!
IF SHE FINDS OUT, WE AIN'T GOT NOTHIN'!
D'Y'GIT WHATCHA JUST DID? DAMN!
OU... OUCH...
NAG NAG NAG NAG NAG NAG NAG NAG NAG
....
Sob...

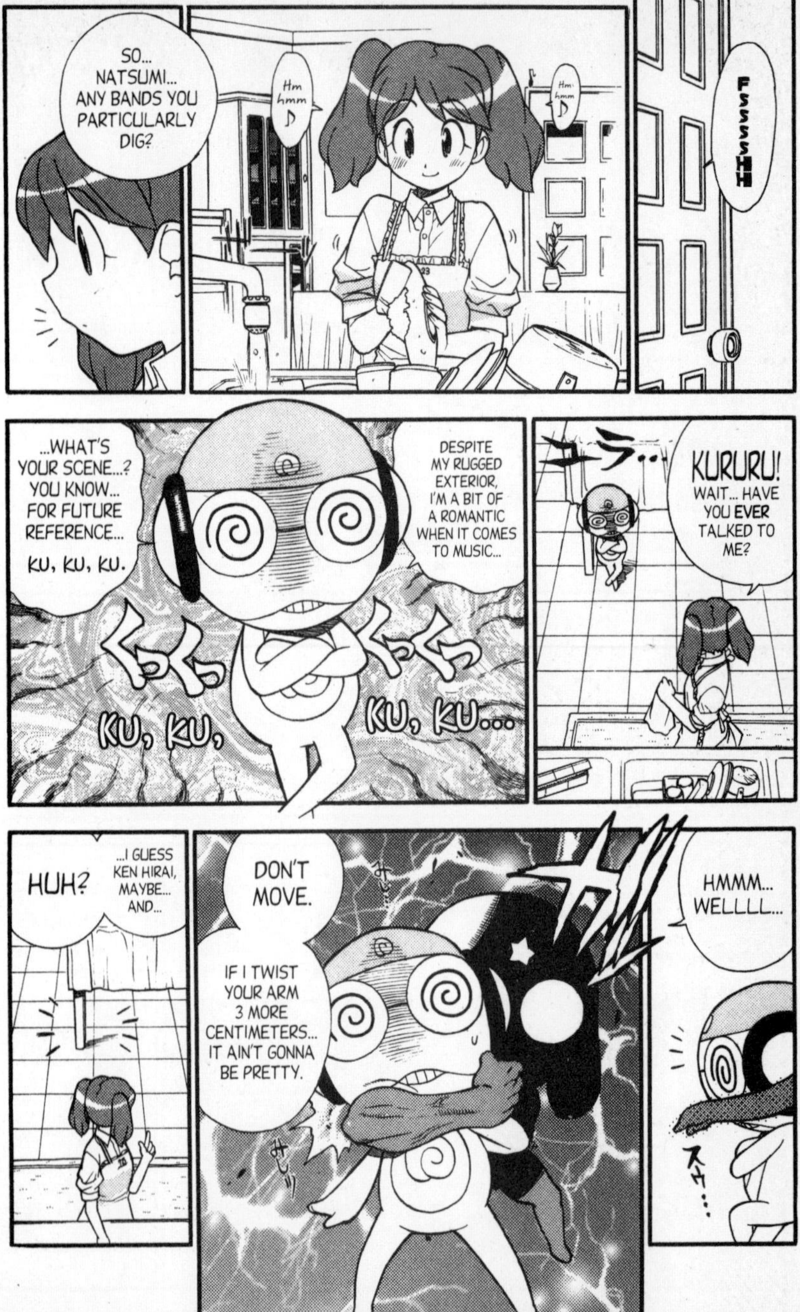
FSSSSHH
Hm-hmm ♪
Hm hmm ♪
SO... NATSUMI... ANY BANDS YOU PARTICULARLY DIG?
コラ…
KURURU! WAIT... HAVE YOU EVER TALKED TO ME?
DESPITE MY RUGGED EXTERIOR, I'M A BIT OF A ROMANTIC WHEN IT COMES TO MUSIC...
...WHAT'S YOUR SCENE...? YOU KNOW... FOR FUTURE REFERENCE...
KU, KU, KU.
くっくっ
KU, KU...
くっくっ
KU, KU,
HMMM... WELLLL...
スッ…
ガッ
DON'T MOVE.
IF I TWIST YOUR ARM 3 MORE CENTIMETERS... IT AIN'T GONNA BE PRETTY.
...I GUESS KEN HIRAI, MAYBE... AND...
HUH?

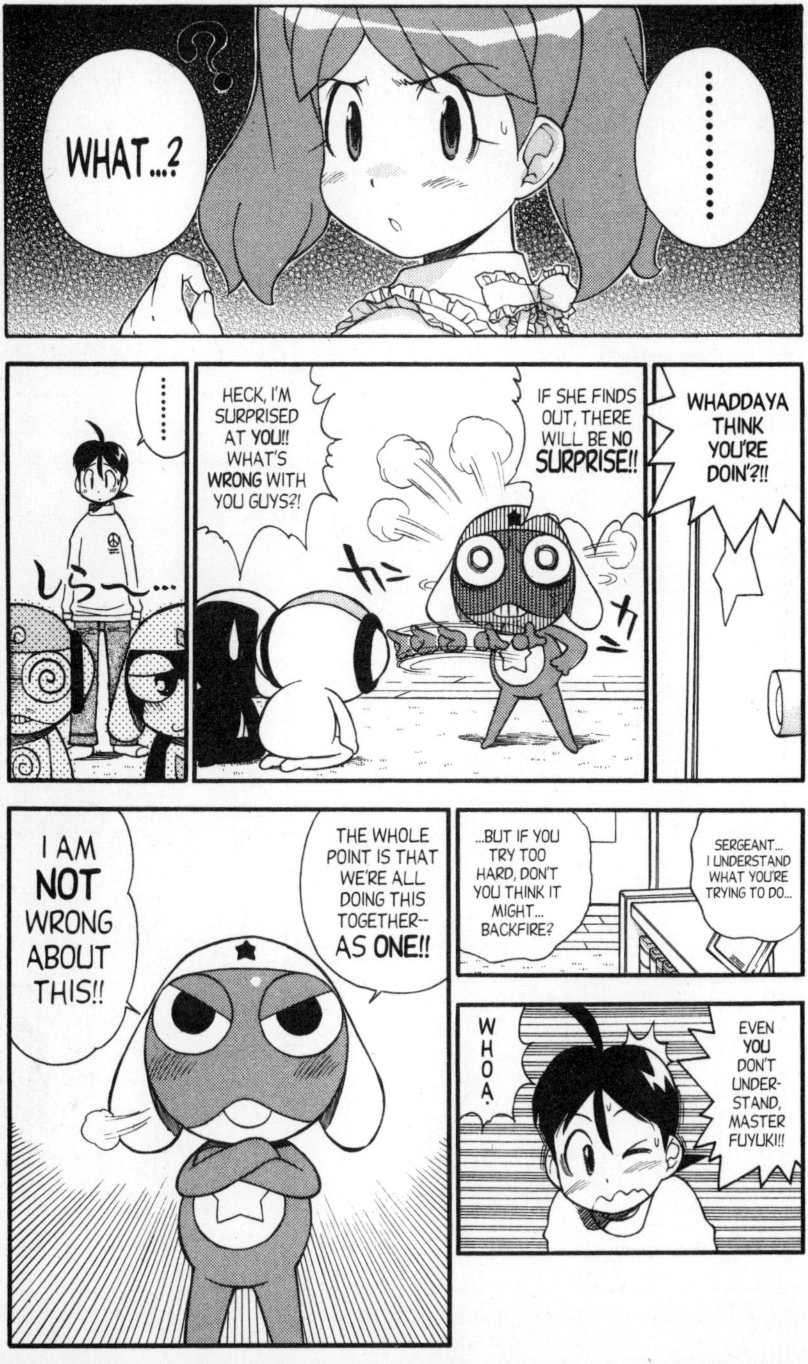

......
WHAT...?
WHADDAYA THINK YOU'RE DOIN'?!!
IF SHE FINDS OUT, THERE WILL BE NO SURPRISE!!
HECK, I'M SURPRISED AT YOU!! WHAT'S WRONG WITH YOU GUYS?!
......
しら〜...
SERGEANT... I UNDERSTAND WHAT YOU'RE TRYING TO DO...
...BUT IF YOU TRY TOO HARD, DON'T YOU THINK IT MIGHT... BACKFIRE?
EVEN YOU DON'T UNDER-STAND, MASTER FUYUKI!!
WHOA.
THE WHOLE POINT IS THAT WE'RE ALL DOING THIS TOGETHER-- AS ONE!!
I AM NOT WRONG ABOUT THIS!!

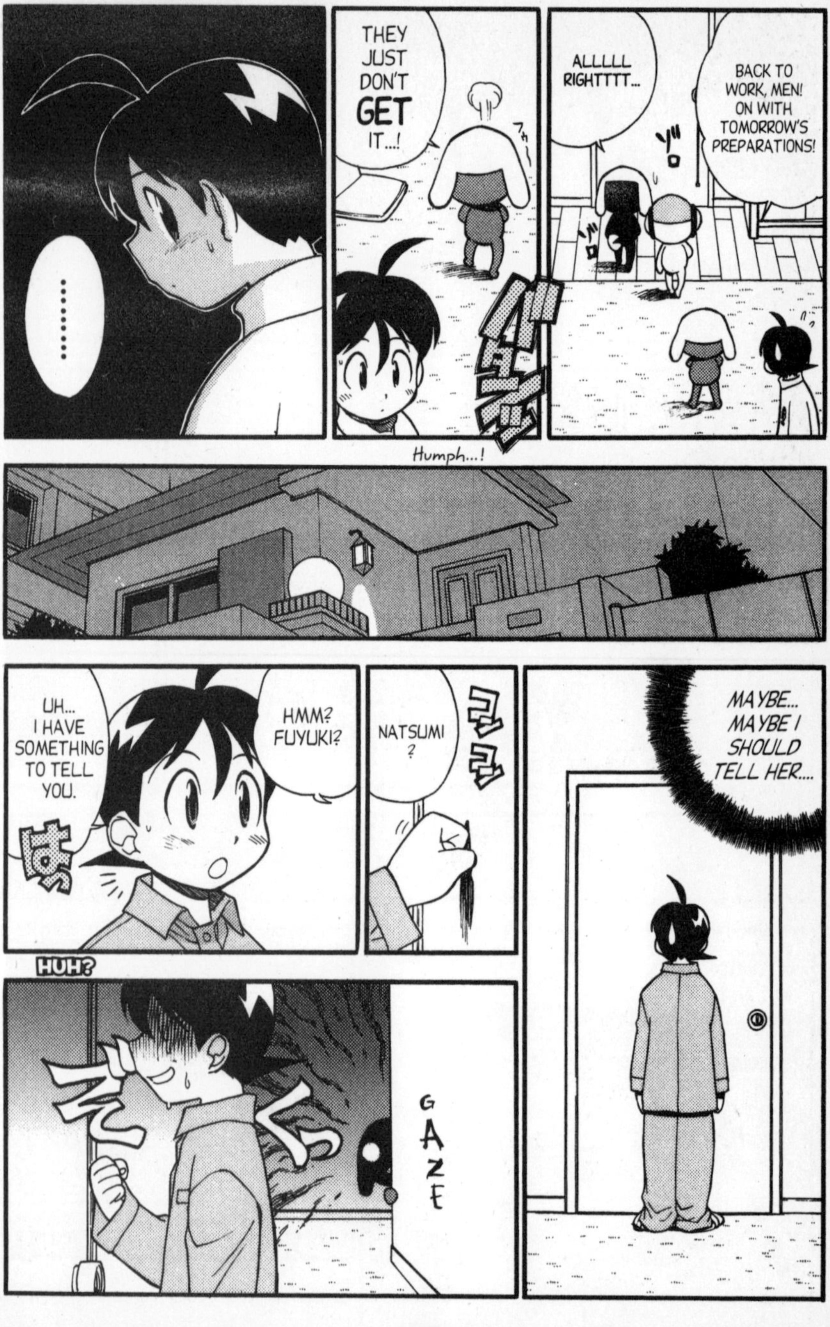
BACK TO WORK, MEN! ON WITH TOMORROW'S PREPARATIONS!
ALLLLL RIGHTTTT...
THEY JUST DON'T GET IT...!
Humph...!
....
MAYBE... MAYBE I SHOULD TELL HER....
NATSUMI?
HMM? FUYUKI?
UH... I HAVE SOMETHING TO TELL YOU.
HUH?
GAZE

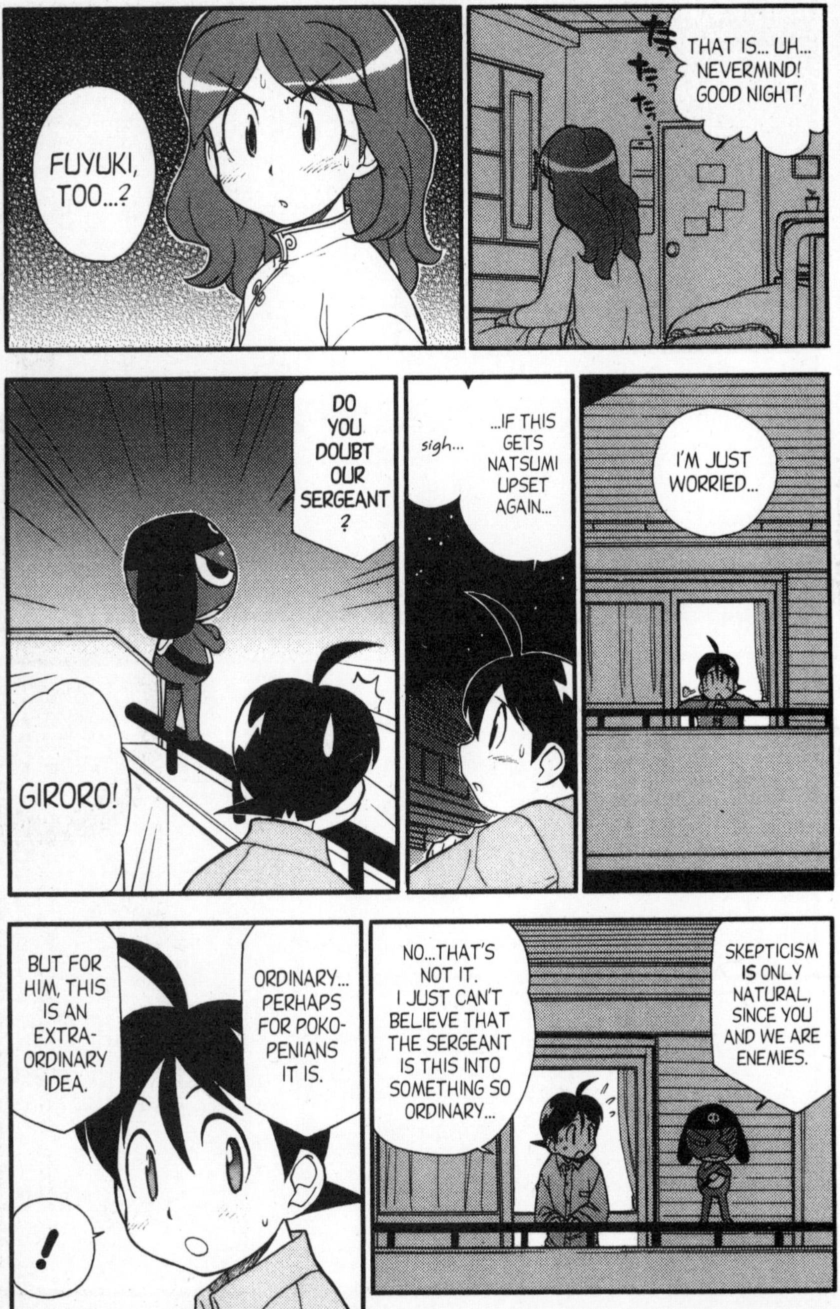

THAT IS... UH... NEVERMIND! GOOD NIGHT!
FUYUKI, TOO...?
I'M JUST WORRIED...
...IF THIS GETS NATSUMI UPSET AGAIN...
sigh...
DO YOU DOUBT OUR SERGEANT?
GIRORO!
SKEPTICISM IS ONLY NATURAL, SINCE YOU AND WE ARE ENEMIES.
NO...THAT'S NOT IT. I JUST CAN'T BELIEVE THAT THE SERGEANT IS THIS INTO SOMETHING SO ORDINARY...
ORDINARY... PERHAPS FOR POKO-PENIANS IT IS.
BUT FOR HIM, THIS IS AN EXTRA-ORDINARY IDEA.
!

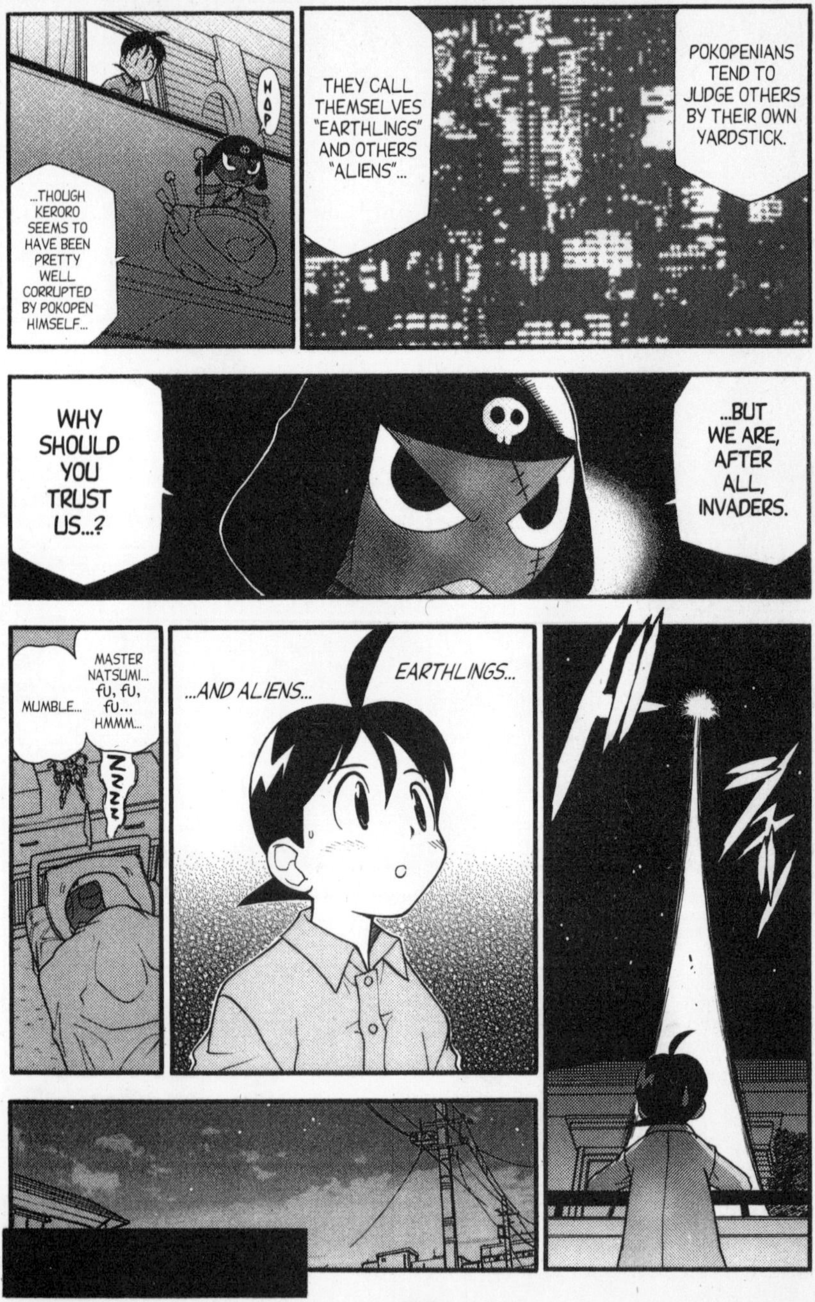
POKOPENIANS TEND TO JUDGE OTHERS BY THEIR OWN YARDSTICK.
THEY CALL THEMSELVES "EARTHLINGS" AND OTHERS "ALIENS"...
HOP
...THOUGH KERORO SEEMS TO HAVE BEEN PRETTY WELL CORRUPTED BY POKOPEN HIMSELF...
...BUT WE ARE, AFTER ALL, INVADERS.
WHY SHOULD YOU TRUST US...?
EARTHLINGS...
...AND ALIENS...
MASTER NATSUMI... FU, FU, FU... HMMM...
MUMBLE...
ZZZZ
[redacted]

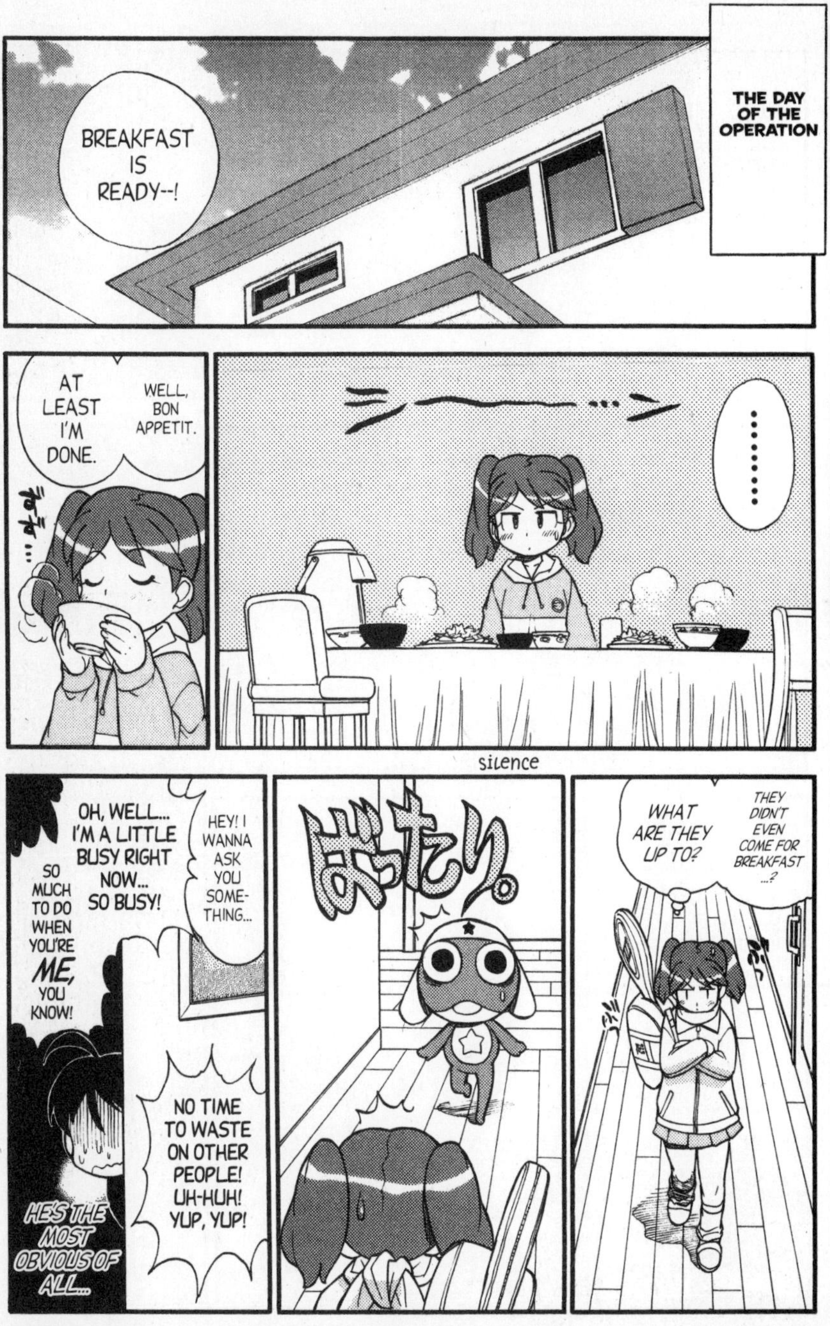
THE DAY OF THE OPERATION
BREAKFAST IS READY--!
......
silence
WELL, BON APPETIT.
AT LEAST I'M DONE.
THEY DIDN'T EVEN COME FOR BREAKFAST ...?
WHAT ARE THEY UP TO?
ぱったり。
HEY! I WANNA ASK YOU SOMETHING...
OH, WELL... I'M A LITTLE BUSY RIGHT NOW... SO BUSY!
SO MUCH TO DO WHEN YOU'RE *ME,* YOU KNOW!
NO TIME TO WASTE ON OTHER PEOPLE! UH-HUH! YUP, YUP!
HE'S THE MOST OBVIOUS OF ALL...

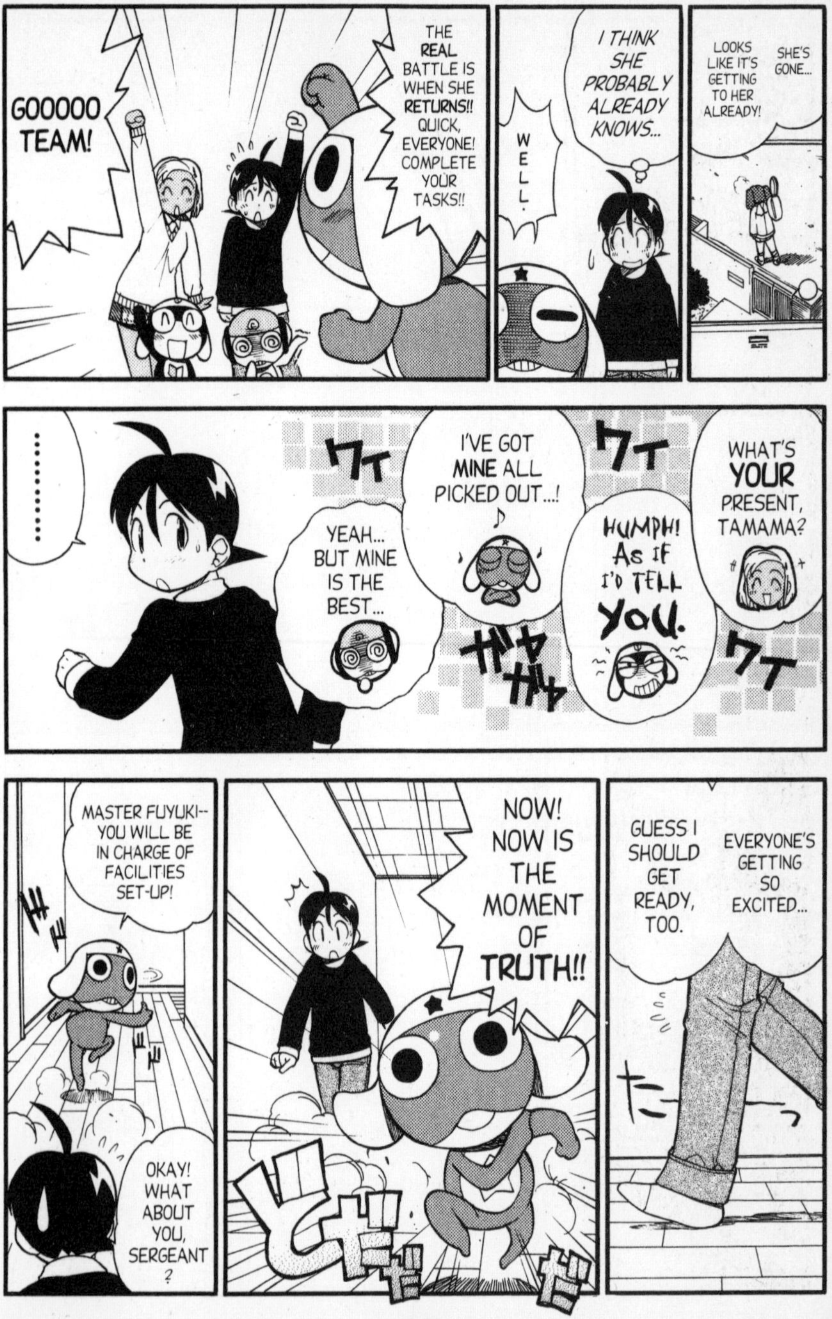
SHE'S GONE...
LOOKS LIKE IT'S GETTING TO HER ALREADY!
I THINK SHE PROBABLY ALREADY KNOWS...
WELL.
THE REAL BATTLE IS WHEN SHE RETURNS!! QUICK, EVERYONE! COMPLETE YOUR TASKS!!
GOOOOO TEAM!
WHAT'S YOUR PRESENT, TAMAMA?
ワイ
HUMPH! As if I'D TELL YOU.
ワイ
I'VE GOT MINE ALL PICKED OUT...! ♪
ワイ
ガヤガヤ
YEAH... BUT MINE IS THE BEST...
....
EVERYONE'S GETTING SO EXCITED...
GUESS I SHOULD GET READY, TOO.
NOW! NOW IS THE MOMENT OF TRUTH!!
MASTER FUYUKI-- YOU WILL BE IN CHARGE OF FACILITIES SET-UP!
OKAY! WHAT ABOUT YOU, SERGEANT?

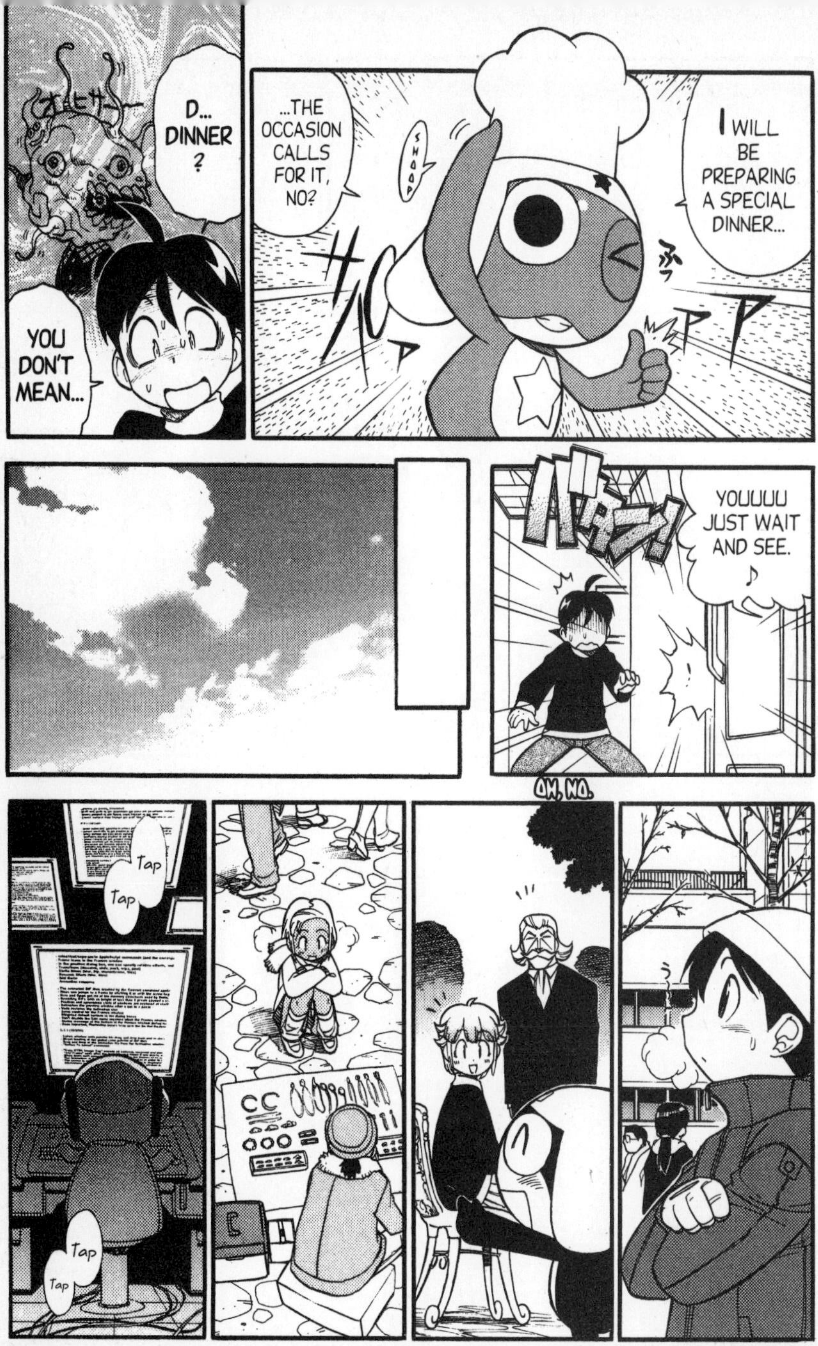
I WILL BE PREPARING A SPECIAL DINNER...
SHOOP
...THE OCCASION CALLS FOR IT, NO?
D... DINNER?
YOU DON'T MEAN...
YOUUUU JUST WAIT AND SEE. ♪
OH, NO.
Tap
Tap
Tap
Tap

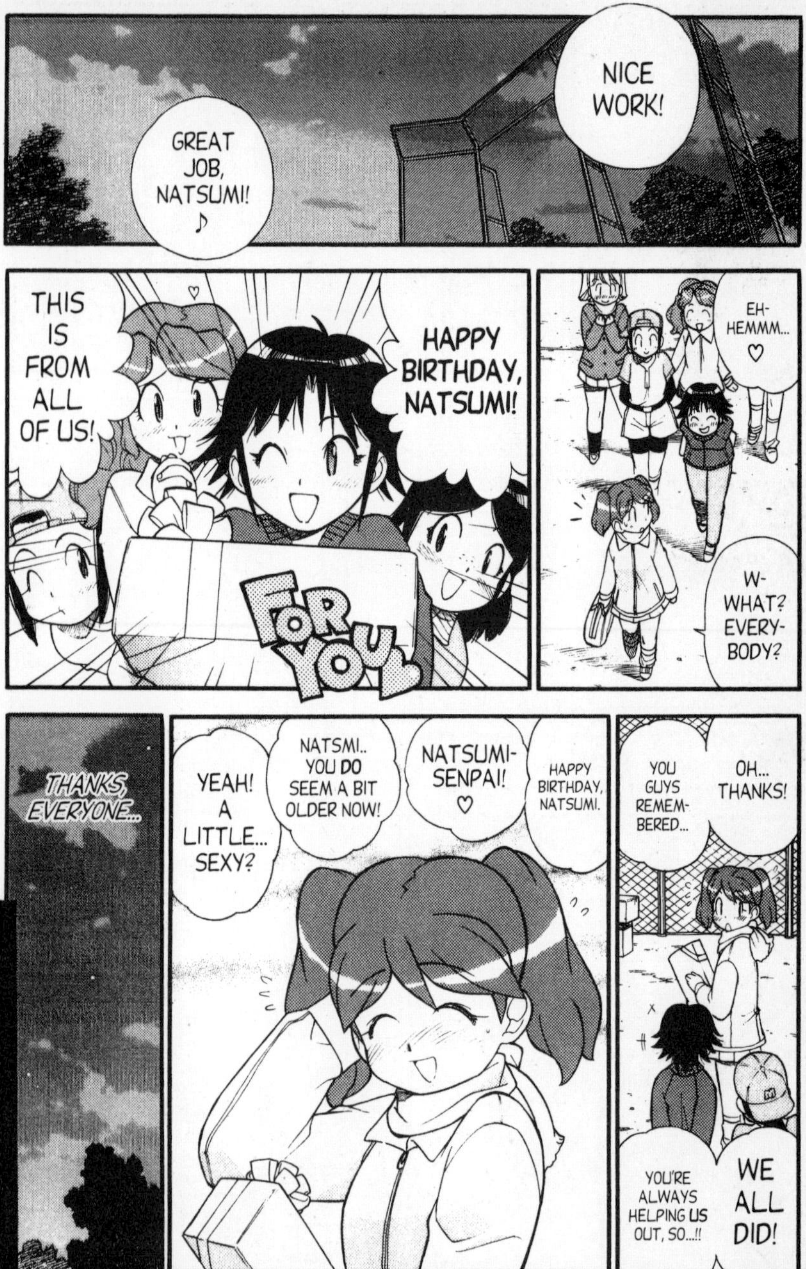
NICE WORK!
GREAT JOB, NATSUMI! ♪
EH-HEMMM... ♡
W-WHAT? EVERYBODY?
HAPPY BIRTHDAY, NATSUMI!
THIS IS FROM ALL OF US!
FOR YOU
OH... THANKS!
YOU GUYS REMEMBERED...
WE ALL DID!
YOU'RE ALWAYS HELPING US OUT, SO...!!
HAPPY BIRTHDAY, NATSUMI.
NATSUMI-SENPAI! ♡
NATSMI.. YOU DO SEEM A BIT OLDER NOW!
YEAH! A LITTLE... SEXY?
THANKS, EVERYONE...

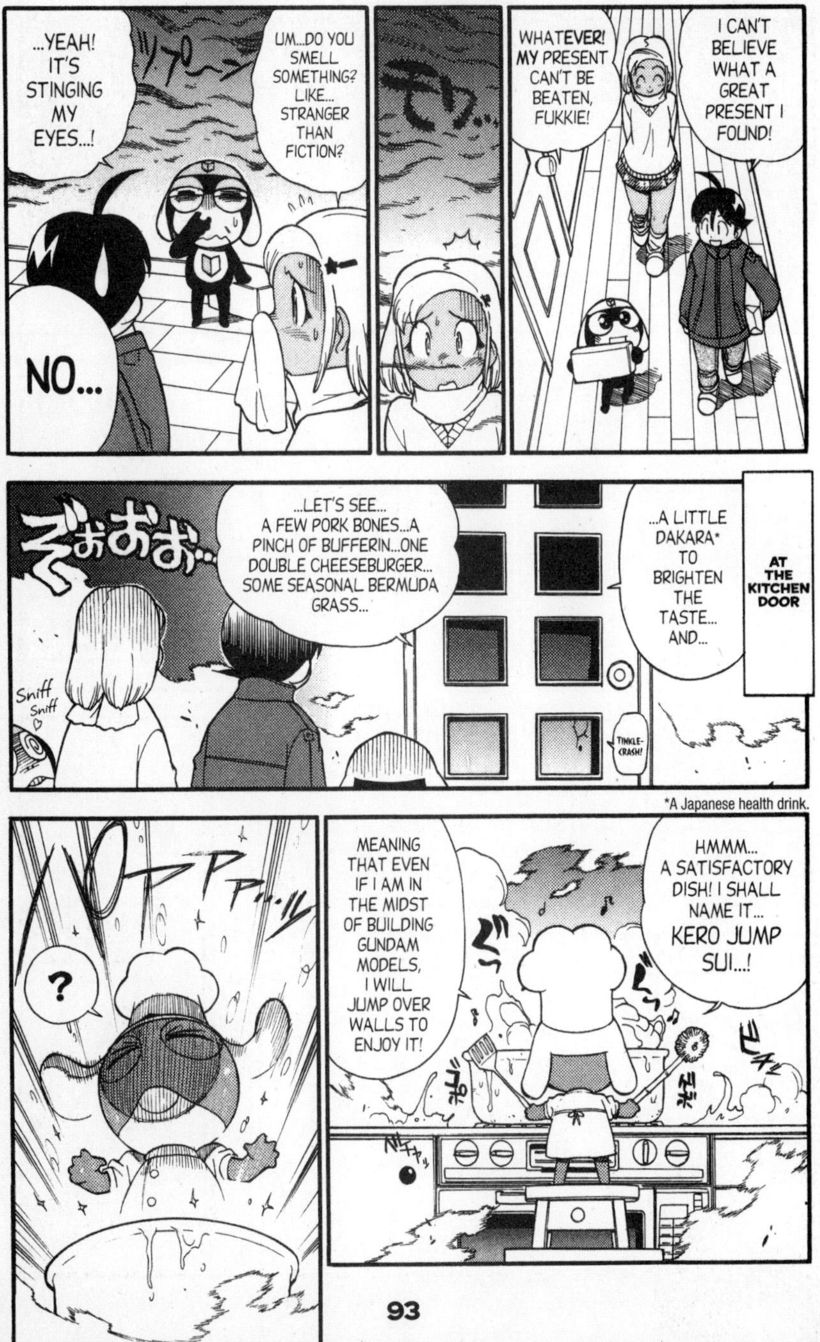
I CAN'T BELIEVE WHAT A GREAT PRESENT I FOUND!
WHATEVER! MY PRESENT CAN'T BE BEATEN, FUKKIE!
UM...DO YOU SMELL SOMETHING? LIKE... STRANGER THAN FICTION?
...YEAH! IT'S STINGING MY EYES...!
NO...
AT THE KITCHEN DOOR
...A LITTLE DAKARA* TO BRIGHTEN THE TASTE... AND...
TINKLE-CRASH!
...LET'S SEE... A FEW PORK BONES...A PINCH OF BUFFERIN...ONE DOUBLE CHEESEBURGER... SOME SEASONAL BERMUDA GRASS...
Sniff Sniff
HMMM... A SATISFACTORY DISH! I SHALL NAME IT... KERO JUMP SUI...!
MEANING THAT EVEN IF I AM IN THE MIDST OF BUILDING GUNDAM MODELS, I WILL JUMP OVER WALLS TO ENJOY IT!
?

*A Japanese health drink.

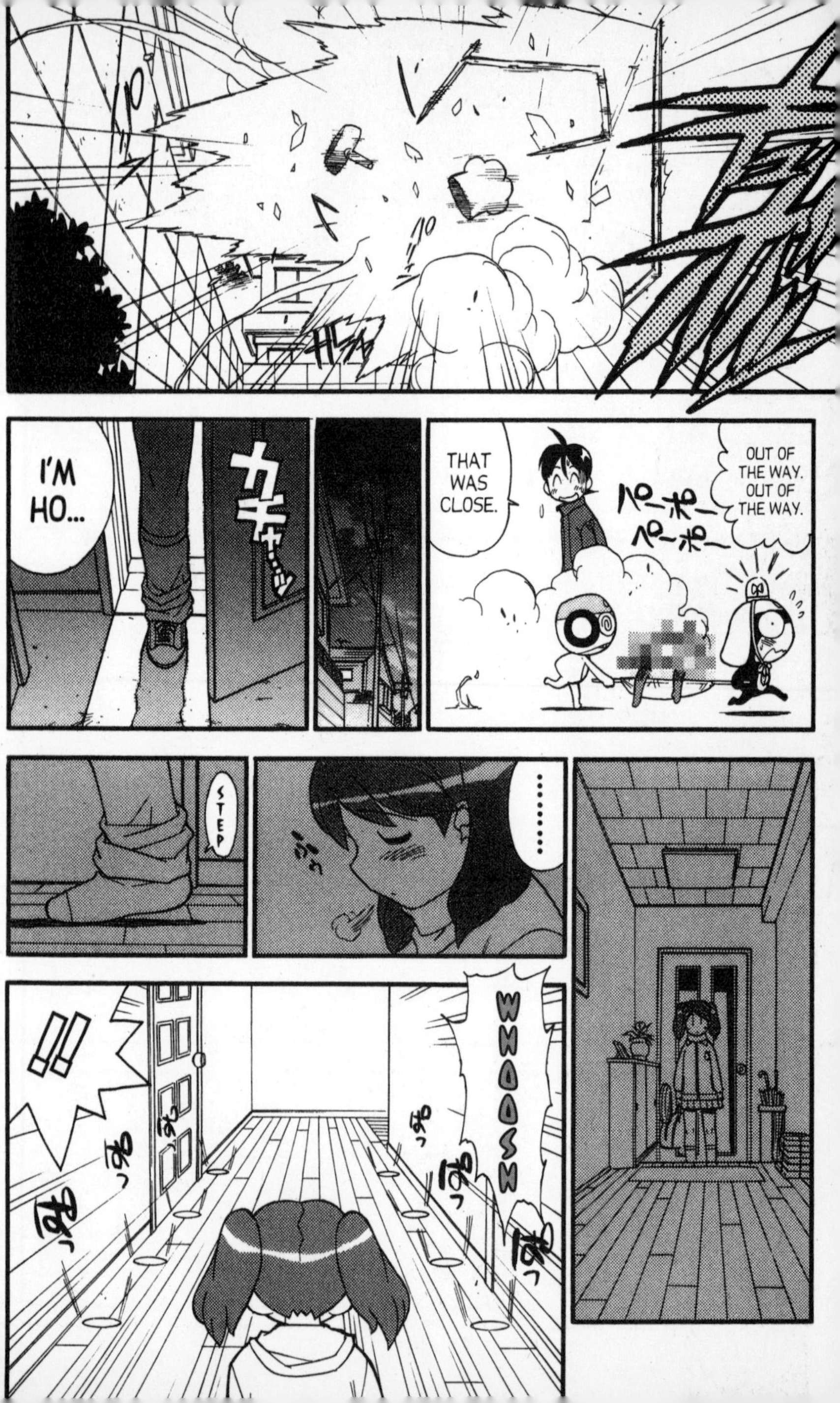

OUT OF THE WAY. OUT OF THE WAY.
ペーポー ペーポー
THAT WAS CLOSE.
I'M HO...
....
STEP
WHOOOSH
!!

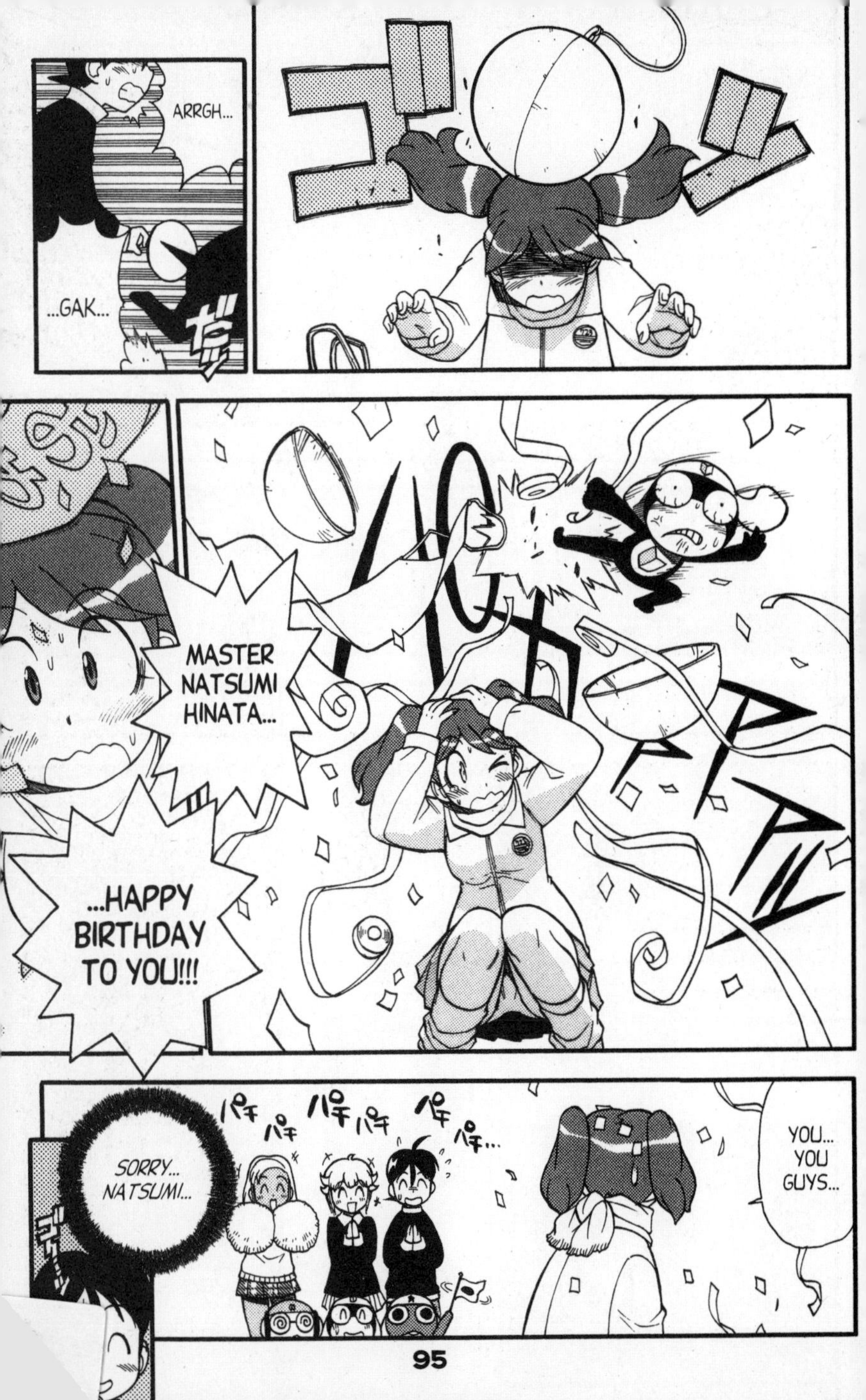
ARRGH...
...GAK...
MASTER NATSUMI HINATA...
...HAPPY BIRTHDAY TO YOU!!!
YOU... YOU GUYS...
SORRY... NATSUMI...

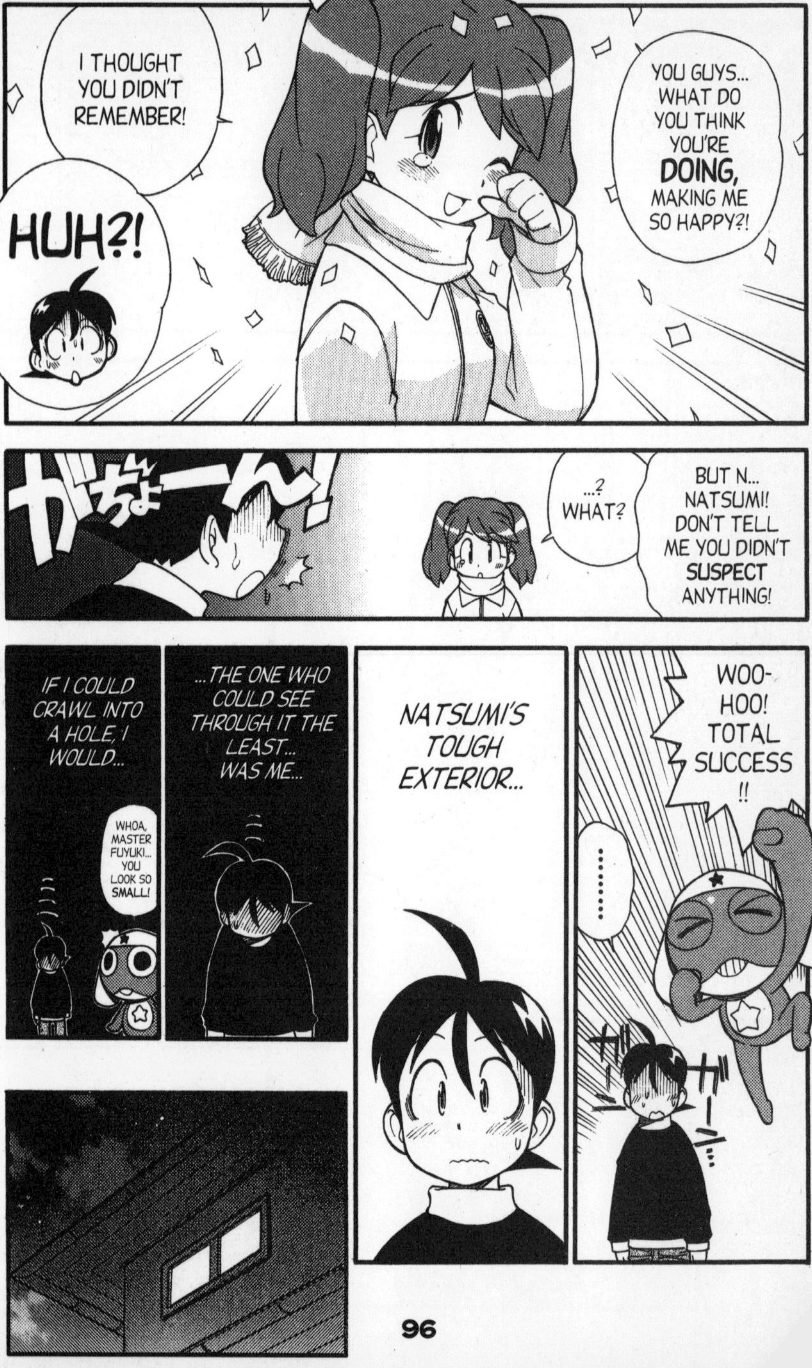
YOU GUYS... WHAT DO YOU THINK YOU'RE **DOING,** MAKING ME SO HAPPY?!
I THOUGHT YOU DIDN'T REMEMBER!
HUH?!
BUT N... NATSUMI! DON'T TELL ME YOU DIDN'T **SUSPECT** ANYTHING!
...? WHAT?
がちょーん!
WOO-HOO! TOTAL SUCCESS !!
....
NATSUMI'S TOUGH EXTERIOR...
...THE ONE WHO COULD SEE THROUGH IT THE LEAST... WAS ME...
IF I COULD CRAWL INTO A HOLE, I WOULD...
WHOA, MASTER FUYUKI... YOU LOOK SO SMALL!

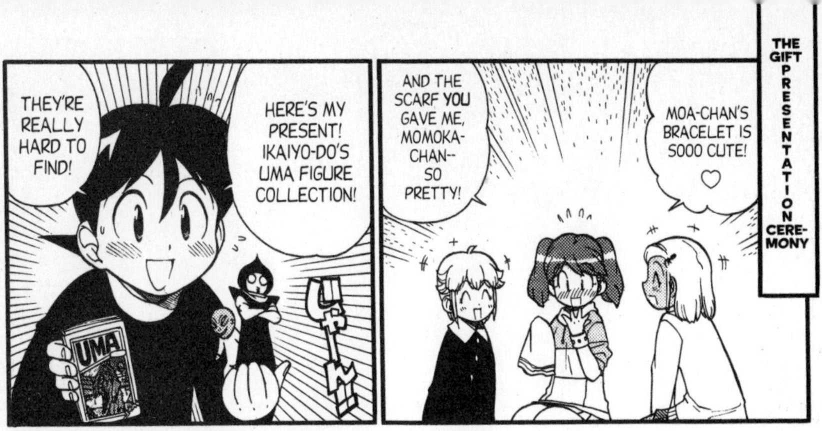
THE GIFT PRESENTATION CEREMONY
MOA-CHAN'S BRACELET IS SOOO CUTE! ♡
AND THE SCARF YOU GAVE ME, MOMOKA-CHAN-- SO PRETTY!
HERE'S MY PRESENT! IKAIYO-DO'S UMA FIGURE COLLECTION!
THEY'RE REALLY HARD TO FIND!
UMA

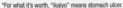

*For what it's worth, "ikaiyo" means stomach ulcer.

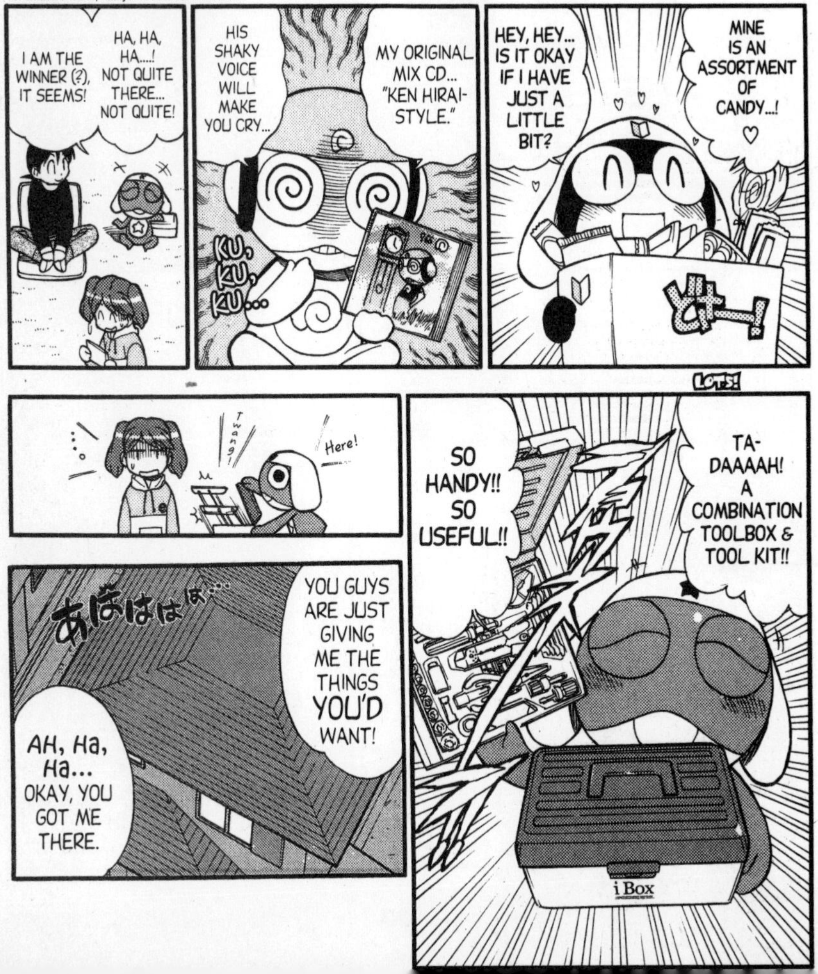
MINE IS AN ASSORTMENT OF CANDY...! ♡
HEY, HEY... IS IT OKAY IF I HAVE JUST A LITTLE BIT?
LOTS!
MY ORIGINAL MIX CD... "KEN HIRAI-STYLE."
HIS SHAKY VOICE WILL MAKE YOU CRY...
KU, KU, KU...
HA, HA, HA...! NOT QUITE THERE... NOT QUITE!
I AM THE WINNER (?), IT SEEMS!
TA-DAAAAH! A COMBINATION TOOLBOX & TOOL KIT!!
SO HANDY!! SO USEFUL!!
i Box
Here!
Twang!
...
あははは...
YOU GUYS ARE JUST GIVING ME THE THINGS YOU'D WANT!
AH, Ha, Ha... OKAY, YOU GOT ME THERE.

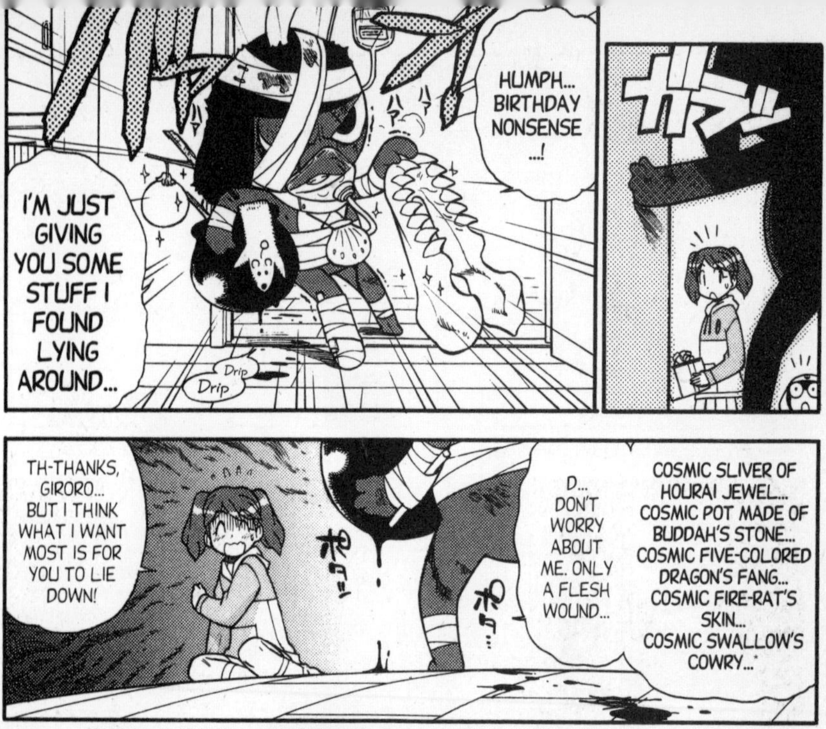
HUMPH... BIRTHDAY NONSENSE ...!
I'M JUST GIVING YOU SOME STUFF I FOUND LYING AROUND...
Drip
Drip
COSMIC SLIVER OF HOURAI JEWEL... COSMIC POT MADE OF BUDDAH'S STONE... COSMIC FIVE-COLORED DRAGON'S FANG... COSMIC FIRE-RAT'S SKIN... COSMIC SWALLOW'S COWRY...*
D... DON'T WORRY ABOUT ME. ONLY A FLESH WOUND...
TH-THANKS, GIRORO... BUT I THINK WHAT I WANT MOST IS FOR YOU TO LIE DOWN!

*Cosmic versions of all the treasures desired by Kaguya-hime (the moon princess in "Taketori Monogatari") when suitors asked for her hand in marriage.

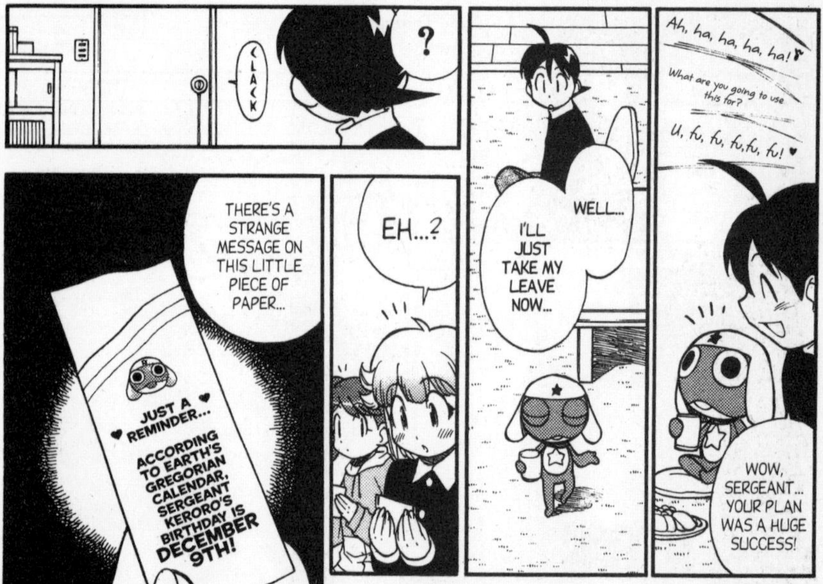
Ah, ha, ha, ha, ha!
What are you going to use this for?
U, fu, fu, fu,fu, fu!
WOW, SERGEANT... YOUR PLAN WAS A HUGE SUCCESS!
WELL...
I'LL JUST TAKE MY LEAVE NOW...
?
CLACK
EH...?
THERE'S A STRANGE MESSAGE ON THIS LITTLE PIECE OF PAPER...
JUST A REMINDER...
ACCORDING TO EARTH'S GREGORIAN CALENDAR, SERGEANT KERORO'S BIRTHDAY IS DECEMBER 9TH!

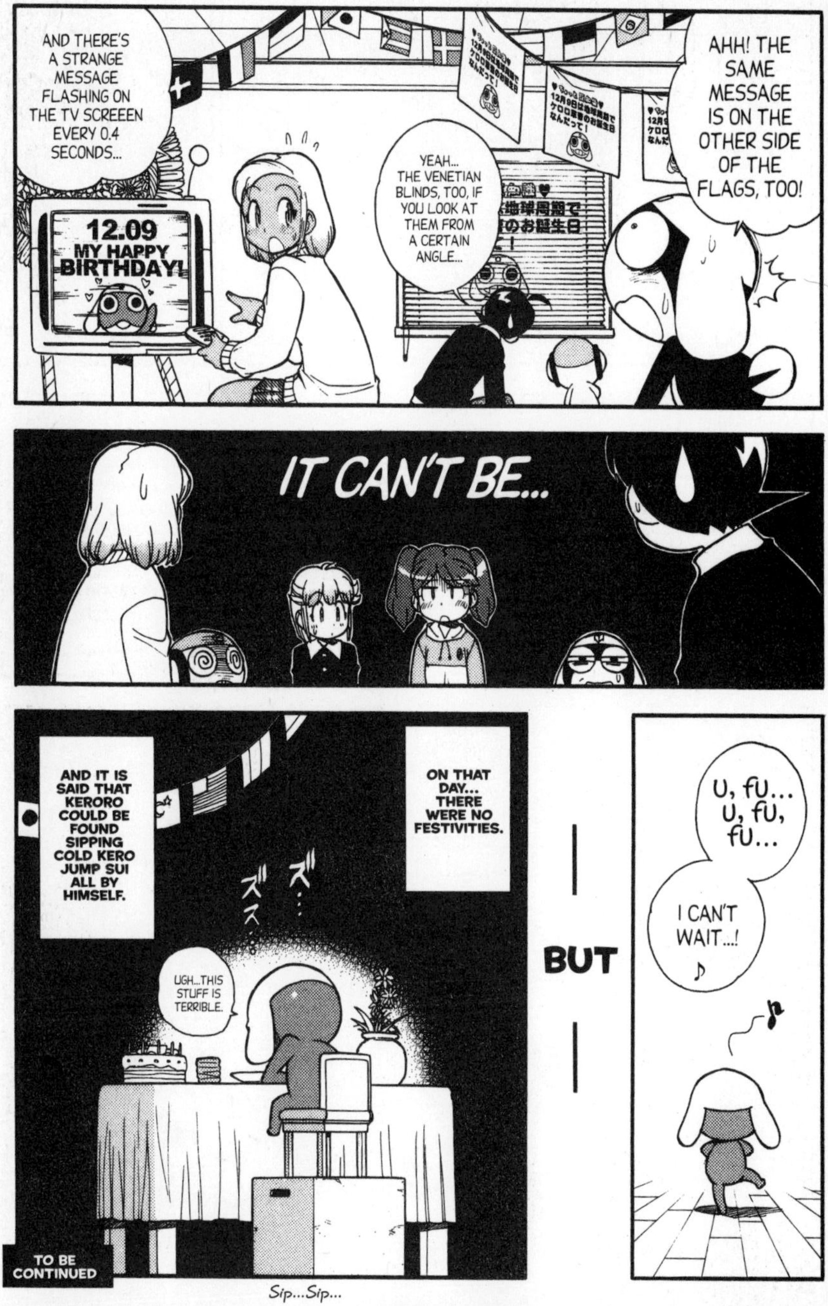
AHH! THE SAME MESSAGE IS ON THE OTHER SIDE OF THE FLAGS, TOO!
AND THERE'S A STRANGE MESSAGE FLASHING ON THE TV SCREEEN EVERY 0.4 SECONDS...
12.09 MY HAPPY BIRTHDAY!
YEAH... THE VENETIAN BLINDS, TOO, IF YOU LOOK AT THEM FROM A CERTAIN ANGLE...
IT CAN'T BE...
U, FU... U, FU, FU...
I CAN'T WAIT...! ♪
BUT
ON THAT DAY... THERE WERE NO FESTIVITIES.
AND IT IS SAID THAT KERORO COULD BE FOUND SIPPING COLD KERO JUMP SUI ALL BY HIMSELF.
ズズ...
ズズ...
UGH...THIS STUFF IS TERRIBLE.
TO BE CONTINUED
Sip...Sip...

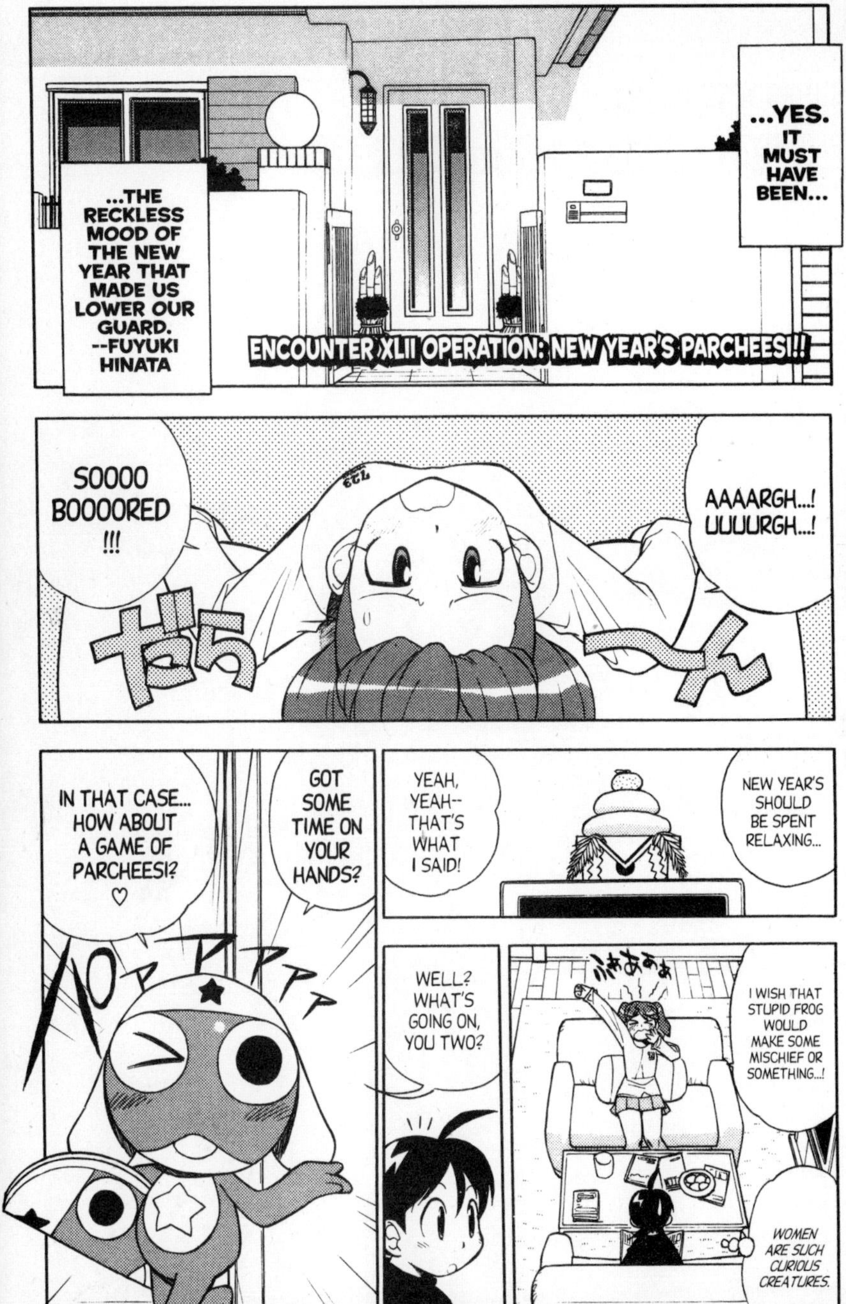
...YES. IT MUST HAVE BEEN...
...THE RECKLESS MOOD OF THE NEW YEAR THAT MADE US LOWER OUR GUARD. --FUYUKI HINATA
ENCOUNTER XLII OPERATION: NEW YEAR'S PARCHEESI!!
AAAARGH...! UUUURGH...!
SOOOO BOOOORED !!!
だら〜ん
NEW YEAR'S SHOULD BE SPENT RELAXING...
YEAH, YEAH-- THAT'S WHAT I SAID!
I WISH THAT STUPID FROG WOULD MAKE SOME MISCHIEF OR SOMETHING...!
ふぁあああ
WOMEN ARE SUCH CURIOUS CREATURES.
Yaa-awn
WELL? WHAT'S GOING ON, YOU TWO?
GOT SOME TIME ON YOUR HANDS?
IN THAT CASE... HOW ABOUT A GAME OF PARCHEESI? ♡

ENCOUNTER XLII
OPERATION: NEW YEAR'S PARCHEESI!!

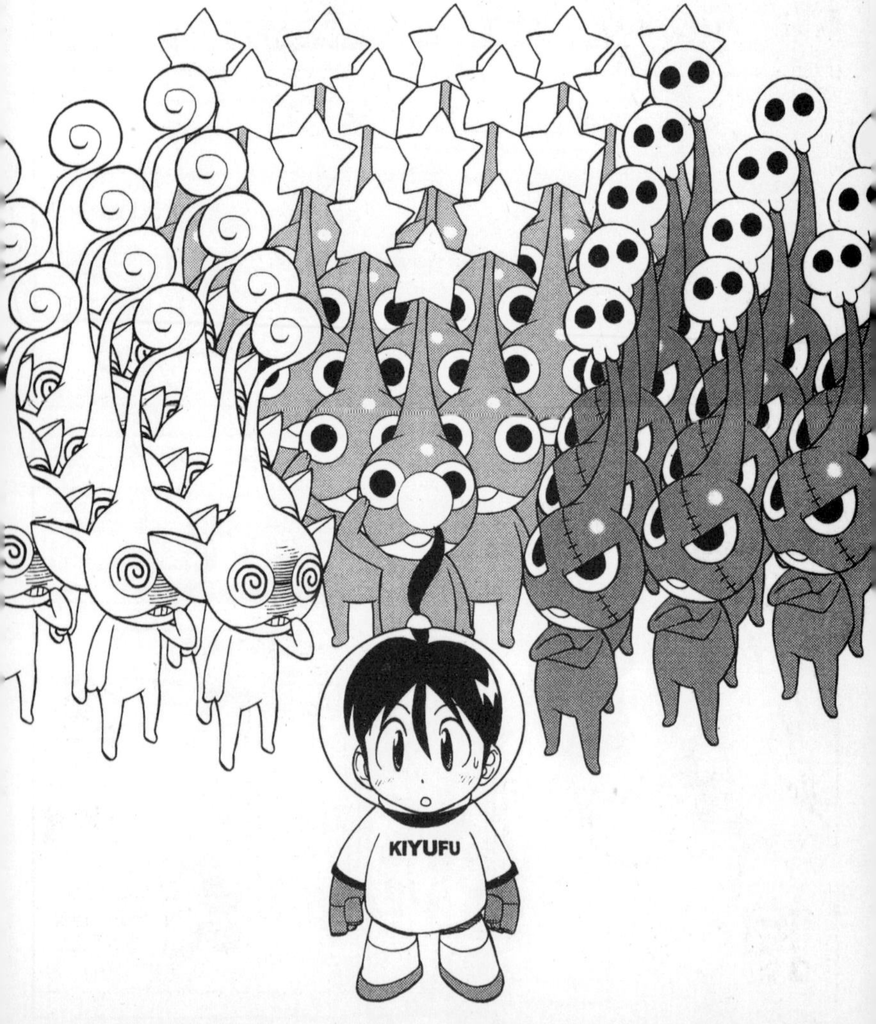
KIYUFU

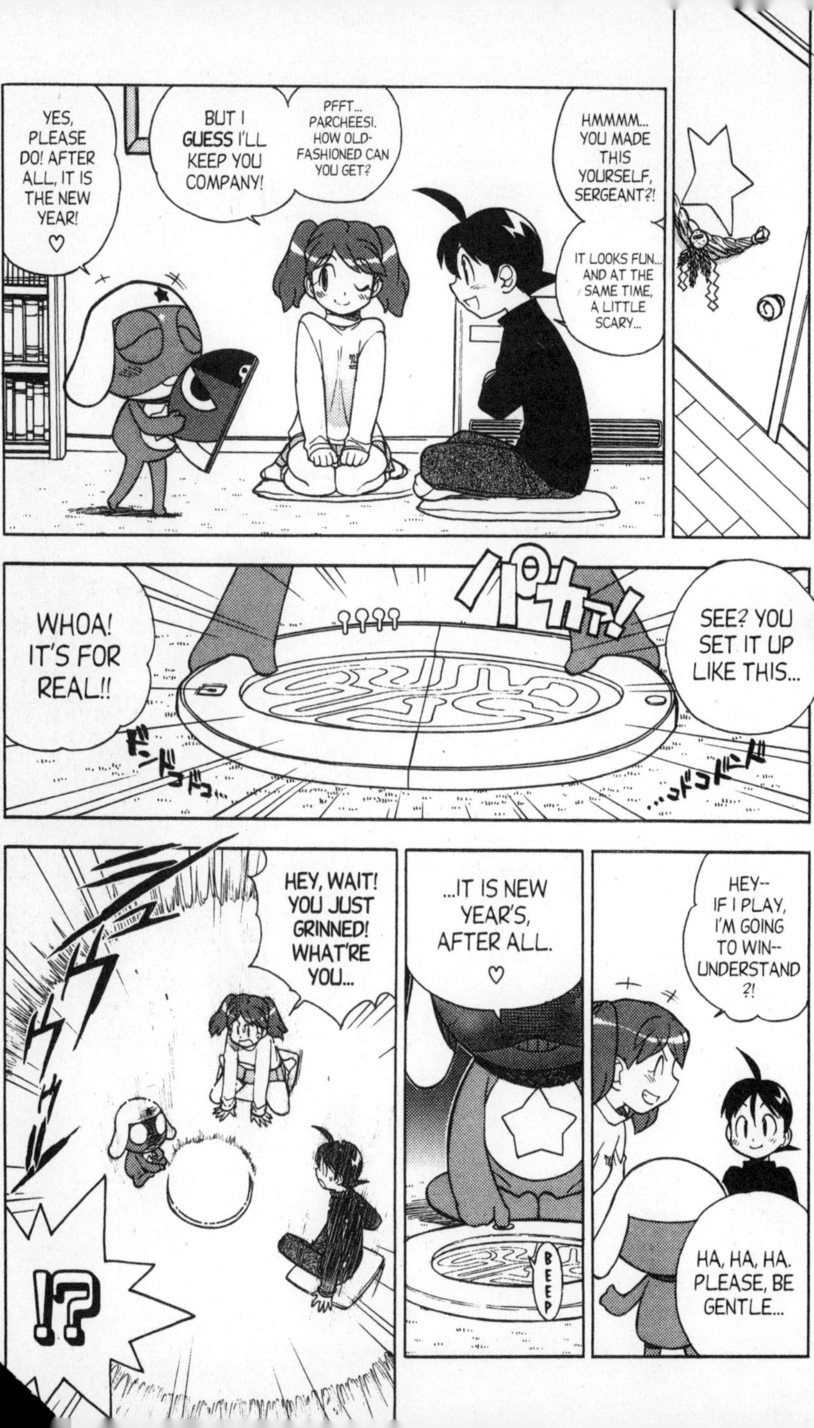
HMMMM... YOU MADE THIS YOURSELF, SERGEANT?!
IT LOOKS FUN... AND AT THE SAME TIME, A LITTLE SCARY...
PFFT... PARCHEESI. HOW OLD-FASHIONED CAN YOU GET?
BUT I GUESS I'LL KEEP YOU COMPANY!
YES, PLEASE DO! AFTER ALL, IT IS THE NEW YEAR! ♡
SEE? YOU SET IT UP LIKE THIS...
WHOA! IT'S FOR REAL!!
HEY-- IF I PLAY, I'M GOING TO WIN-- UNDERSTAND?!
HA, HA, HA. PLEASE, BE GENTLE...
...IT IS NEW YEAR'S, AFTER ALL. ♡
BEEP
HEY, WAIT! YOU JUST GRINNED! WHAT'RE YOU...
!?

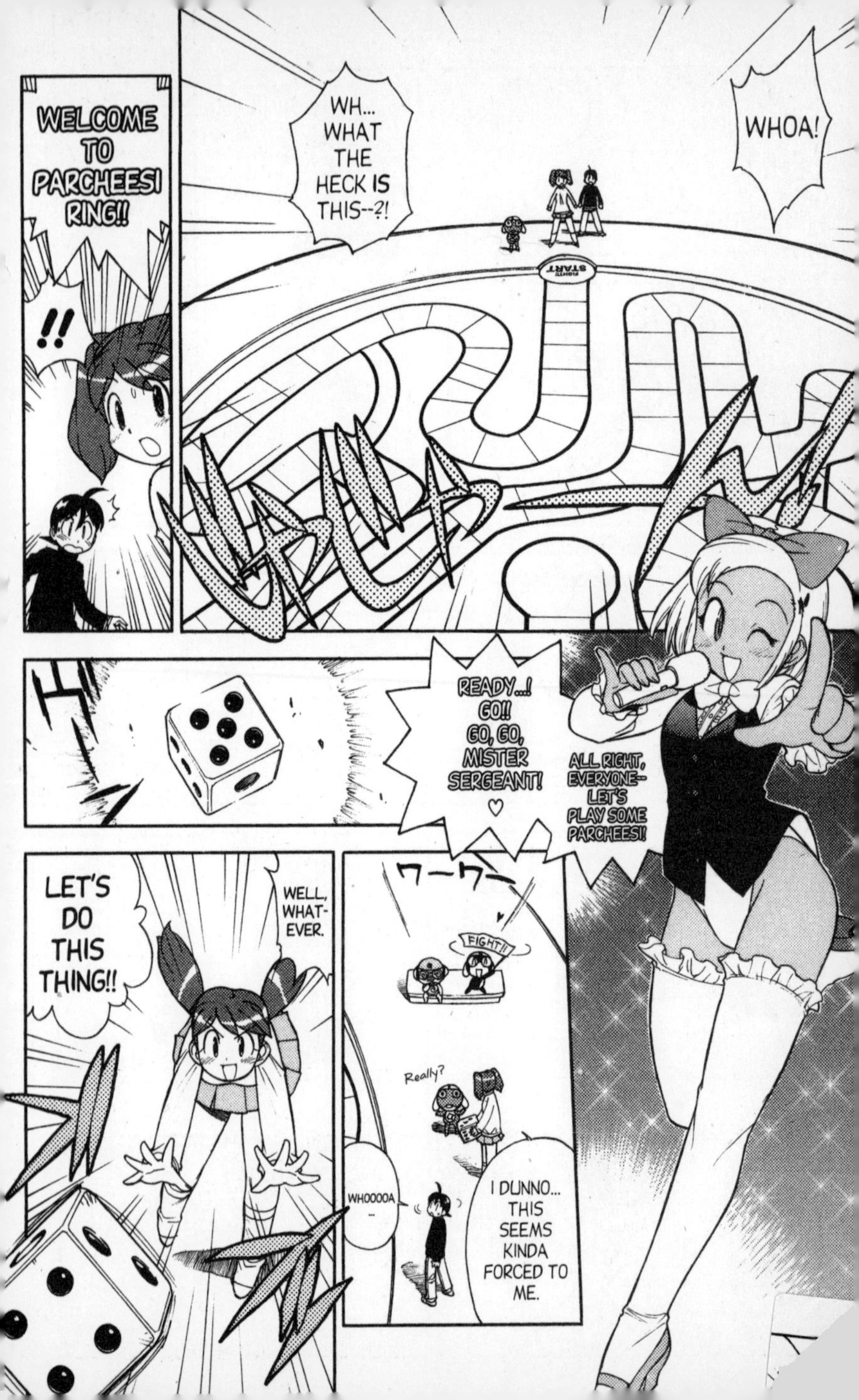
WHOA!
WH... WHAT THE HECK IS THIS--?!
WELCOME TO PARCHEESI RING!!
!!
ALL RIGHT, EVERYONE-- LET'S PLAY SOME PARCHEESI!
READY...! GO!! GO, GO, MISTER SERGEANT! ♡
ワーワー
FIGHT!!
Really?
I DUNNO... THIS SEEMS KINDA FORCED TO ME.
WHOOOOA...
WELL, WHAT-EVER.
LET'S DO THIS THING!!

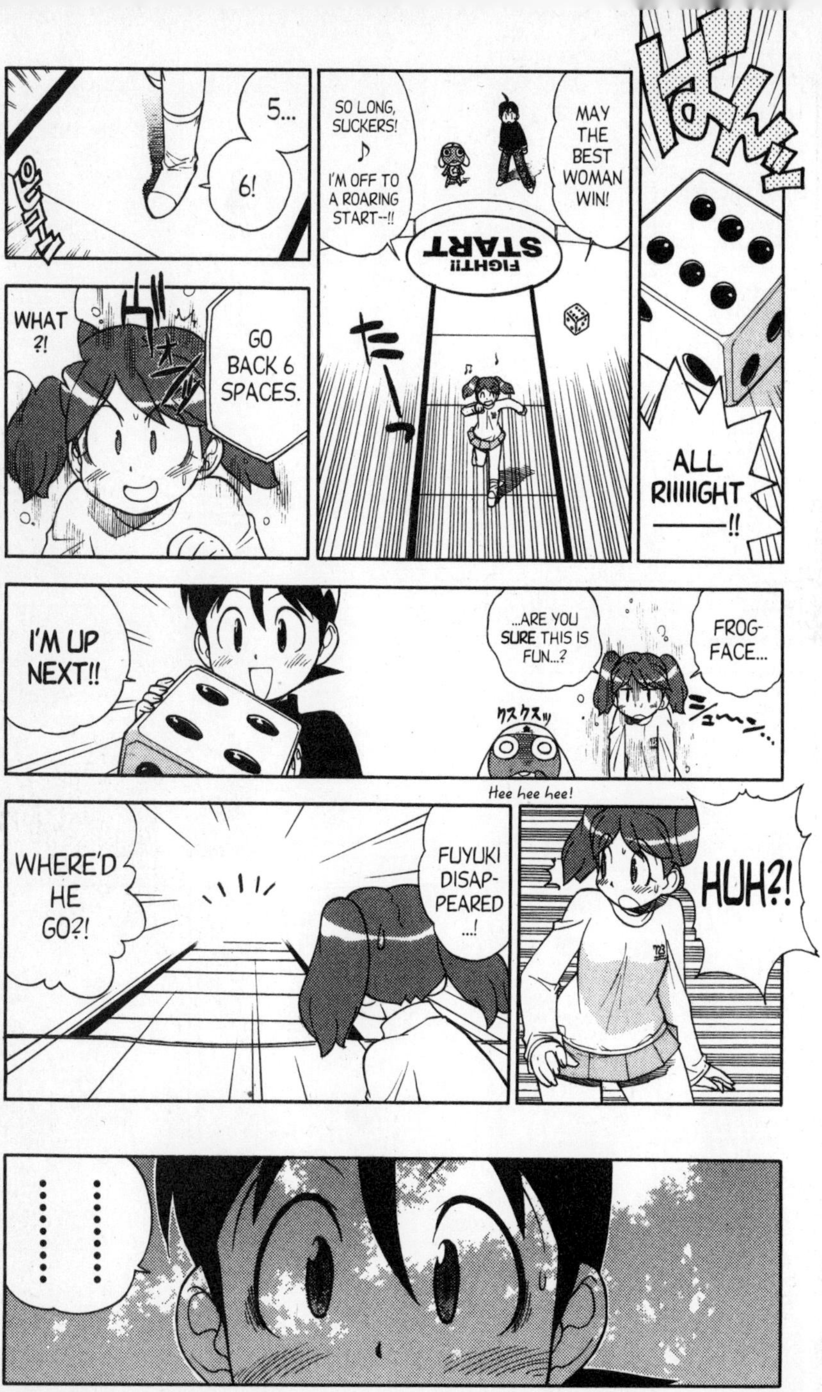
ALL RIIIIGHT ———!!
MAY THE BEST WOMAN WIN!
SO LONG, SUCKERS! ♪ I'M OFF TO A ROARING START--!!
FIGHT!! START
5...
6!
GO BACK 6 SPACES.
WHAT ?!
FROG-FACE...
...ARE YOU SURE THIS IS FUN...?
Hee hee hee!
I'M UP NEXT!!
HUH?!
FUYUKI DISAP-PEARED ...!
WHERE'D HE GO?!
....
....

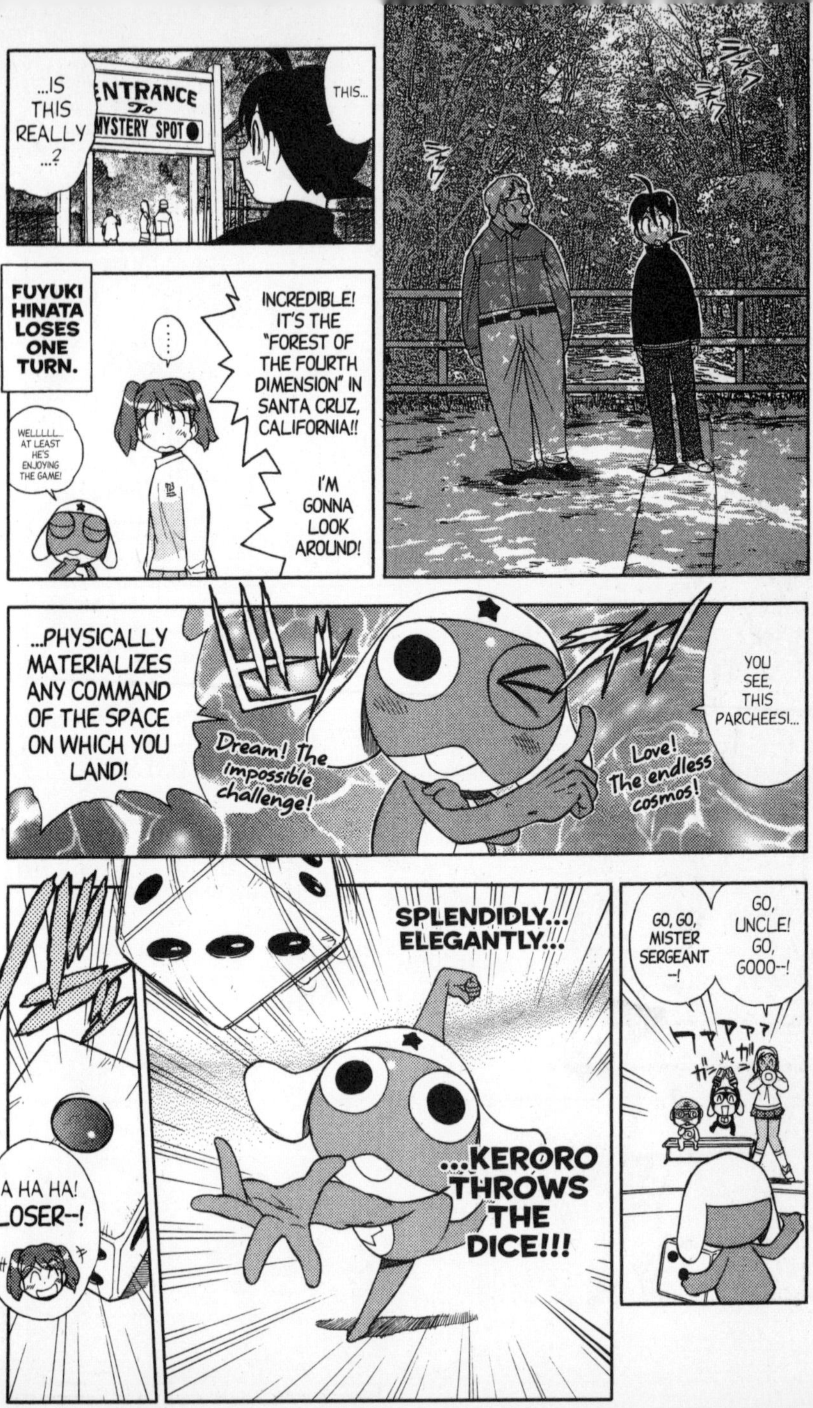
THIS...
...IS THIS REALLY ...?
ENTRANCE To MYSTERY SPOT
INCREDIBLE! IT'S THE "FOREST OF THE FOURTH DIMENSION" IN SANTA CRUZ, CALIFORNIA!!
I'M GONNA LOOK AROUND!
......
WELLLLL... AT LEAST HE'S ENJOYING THE GAME!
FUYUKI HINATA LOSES ONE TURN.
YOU SEE, THIS PARCHEESI...
Love! The endless cosmos!
Dream! The impossible challenge!
...PHYSICALLY MATERIALIZES ANY COMMAND OF THE SPACE ON WHICH YOU LAND!
GO, UNCLE! GO, GOOO--!
GO, GO, MISTER SERGEANT--!
SPLENDIDLY... ELEGANTLY...
...KERORO THROWS THE DICE!!!
A HA HA! LOSER--!

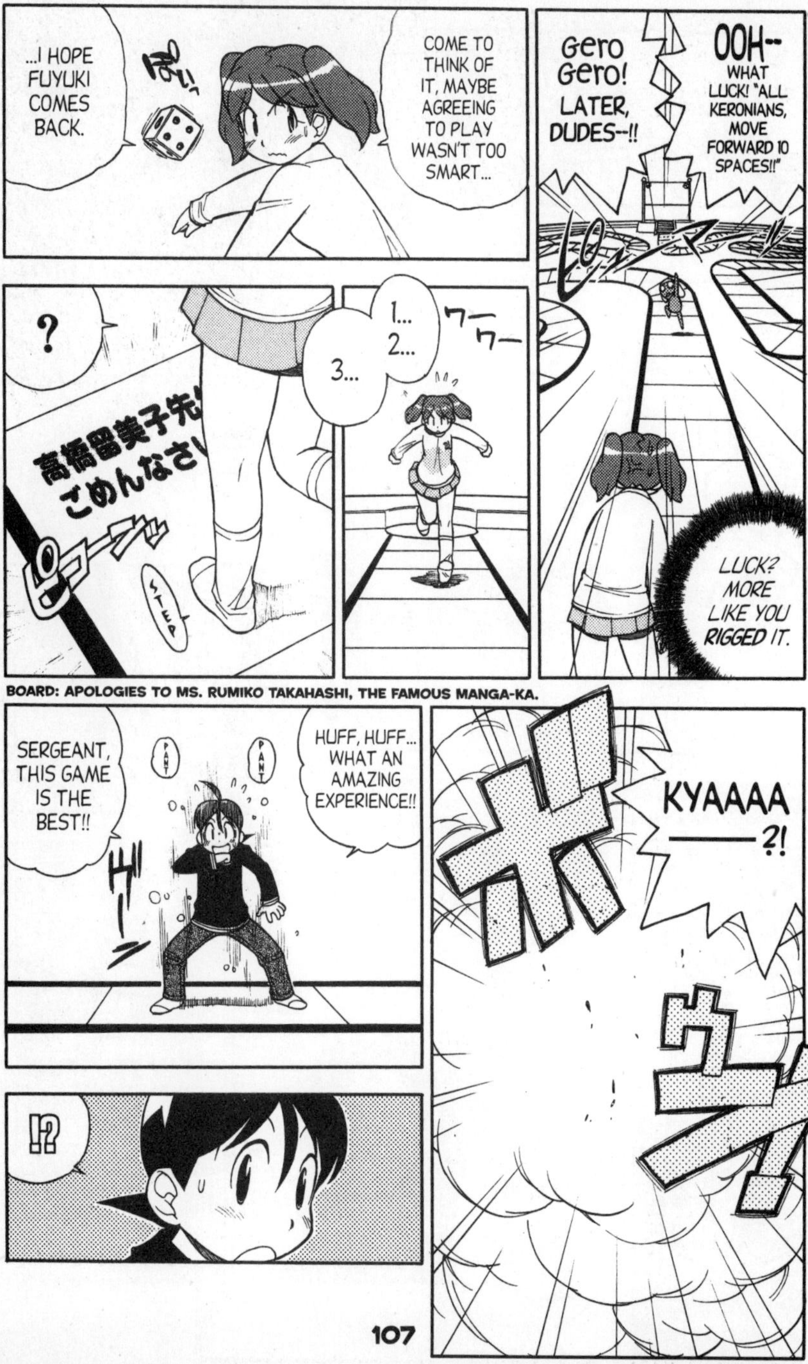
OOH-- WHAT LUCK! "ALL KERONIANS, MOVE FORWARD 10 SPACES!!"
Gero Gero! LATER, DUDES--!!
LUCK? MORE LIKE YOU RIGGED IT.
COME TO THINK OF IT, MAYBE AGREEING TO PLAY WASN'T TOO SMART...
...I HOPE FUYUKI COMES BACK.
1... 2...
3...
?
高橋留美子先
ごめんなさい
STEP
KYAAAA——?!
HUFF, HUFF... WHAT AN AMAZING EXPERIENCE!!
PANT
PANT
SERGEANT, THIS GAME IS THE BEST!!
!?

BOARD: APOLOGIES TO MS. RUMIKO TAKAHASHI, THE FAMOUS MANGA-KA.

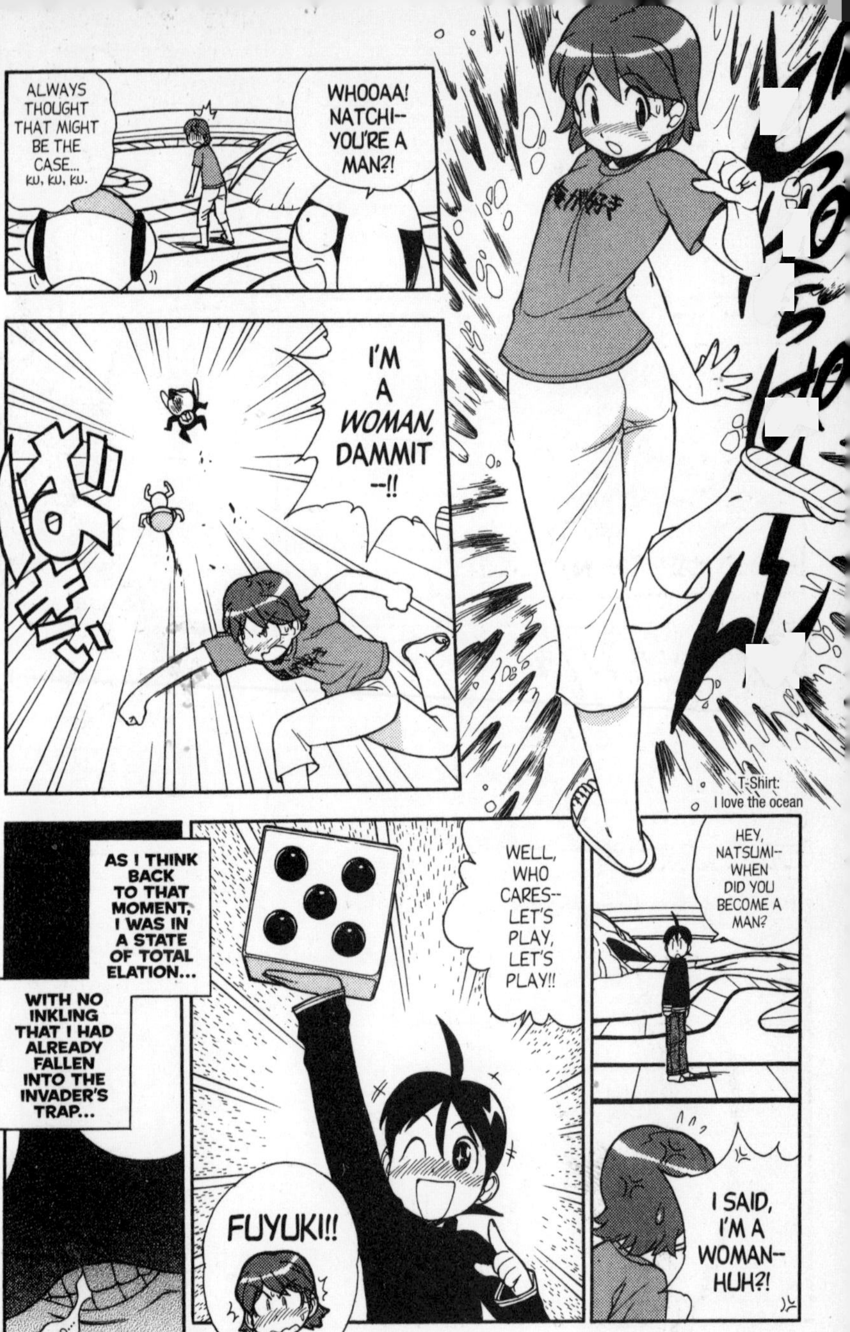
T-Shirt:
I love the ocean
WHOOAA! NATCHI-- YOU'RE A MAN?!
ALWAYS THOUGHT THAT MIGHT BE THE CASE... KU, KU, KU.
I'M A *WOMAN,* DAMMIT--!!
HEY, NATSUMI-- WHEN DID YOU BECOME A MAN?
I SAID, I'M A WOMAN-- HUH?!
WELL, WHO CARES-- LET'S PLAY, LET'S PLAY!!
FUYUKI!!
AS I THINK BACK TO THAT MOMENT, I WAS IN A STATE OF TOTAL ELATION...
WITH NO INKLING THAT I HAD ALREADY FALLEN INTO THE INVADER'S TRAP...
Kero Kero Kero...

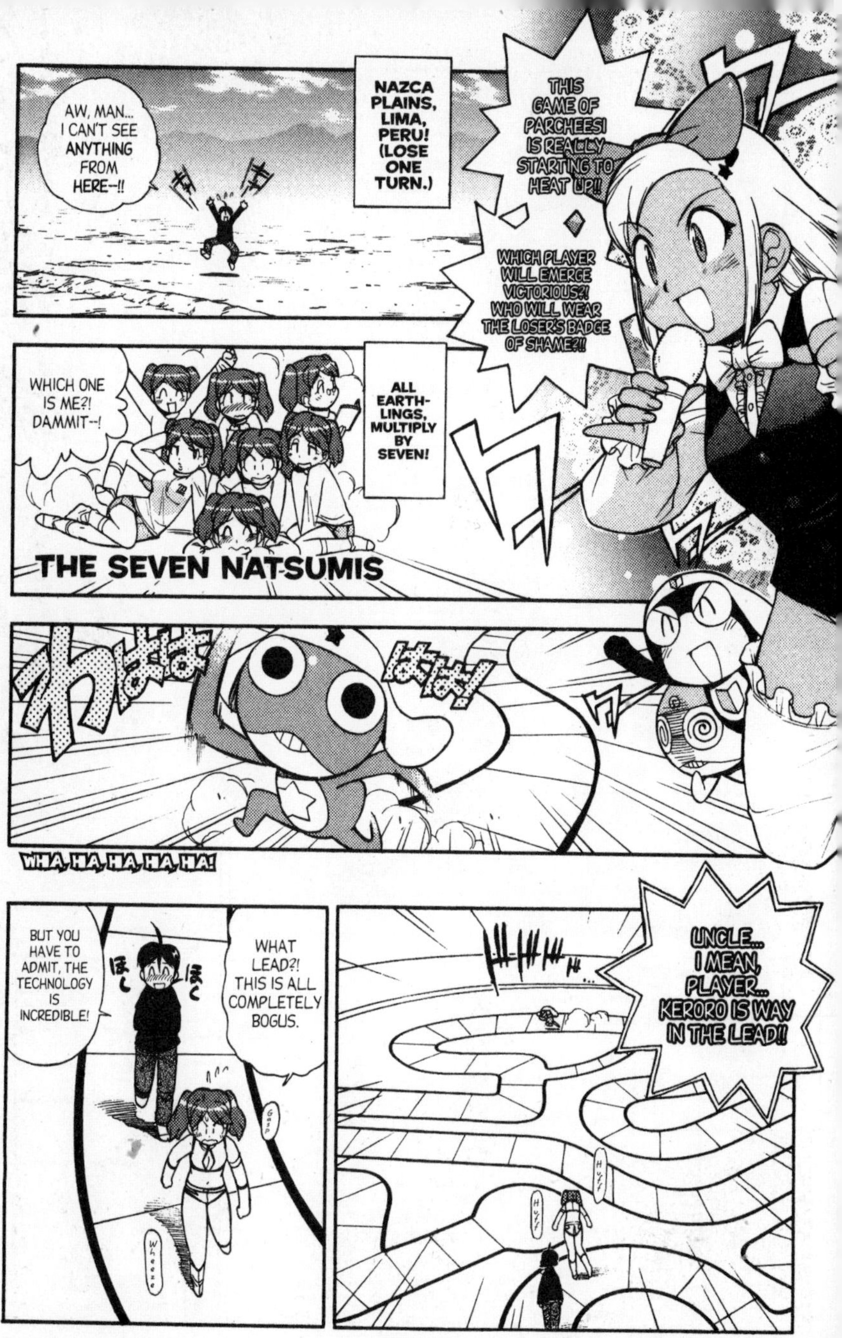
THIS GAME OF PARCHEESI IS REALLY STARTING TO HEAT UP!!
WHICH PLAYER WILL EMERGE VICTORIOUS?! WHO WILL WEAR THE LOSER'S BADGE OF SHAME?!!
NAZCA PLAINS, LIMA, PERU! (LOSE ONE TURN.)
AW, MAN... I CAN'T SEE ANYTHING FROM HERE--!!
ALL EARTHLINGS, MULTIPLY BY SEVEN!
WHICH ONE IS ME?! DAMMIT--!
THE SEVEN NATSUMIS
WHA, HA, HA, HA, HA!
UNCLE... I MEAN, PLAYER... KERORO IS WAY IN THE LEAD!!
Huff
Huff
WHAT LEAD?! THIS IS ALL COMPLETELY BOGUS.
Gasp
Wheeze
BUT YOU HAVE TO ADMIT, THE TECHNOLOGY IS INCREDIBLE!

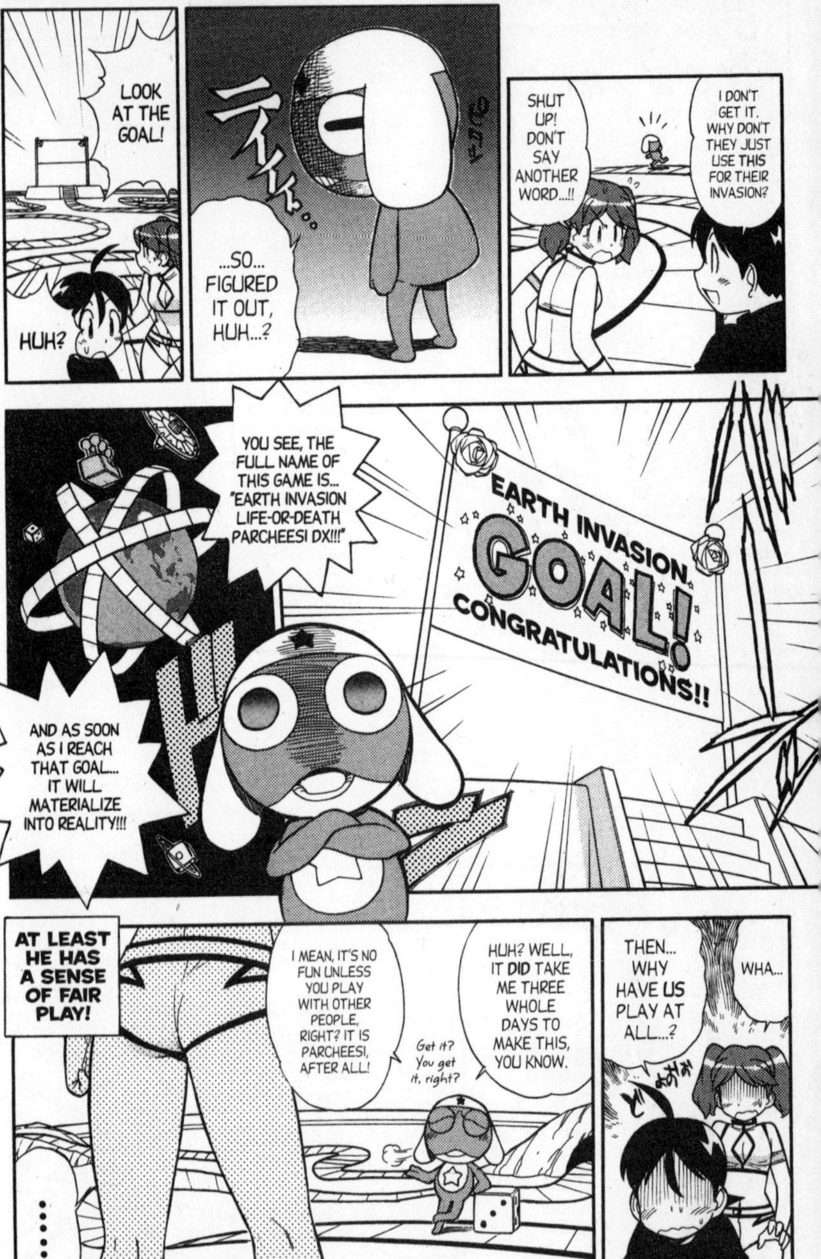
I DON'T GET IT. WHY DON'T THEY JUST USE THIS FOR THEIR INVASION?
SHUT UP! DON'T SAY ANOTHER WORD...!!
...SO... FIGURED IT OUT, HUH...?
LOOK AT THE GOAL!
HUH?
YOU SEE, THE FULL NAME OF THIS GAME IS... "EARTH INVASION LIFE-OR-DEATH PARCHEESI DX!!!"
EARTH INVASION GOAL! CONGRATULATIONS!!
AND AS SOON AS I REACH THAT GOAL... IT WILL MATERIALIZE INTO REALITY!!!
WHA...
THEN... WHY HAVE US PLAY AT ALL...?
HUH? WELL, IT DID TAKE ME THREE WHOLE DAYS TO MAKE THIS, YOU KNOW.
I MEAN, IT'S NO FUN UNLESS YOU PLAY WITH OTHER PEOPLE, RIGHT? IT IS PARCHEESI, AFTER ALL!
Get it? You get it, right?
AT LEAST HE HAS A SENSE OF FAIR PLAY!
......

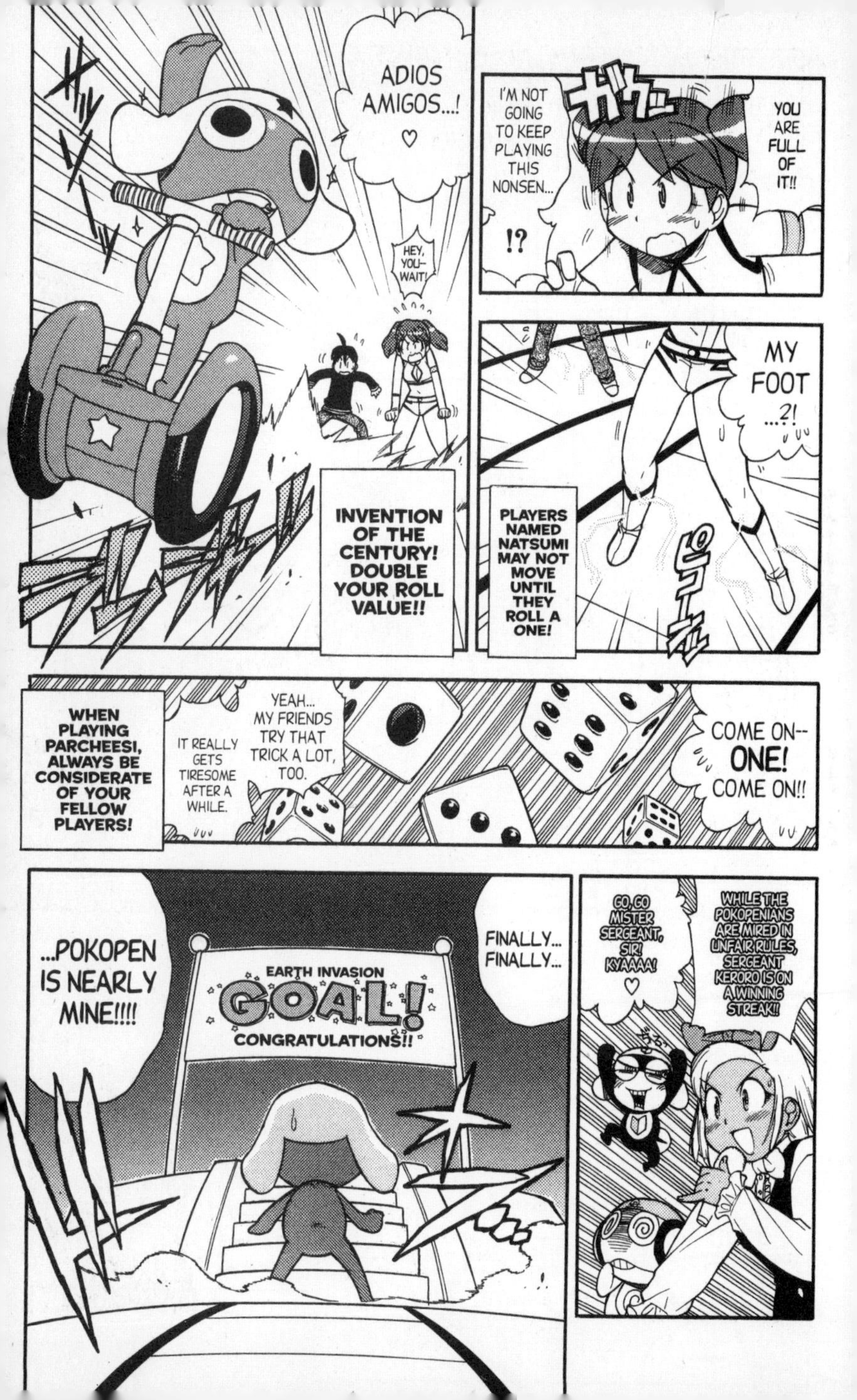
YOU ARE FULL OF IT!!
I'M NOT GOING TO KEEP PLAYING THIS NONSEN...
!?
MY FOOT ...?!
PLAYERS NAMED NATSUMI MAY NOT MOVE UNTIL THEY ROLL A ONE!
ADIOS AMIGOS...! ♡
HEY, YOU— WAIT!
INVENTION OF THE CENTURY! DOUBLE YOUR ROLL VALUE!!
COME ON-- ONE! COME ON!!
YEAH... MY FRIENDS TRY THAT TRICK A LOT, TOO.
IT REALLY GETS TIRESOME AFTER A WHILE.
WHEN PLAYING PARCHEESI, ALWAYS BE CONSIDERATE OF YOUR FELLOW PLAYERS!
WHILE THE POKOPENIANS ARE MIRED IN UNFAIR RULES, SERGEANT KERORO IS ON A WINNING STREAK!!
GO, GO MISTER SERGEANT, SIR! KYAAAA! ♡
FINALLY... FINALLY...
EARTH INVASION GOAL! CONGRATULATIONS!!
...POKOPEN IS NEARLY MINE!!!!

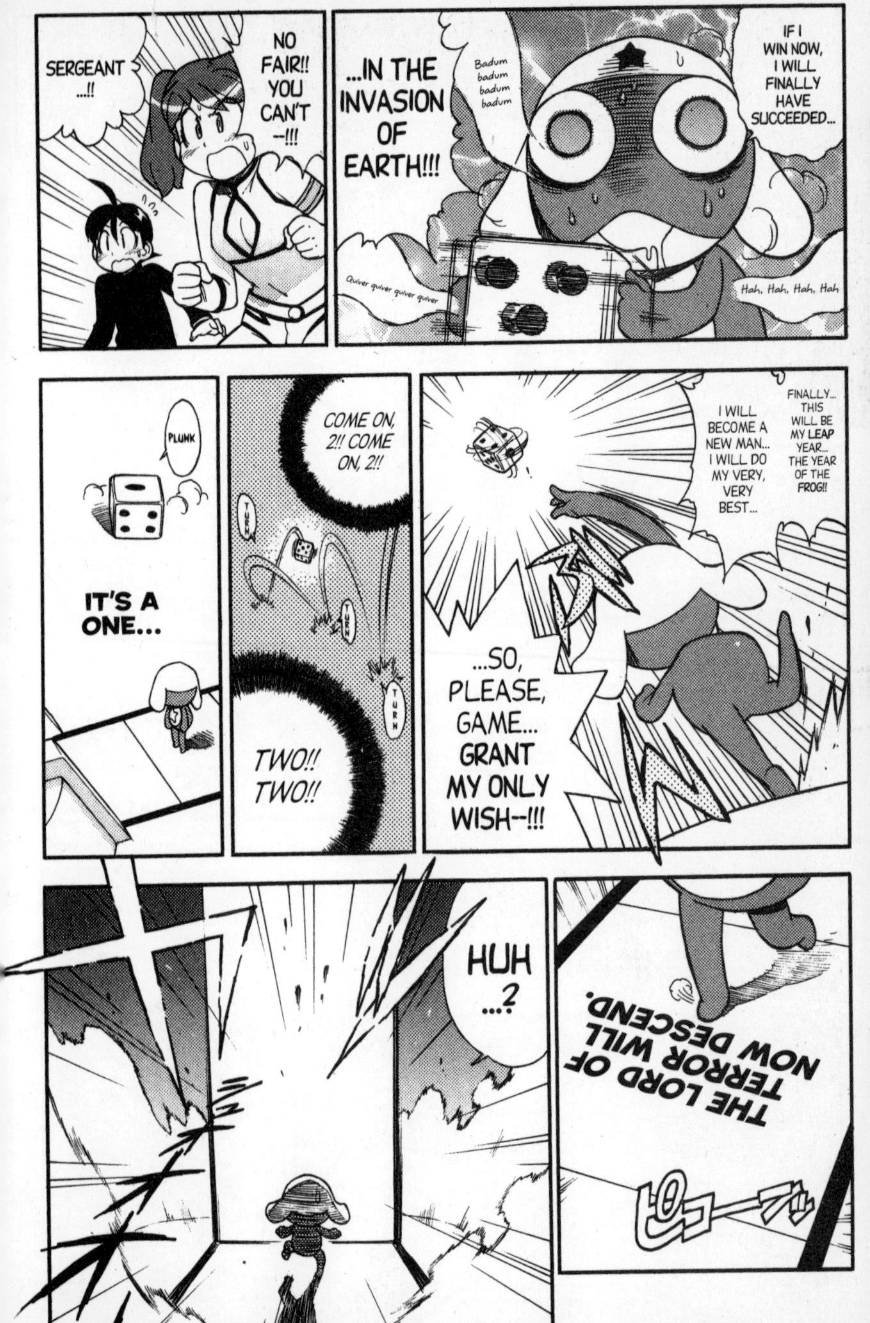
IF I WIN NOW, I WILL FINALLY HAVE SUCCEEDED...
Badum badum badum badum
...IN THE INVASION OF EARTH!!!
Hah, Hah, Hah, Hah
Quiver quiver quiver quiver
NO FAIR!! YOU CAN'T --!!!
SERGEANT ...!!
FINALLY... THIS WILL BE MY LEAP YEAR... THE YEAR OF THE FROG!!
I WILL BECOME A NEW MAN... I WILL DO MY VERY, VERY BEST...
...SO, PLEASE, GAME... GRANT MY ONLY WISH--!!!
COME ON, 2!! COME ON, 2!!
TURN
TURN
TURN
TWO!! TWO!!
PLUNK
IT'S A ONE...
THE LORD OF TERROR WILL NOW DESCEND.
HUH ...?

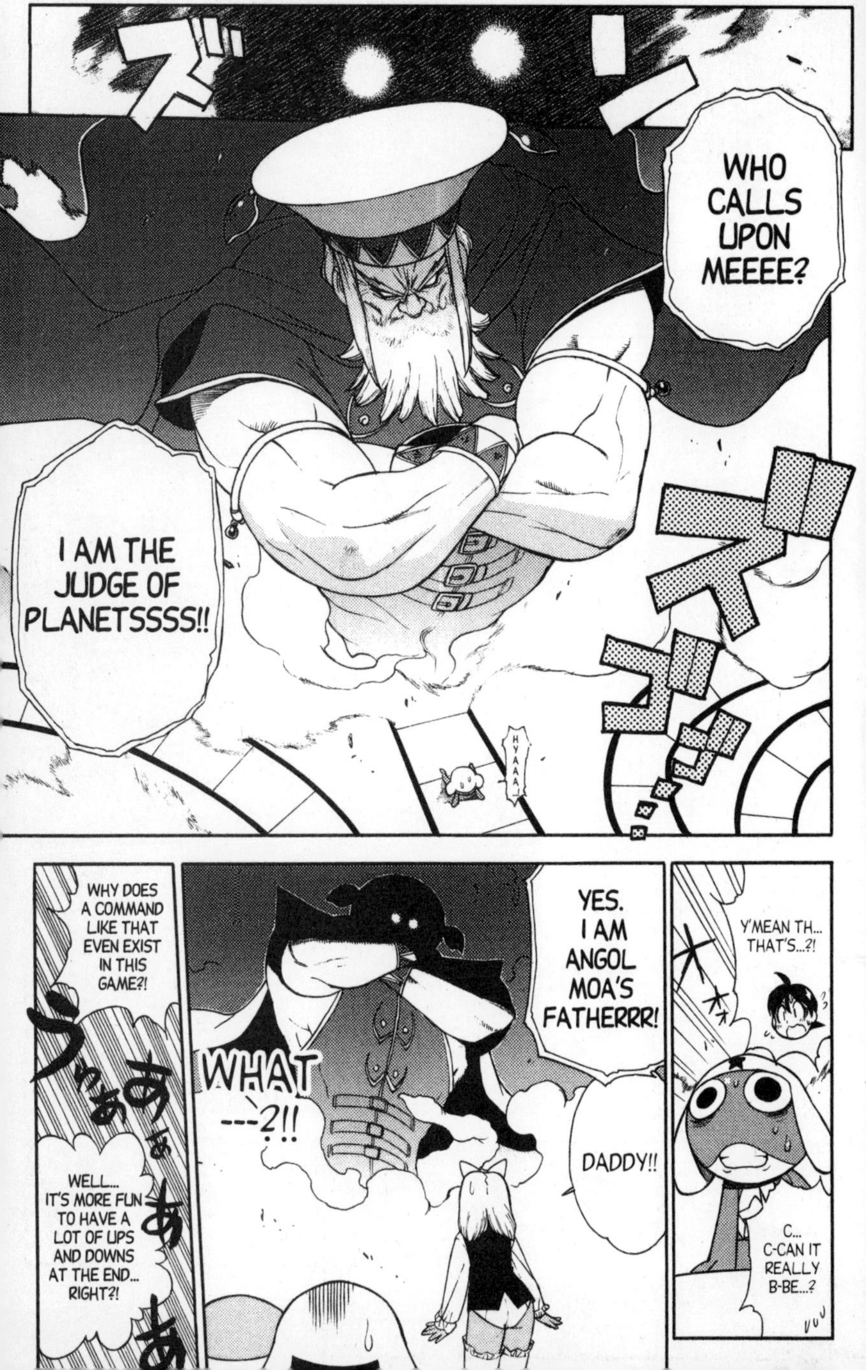
WHO CALLS UPON MEEEE?
I AM THE JUDGE OF PLANETSSSS!!
HYAAA...
Y'MEAN TH... THAT'S...?!
C... C-CAN IT REALLY B-BE...?
YES. I AM ANGOL MOA'S FATHERRR!
WHAT---?!!
DADDY!!
WHY DOES A COMMAND LIKE THAT EVEN EXIST IN THIS GAME?!
WELL... IT'S MORE FUN TO HAVE A LOT OF UPS AND DOWNS AT THE END... RIGHT?!

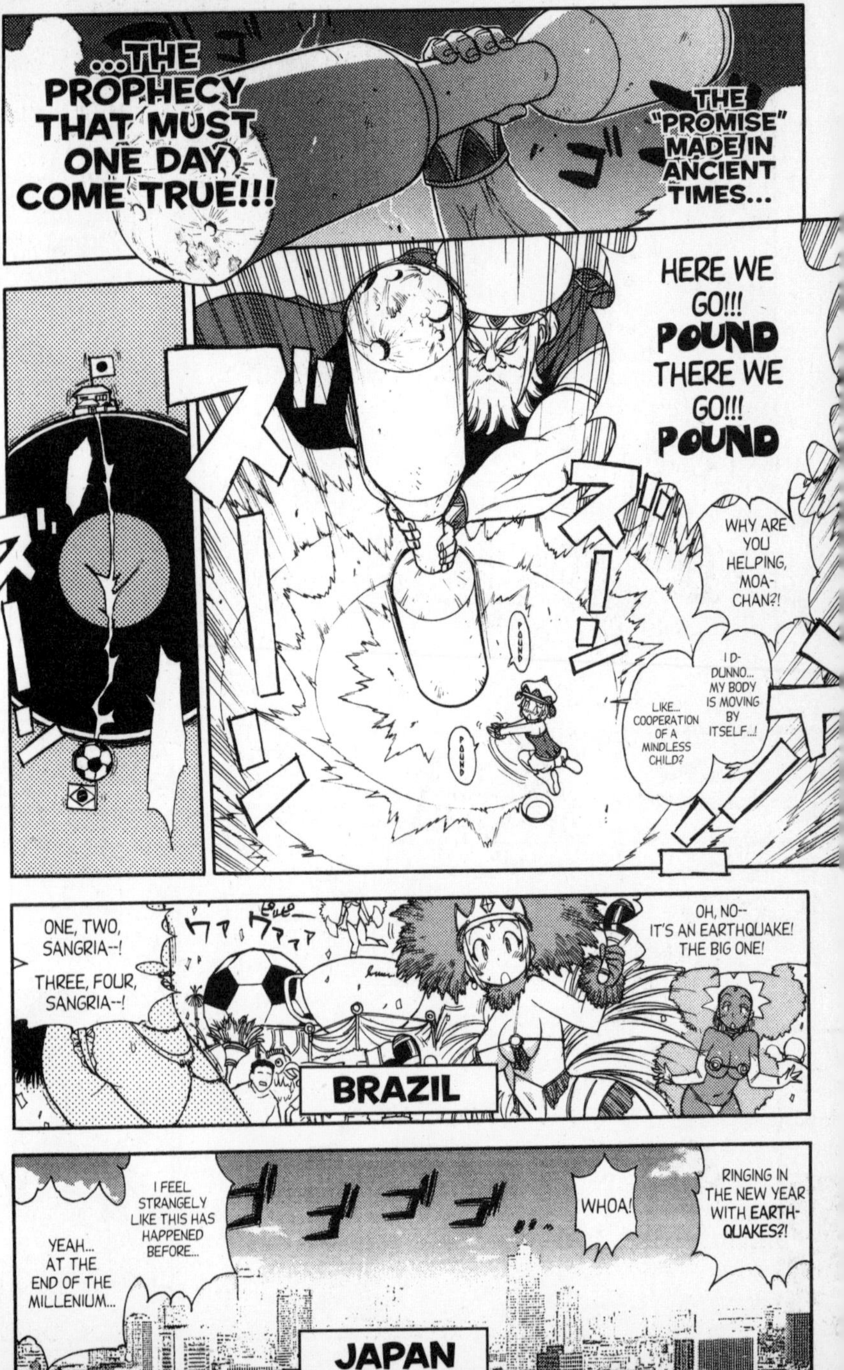
THE "PROMISE" MADE IN ANCIENT TIMES...
...THE PROPHECY THAT MUST ONE DAY COME TRUE!!!
HERE WE GO!!! POUND THERE WE GO!!! POUND
WHY ARE YOU HELPING, MOA-CHAN?!
I D-DUNNO... MY BODY IS MOVING BY ITSELF...!
LIKE... COOPERATION OF A MINDLESS CHILD?
POUND
POUND
OH, NO-- IT'S AN EARTHQUAKE! THE BIG ONE!
ONE, TWO, SANGRIA--!
THREE, FOUR, SANGRIA--!
BRAZIL
RINGING IN THE NEW YEAR WITH EARTHQUAKES?!
WHOA!
I FEEL STRANGELY LIKE THIS HAS HAPPENED BEFORE...
YEAH... AT THE END OF THE MILLENIUM...
JAPAN

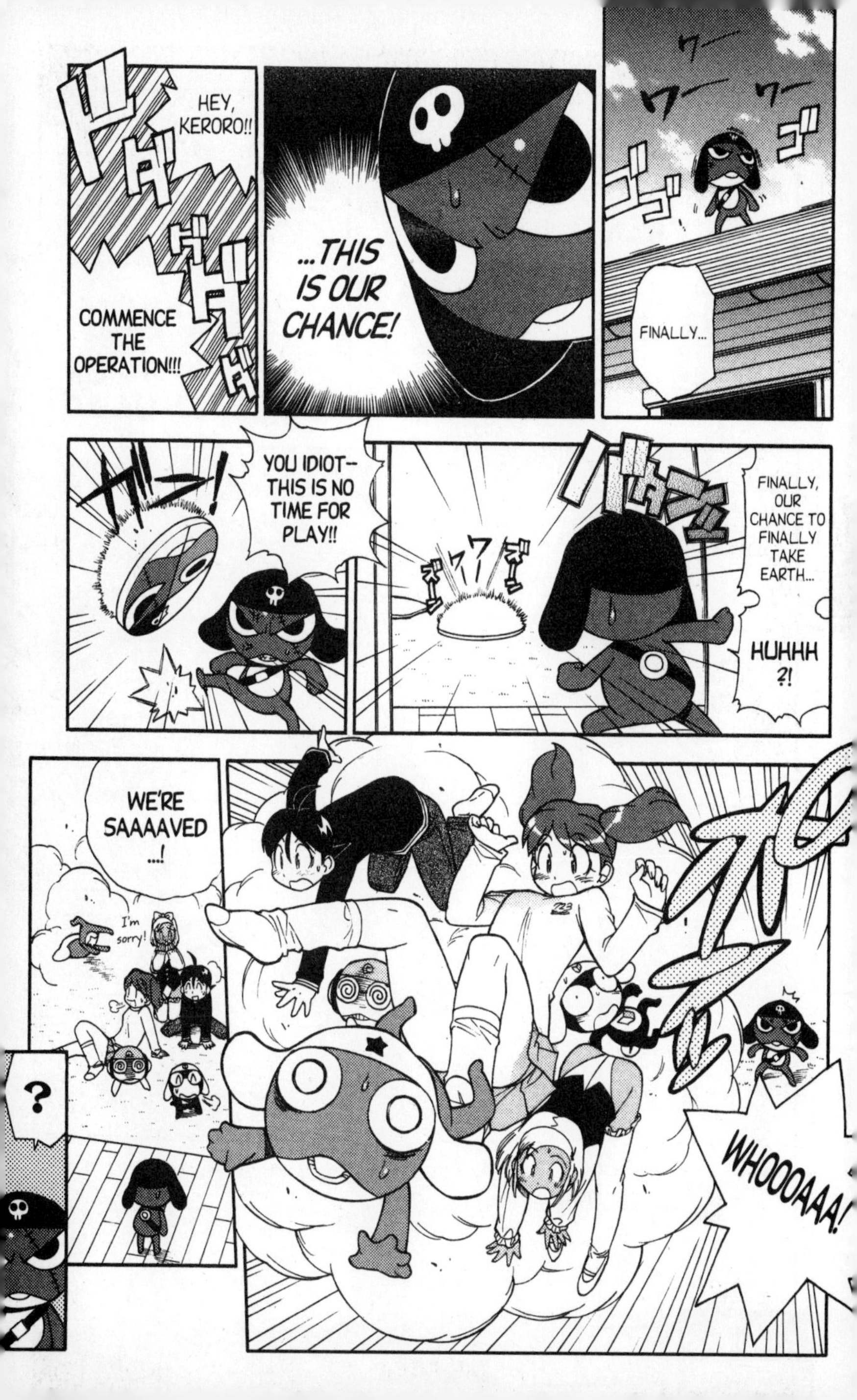
FINALLY...
...THIS IS OUR CHANCE!
HEY, KERORO!!
COMMENCE THE OPERATION!!!
FINALLY, OUR CHANCE TO FINALLY TAKE EARTH...
HUHHH ?!
YOU IDIOT-- THIS IS NO TIME FOR PLAY!!
WHOOOAAA!
WE'RE SAAAAVED ...!
I'm sorry!
?

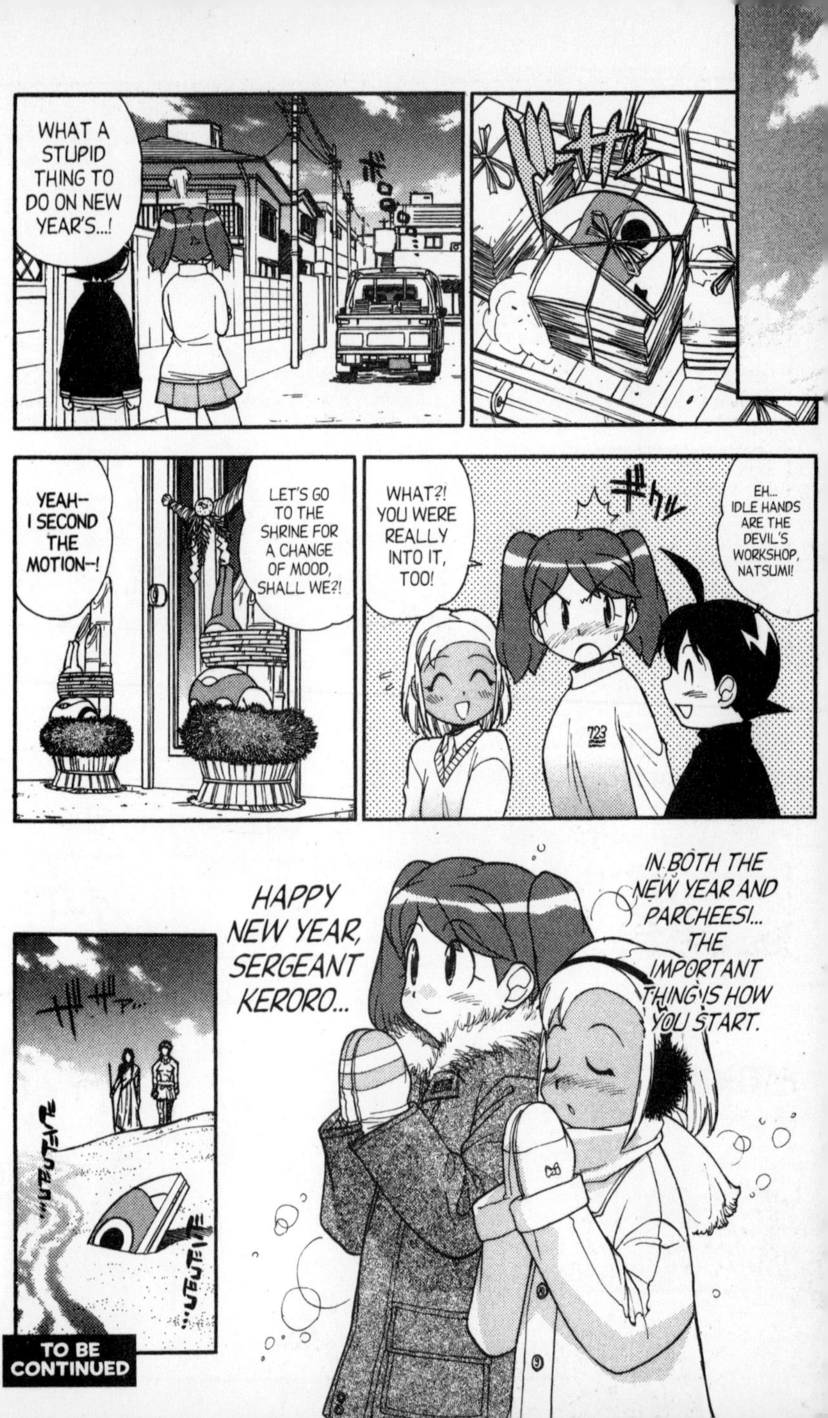
WHAT A STUPID THING TO DO ON NEW YEAR'S...!
EH... IDLE HANDS ARE THE DEVIL'S WORKSHOP, NATSUMI!
WHAT?! YOU WERE REALLY INTO IT, TOO!
LET'S GO TO THE SHRINE FOR A CHANGE OF MOOD, SHALL WE?!
YEAH-- I SECOND THE MOTION--!
IN BOTH THE NEW YEAR AND PARCHEESI... THE IMPORTANT THING IS HOW YOU START.
HAPPY NEW YEAR, SERGEANT KERORO...
TO BE CONTINUED

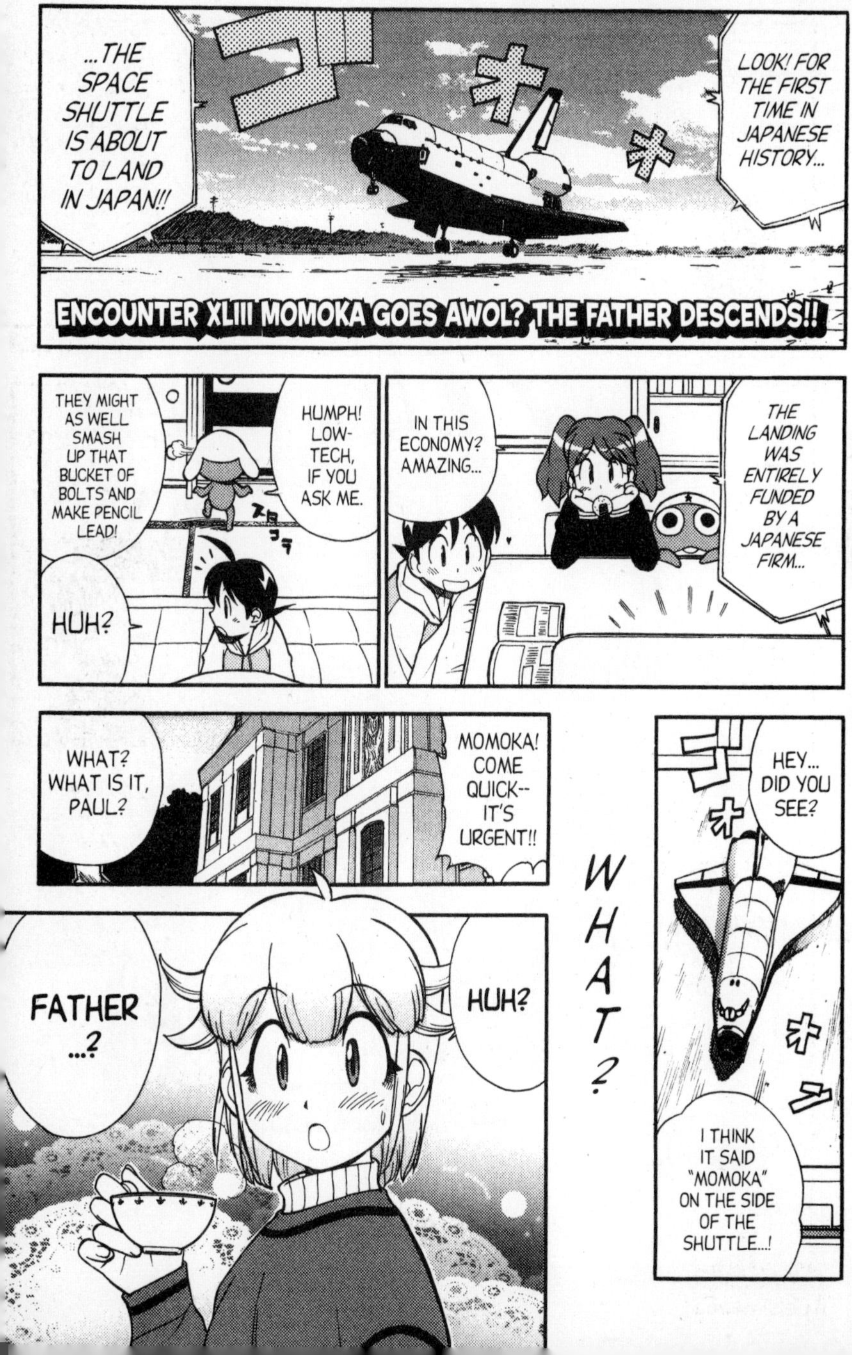
LOOK! FOR THE FIRST TIME IN JAPANESE HISTORY...
...THE SPACE SHUTTLE IS ABOUT TO LAND IN JAPAN!!
ENCOUNTER XLIII MOMOKA GOES AWOL? THE FATHER DESCENDS!!
THE LANDING WAS ENTIRELY FUNDED BY A JAPANESE FIRM...
IN THIS ECONOMY? AMAZING...
HUMPH! LOW-TECH, IF YOU ASK ME.
THEY MIGHT AS WELL SMASH UP THAT BUCKET OF BOLTS AND MAKE PENCIL LEAD!
HUH?
HEY... DID YOU SEE?
I THINK IT SAID "MOMOKA" ON THE SIDE OF THE SHUTTLE...!
WHAT?
MOMOKA! COME QUICK-- IT'S URGENT!!
WHAT? WHAT IS IT, PAUL?
HUH?
FATHER ...?

ENCOUNTER XLIII
MOMOKA GOES AWOL? THE FATHER DESCENDS!!

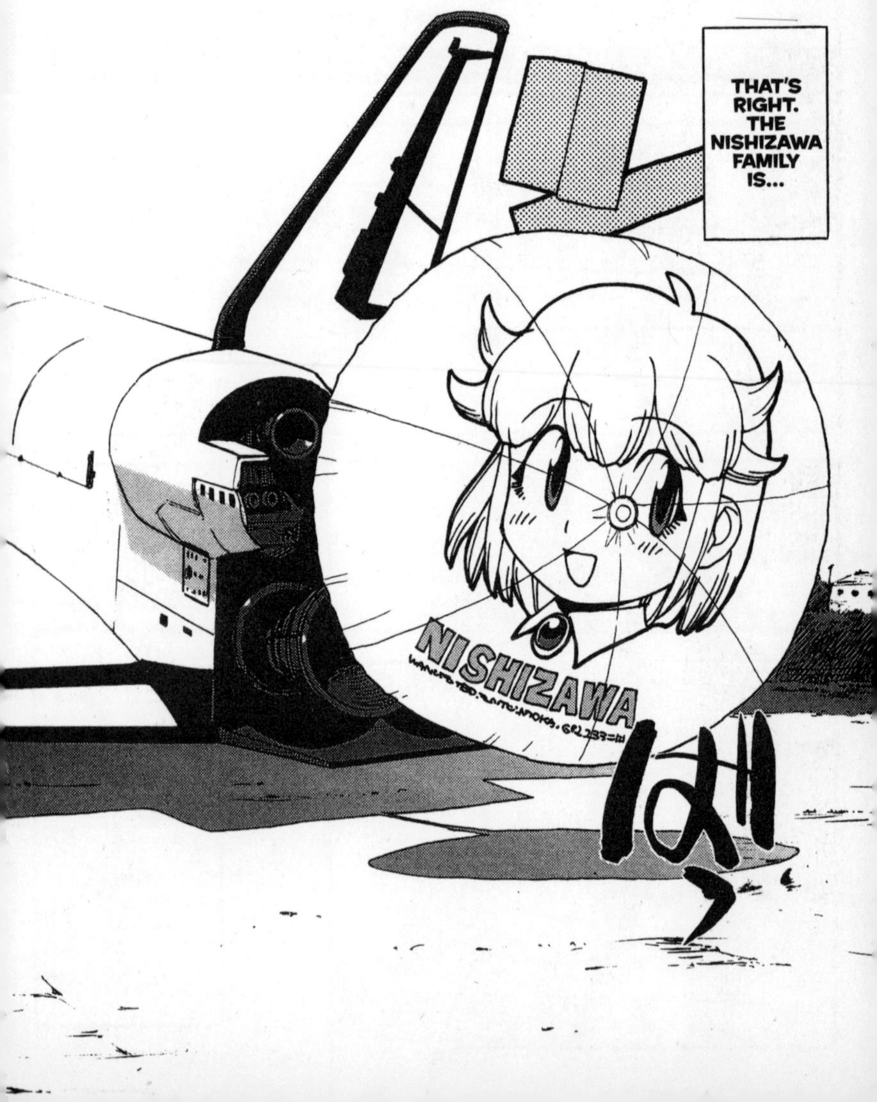
THAT'S RIGHT. THE NISHIZAWA FAMILY IS...
NISHIZAWA

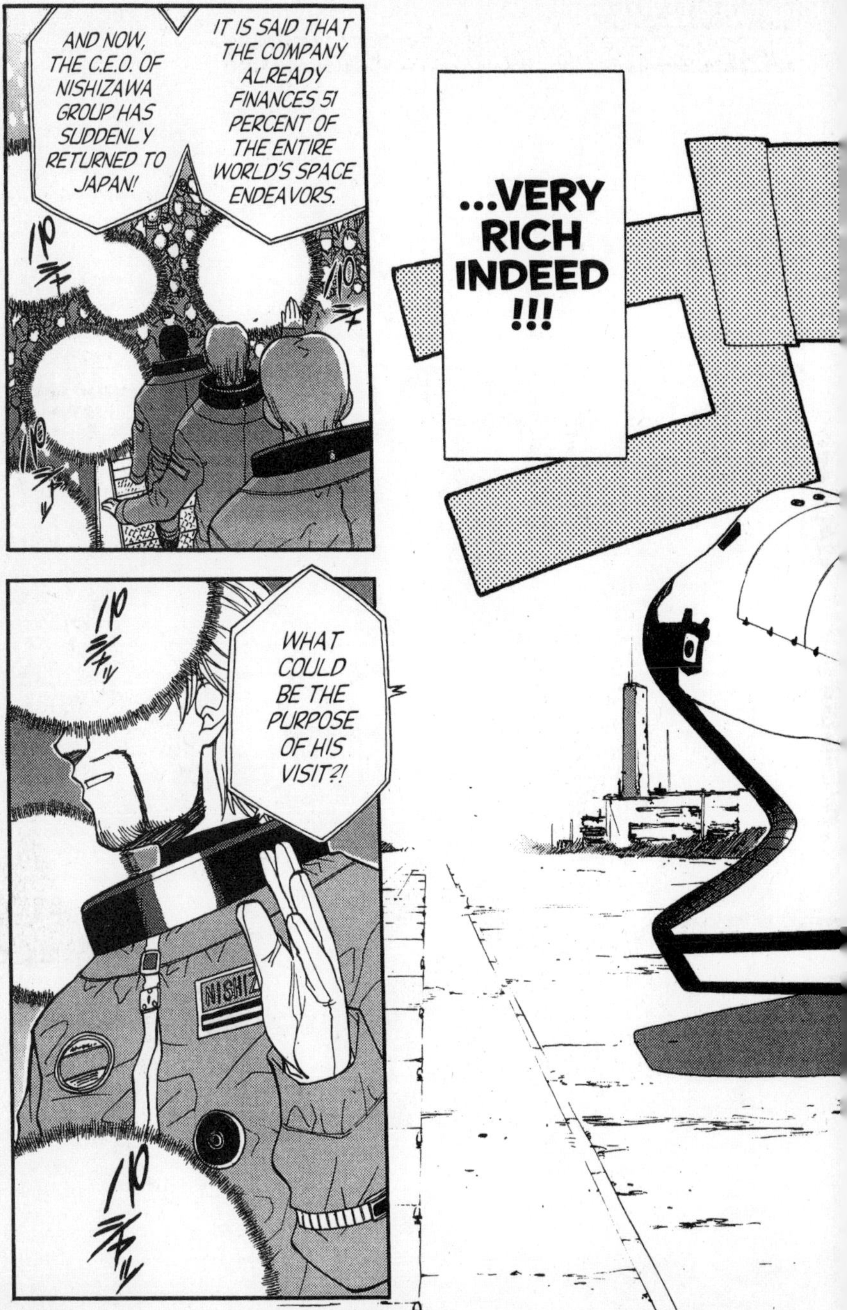
...VERY RICH INDEED!!!
AND NOW, THE C.E.O. OF NISHIZAWA GROUP HAS SUDDENLY RETURNED TO JAPAN!
IT IS SAID THAT THE COMPANY ALREADY FINANCES 51 PERCENT OF THE ENTIRE WORLD'S SPACE ENDEAVORS.
WHAT COULD BE THE PURPOSE OF HIS VISIT?!
NISHIZ

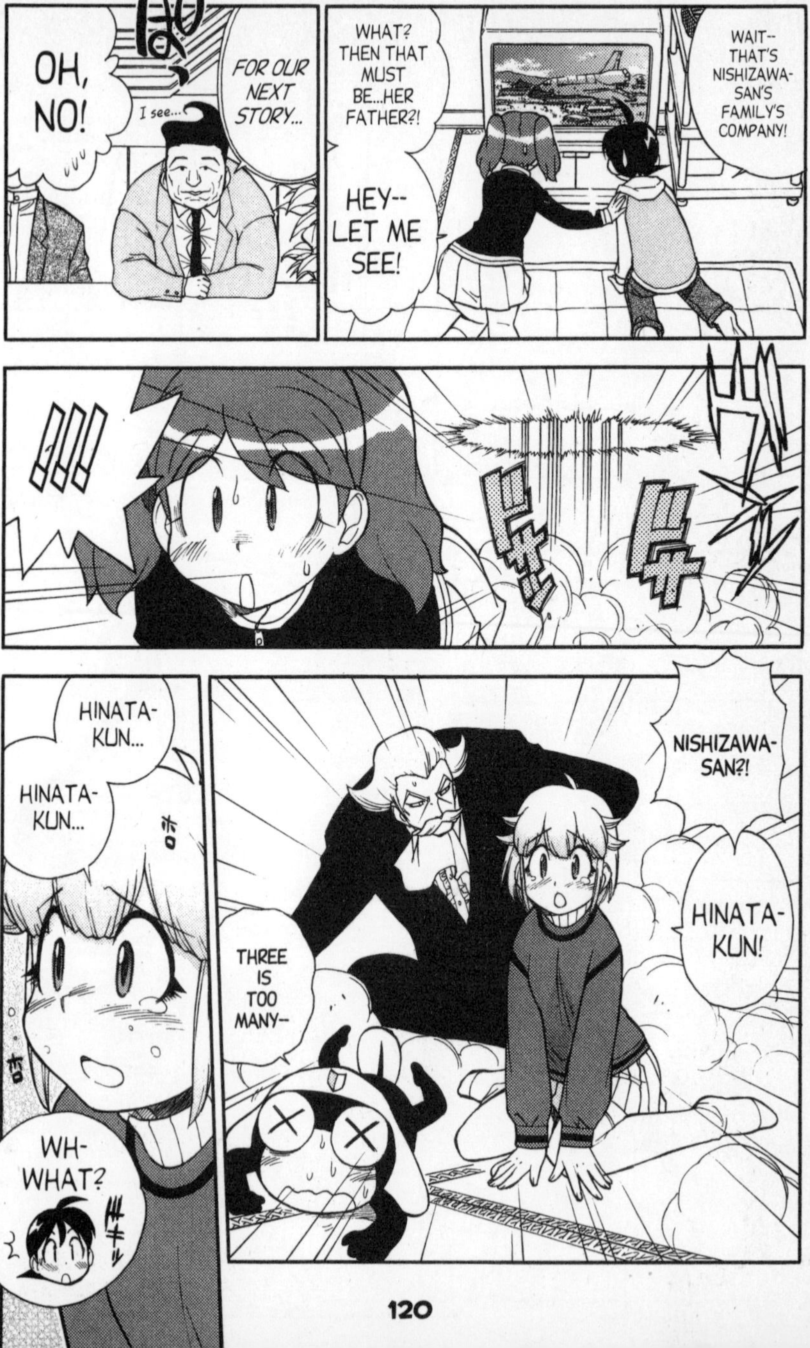
WAIT-- THAT'S NISHIZAWA-SAN'S FAMILY'S COMPANY!
WHAT? THEN THAT MUST BE...HER FATHER?!
HEY-- LET ME SEE!
FOR OUR NEXT STORY...
I see...
OH, NO!
NISHIZAWA-SAN?!
HINATA-KUN!
THREE IS TOO MANY--
HINATA-KUN...
HINATA-KUN...
WH-WHAT?

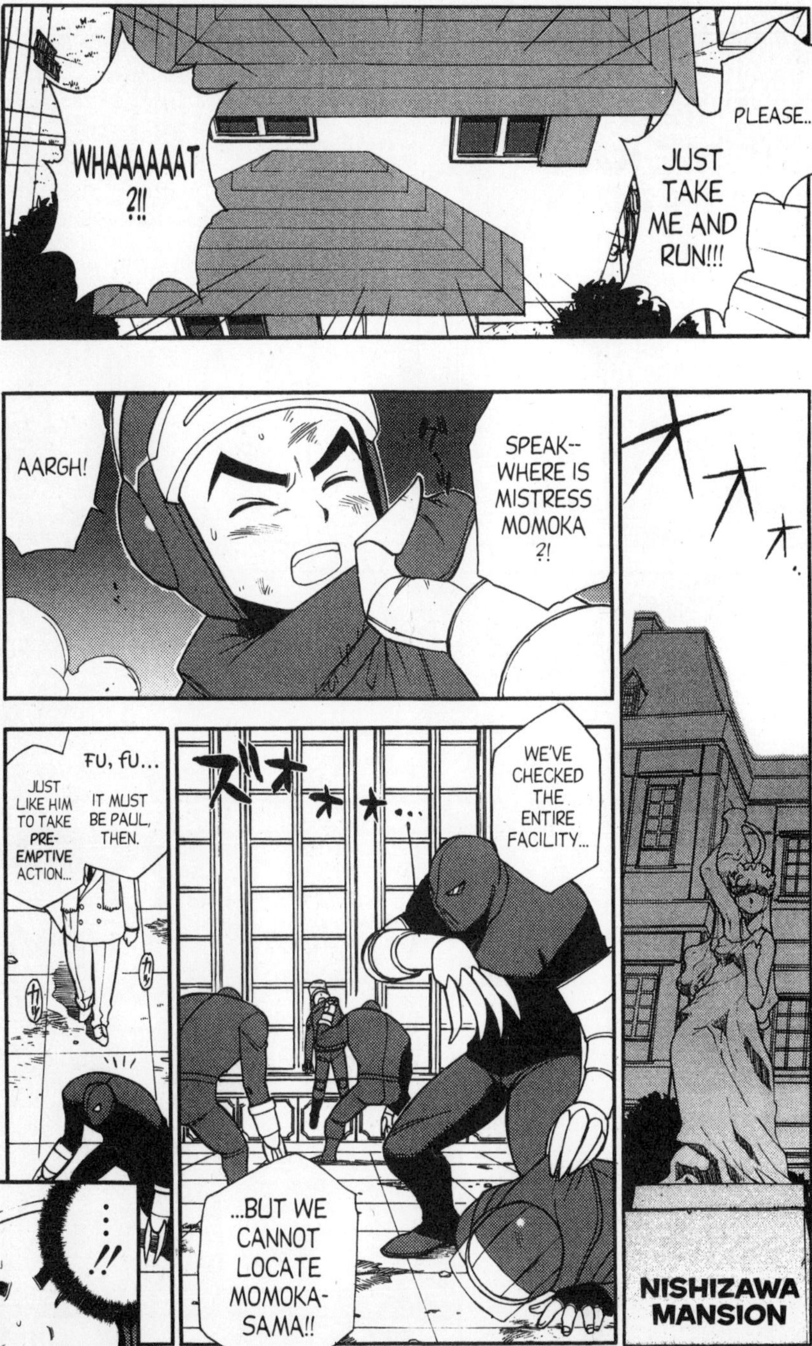
PLEASE...
JUST TAKE ME AND RUN!!!
WHAAAAAAT?!!
NISHIZAWA MANSION
SPEAK-- WHERE IS MISTRESS MOMOKA?!
AARGH!
WE'VE CHECKED THE ENTIRE FACILITY...
...BUT WE CANNOT LOCATE MOMOKA-SAMA!!
FU, FU...
IT MUST BE PAUL, THEN.
JUST LIKE HIM TO TAKE PRE-EMPTIVE ACTION...
...!!

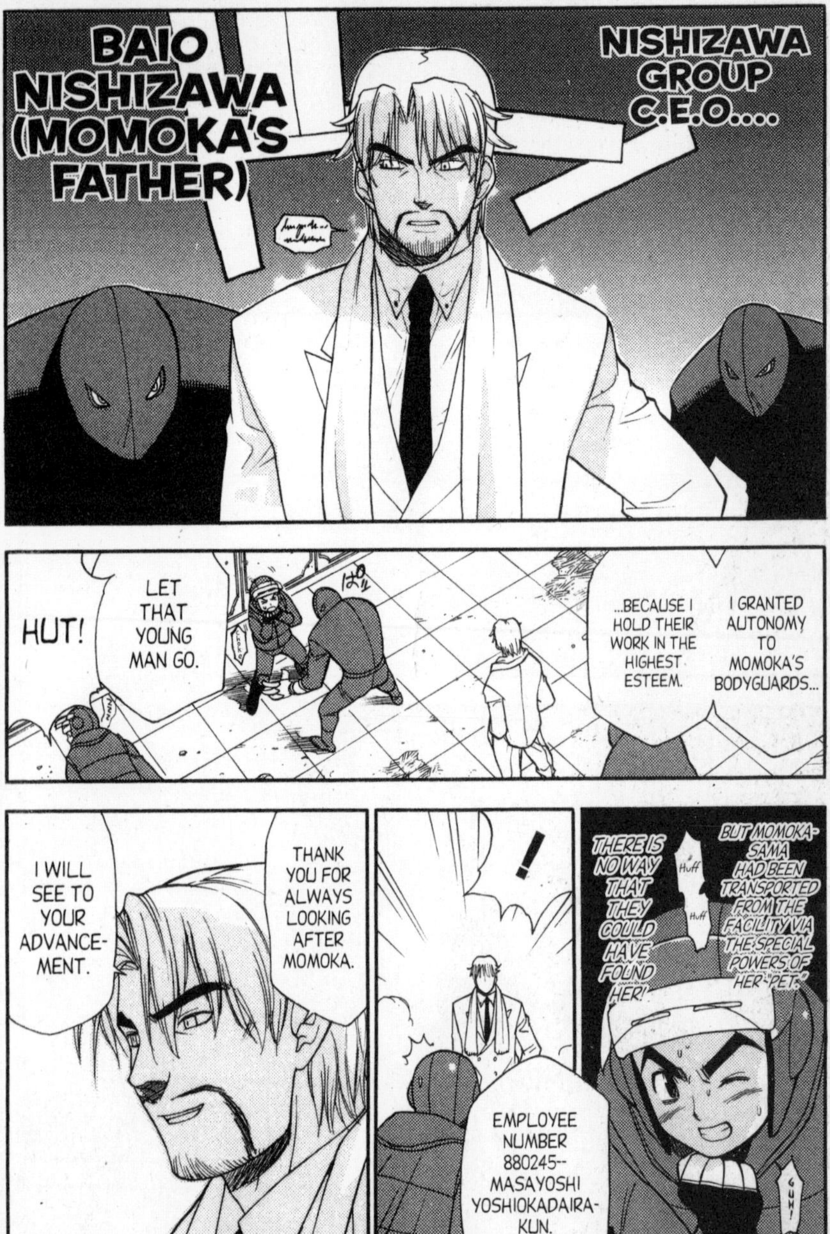
NISHIZAWA GROUP C.E.O....
BAIO NISHIZAWA (MOMOKA'S FATHER)
I GRANTED AUTONOMY TO MOMOKA'S BODYGUARDS...
...BECAUSE I HOLD THEIR WORK IN THE HIGHEST ESTEEM.
LET THAT YOUNG MAN GO.
HUT!
BUT MOMOKA-SAMA HAD BEEN TRANSPORTED FROM THE FACILITY VIA THE SPECIAL POWERS OF HER "PET."
THERE IS NO WAY THAT THEY COULD HAVE FOUND HER!
Huff
Huff
GUH!
!
EMPLOYEE NUMBER 880245-- MASAYOSHI YOSHIOKADAIRA-KUN.
THANK YOU FOR ALWAYS LOOKING AFTER MOMOKA.
I WILL SEE TO YOUR ADVANCE-MENT.

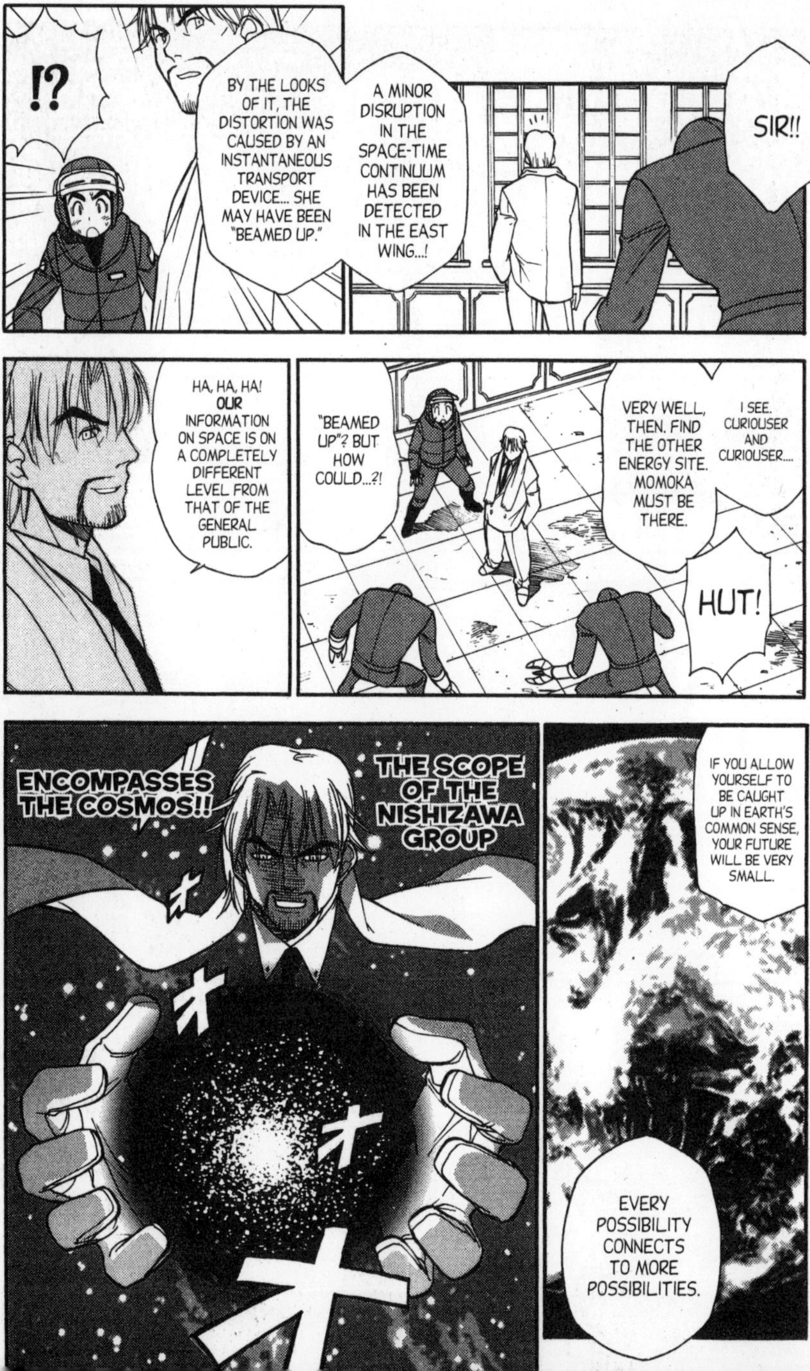
SIR!!
A MINOR DISRUPTION IN THE SPACE-TIME CONTINUUM HAS BEEN DETECTED IN THE EAST WING...!
BY THE LOOKS OF IT, THE DISTORTION WAS CAUSED BY AN INSTANTANEOUS TRANSPORT DEVICE... SHE MAY HAVE BEEN "BEAMED UP."
!?
I SEE. CURIOUSER AND CURIOUSER....
VERY WELL, THEN. FIND THE OTHER ENERGY SITE. MOMOKA MUST BE THERE.
HUT!
"BEAMED UP"? BUT HOW COULD...?!
HA, HA, HA! **OUR** INFORMATION ON SPACE IS ON A COMPLETELY DIFFERENT LEVEL FROM THAT OF THE GENERAL PUBLIC.
IF YOU ALLOW YOURSELF TO BE CAUGHT UP IN EARTH'S COMMON SENSE, YOUR FUTURE WILL BE VERY SMALL.
EVERY POSSIBILITY CONNECTS TO MORE POSSIBILITIES.
THE SCOPE OF THE NISHIZAWA GROUP
ENCOMPASSES THE COSMOS!!

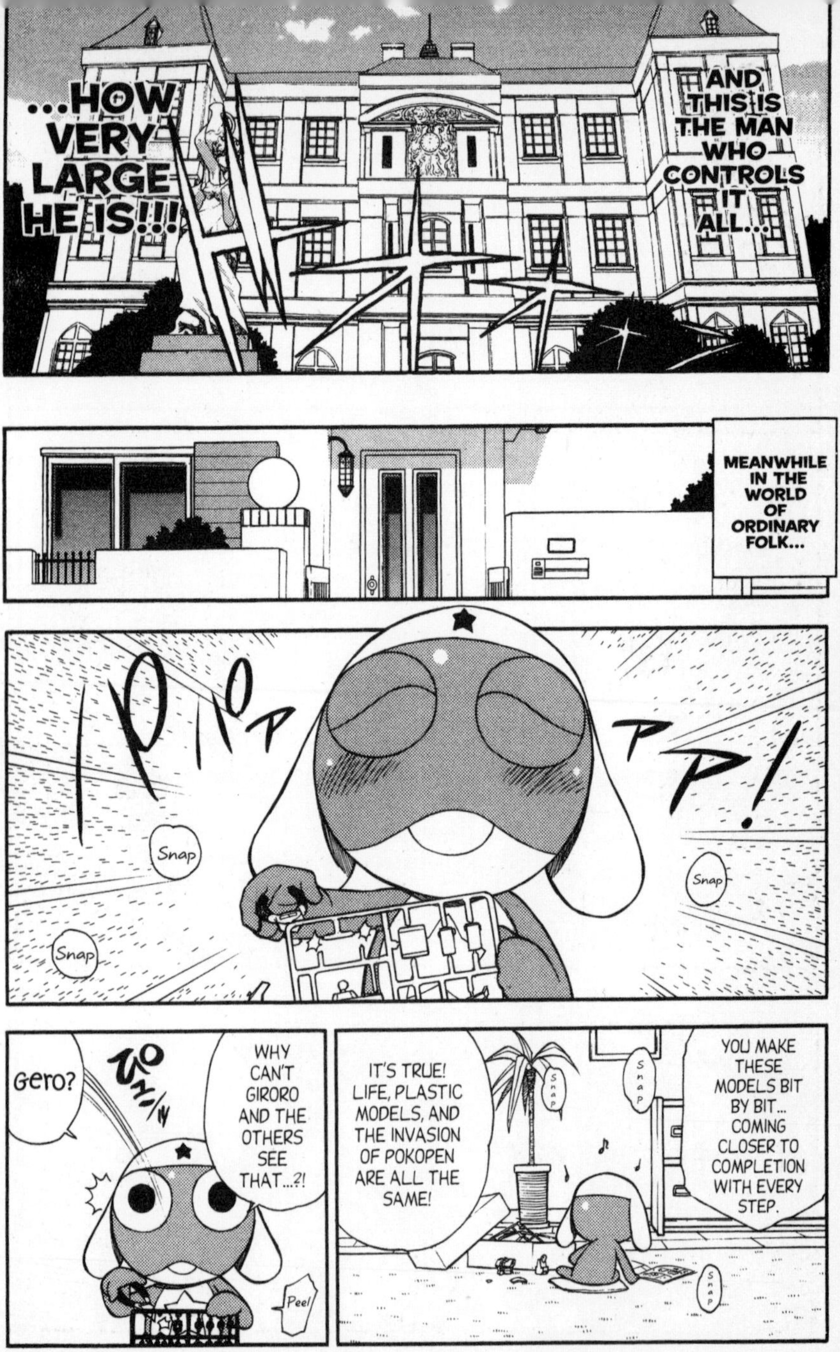

AND THIS IS THE MAN WHO CONTROLS IT ALL...
...HOW VERY LARGE HE IS!!!
MEANWHILE IN THE WORLD OF ORDINARY FOLK...
Snap
Snap
Snap
YOU MAKE THESE MODELS BIT BY BIT... COMING CLOSER TO COMPLETION WITH EVERY STEP.
IT'S TRUE! LIFE, PLASTIC MODELS, AND THE INVASION OF POKOPEN ARE ALL THE SAME!
Snap
Snap
Snap
WHY CAN'T GIRORO AND THE OTHERS SEE THAT...?!
Gero?
Peel

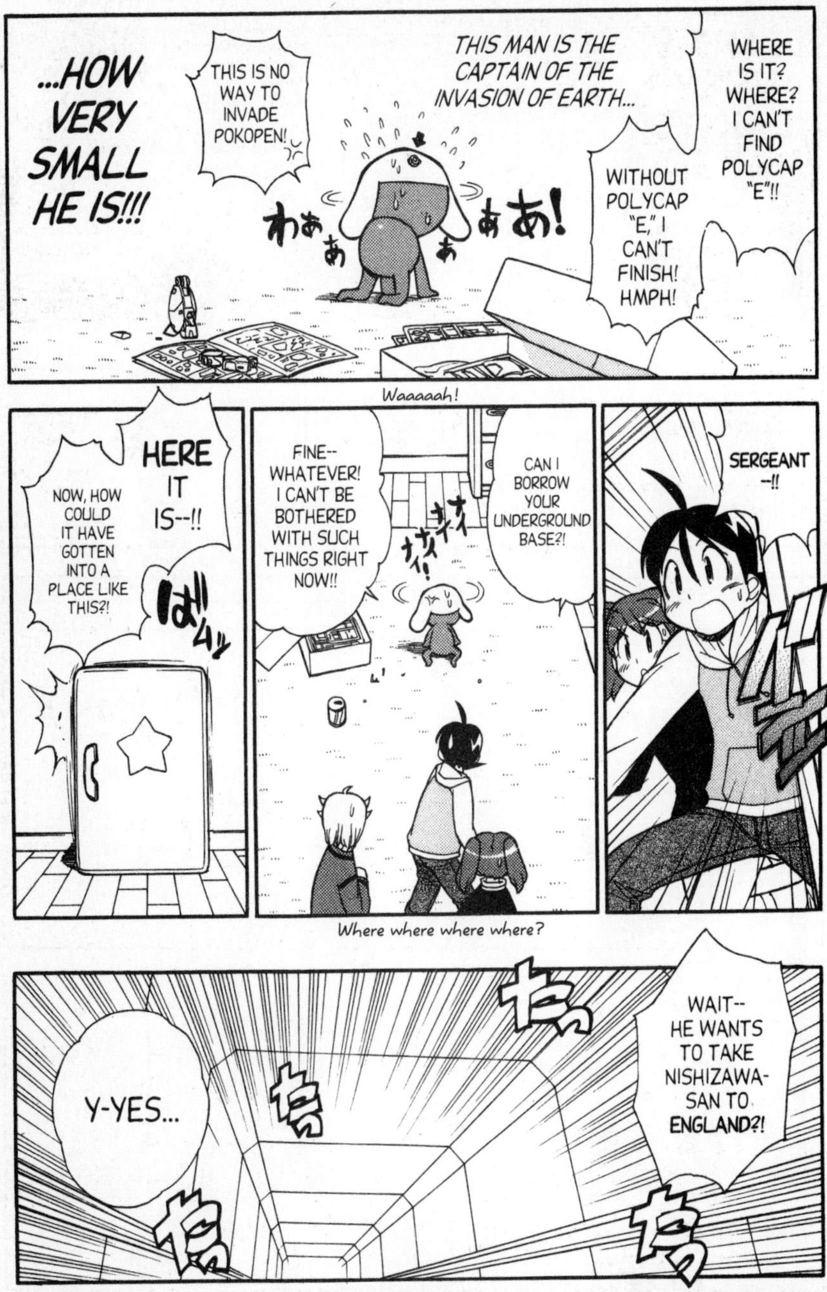
WHERE IS IT? WHERE? I CAN'T FIND POLYCAP "E"!!
THIS MAN IS THE CAPTAIN OF THE INVASION OF EARTH...
WITHOUT POLYCAP "E," I CAN'T FINISH! HMPH!
THIS IS NO WAY TO INVADE POKOPEN!
わぁぁぁぁあ!
...HOW VERY SMALL HE IS!!!
Waaaaah!
SERGEANT--!!
CAN I BORROW YOUR UNDERGROUND BASE?!
FINE--WHATEVER! I CAN'T BE BOTHERED WITH SUCH THINGS RIGHT NOW!!
HERE IT IS--!!
NOW, HOW COULD IT HAVE GOTTEN INTO A PLACE LIKE THIS?!
Where where where where?
WAIT-- HE WANTS TO TAKE NISHIZAWA-SAN TO ENGLAND?!
Y-YES...

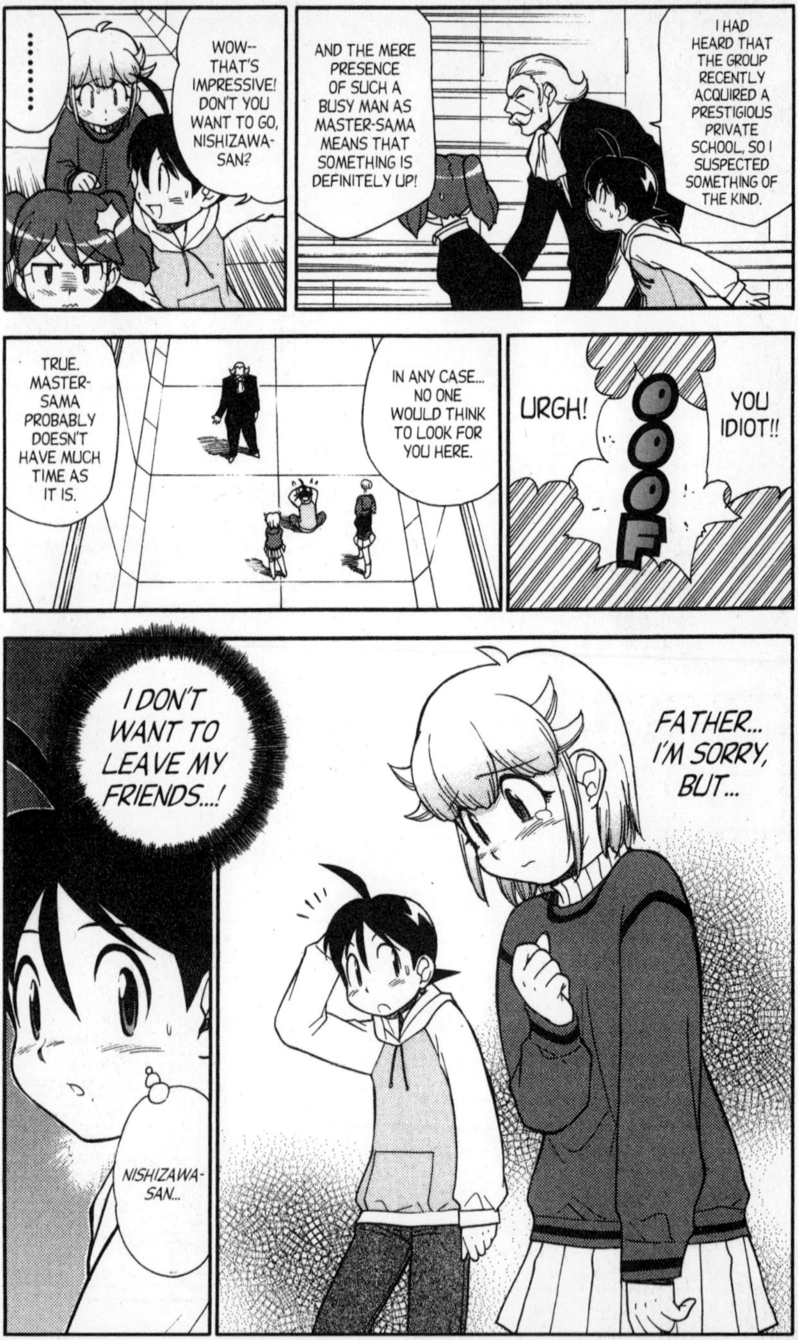
I HAD HEARD THAT THE GROUP RECENTLY ACQUIRED A PRESTIGIOUS PRIVATE SCHOOL, SO I SUSPECTED SOMETHING OF THE KIND.
AND THE MERE PRESENCE OF SUCH A BUSY MAN AS MASTER-SAMA MEANS THAT SOMETHING IS DEFINITELY UP!
WOW-- THAT'S IMPRESSIVE! DON'T YOU WANT TO GO, NISHIZAWA-SAN?
....
YOU IDIOT!!
OOOOF
URGH!
IN ANY CASE... NO ONE WOULD THINK TO LOOK FOR YOU HERE.
TRUE. MASTER-SAMA PROBABLY DOESN'T HAVE MUCH TIME AS IT IS.
FATHER... I'M SORRY, BUT...
I DON'T WANT TO LEAVE MY FRIENDS...!
NISHIZAWA-SAN...

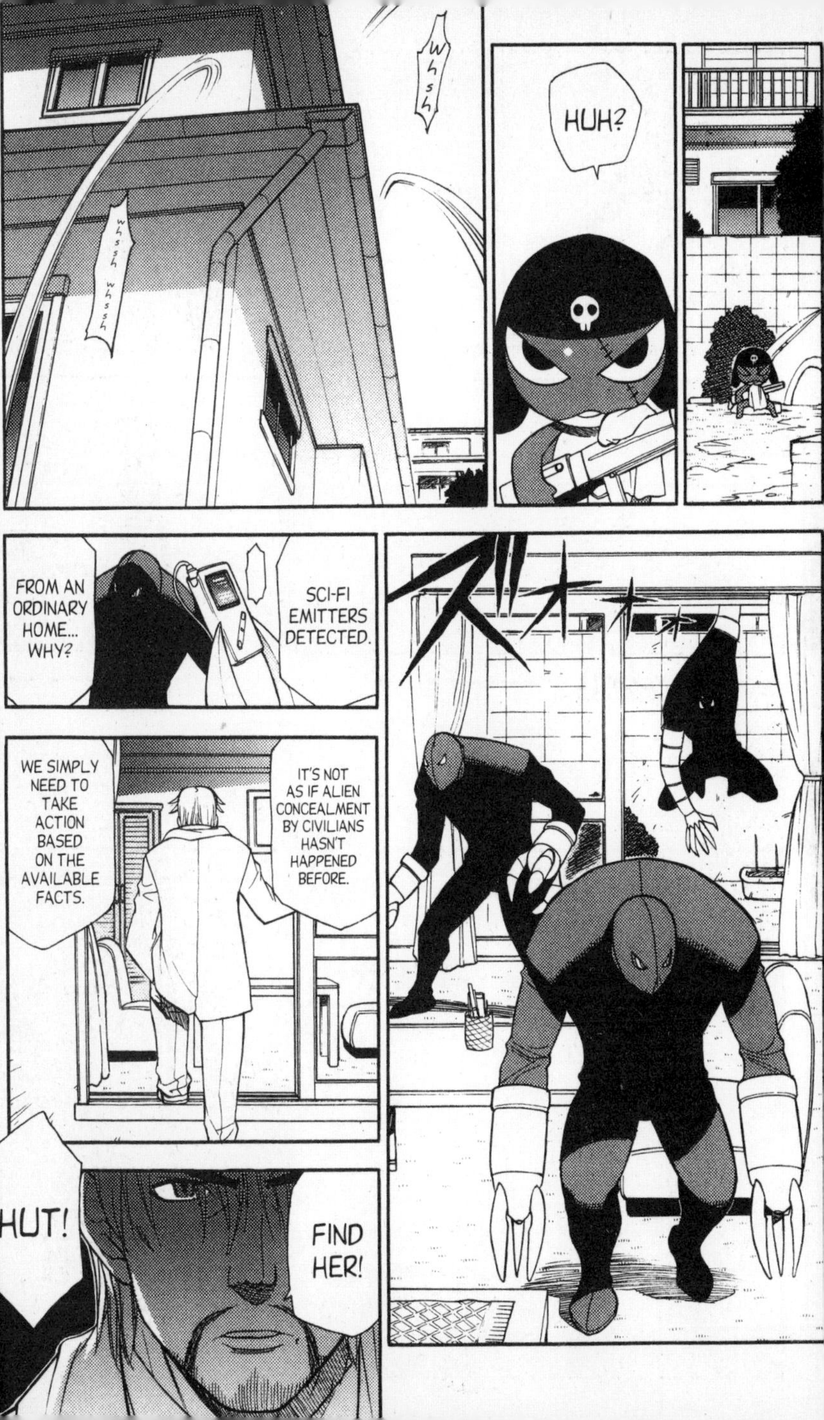
HUH?
whsh
whssh whsssh
SCI-FI EMITTERS DETECTED.
FROM AN ORDINARY HOME... WHY?
IT'S NOT AS IF ALIEN CONCEALMENT BY CIVILIANS HASN'T HAPPENED BEFORE.
WE SIMPLY NEED TO TAKE ACTION BASED ON THE AVAILABLE FACTS.
FIND HER!
HUT!

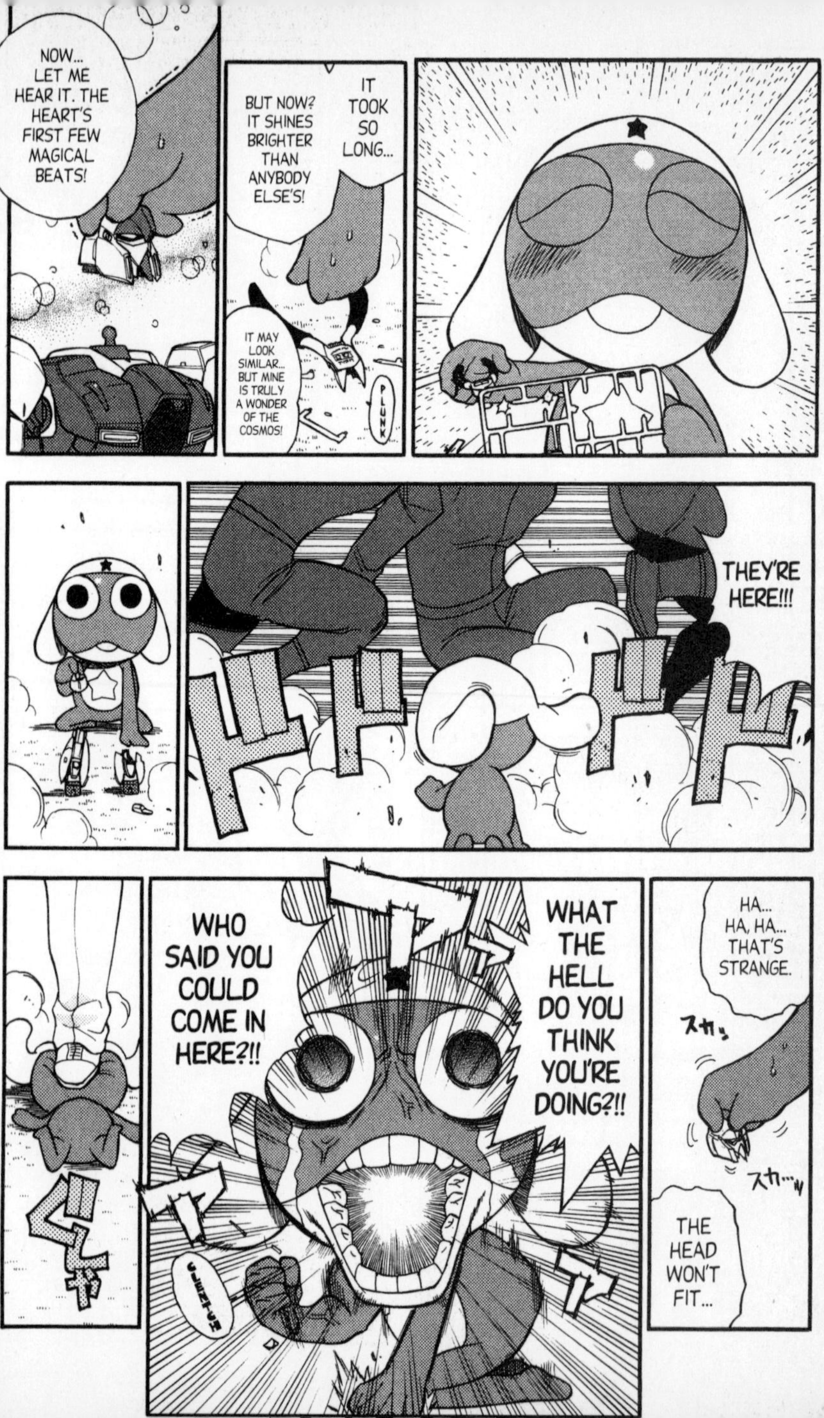
IT TOOK SO LONG...
BUT NOW? IT SHINES BRIGHTER THAN ANYBODY ELSE'S!
IT MAY LOOK SIMILAR... BUT MINE IS TRULY A WONDER OF THE COSMOS!
PLUNK
NOW... LET ME HEAR IT. THE HEART'S FIRST FEW MAGICAL BEATS!
THEY'RE HERE!!!
HA... HA, HA... THAT'S STRANGE.
スカッ
スカ…
THE HEAD WON'T FIT...
WHAT THE HELL DO YOU THINK YOU'RE DOING?!!
WHO SAID YOU COULD COME IN HERE?!!
CLENTCH

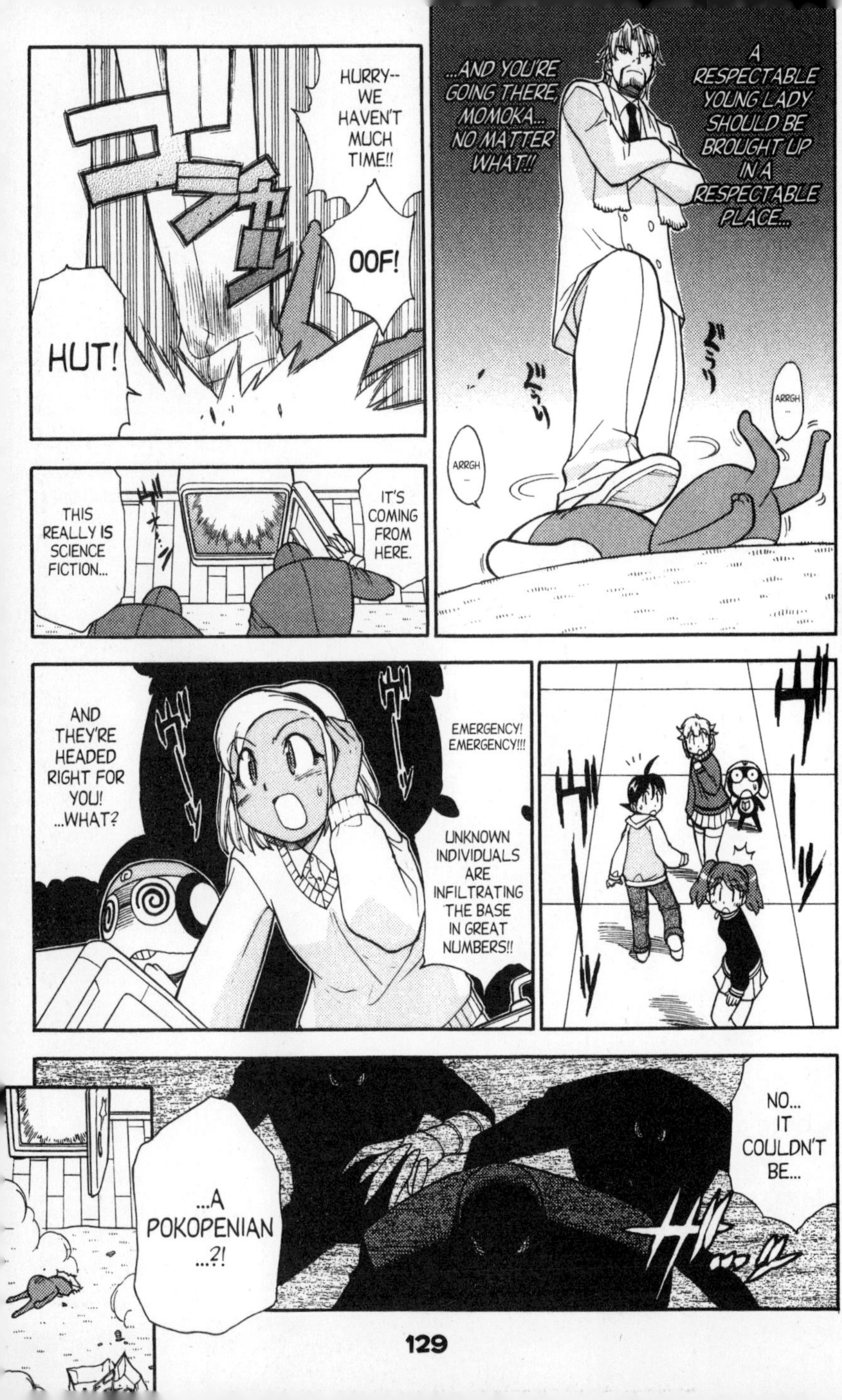
A RESPECTABLE YOUNG LADY SHOULD BE BROUGHT UP IN A RESPECTABLE PLACE...
...AND YOU'RE GOING THERE, MOMOKA... NO MATTER WHAT!!
ARRGH...
ARRGH...
HURRY-- WE HAVEN'T MUCH TIME!!
OOF!
HUT!
IT'S COMING FROM HERE.
THIS REALLY IS SCIENCE FICTION...
EMERGENCY! EMERGENCY!!!
UNKNOWN INDIVIDUALS ARE INFILTRATING THE BASE IN GREAT NUMBERS!!
AND THEY'RE HEADED RIGHT FOR YOU! ...WHAT?
NO... IT COULDN'T BE...
...A POKOPENIAN ...?!

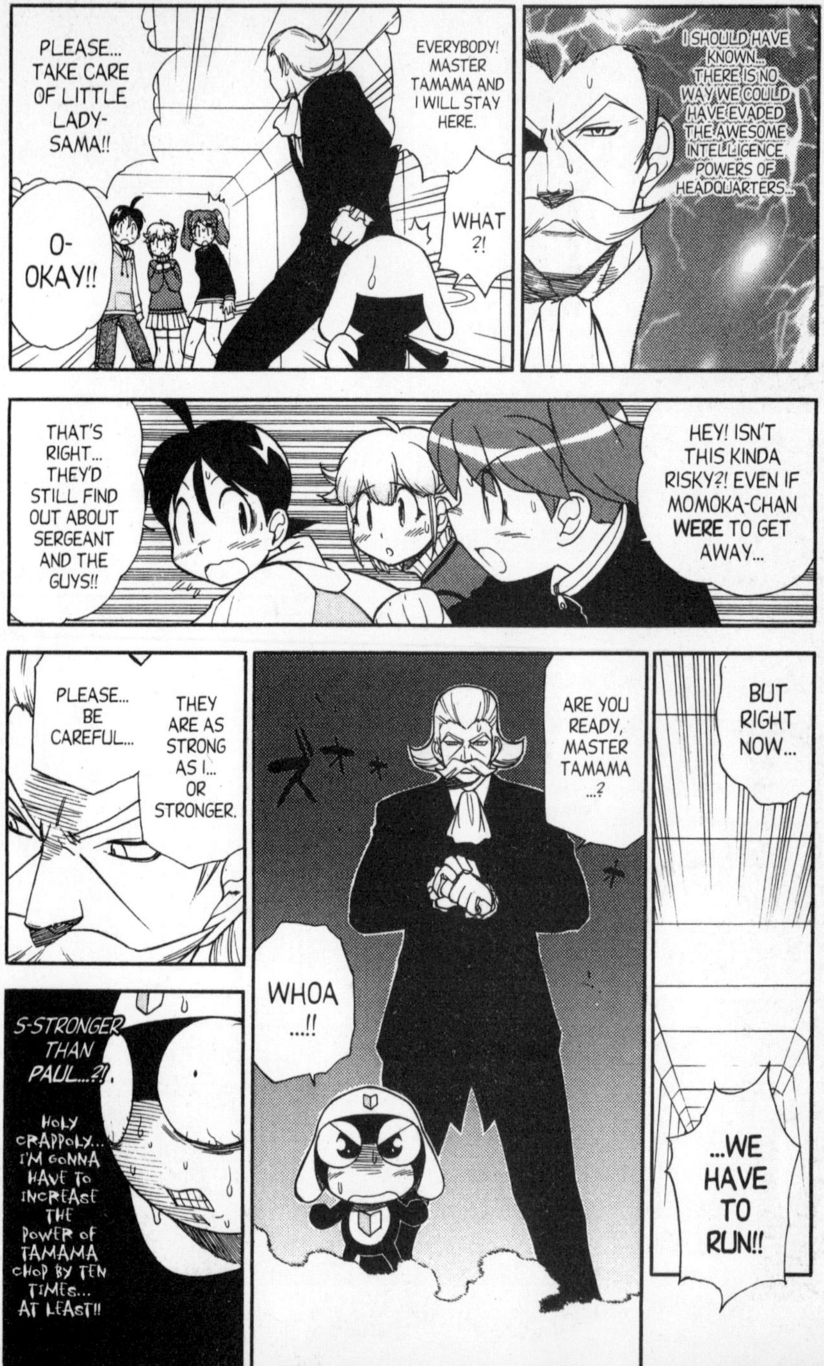
I SHOULD HAVE KNOWN... THERE IS NO WAY WE COULD HAVE EVADED THE AWESOME INTELLIGENCE POWERS OF HEADQUARTERS...
EVERYBODY! MASTER TAMAMA AND I WILL STAY HERE.
WHAT?!
PLEASE... TAKE CARE OF LITTLE LADY-SAMA!!
O-OKAY!!
HEY! ISN'T THIS KINDA RISKY?! EVEN IF MOMOKA-CHAN WERE TO GET AWAY...
THAT'S RIGHT... THEY'D STILL FIND OUT ABOUT SERGEANT AND THE GUYS!!
BUT RIGHT NOW...
...WE HAVE TO RUN!!
ARE YOU READY, MASTER TAMAMA...?
WHOA...!!
PLEASE... BE CAREFUL...
THEY ARE AS STRONG AS I... OR STRONGER.
S-STRONGER THAN PAUL...?!
HOLY CRAPPOLY... I'M GONNA HAVE TO INCREASE THE POWER OF TAMAMA CHOP BY TEN TIMES... AT LEAST!!

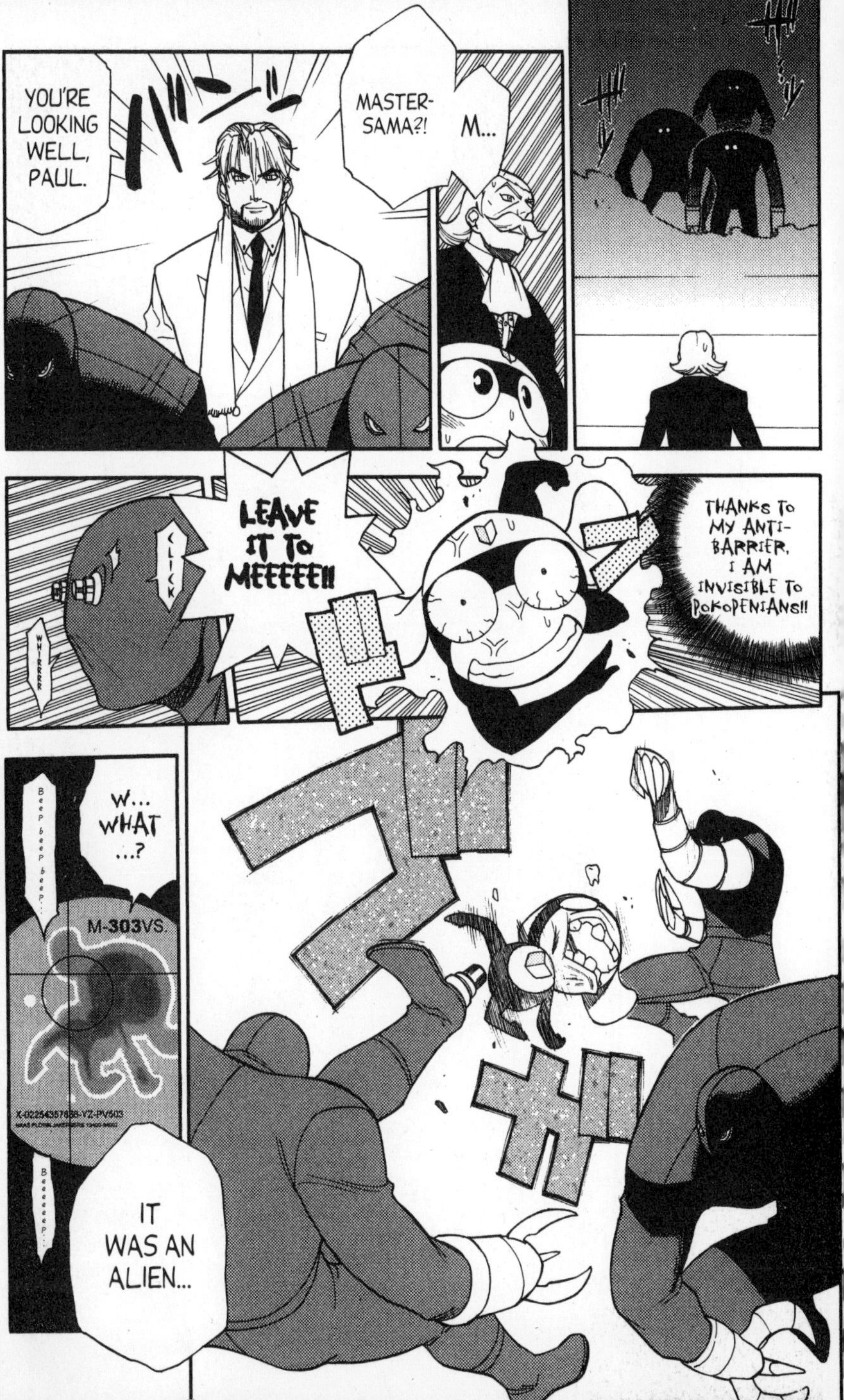
M...
MASTER-SAMA?!
YOU'RE LOOKING WELL, PAUL.
THANKS TO MY ANTI-BARRIER, I AM INVISIBLE TO POKOPENIANS!!
LEAVE IT TO MEEEEE!!
CLICK
WHIRRRR
Beep beep beep...
W... WHAT ...?
M-303VS.
X-02254357638-VZ-PV503
IT WAS AN ALIEN...
Beeeeeep...

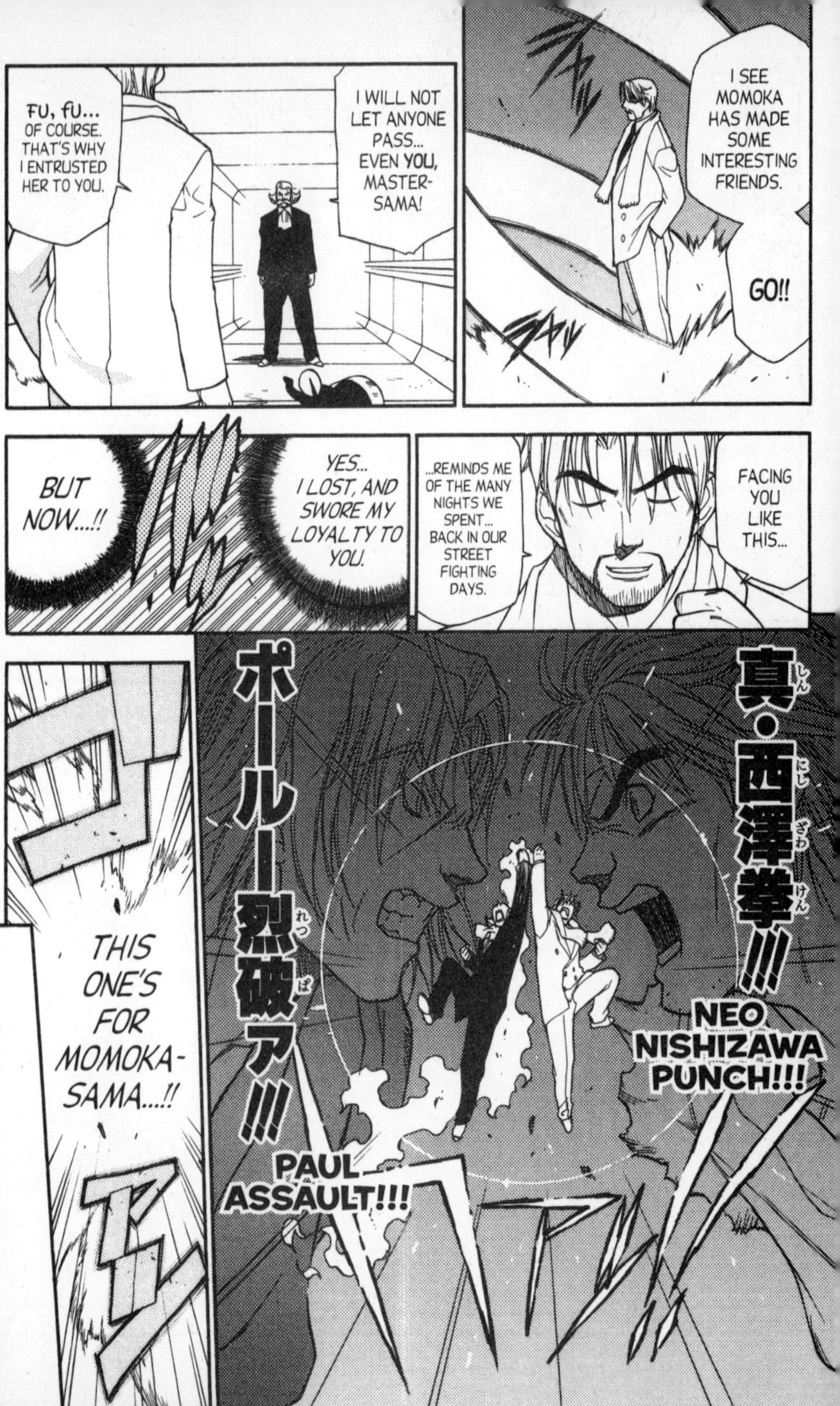
I SEE MOMOKA HAS MADE SOME INTERESTING FRIENDS.
GO!!
I WILL NOT LET ANYONE PASS... EVEN YOU, MASTER-SAMA!
FU, FU... OF COURSE. THAT'S WHY I ENTRUSTED HER TO YOU.
FACING YOU LIKE THIS...
...REMINDS ME OF THE MANY NIGHTS WE SPENT... BACK IN OUR STREET FIGHTING DAYS.
YES... I LOST, AND SWORE MY LOYALTY TO YOU.
BUT NOW...!!
真・西澤拳!!!
NEO NISHIZAWA PUNCH!!!
ポール烈破ア!!!
PAUL ASSAULT!!!
THIS ONE'S FOR MOMOKA-SAMA...!!

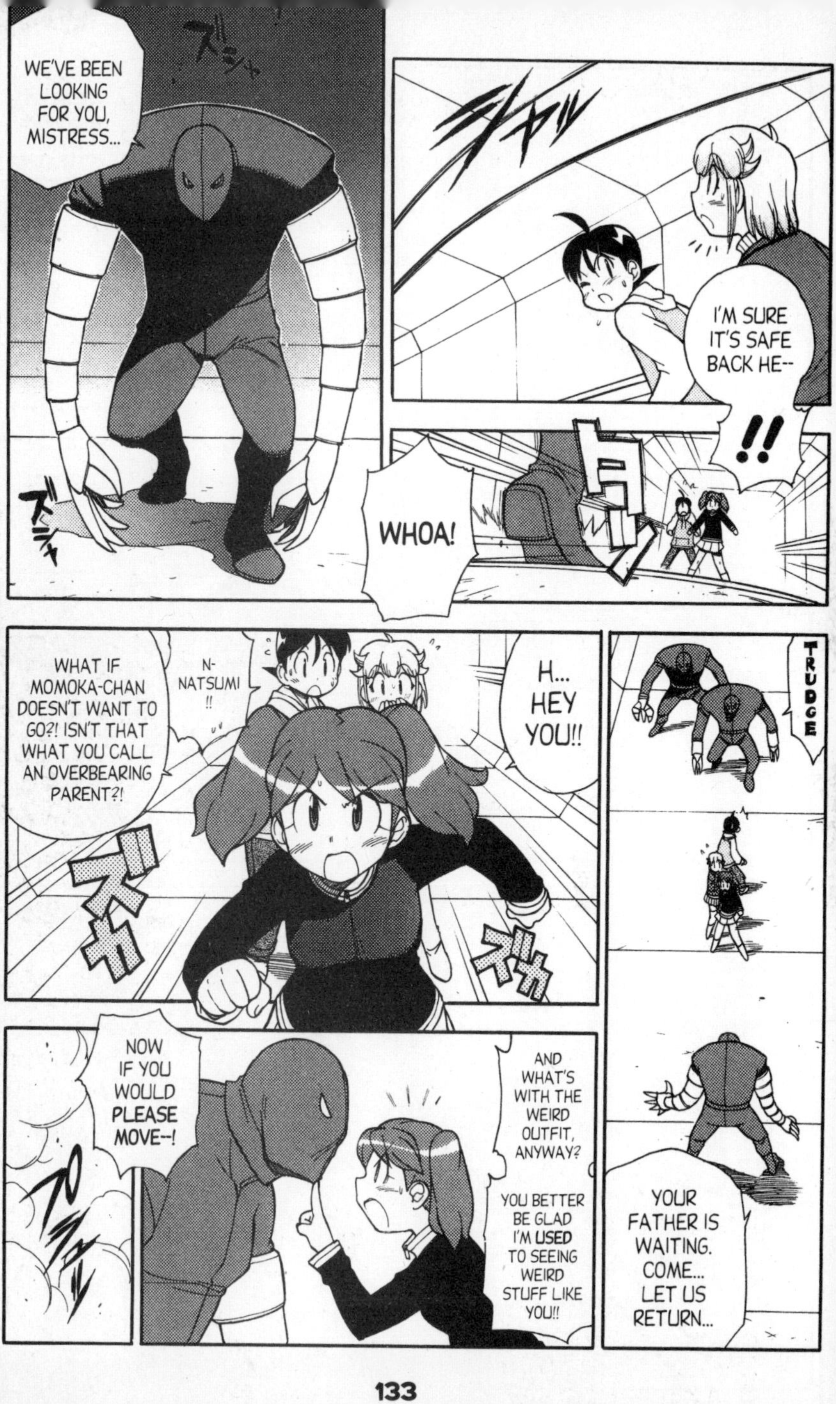
I'M SURE IT'S SAFE BACK HE--
!!
WHOA!
WE'VE BEEN LOOKING FOR YOU, MISTRESS...
TRUDGE
YOUR FATHER IS WAITING. COME... LET US RETURN...
H... HEY YOU!!
N-NATSUMI!!
WHAT IF MOMOKA-CHAN DOESN'T WANT TO GO?! ISN'T THAT WHAT YOU CALL AN OVERBEARING PARENT?!
AND WHAT'S WITH THE WEIRD OUTFIT, ANYWAY?
YOU BETTER BE GLAD I'M USED TO SEEING WEIRD STUFF LIKE YOU!!
NOW IF YOU WOULD PLEASE MOVE--!

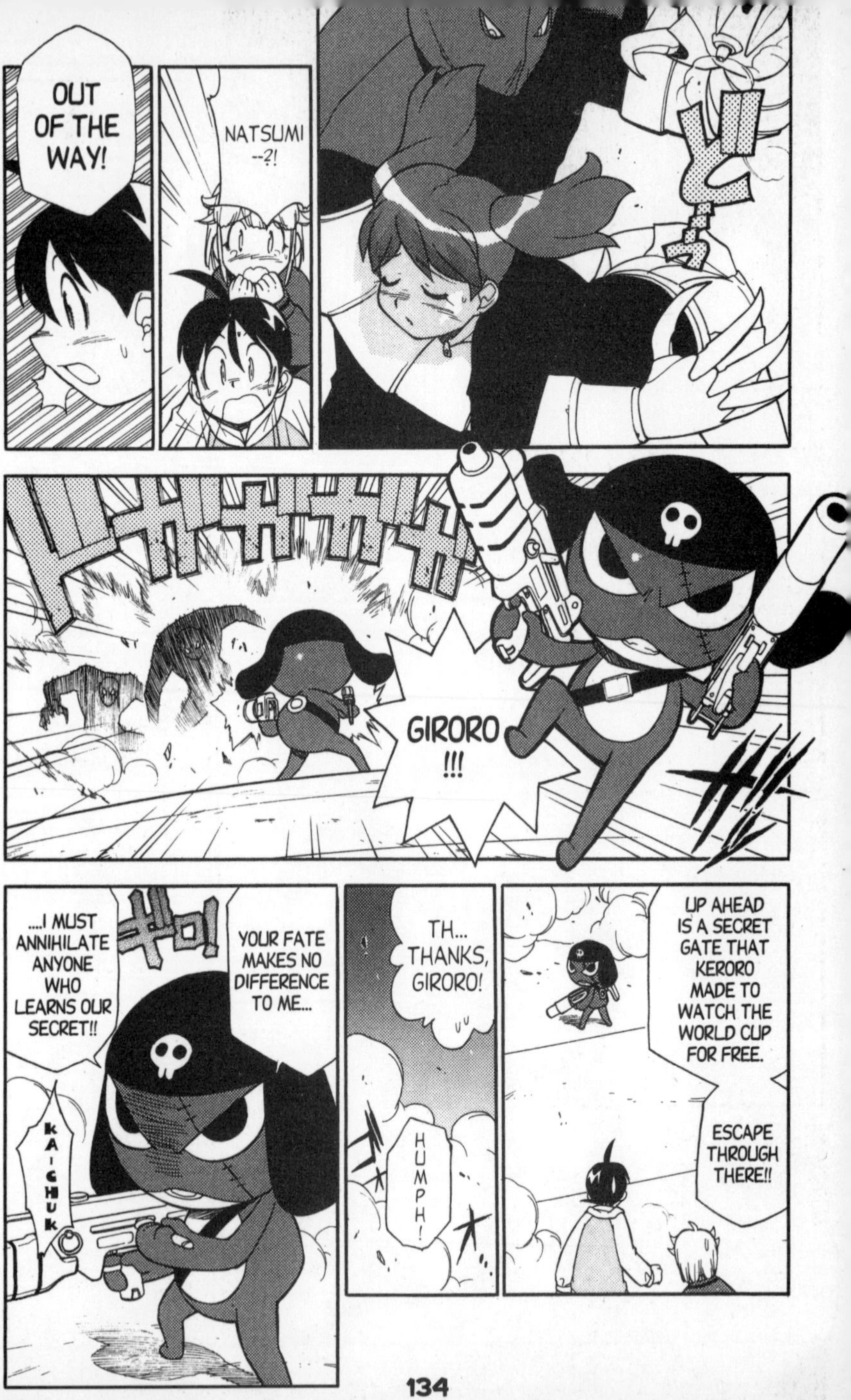
NATSUMI --?!
OUT OF THE WAY!
GIRORO !!!
UP AHEAD IS A SECRET GATE THAT KERORO MADE TO WATCH THE WORLD CUP FOR FREE.
ESCAPE THROUGH THERE!!
TH... THANKS, GIRORO!
HUMPH!
YOUR FATE MAKES NO DIFFERENCE TO ME...
ギロ!
....I MUST ANNIHILATE ANYONE WHO LEARNS OUR SECRET!!
KAICHUK

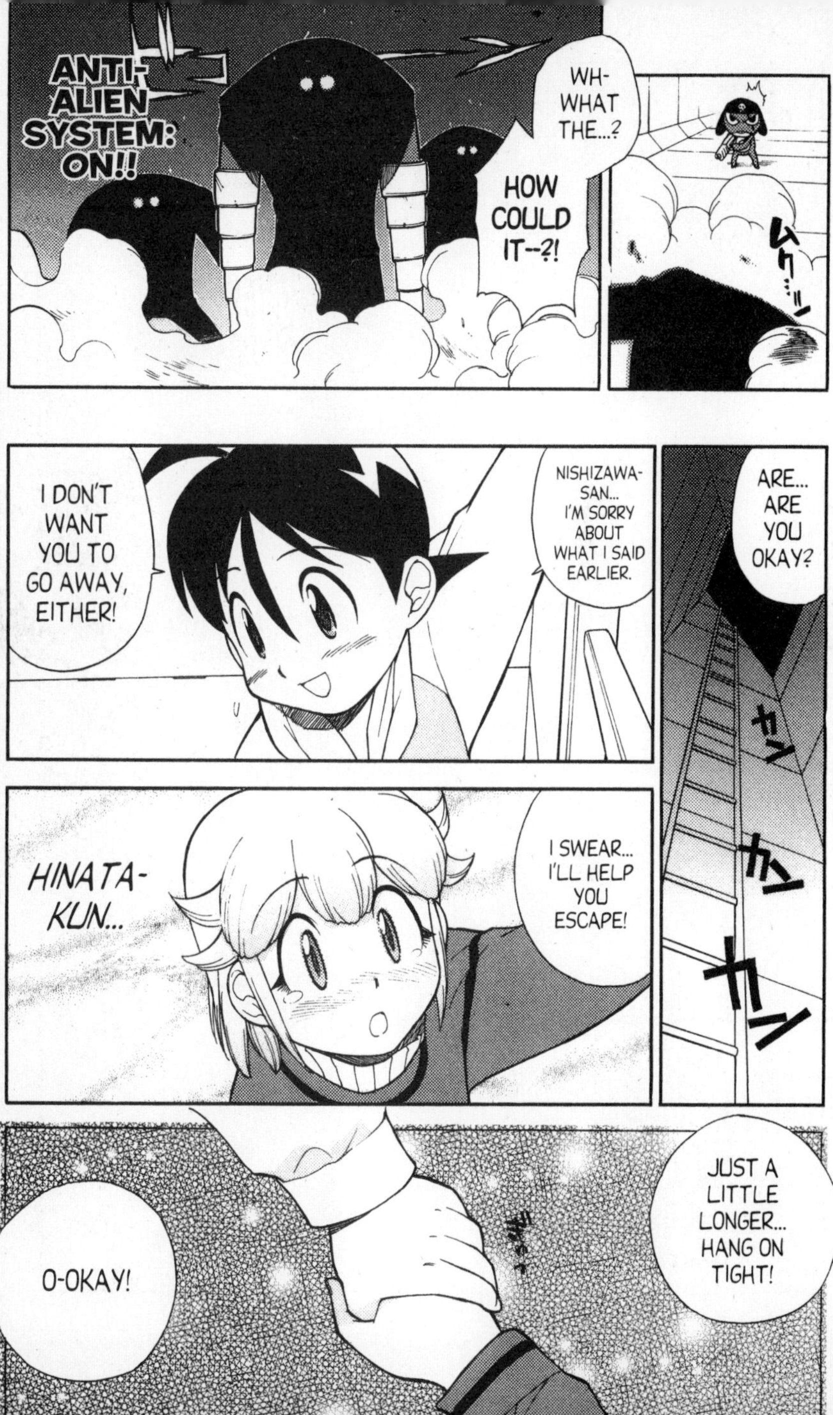

WH-WHAT THE...?
HOW COULD IT--?!
ANTI-ALIEN SYSTEM: ON!!
ARE... ARE YOU OKAY?
NISHIZAWA-SAN... I'M SORRY ABOUT WHAT I SAID EARLIER.
I DON'T WANT YOU TO GO AWAY, EITHER!
I SWEAR... I'LL HELP YOU ESCAPE!
HINATA-KUN...
JUST A LITTLE LONGER... HANG ON TIGHT!
O-OKAY!

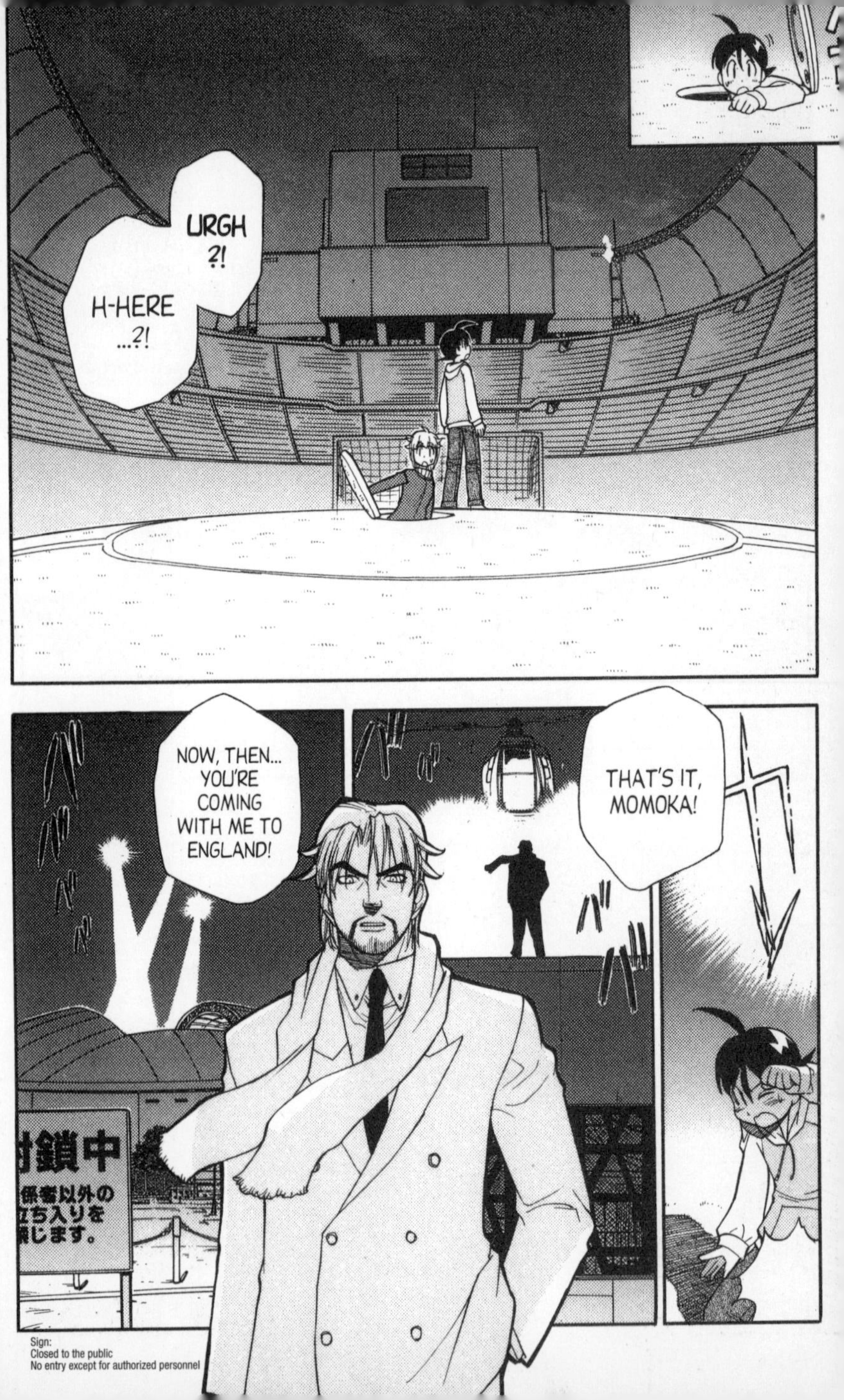
URGH ?!
H-HERE ...?!
THAT'S IT, MOMOKA!
NOW, THEN... YOU'RE COMING WITH ME TO ENGLAND!
鎖中
係者以外の
立ち入りを
じます。

Sign:
Closed to the public
No entry except for authorized personnel

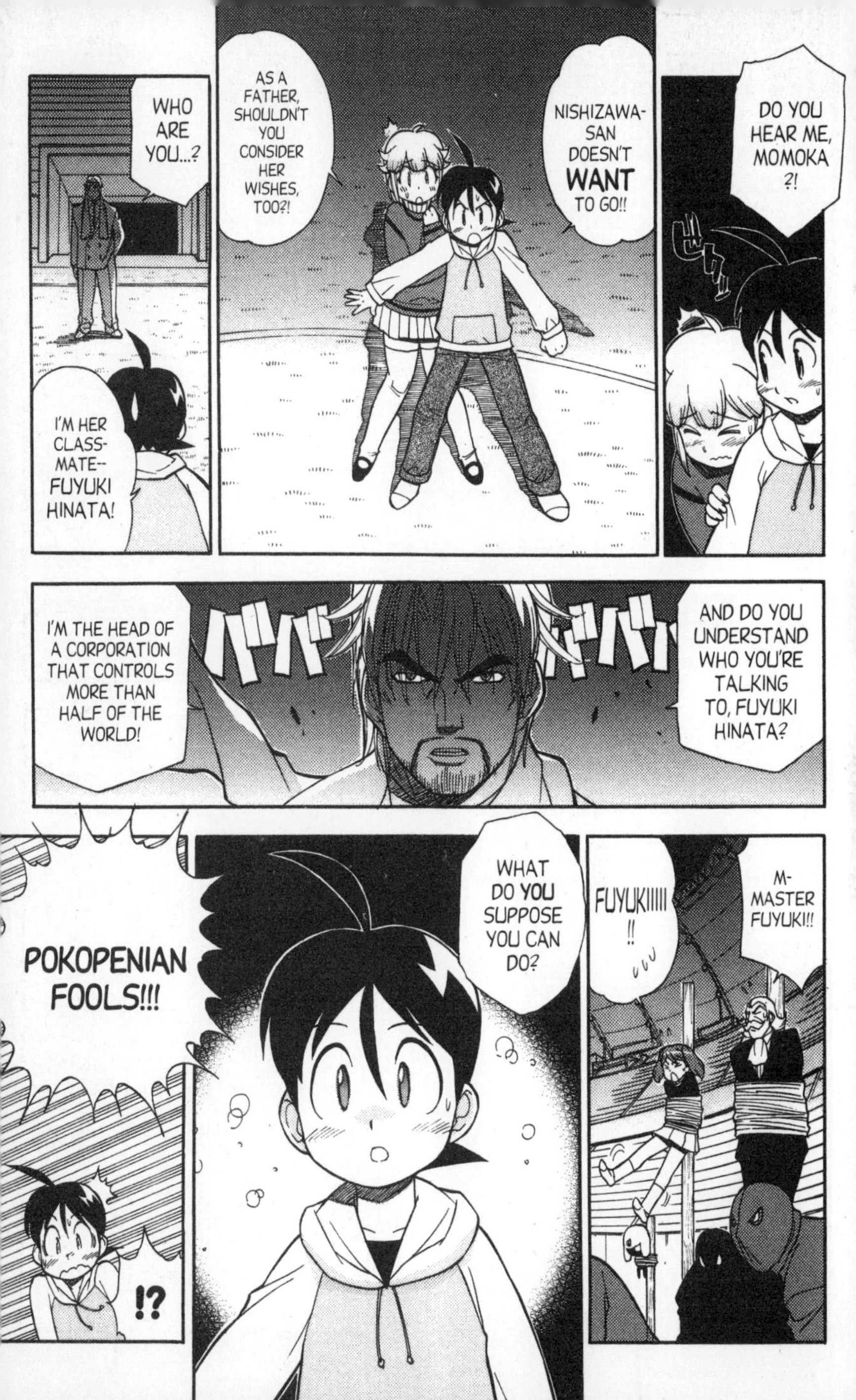
DO YOU HEAR ME, MOMOKA?!
NISHIZAWA-SAN DOESN'T WANT TO GO!!
AS A FATHER, SHOULDN'T YOU CONSIDER HER WISHES, TOO?!
WHO ARE YOU...?
I'M HER CLASSMATE--FUYUKI HINATA!
AND DO YOU UNDERSTAND WHO YOU'RE TALKING TO, FUYUKI HINATA?
I'M THE HEAD OF A CORPORATION THAT CONTROLS MORE THAN HALF OF THE WORLD!
M-MASTER FUYUKI!!
FUYUKIIIII!!
WHAT DO YOU SUPPOSE YOU CAN DO?
POKOPENIAN FOOLS!!!
!?

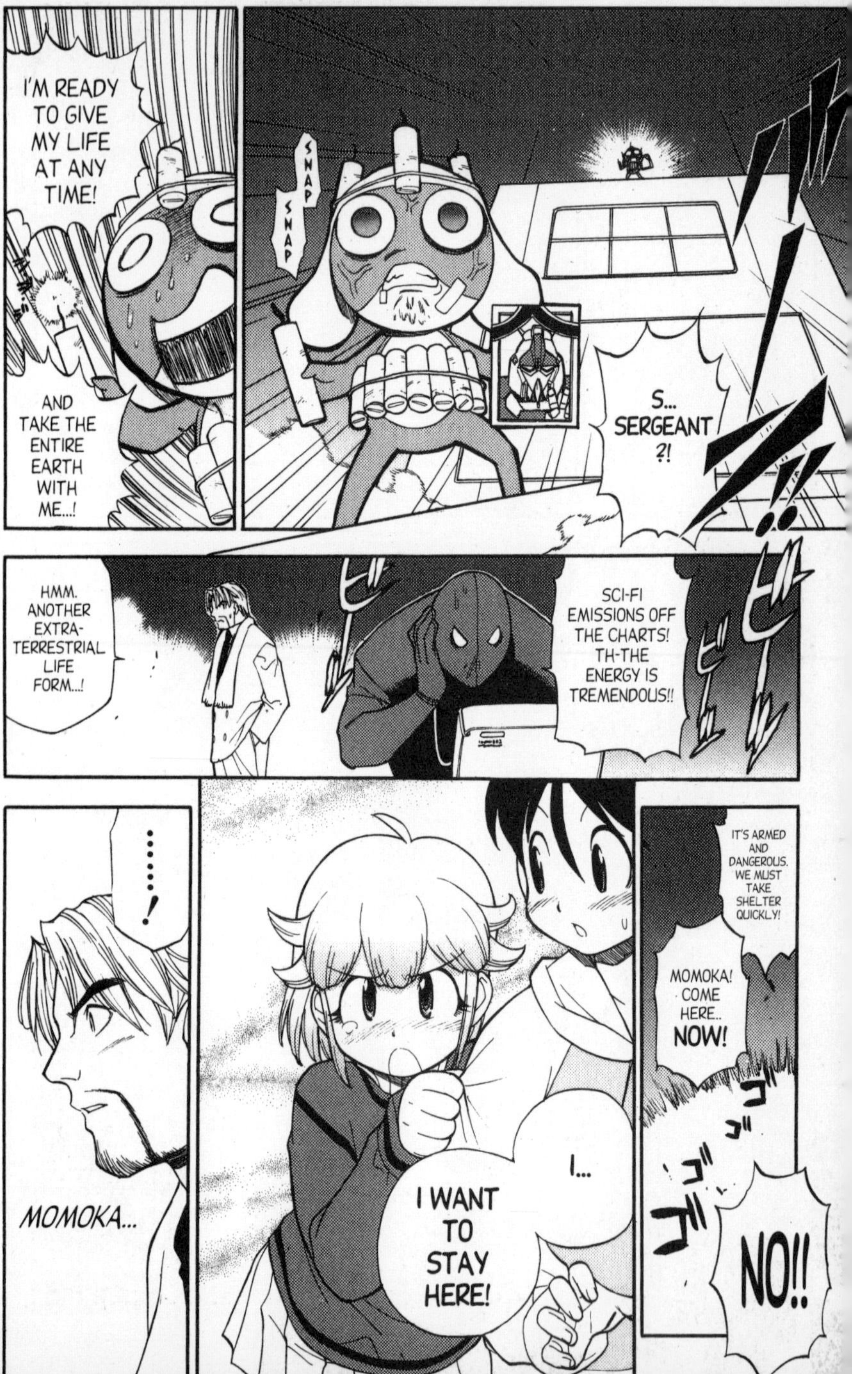
S... SERGEANT ?!
SNAP SNAP
I'M READY TO GIVE MY LIFE AT ANY TIME!
AND TAKE THE ENTIRE EARTH WITH ME...!
SCI-FI EMISSIONS OFF THE CHARTS! TH-THE ENERGY IS TREMENDOUS!!
HMM. ANOTHER EXTRA-TERRESTRIAL LIFE FORM...!
IT'S ARMED AND DANGEROUS. WE MUST TAKE SHELTER QUICKLY!
MOMOKA! COME HERE.. NOW!
NO!!
I...
I WANT TO STAY HERE!
......!
MOMOKA...

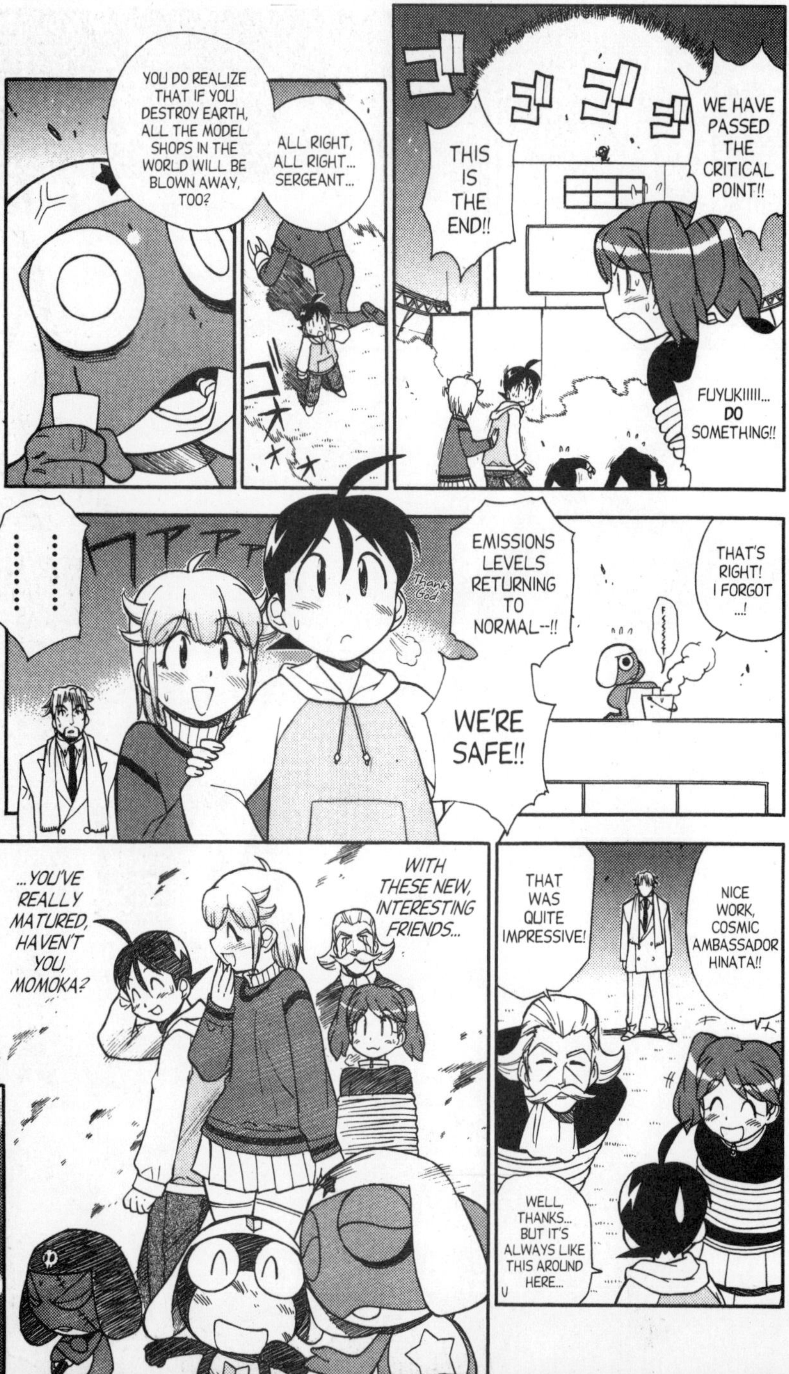
WE HAVE PASSED THE CRITICAL POINT!!
THIS IS THE END!!
FUYUKIIIII... DO SOMETHING!!
ALL RIGHT, ALL RIGHT... SERGEANT...
YOU DO REALIZE THAT IF YOU DESTROY EARTH, ALL THE MODEL SHOPS IN THE WORLD WILL BE BLOWN AWAY, TOO?
THAT'S RIGHT! I FORGOT ...!
EMISSIONS LEVELS RETURNING TO NORMAL--!!
WE'RE SAFE!!
Thank God
......
NICE WORK, COSMIC AMBASSADOR HINATA!!
THAT WAS QUITE IMPRESSIVE!
WELL, THANKS... BUT IT'S ALWAYS LIKE THIS AROUND HERE...
WITH THESE NEW, INTERESTING FRIENDS...
...YOU'VE REALLY MATURED, HAVEN'T YOU, MOMOKA?

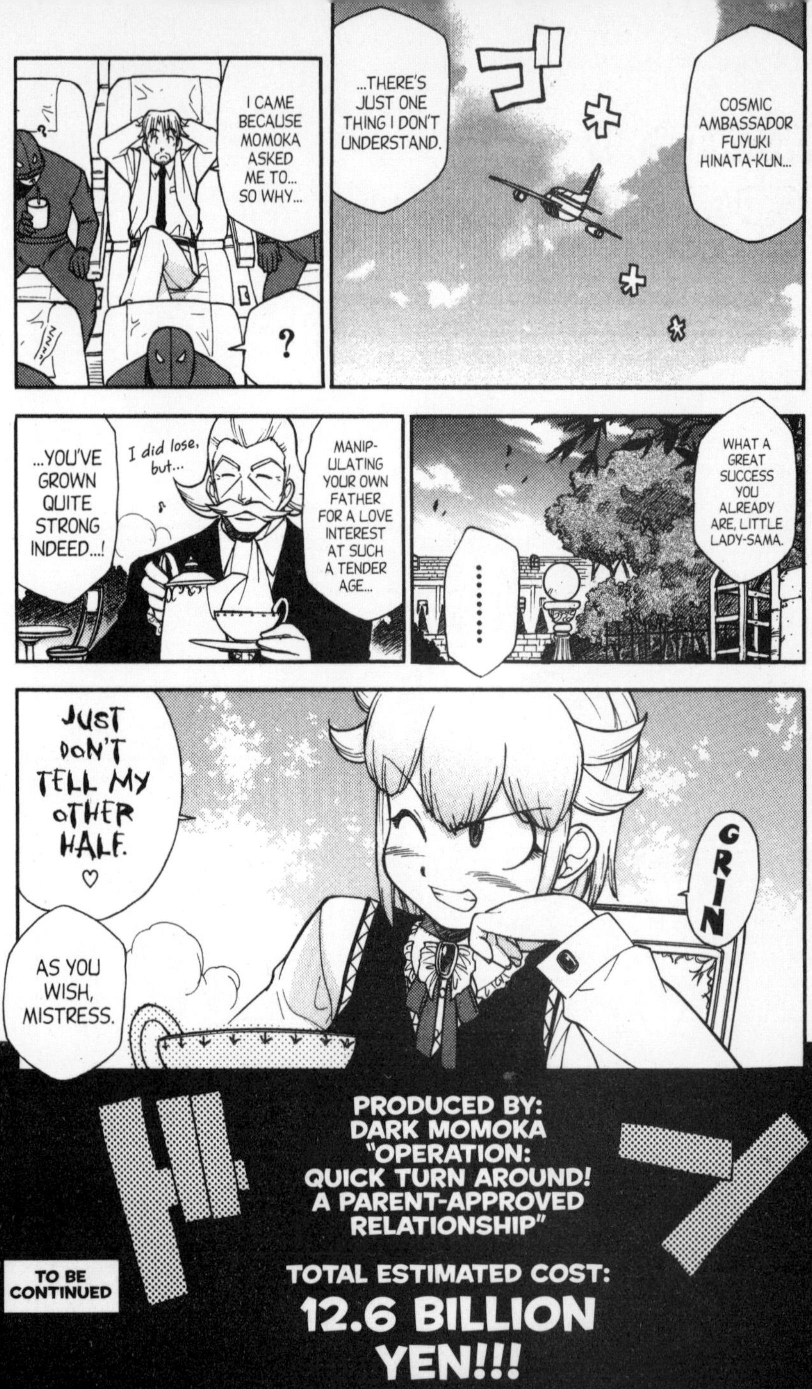
COSMIC AMBASSADOR FUYUKI HINATA-KUN...
...THERE'S JUST ONE THING I DON'T UNDERSTAND.
I CAME BECAUSE MOMOKA ASKED ME TO... SO WHY...
?
WHAT A GREAT SUCCESS YOU ALREADY ARE, LITTLE LADY-SAMA.
....
MANIP-ULATING YOUR OWN FATHER FOR A LOVE INTEREST AT SUCH A TENDER AGE...
I did lose, but...
...YOU'VE GROWN QUITE STRONG INDEED...!
GRIN
JUST DON'T TELL MY OTHER HALF. ♡
AS YOU WISH, MISTRESS.
PRODUCED BY: DARK MOMOKA "OPERATION: QUICK TURN AROUND! A PARENT-APPROVED RELATIONSHIP"
TOTAL ESTIMATED COST: 12.6 BILLION YEN!!!
TO BE CONTINUED

ENCOUNTER XLIV
LORD OF TERROR, GO! GO! GO!

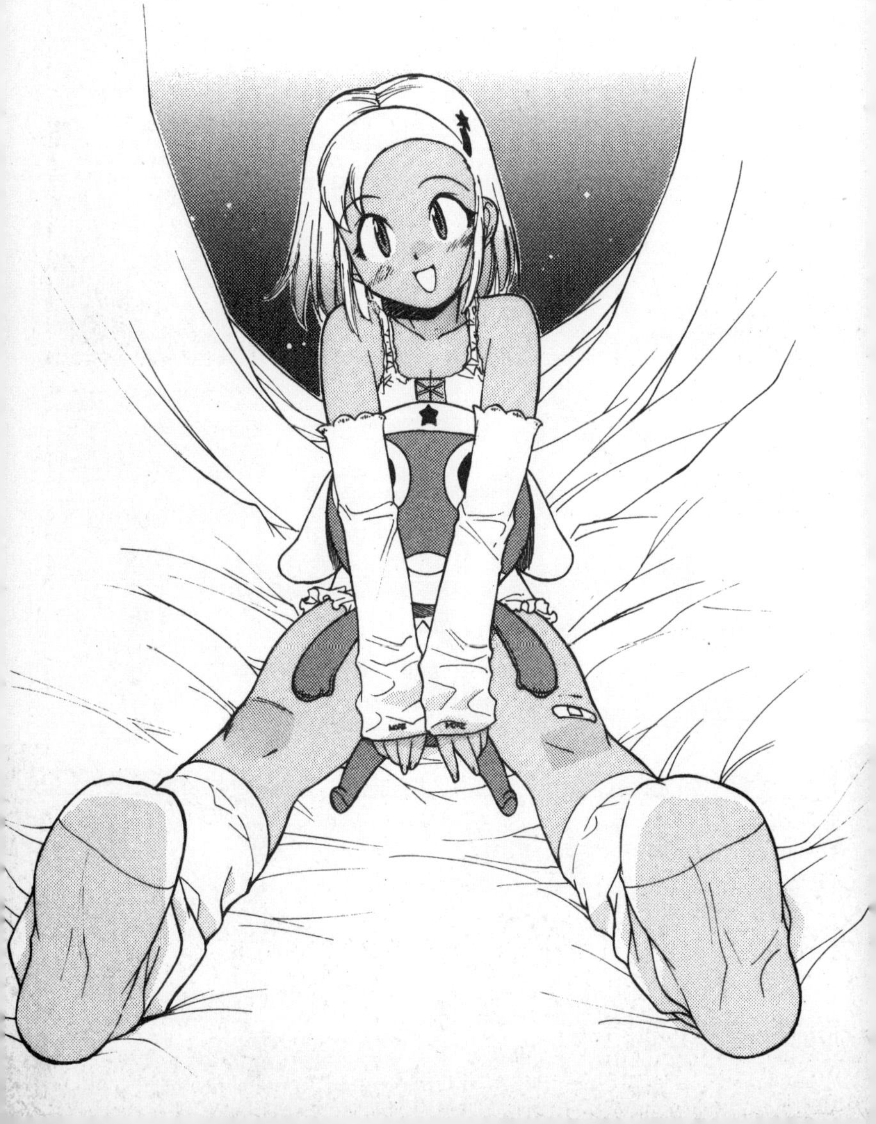

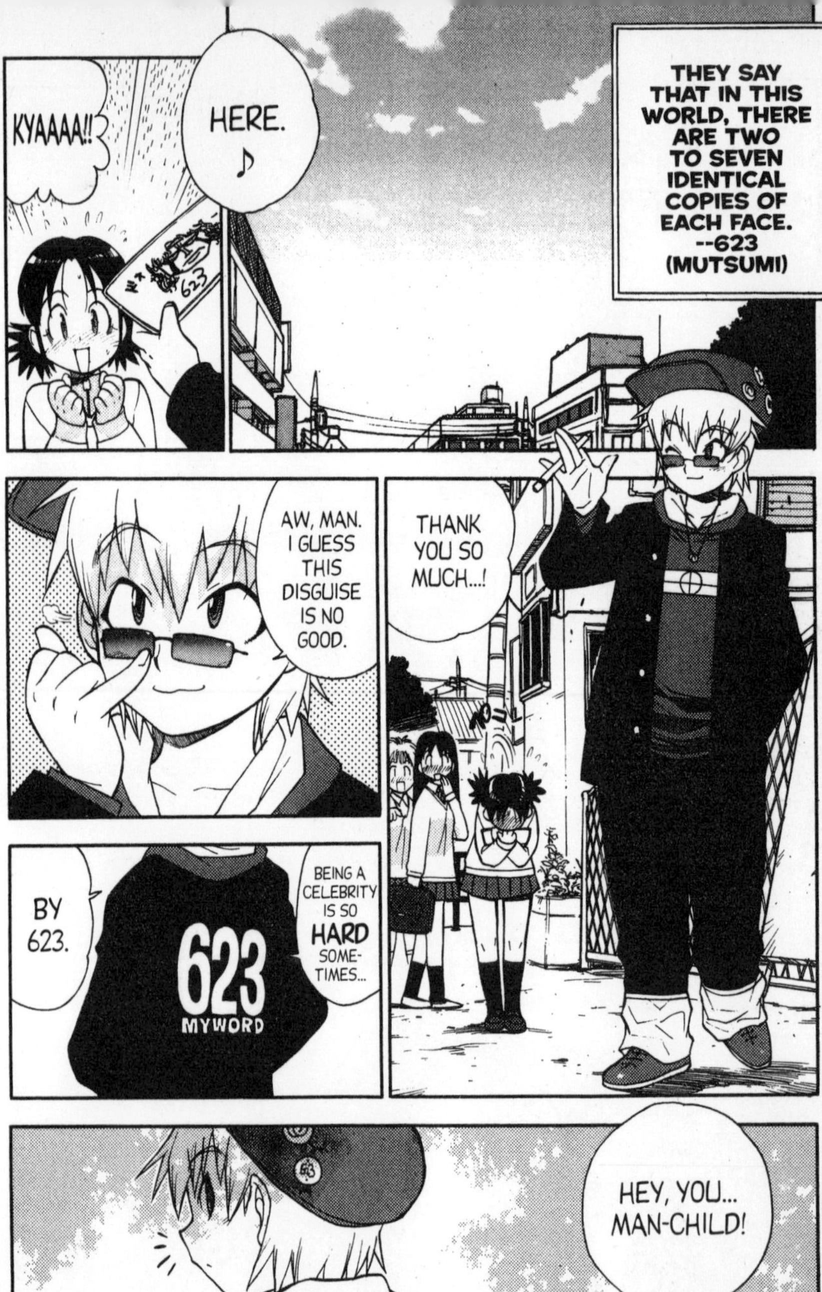
THEY SAY THAT IN THIS WORLD, THERE ARE TWO TO SEVEN IDENTICAL COPIES OF EACH FACE. --623 (MUTSUMI)
HERE. ♪
KYAAAA!!
623
THANK YOU SO MUCH...!
AW, MAN. I GUESS THIS DISGUISE IS NO GOOD.
BEING A CELEBRITY IS SO HARD SOMETIMES...
623 MYWORD
BY 623.
HEY, YOU... MAN-CHILD!

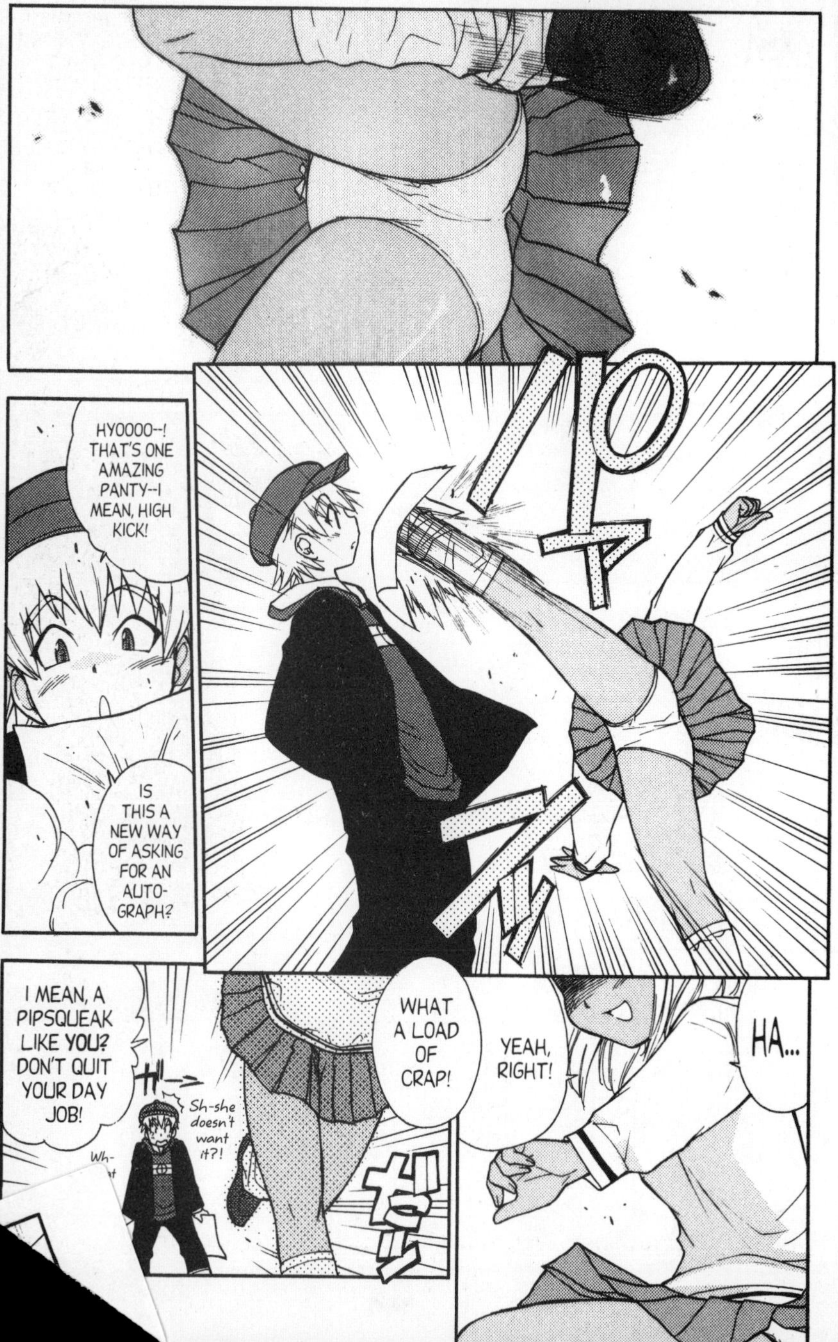
HYOOOO--! THAT'S ONE AMAZING PANTY--I MEAN, HIGH KICK!
IS THIS A NEW WAY OF ASKING FOR AN AUTO-GRAPH?
HA...
YEAH, RIGHT!
WHAT A LOAD OF CRAP!
I MEAN, A PIPSQUEAK LIKE **YOU?** DON'T QUIT YOUR DAY JOB!
Sh-she doesn't want it?!

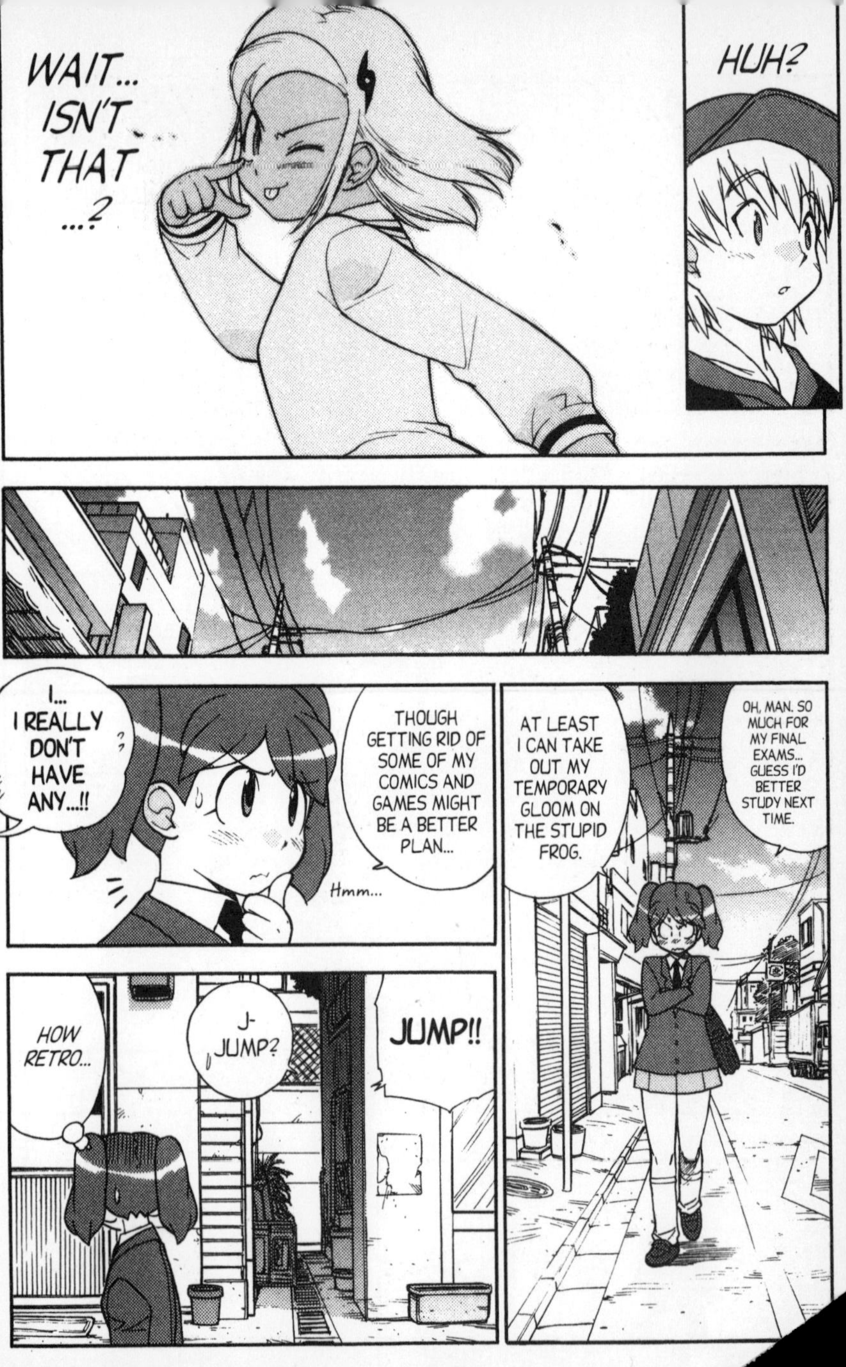
HUH?
WAIT... ISN'T THAT ...?
OH, MAN. SO MUCH FOR MY FINAL EXAMS... GUESS I'D BETTER STUDY NEXT TIME.
AT LEAST I CAN TAKE OUT MY TEMPORARY GLOOM ON THE STUPID FROG.
THOUGH GETTING RID OF SOME OF MY COMICS AND GAMES MIGHT BE A BETTER PLAN...
I... I REALLY DON'T HAVE ANY...!!
Hmm...
JUMP!!
J- JUMP?
HOW RETRO...

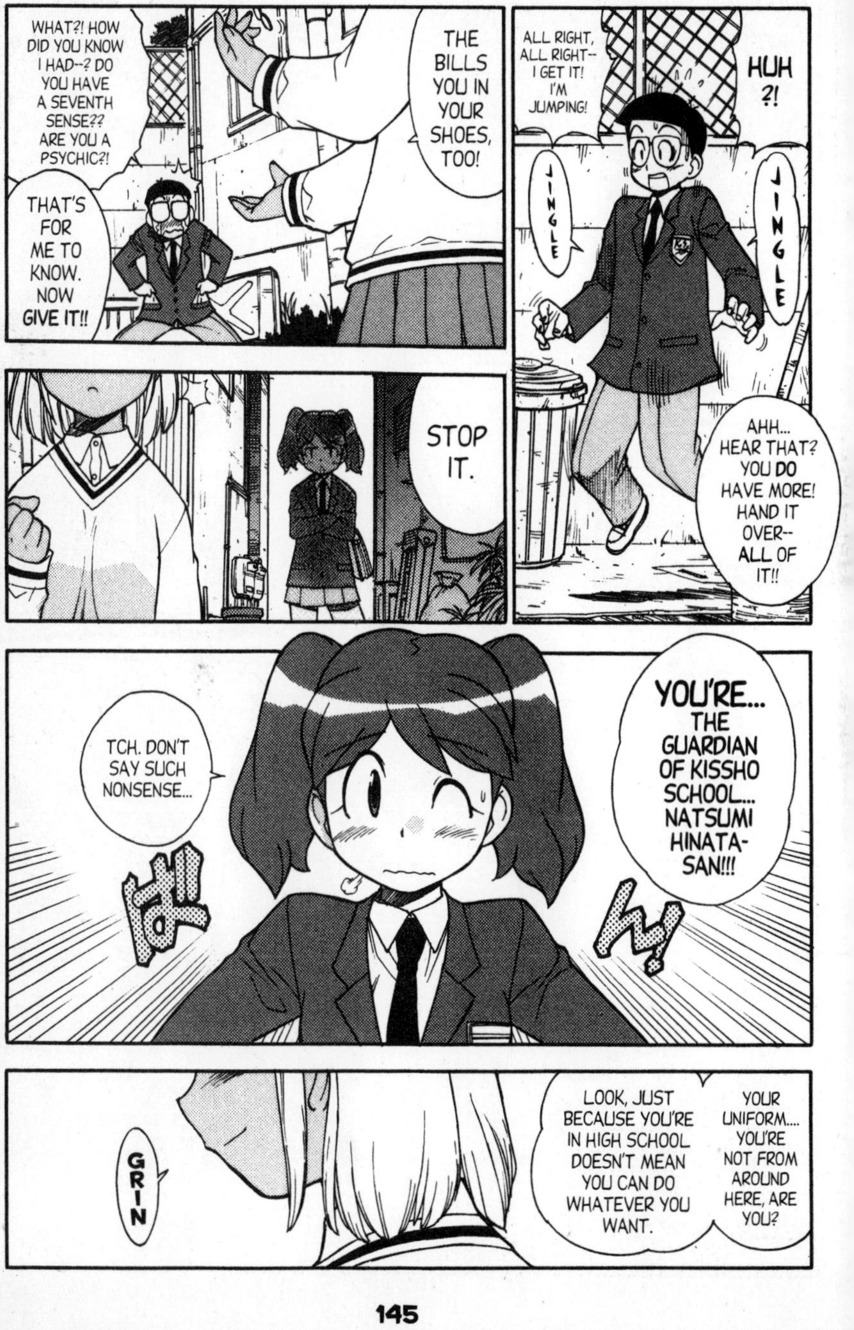

HUH ?!
ALL RIGHT, ALL RIGHT-- I GET IT! I'M JUMPING!
JINGLE
JINGLE
AHH... HEAR THAT? YOU DO HAVE MORE! HAND IT OVER-- ALL OF IT!!
THE BILLS YOU IN YOUR SHOES, TOO!
WHAT?! HOW DID YOU KNOW I HAD--? DO YOU HAVE A SEVENTH SENSE?? ARE YOU A PSYCHIC?!
THAT'S FOR ME TO KNOW. NOW GIVE IT!!
STOP IT.
YOU'RE... THE GUARDIAN OF KISSHO SCHOOL... NATSUMI HINATA-SAN!!!
ばん!
TCH. DON'T SAY SUCH NONSENSE...
YOUR UNIFORM.... YOU'RE NOT FROM AROUND HERE, ARE YOU?
LOOK, JUST BECAUSE YOU'RE IN HIGH SCHOOL DOESN'T MEAN YOU CAN DO WHATEVER YOU WANT.
GRIN

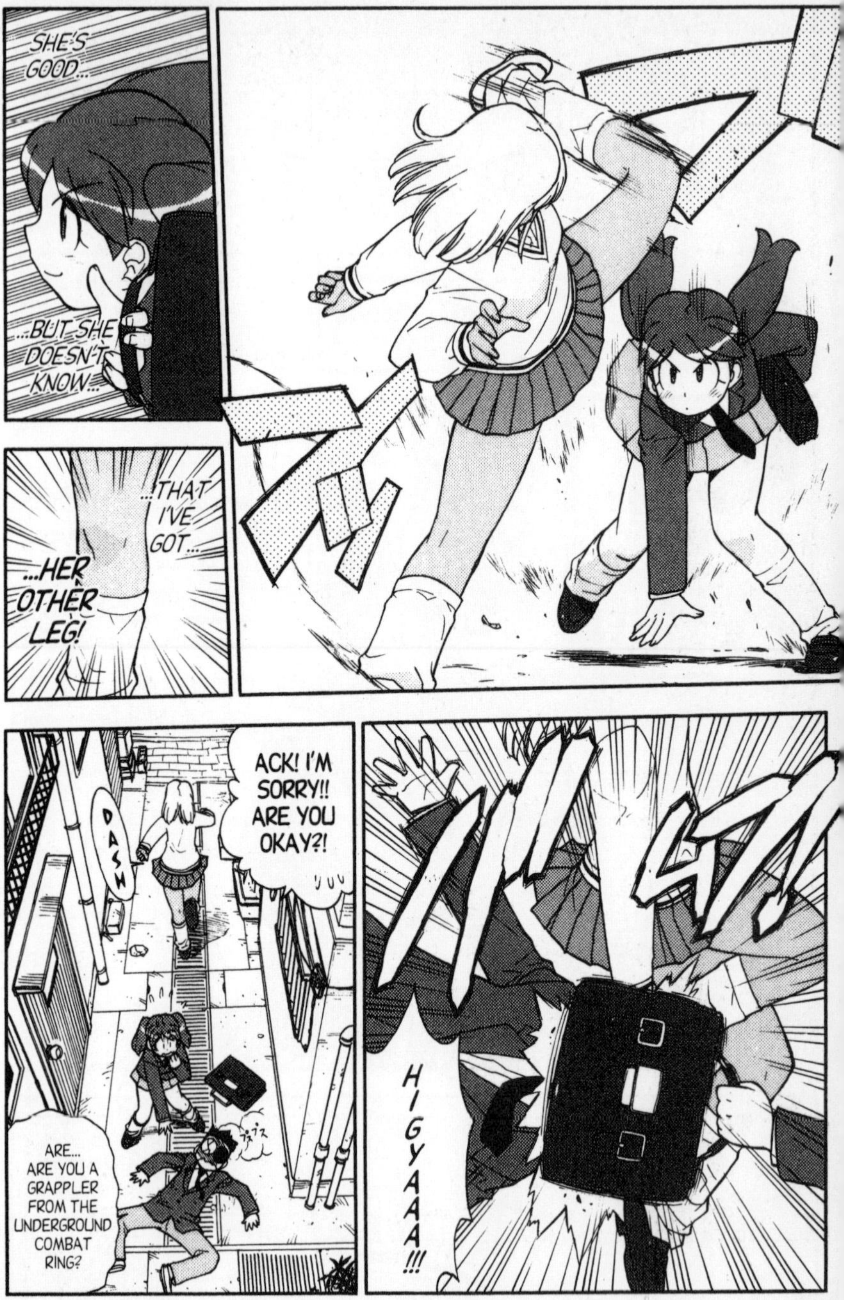
SHE'S GOOD...
...BUT SHE DOESN'T KNOW...
...THAT I'VE GOT...
...HER OTHER LEG!
HIGYAAA!!!
ACK! I'M SORRY!! ARE YOU OKAY?!
DASH
ARE... ARE YOU A GRAPPLER FROM THE UNDERGROUND COMBAT RING?

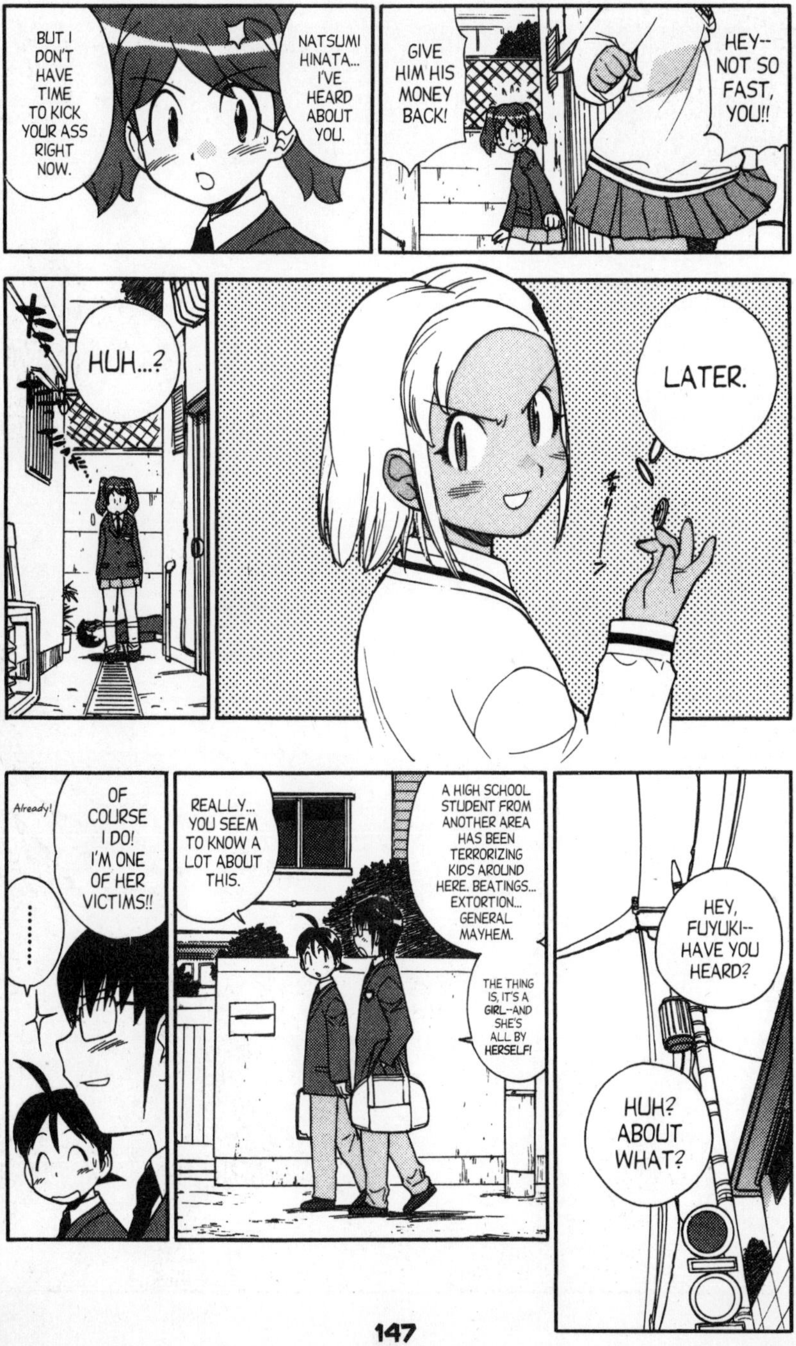
HEY-- NOT SO FAST, YOU!!
GIVE HIM HIS MONEY BACK!
NATSUMI HINATA... I'VE HEARD ABOUT YOU.
BUT I DON'T HAVE TIME TO KICK YOUR ASS RIGHT NOW.
LATER.
HUH...?
HEY, FUYUKI-- HAVE YOU HEARD?
HUH? ABOUT WHAT?
A HIGH SCHOOL STUDENT FROM ANOTHER AREA HAS BEEN TERRORIZING KIDS AROUND HERE. BEATINGS... EXTORTION... GENERAL MAYHEM.
THE THING IS, IT'S A GIRL--AND SHE'S ALL BY HERSELF!
REALLY... YOU SEEM TO KNOW A LOT ABOUT THIS.
OF COURSE I DO! I'M ONE OF HER VICTIMS!!
Already!
......

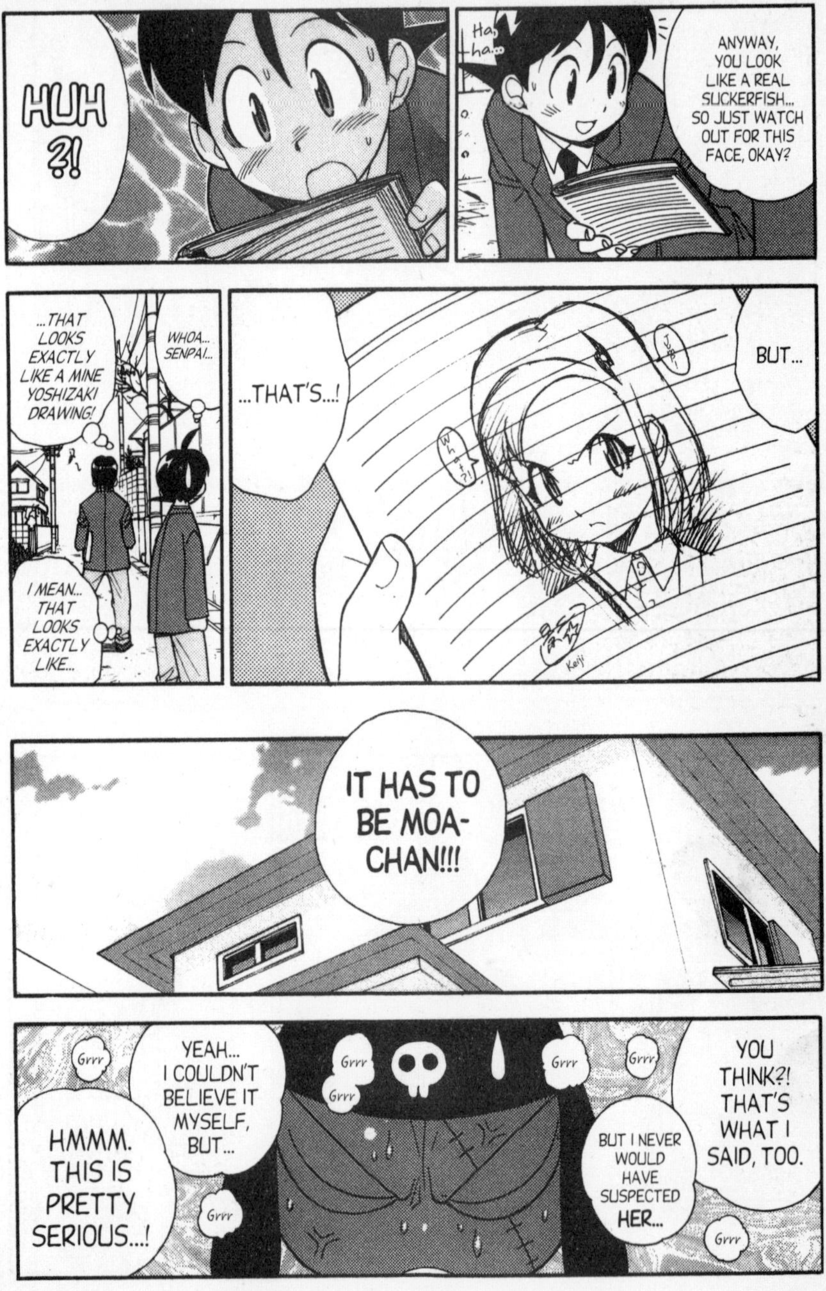
Ha, ha...
ANYWAY, YOU LOOK LIKE A REAL SUCKERFISH... SO JUST WATCH OUT FOR THIS FACE, OKAY?
HUH ?!
BUT...
What?!
Keiji
...THAT'S...!
WHOA... SENPAI...
...THAT LOOKS EXACTLY LIKE A MINE YOSHIZAKI DRAWING!
I MEAN... THAT LOOKS EXACTLY LIKE...
IT HAS TO BE MOA-CHAN!!!
YOU THINK?! THAT'S WHAT I SAID, TOO.
Grrr
BUT I NEVER WOULD HAVE SUSPECTED HER...
Grrr
Grrr
Grrr
YEAH... I COULDN'T BELIEVE IT MYSELF, BUT...
Grrr
HMMM. THIS IS PRETTY SERIOUS...!
Grrr
Grrr

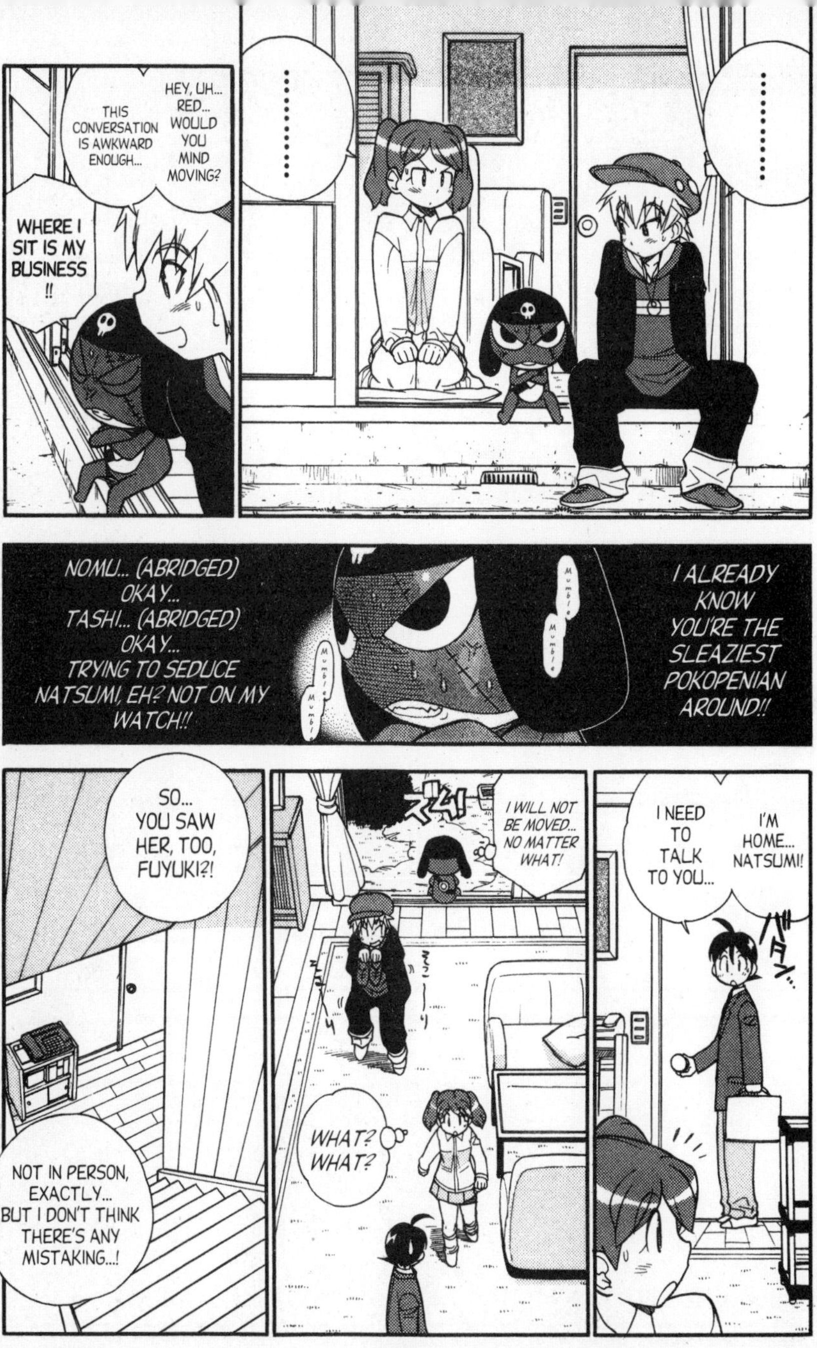
......
......
HEY, UH... RED... WOULD YOU MIND MOVING?
THIS CONVERSATION IS AWKWARD ENOUGH...
WHERE I SIT IS MY BUSINESS!!
I ALREADY KNOW YOU'RE THE SLEAZIEST POKOPENIAN AROUND!!
Mumble Mumble
Mumble Mumble
NOMU... (ABRIDGED) OKAY... TASHI... (ABRIDGED) OKAY... TRYING TO SEDUCE NATSUMI, EH? NOT ON MY WATCH!!
I'M HOME... NATSUMI!
I NEED TO TALK TO YOU...
I WILL NOT BE MOVED... NO MATTER WHAT!
WHAT? WHAT?
SO... YOU SAW HER, TOO, FUYUKI?!
NOT IN PERSON, EXACTLY... BUT I DON'T THINK THERE'S ANY MISTAKING...!

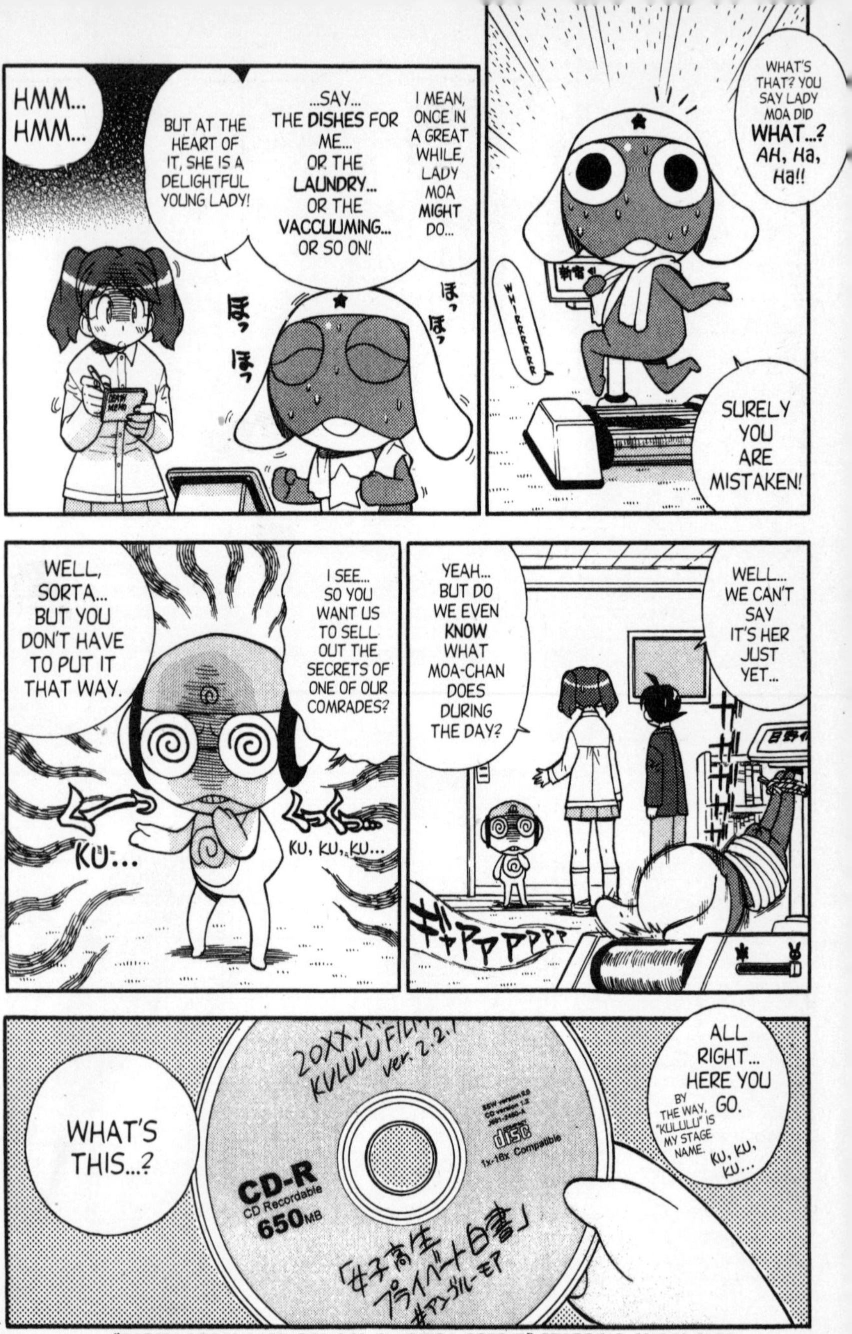
WHAT'S THAT? YOU SAY LADY MOA DID WHAT...? AH, Ha, Ha!!
WHIRRRRRRRR
SURELY YOU ARE MISTAKEN!
I MEAN, ONCE IN A GREAT WHILE, LADY MOA MIGHT DO...
...SAY... THE DISHES FOR ME... OR THE LAUNDRY... OR THE VACCUUMING... OR SO ON!
BUT AT THE HEART OF IT, SHE IS A DELIGHTFUL YOUNG LADY!
HMM... HMM...
ほっ ほっ
ほっ ほっ
WELL... WE CAN'T SAY IT'S HER JUST YET...
YEAH... BUT DO WE EVEN KNOW WHAT MOA-CHAN DOES DURING THE DAY?
I SEE... SO YOU WANT US TO SELL OUT THE SECRETS OF ONE OF OUR COMRADES?
WELL, SORTA... BUT YOU DON'T HAVE TO PUT IT THAT WAY.
くっくっ... KU, KU, KU...
く... KU...
ALL RIGHT... HERE YOU GO.
BY THE WAY, "KULULU" IS MY STAGE NAME.
KU, KU, KU...
20XX.X. KULULU FILM ver. 2.2.1
1x-16x Compatible
CD-R CD Recordable 650MB
「女子高生プライベート白書」
#アンゴルモア
WHAT'S THIS...?

"BARELY LEGAL HIGH SCHOOL IV: EXTRA CREDIT" STARRING ANGOL MOA

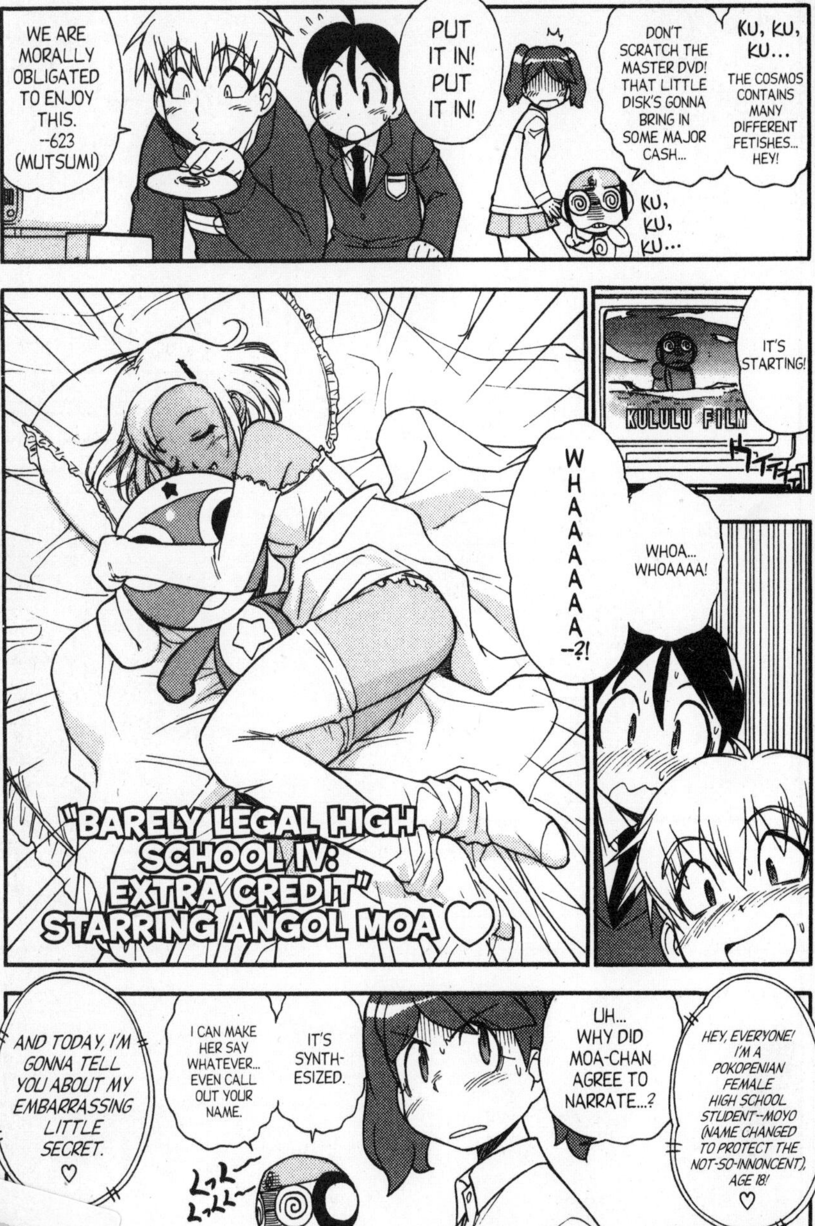
KU, KU, KU... THE COSMOS CONTAINS MANY DIFFERENT FETISHES... HEY!
DON'T SCRATCH THE MASTER DVD! THAT LITTLE DISK'S GONNA BRING IN SOME MAJOR CASH...
KU, KU, KU...
PUT IT IN! PUT IT IN!
WE ARE MORALLY OBLIGATED TO ENJOY THIS. --623 (MUTSUMI)
KULULU FILM
IT'S STARTING!
WHOA... WHOAAAA!
WHAAAAAAA--?!
"BARELY LEGAL HIGH SCHOOL IV: EXTRA CREDIT" STARRING ANGOL MOA ♡
HEY, EVERYONE! I'M A POKOPENIAN FEMALE HIGH SCHOOL STUDENT--MOYO (NAME CHANGED TO PROTECT THE NOT-SO-INNONCENT), AGE 18! ♡
UH... WHY DID MOA-CHAN AGREE TO NARRATE...?
IT'S SYNTH-ESIZED.
I CAN MAKE HER SAY WHATEVER... EVEN CALL OUT YOUR NAME.
AND TODAY, I'M GONNA TELL YOU ABOUT MY EMBARRASSING LITTLE SECRET. ♡

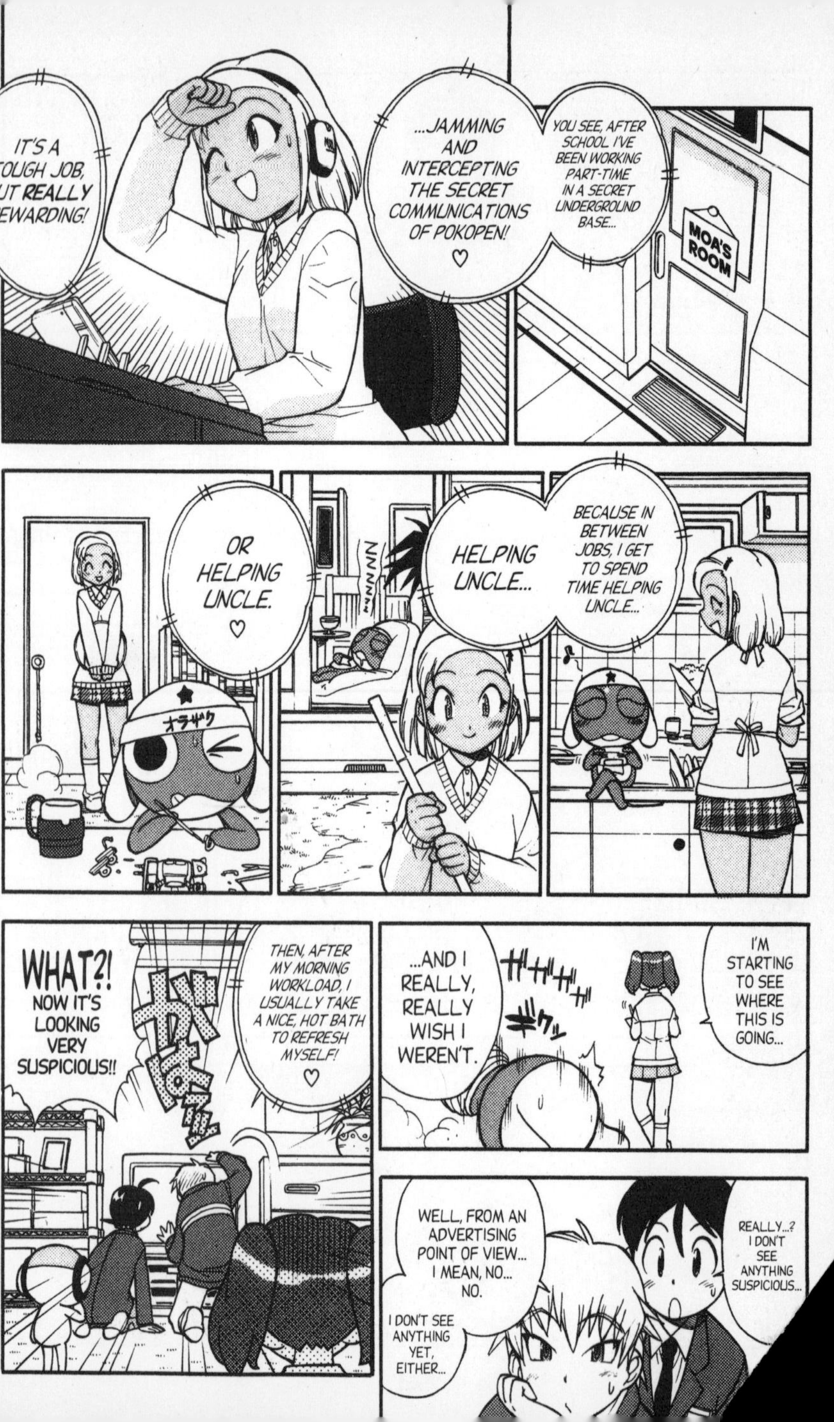

YOU SEE, AFTER SCHOOL I'VE BEEN WORKING PART-TIME IN A SECRET UNDERGROUND BASE...
MOA'S ROOM
...JAMMING AND INTERCEPTING THE SECRET COMMUNICATIONS OF POKOPEN! ♡
IT'S A TOUGH JOB, BUT REALLY REWARDING!
BECAUSE IN BETWEEN JOBS, I GET TO SPEND TIME HELPING UNCLE...
HELPING UNCLE...
OR HELPING UNCLE. ♡
オラザク
I'M STARTING TO SEE WHERE THIS IS GOING...
...AND I REALLY, REALLY WISH I WEREN'T.
REALLY...? I DON'T SEE ANYTHING SUSPICIOUS...
WELL, FROM AN ADVERTISING POINT OF VIEW... I MEAN, NO... NO.
I DON'T SEE ANYTHING YET, EITHER...
THEN, AFTER MY MORNING WORKLOAD, I USUALLY TAKE A NICE, HOT BATH TO REFRESH MYSELF! ♡
WHAT?! NOW IT'S LOOKING VERY SUSPICIOUS!!

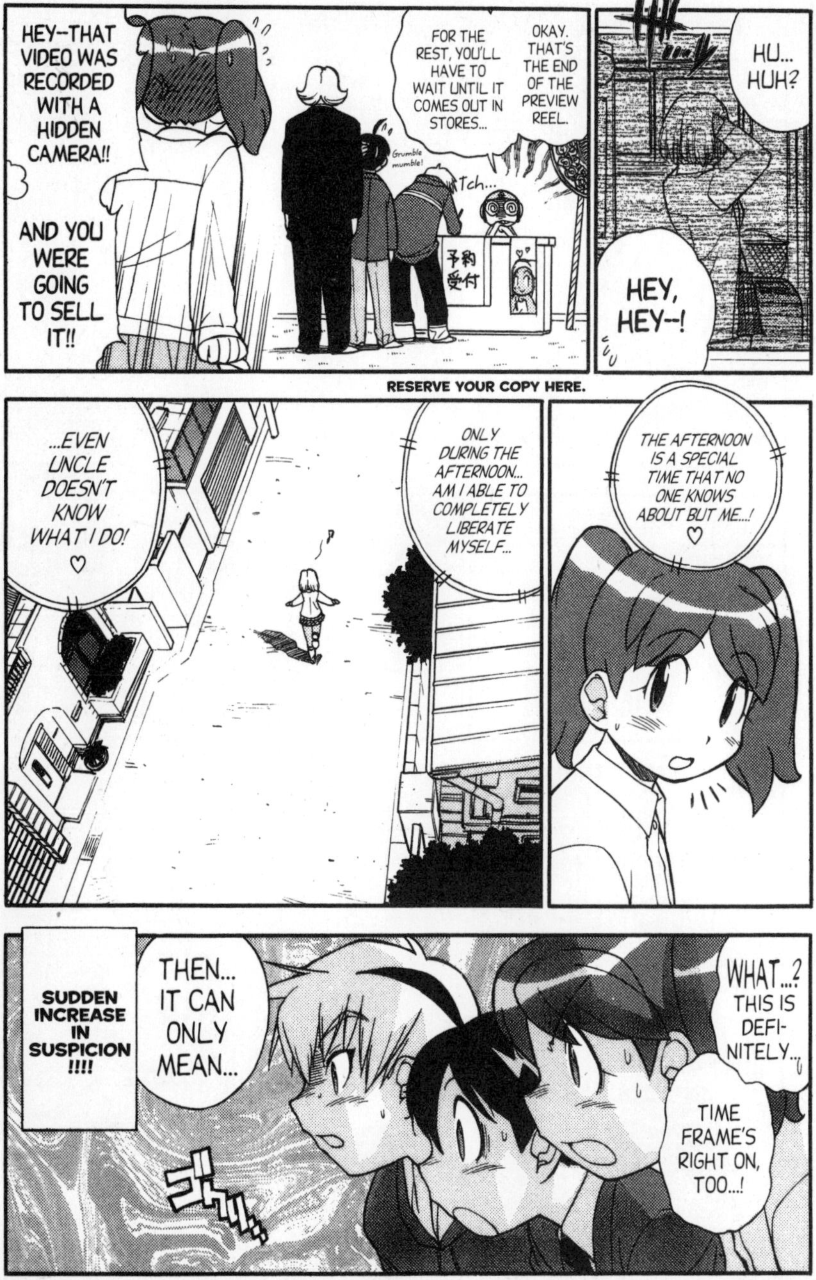
HU... HUH?
HEY, HEY--!
OKAY. THAT'S THE END OF THE PREVIEW REEL.
FOR THE REST, YOU'LL HAVE TO WAIT UNTIL IT COMES OUT IN STORES...
Tch...
Grumble mumble!
予約受付
HEY--THAT VIDEO WAS RECORDED WITH A HIDDEN CAMERA!!
AND YOU WERE GOING TO SELL IT!!
THE AFTERNOON IS A SPECIAL TIME THAT NO ONE KNOWS ABOUT BUT ME...! ♡
ONLY DURING THE AFTERNOON... AM I ABLE TO COMPLETELY LIBERATE MYSELF...
...EVEN UNCLE DOESN'T KNOW WHAT I DO! ♡
WHAT...? THIS IS DEFINITELY...
TIME FRAME'S RIGHT ON, TOO...!
THEN... IT CAN ONLY MEAN...
SUDDEN INCREASE IN SUSPICION !!!!
RESERVE YOUR COPY HERE.

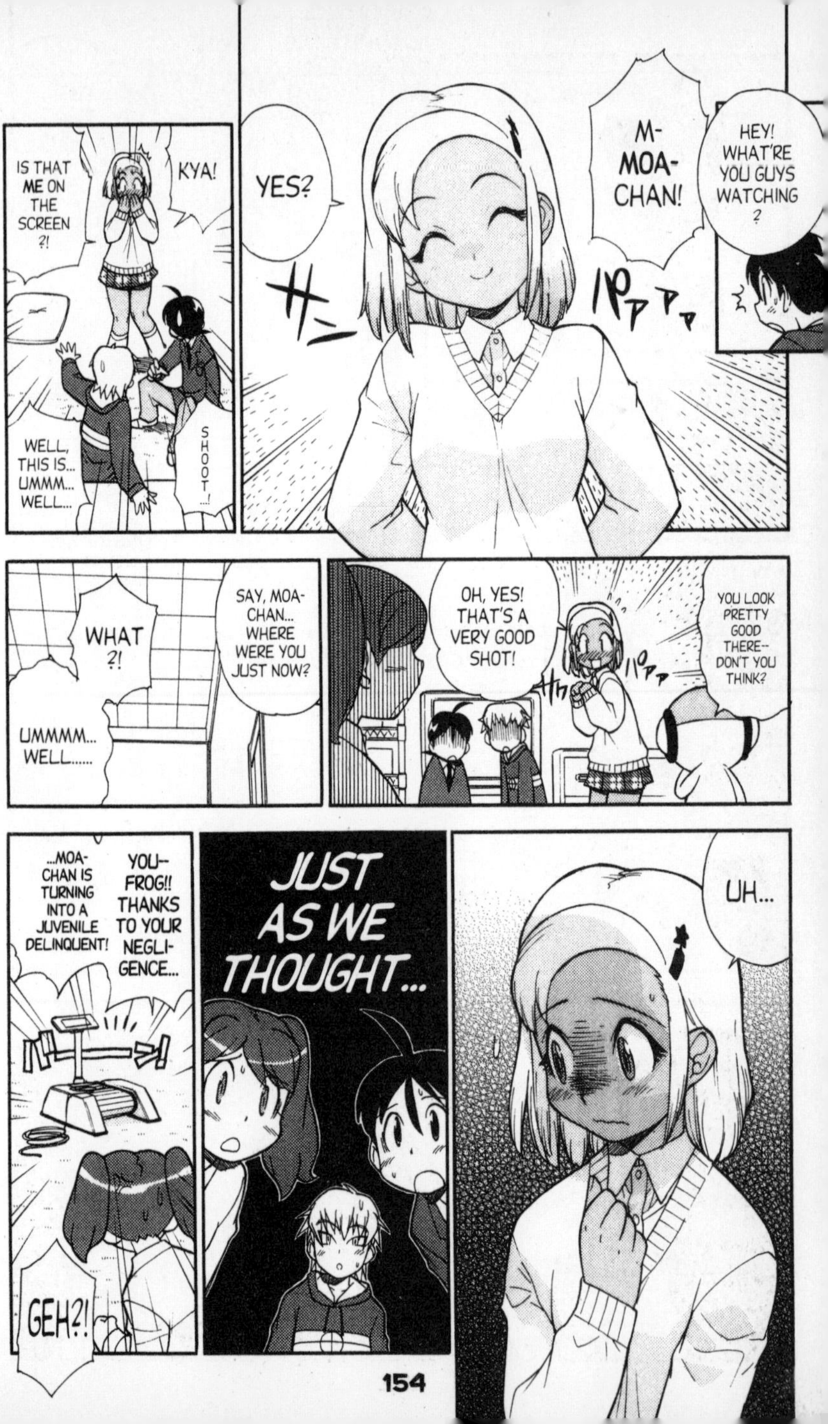
HEY! WHAT'RE YOU GUYS WATCHING?
M- MOA- CHAN!
YES?
KYA!
IS THAT ME ON THE SCREEN?!
SHOOT...!
WELL, THIS IS... UMMM... WELL...
YOU LOOK PRETTY GOOD THERE-- DON'T YOU THINK?
OH, YES! THAT'S A VERY GOOD SHOT!
SAY, MOA- CHAN... WHERE WERE YOU JUST NOW?
WHAT?!
UMMMM... WELL......
UH...
JUST AS WE THOUGHT...
YOU-- FROG!! THANKS TO YOUR NEGLI- GENCE...
...MOA- CHAN IS TURNING INTO A JUVENILE DELINQUENT!
GEH?!

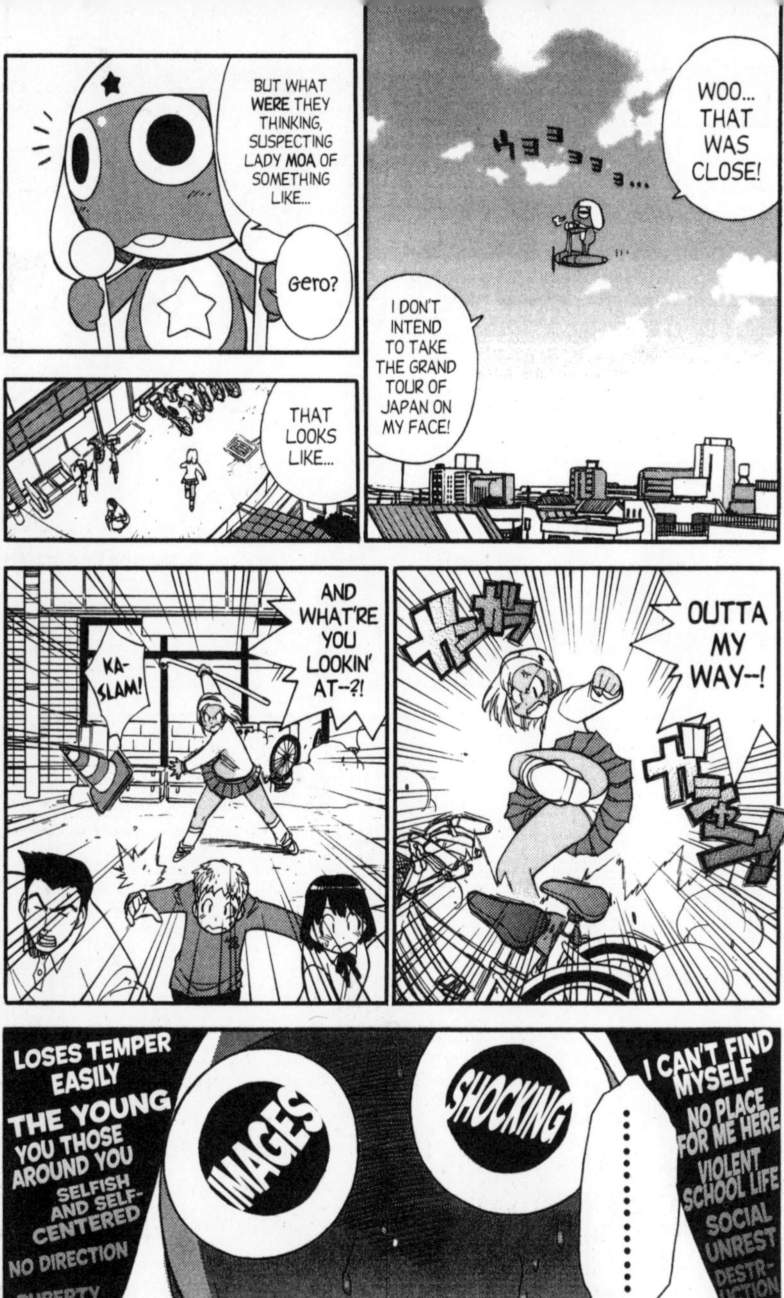
WOO... THAT WAS CLOSE!
I DON'T INTEND TO TAKE THE GRAND TOUR OF JAPAN ON MY FACE!
BUT WHAT WERE THEY THINKING, SUSPECTING LADY MOA OF SOMETHING LIKE...
Gero?
THAT LOOKS LIKE...
OUTTA MY WAY--!
AND WHAT'RE YOU LOOKIN' AT--?!
KA-SLAM!
SHOCKING
IMAGES
......
I CAN'T FIND MYSELF
NO PLACE FOR ME HERE
VIOLENT SCHOOL LIFE
SOCIAL UNREST
LOSES TEMPER EASILY
THE YOUNG
YOU THOSE AROUND YOU
SELFISH AND SELF-CENTERED
NO DIRECTION
PUBERTY
DEBAUCHED

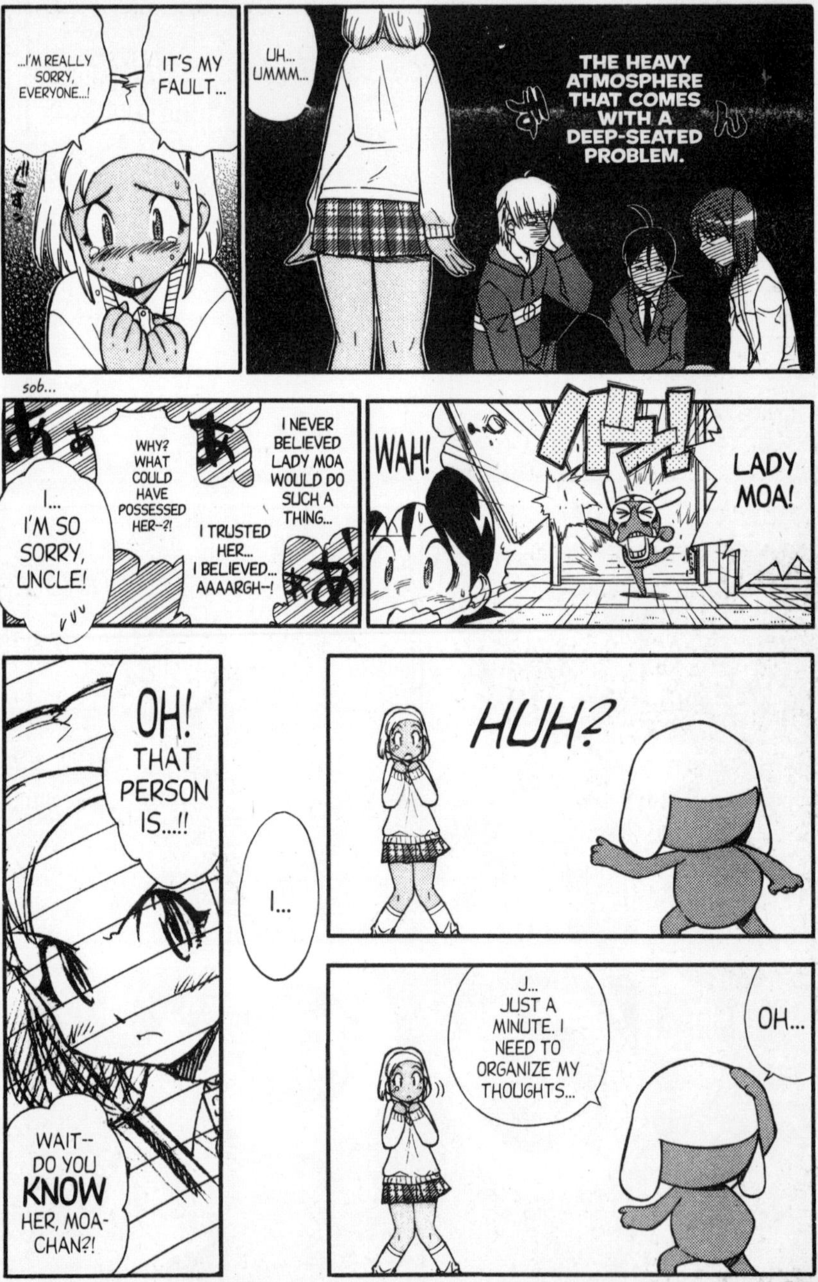
UH... UMMM...
THE HEAVY ATMOSPHERE THAT COMES WITH A DEEP-SEATED PROBLEM.
IT'S MY FAULT...
...I'M REALLY SORRY, EVERYONE...!
sob...
LADY MOA!
WAH!
I NEVER BELIEVED LADY MOA WOULD DO SUCH A THING...
WHY? WHAT COULD HAVE POSSESSED HER--?!
I TRUSTED HER... I BELIEVED... AAAARGH--!
I... I'M SO SORRY, UNCLE!
HUH?
OH...
J... JUST A MINUTE. I NEED TO ORGANIZE MY THOUGHTS...
I...
OH! THAT PERSON IS...!!
WAIT-- DO YOU KNOW HER, MOA-CHAN?!

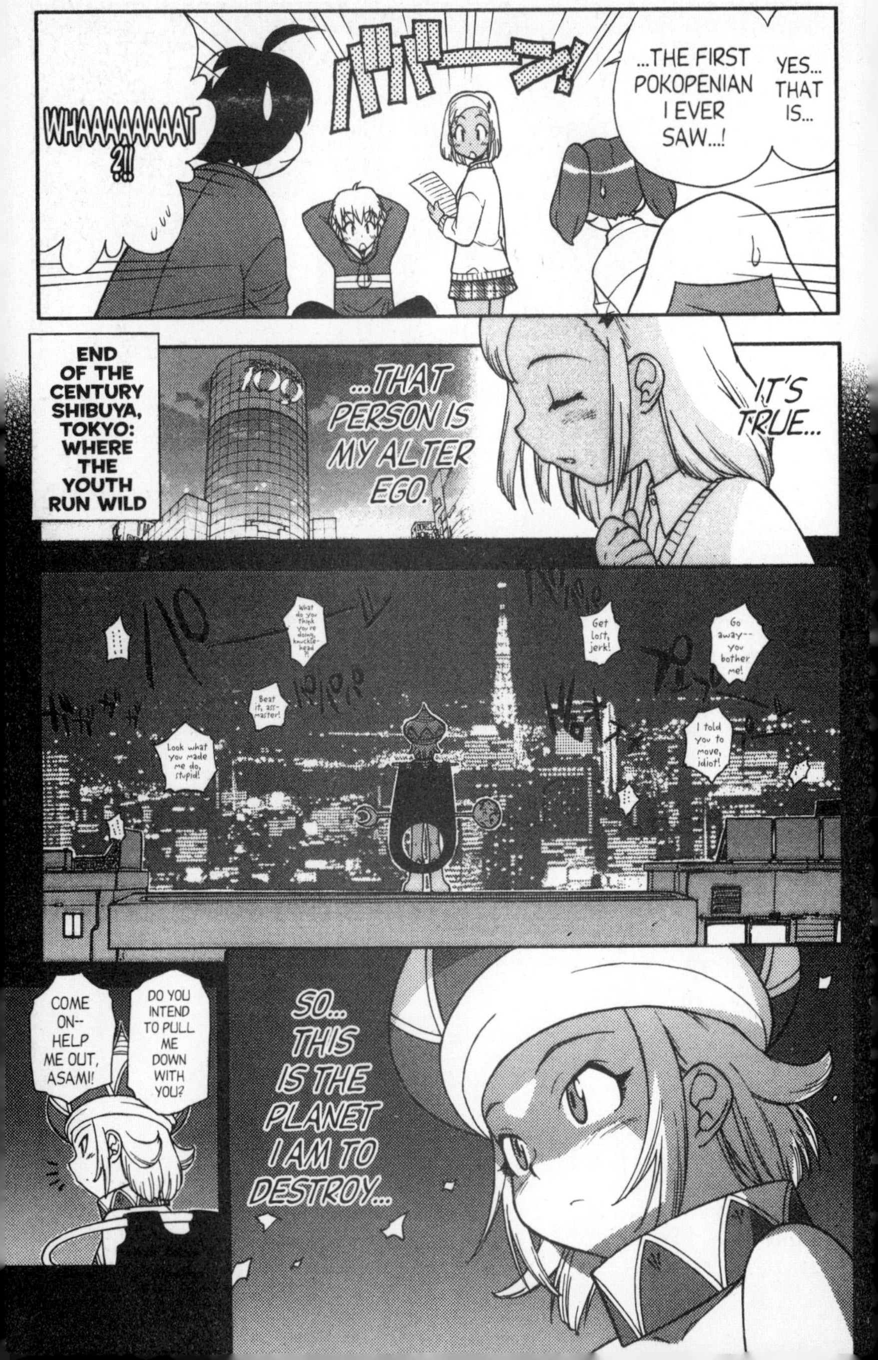
YES... THAT IS...
...THE FIRST POKOPENIAN I EVER SAW...!
WHAAAAAAAAT?!!
IT'S TRUE...
...THAT PERSON IS MY ALTER EGO.
END OF THE CENTURY SHIBUYA, TOKYO: WHERE THE YOUTH RUN WILD
Go away--you bother me!
Get lost, jerk!
What do you think you're doing, knuckle-head?!
I told you to move, idiot!
Beat it, ass-master!
Look what you made me do, stupid!
SO... THIS IS THE PLANET I AM TO DESTROY...
DO YOU INTEND TO PULL ME DOWN WITH YOU?
COME ON--HELP ME OUT, ASAMI!

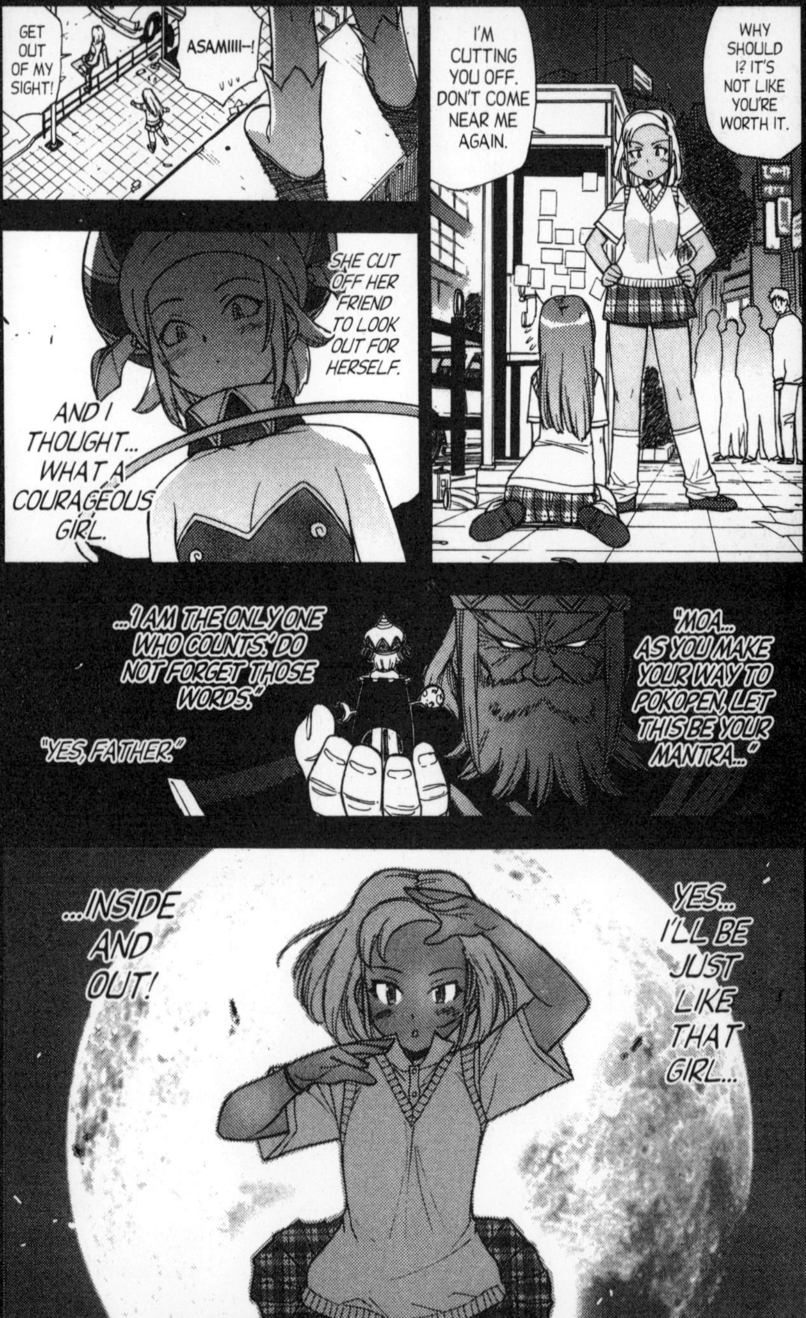
WHY SHOULD I? IT'S NOT LIKE YOU'RE WORTH IT.
I'M CUTTING YOU OFF. DON'T COME NEAR ME AGAIN.
ASAMIIII—!
GET OUT OF MY SIGHT!
SHE CUT OFF HER FRIEND TO LOOK OUT FOR HERSELF.
AND I THOUGHT... WHAT A COURAGEOUS GIRL.
"MOA... AS YOU MAKE YOUR WAY TO POKOPEN, LET THIS BE YOUR MANTRA..."
..."I AM THE ONLY ONE WHO COUNTS.' DO NOT FORGET THOSE WORDS."
"YES, FATHER."
YES... I'LL BE JUST LIKE THAT GIRL...
...INSIDE AND OUT!

REFER TO VOLUME ONE, ENCOUNTER X

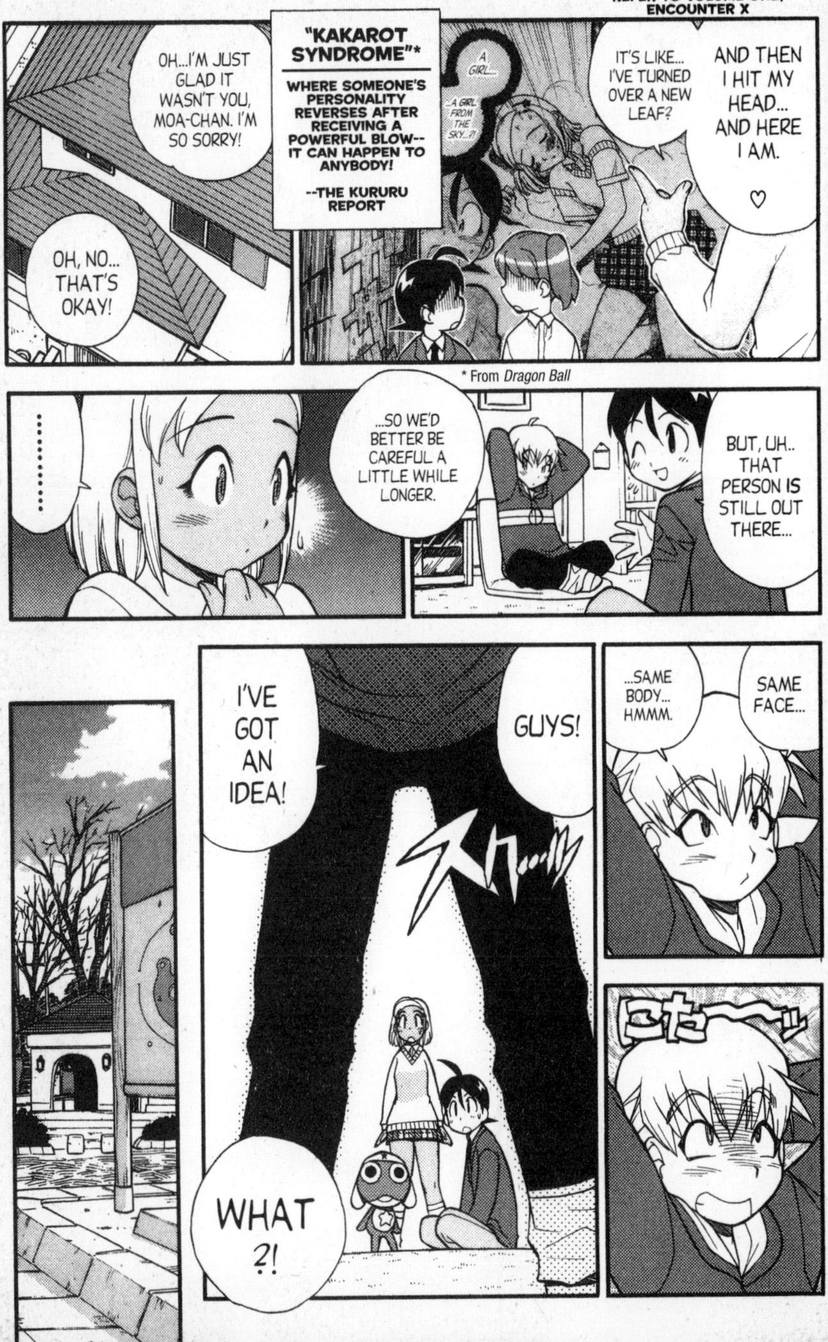
AND THEN I HIT MY HEAD... AND HERE I AM. ♡
IT'S LIKE... I'VE TURNED OVER A NEW LEAF?
A GIRL...
...A GIRL FROM THE SKY...?!
"KAKAROT SYNDROME"* WHERE SOMEONE'S PERSONALITY REVERSES AFTER RECEIVING A POWERFUL BLOW--IT CAN HAPPEN TO ANYBODY! --THE KURURU REPORT
OH...I'M JUST GLAD IT WASN'T YOU, MOA-CHAN. I'M SO SORRY!
OH, NO... THAT'S OKAY!
BUT, UH.. THAT PERSON IS STILL OUT THERE...
...SO WE'D BETTER BE CAREFUL A LITTLE WHILE LONGER.
....
SAME FACE...
...SAME BODY... HMMM.
にたーッ
GUYS!
I'VE GOT AN IDEA!
WHAT?!

* From *Dragon Ball*

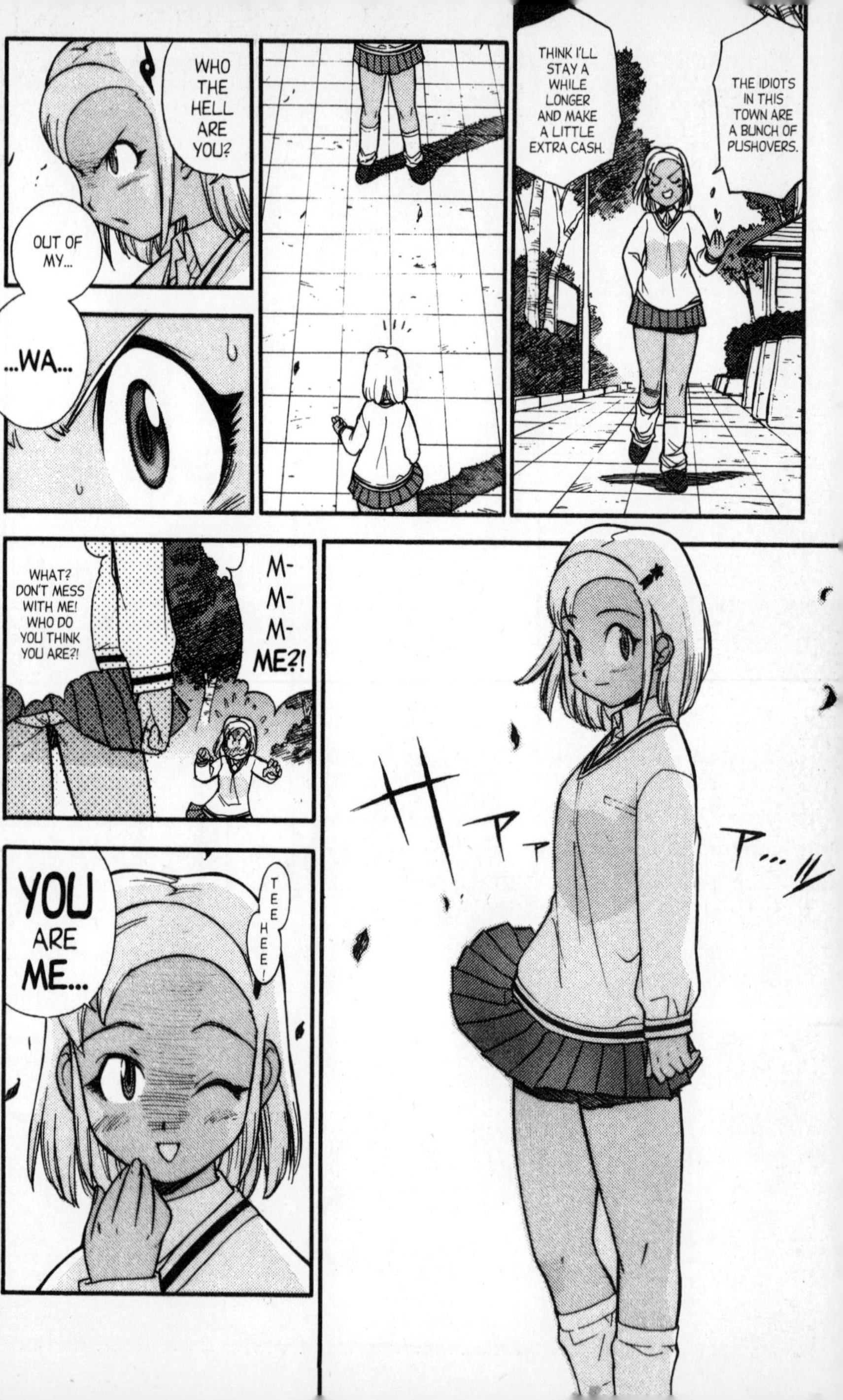
THE IDIOTS IN THIS TOWN ARE A BUNCH OF PUSHOVERS.
THINK I'LL STAY A WHILE LONGER AND MAKE A LITTLE EXTRA CASH.
WHO THE HELL ARE YOU?
OUT OF MY...
...WA...
M-M-M-ME?!
WHAT? DON'T MESS WITH ME! WHO DO YOU THINK YOU ARE?!
TEE HEE!
YOU ARE ME...

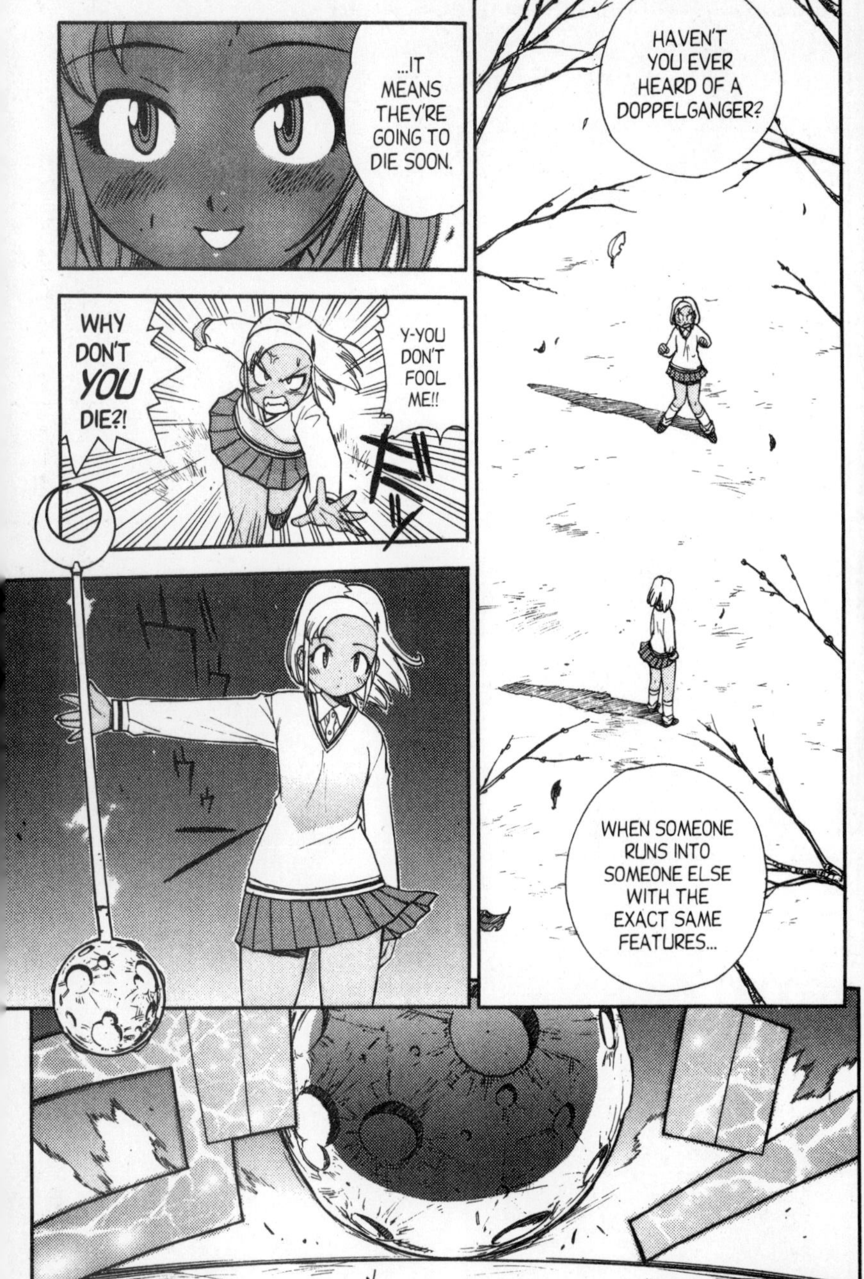
HAVEN'T YOU EVER HEARD OF A DOPPELGANGER?
WHEN SOMEONE RUNS INTO SOMEONE ELSE WITH THE EXACT SAME FEATURES...
...IT MEANS THEY'RE GOING TO DIE SOON.
Y-YOU DON'T FOOL ME!!
WHY DON'T *YOU* DIE?!

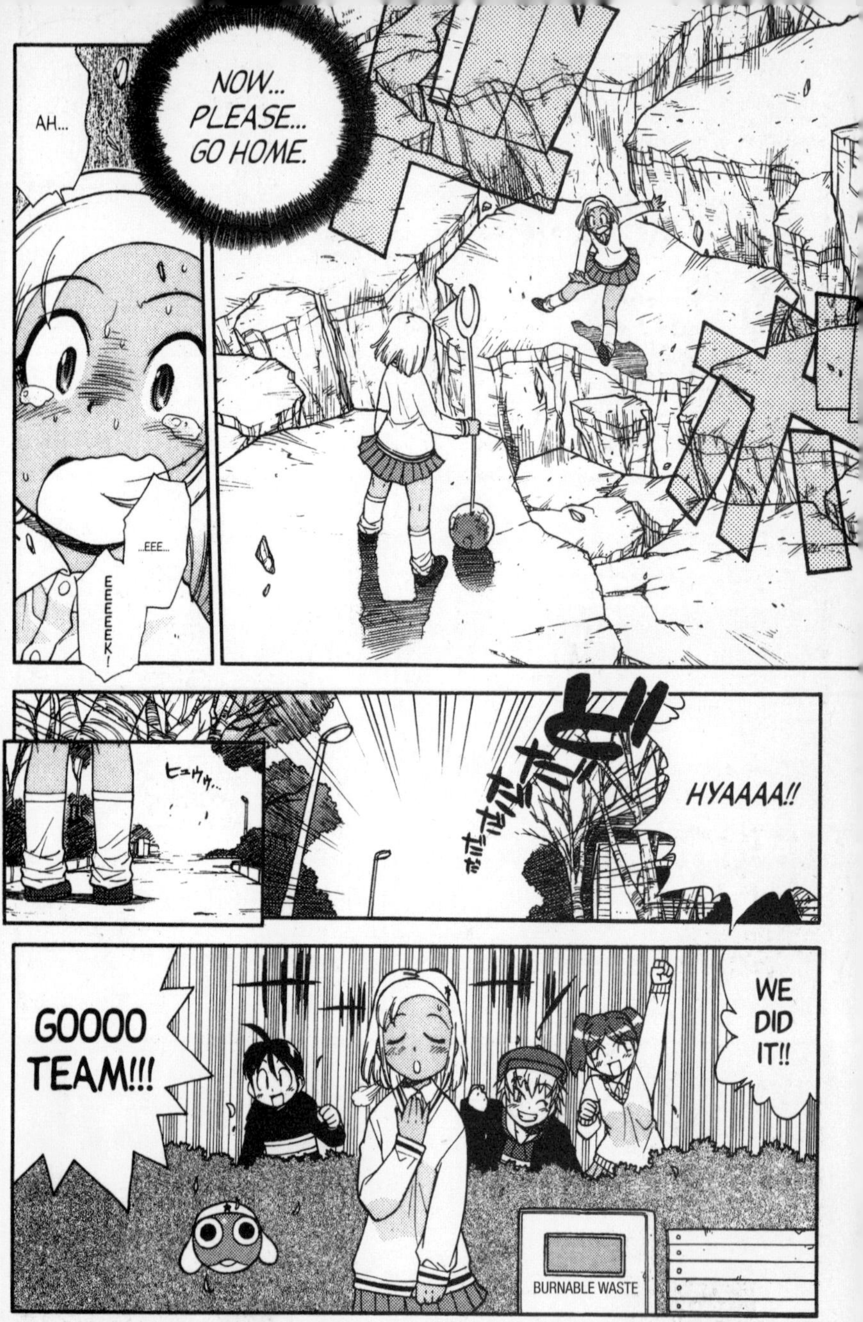
NOW... PLEASE... GO HOME.
AH...
...EEE...
EEEEEK!
HYAAAA!!
ヒュウゥ...
WE DID IT!!
GOOOO TEAM!!!
BURNABLE WASTE

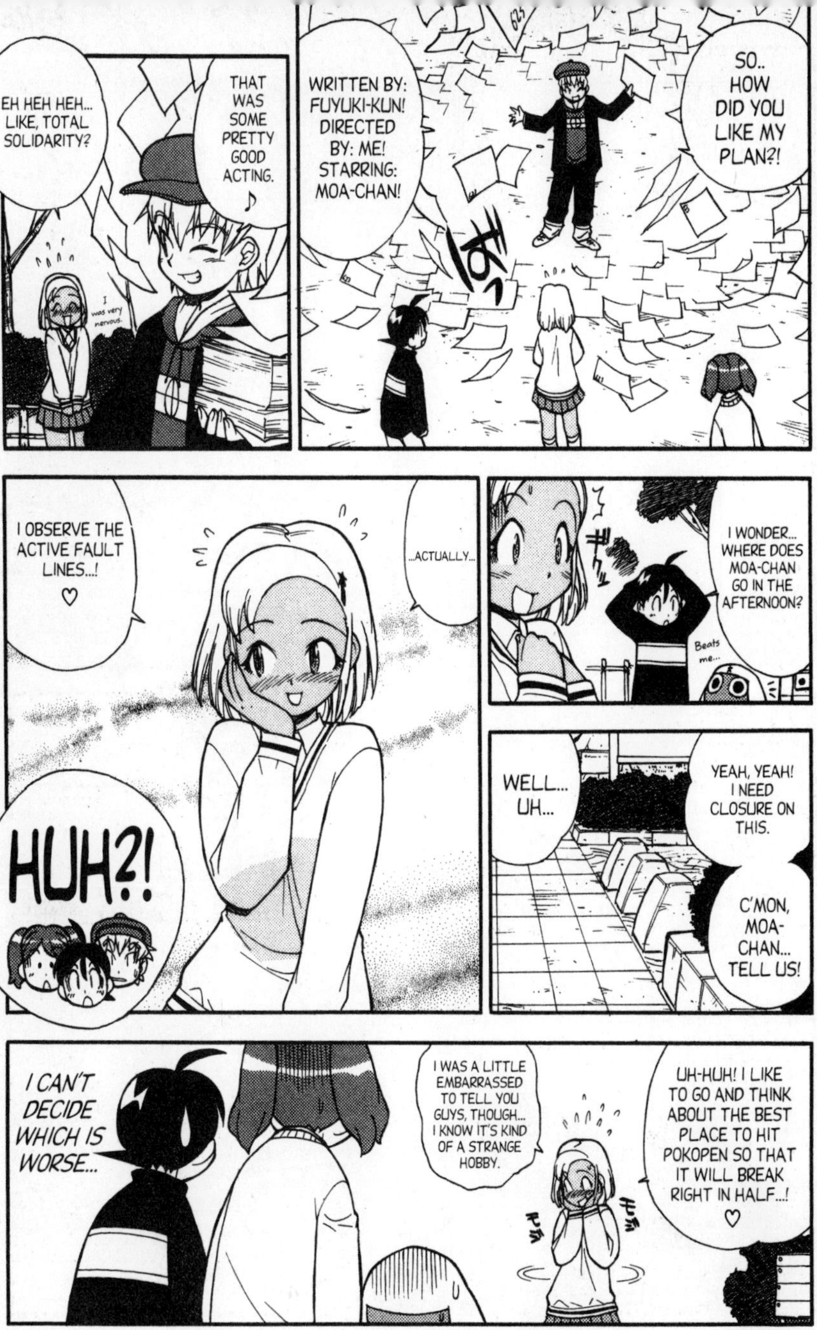
SO.. HOW DID YOU LIKE MY PLAN?!
WRITTEN BY: FUYUKI-KUN! DIRECTED BY: ME! STARRING: MOA-CHAN!
THAT WAS SOME PRETTY GOOD ACTING. ♪
EH HEH HEH... LIKE, TOTAL SOLIDARITY?
I was very nervous.
I WONDER... WHERE DOES MOA-CHAN GO IN THE AFTERNOON?
Beats me...
YEAH, YEAH! I NEED CLOSURE ON THIS.
C'MON, MOA-CHAN... TELL US!
WELL... UH...
...ACTUALLY...
I OBSERVE THE ACTIVE FAULT LINES...! ♡
HUH?!
UH-HUH! I LIKE TO GO AND THINK ABOUT THE BEST PLACE TO HIT POKOPEN SO THAT IT WILL BREAK RIGHT IN HALF...! ♡
I WAS A LITTLE EMBARRASSED TO TELL YOU GUYS, THOUGH... I KNOW IT'S KIND OF A STRANGE HOBBY.
I CAN'T DECIDE WHICH IS WORSE...

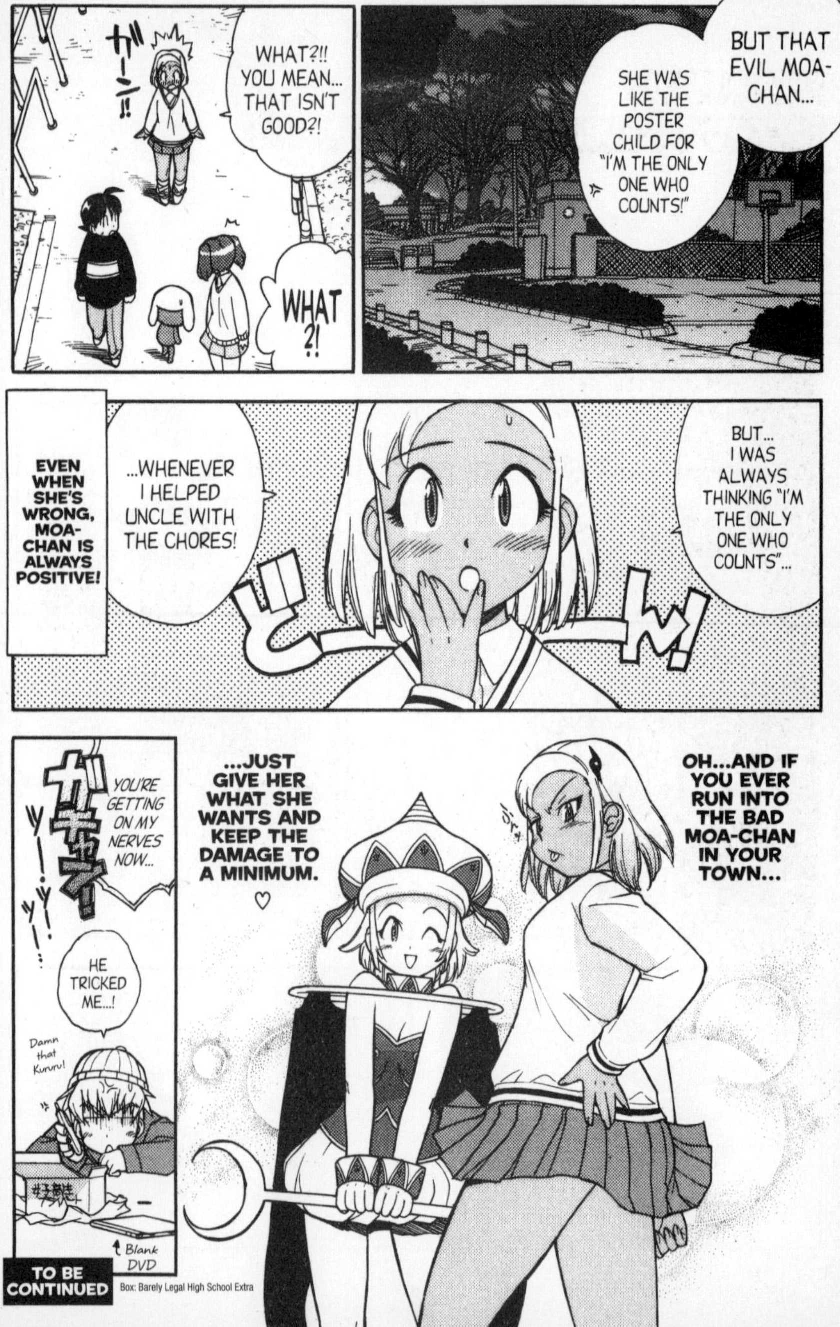
BUT THAT EVIL MOA-CHAN...
SHE WAS LIKE THE POSTER CHILD FOR "I'M THE ONLY ONE WHO COUNTS!"
WHAT?!! YOU MEAN... THAT ISN'T GOOD?!
WHAT ?!
BUT... I WAS ALWAYS THINKING "I'M THE ONLY ONE WHO COUNTS"...
...WHENEVER I HELPED UNCLE WITH THE CHORES!
EVEN WHEN SHE'S WRONG, MOA-CHAN IS ALWAYS POSITIVE!
OH...AND IF YOU EVER RUN INTO THE BAD MOA-CHAN IN YOUR TOWN...
...JUST GIVE HER WHAT SHE WANTS AND KEEP THE DAMAGE TO A MINIMUM. ♡
YOU'RE GETTING ON MY NERVES NOW...
HE TRICKED ME...!
Damn that Kururu!
Blank DVD
TO BE CONTINUED
Box: Barely Legal High School Extra

ENCOUNTER XLV
BACK TO THE SUBJECT--FORWARD MARCH!!

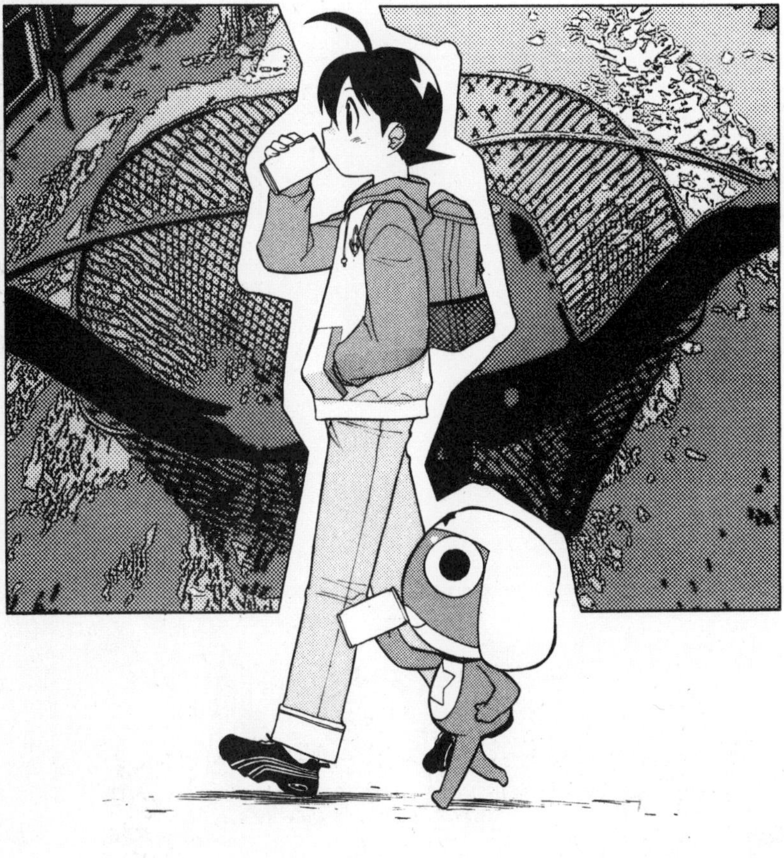

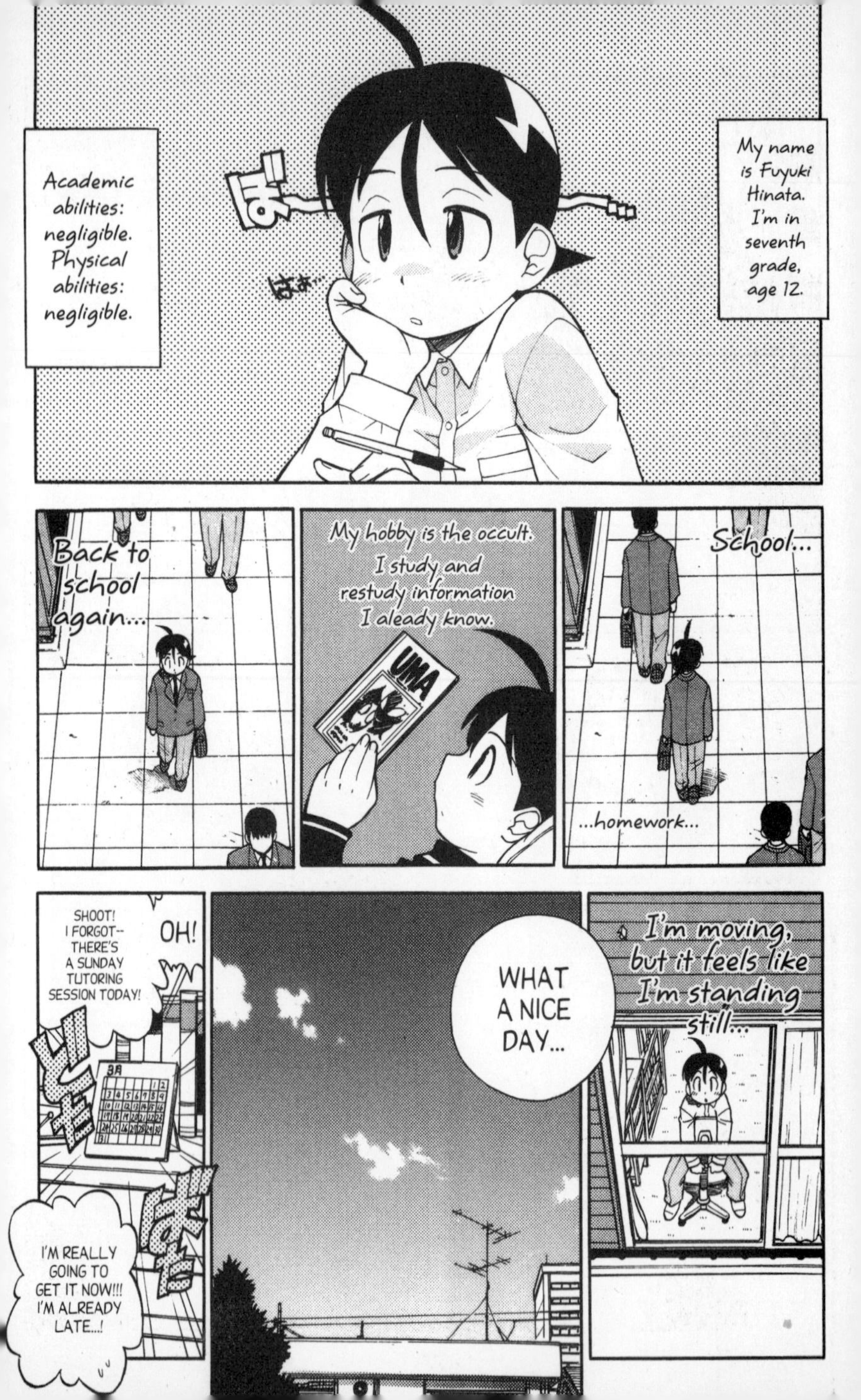
My name is Fuyuki Hinata. I'm in seventh grade, age 12.
Academic abilities: negligible. Physical abilities: negligible.
School...
...homework...
My hobby is the occult. I study and restudy information I aleady know.
UMA
Back to school again...
I'm moving, but it feels like I'm standing still...
WHAT A NICE DAY...
OH!
SHOOT! I FORGOT-- THERE'S A SUNDAY TUTORING SESSION TODAY!
I'M REALLY GOING TO GET IT NOW!!! I'M ALREADY LATE...!

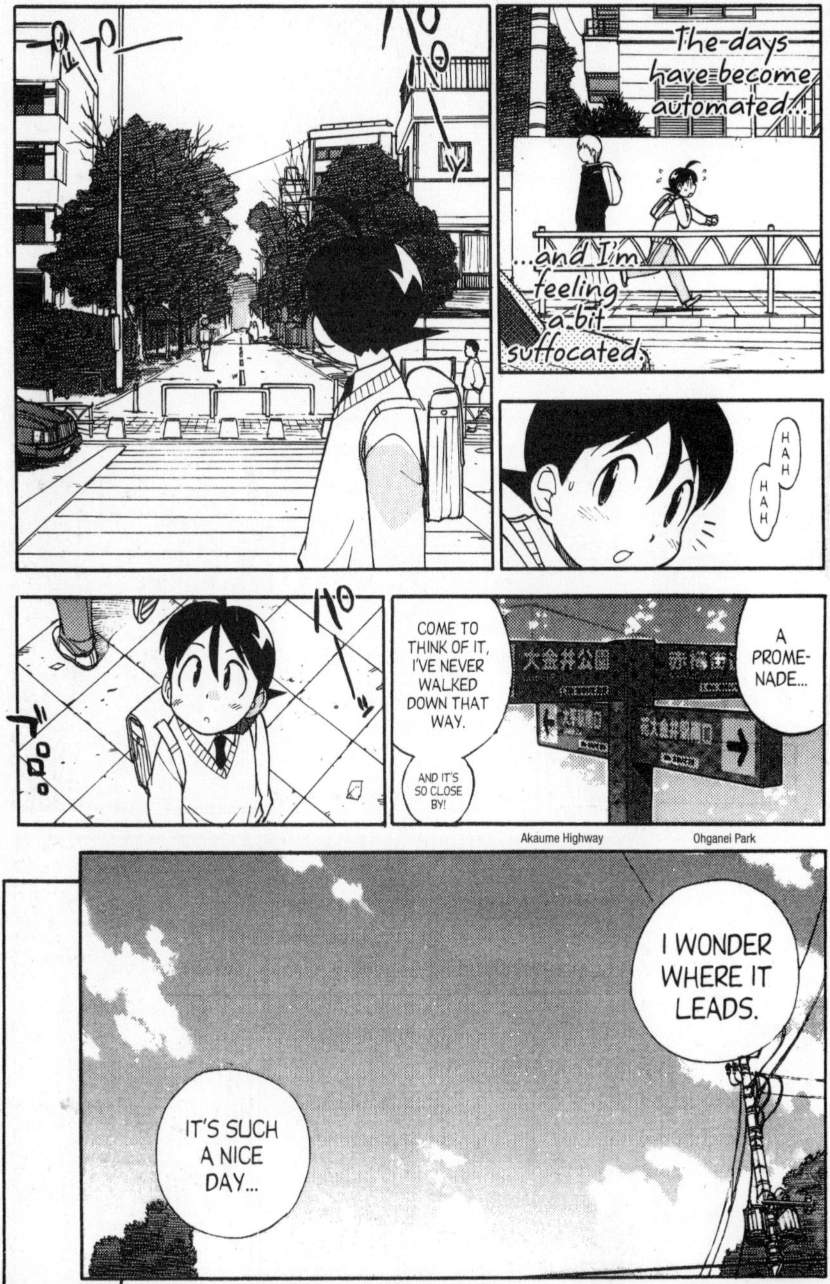
The days have become automated...
...and I'm feeling a bit suffocated.
HAH HAH
A PROMENADE...
COME TO THINK OF IT, I'VE NEVER WALKED DOWN THAT WAY.
AND IT'S SO CLOSE BY!
Akaume Highway
Ohganei Park
I WONDER WHERE IT LEADS.
IT'S SUCH A NICE DAY...

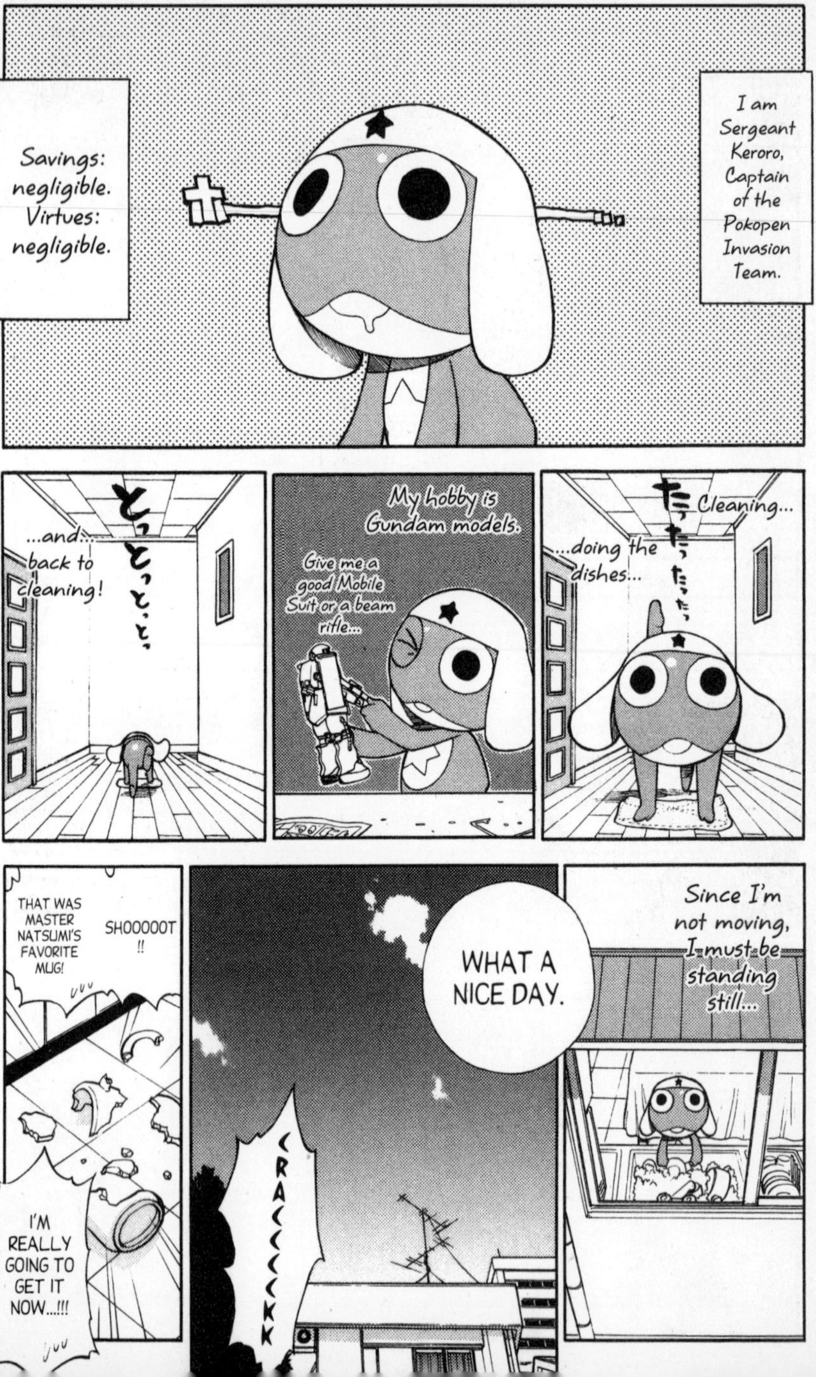
I am Sergeant Keroro, Captain of the Pokopen Invasion Team.
Savings: negligible. Virtues: negligible.
Cleaning...
...doing the dishes...
My hobby is Gundam models.
Give me a good Mobile Suit or a beam rifle...
...and... back to cleaning!
Since I'm not moving, I must be standing still...
WHAT A NICE DAY.
CRACCCCKK
SHOOOOOT !!
THAT WAS MASTER NATSUMI'S FAVORITE MUG!
I'M REALLY GOING TO GET IT NOW...!!!

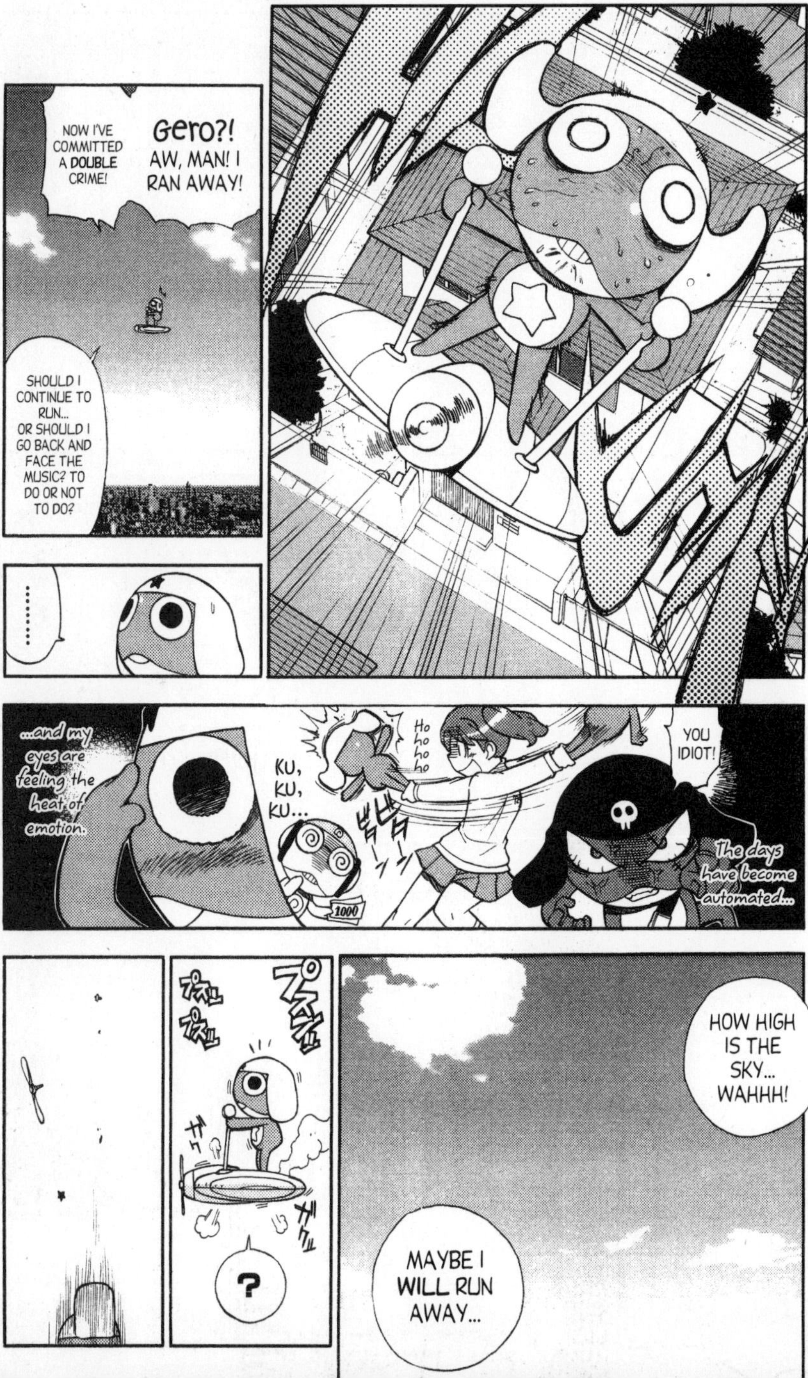
Gero?! AW, MAN! I RAN AWAY!
NOW I'VE COMMITTED A DOUBLE CRIME!
SHOULD I CONTINUE TO RUN... OR SHOULD I GO BACK AND FACE THE MUSIC? TO DO OR NOT TO DO?
....
The days have become automated...
YOU IDIOT!
Ho ho ho ho
KU, KU, KU...
1000
...and my eyes are feeling the heat of emotion.
HOW HIGH IS THE SKY... WAHHH!
MAYBE I WILL RUN AWAY...
?

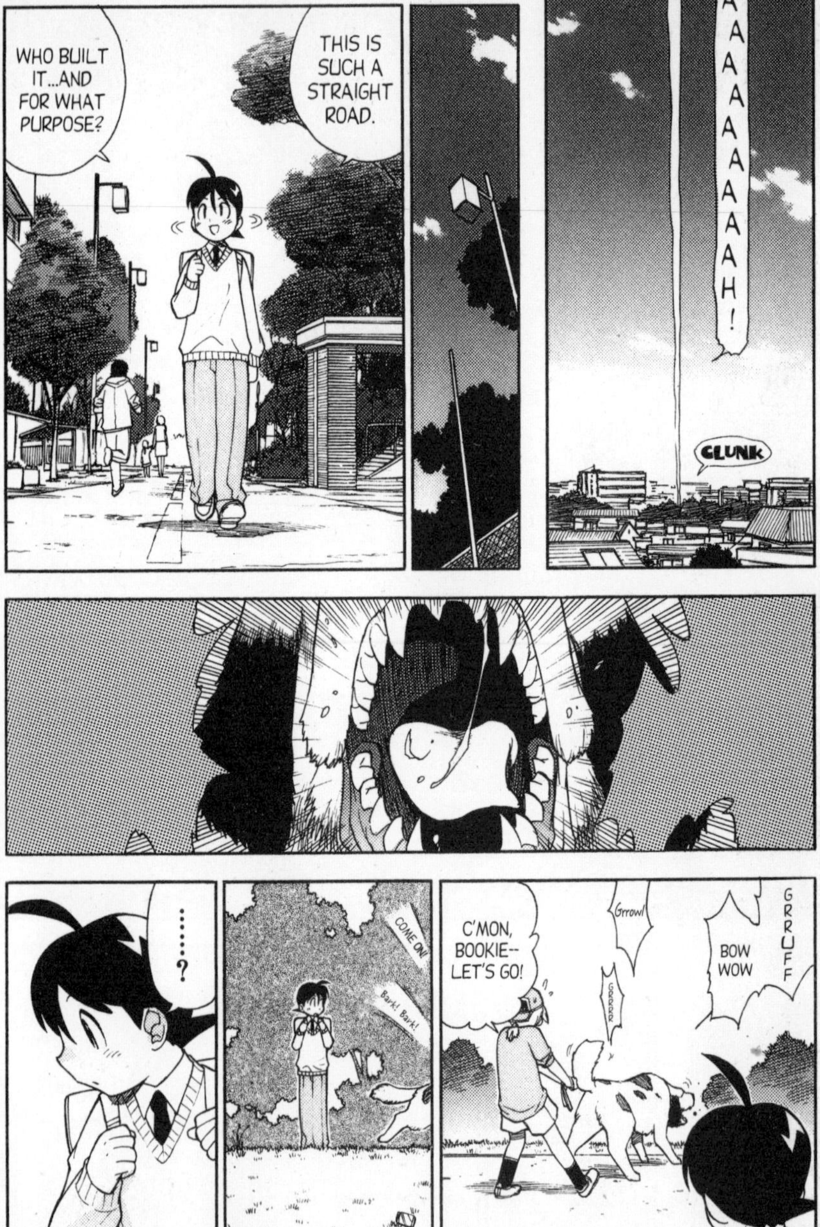
AAAAAAAAAAAH!
GLUNK
THIS IS SUCH A STRAIGHT ROAD.
WHO BUILT IT...AND FOR WHAT PURPOSE?
GRRUFF
BOW WOW
Grrowl
C'MON, BOOKIE--LET'S GO!
GRRRRR
COME ON!
Bark! Bark!
......?

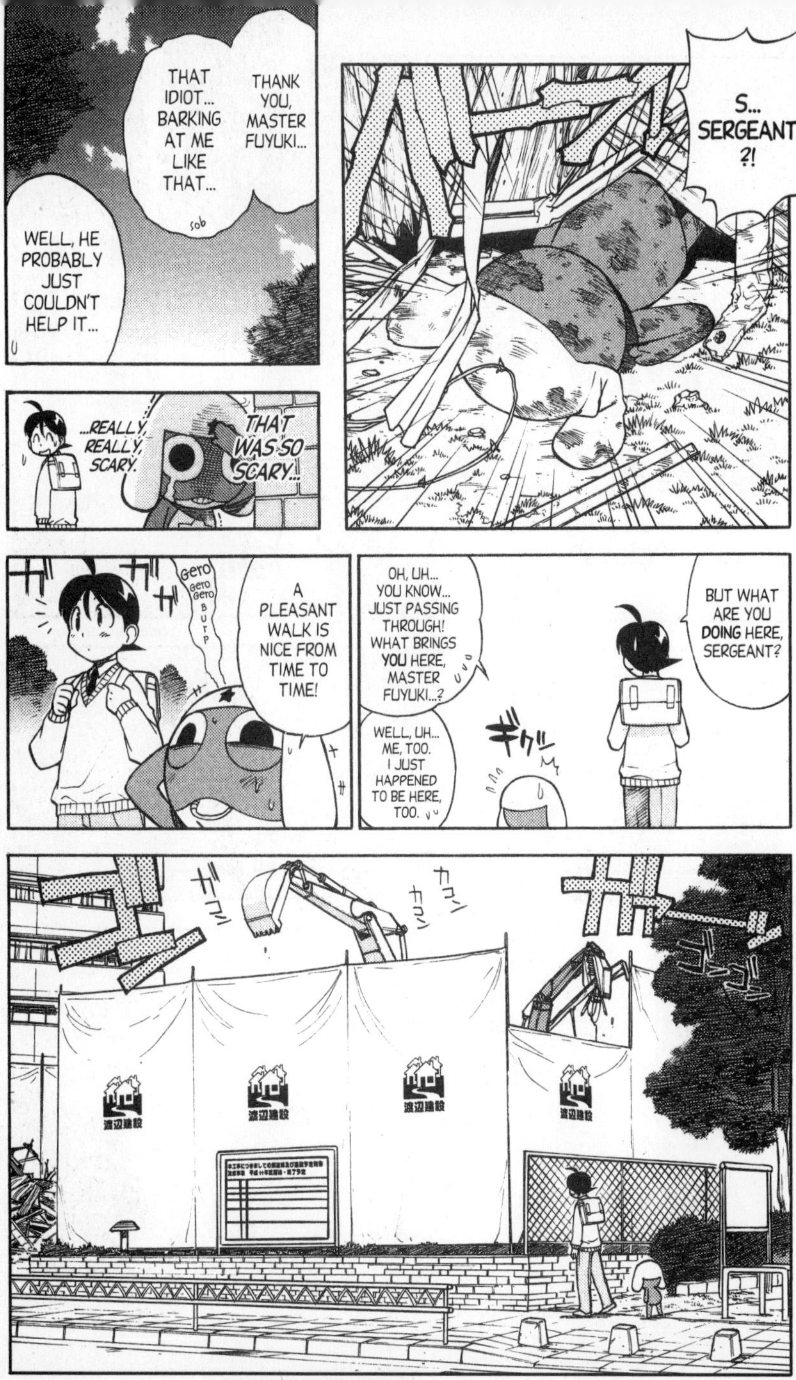
S... SERGEANT ?!
THANK YOU, MASTER FUYUKI...
THAT IDIOT... BARKING AT ME LIKE THAT...
sob
WELL, HE PROBABLY JUST COULDN'T HELP IT...
THAT WAS SO SCARY...
...REALLY, REALLY, SCARY.
BUT WHAT ARE YOU DOING HERE, SERGEANT?
OH, UH... YOU KNOW... JUST PASSING THROUGH! WHAT BRINGS YOU HERE, MASTER FUYUKI...?
WELL, UH... ME, TOO. I JUST HAPPENED TO BE HERE, TOO.
A PLEASANT WALK IS NICE FROM TIME TO TIME!
Gero Gero Gero Burp
渡辺建設
渡辺建設
渡辺建設
渡辺建設
WATANABE CONSTRUCTION

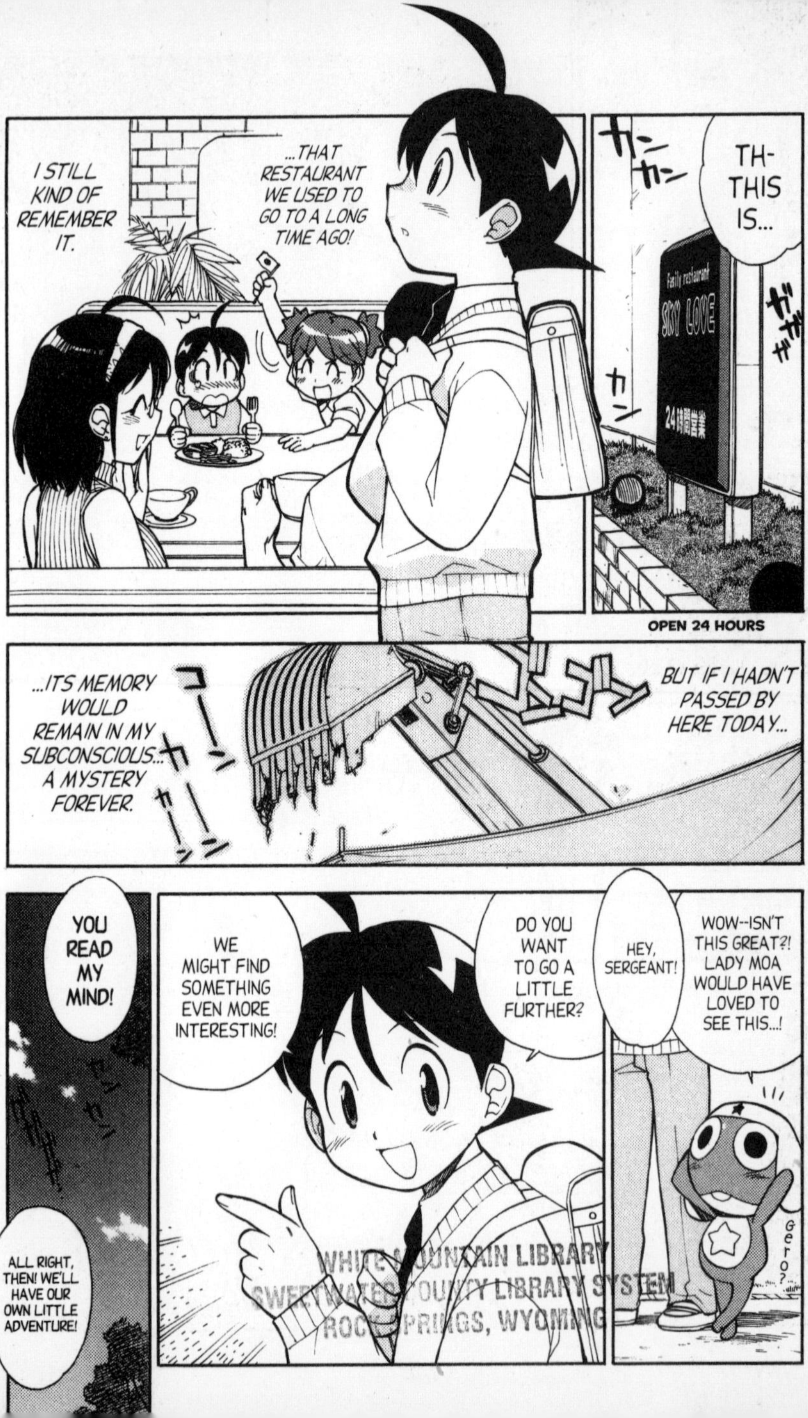
TH- THIS IS...
Family restaurant
SKY LOVE
24時間営業
OPEN 24 HOURS
...THAT RESTAURANT WE USED TO GO TO A LONG TIME AGO!
I STILL KIND OF REMEMBER IT.
BUT IF I HADN'T PASSED BY HERE TODAY...
...ITS MEMORY WOULD REMAIN IN MY SUBCONSCIOUS... A MYSTERY FOREVER.
WOW--ISN'T THIS GREAT?! LADY MOA WOULD HAVE LOVED TO SEE THIS...!
HEY, SERGEANT!
Gero?
DO YOU WANT TO GO A LITTLE FURTHER?
WE MIGHT FIND SOMETHING EVEN MORE INTERESTING!
YOU READ MY MIND!
ALL RIGHT, THEN! WE'LL HAVE OUR OWN LITTLE ADVENTURE!

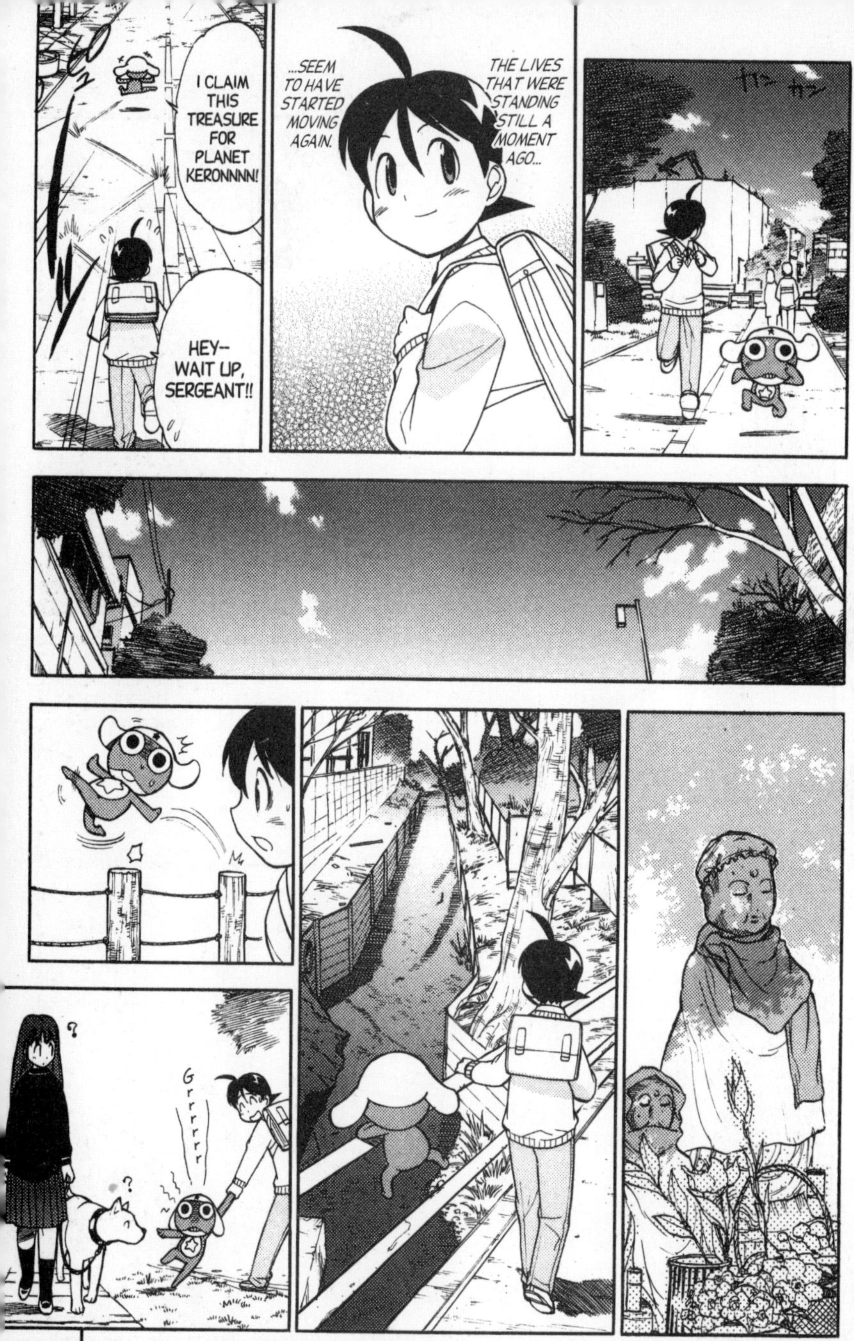
THE LIVES THAT WERE STANDING STILL A MOMENT AGO...
...SEEM TO HAVE STARTED MOVING AGAIN.
I CLAIM THIS TREASURE FOR PLANET KERONNNN!
HEY-- WAIT UP, SERGEANT!!
Grrrrrr

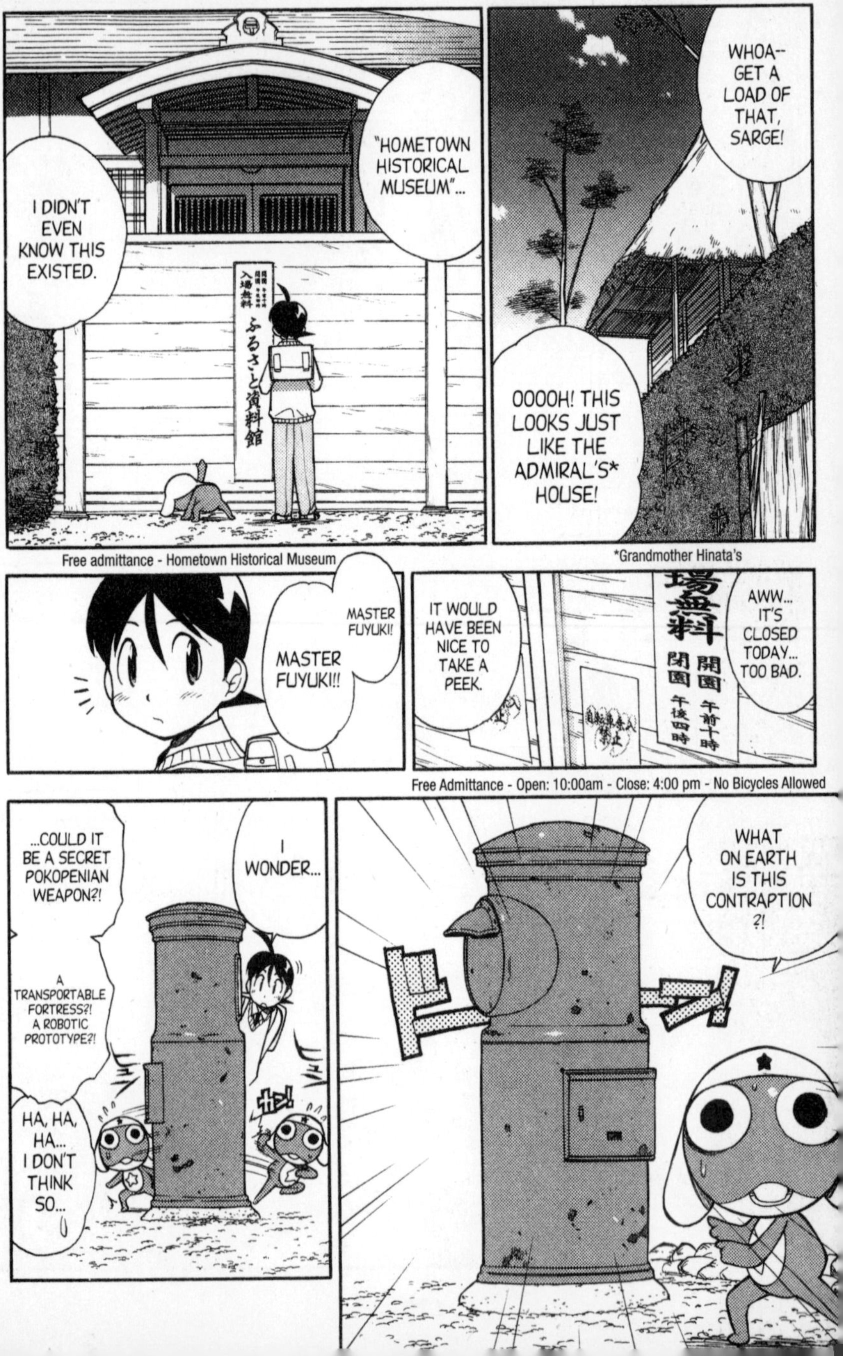
WHOA-- GET A LOAD OF THAT, SARGE!
OOOOH! THIS LOOKS JUST LIKE THE ADMIRAL'S* HOUSE!
*Grandmother Hinata's
"HOMETOWN HISTORICAL MUSEUM"...
I DIDN'T EVEN KNOW THIS EXISTED.
入場無料
ふるさと資料館
Free admittance - Hometown Historical Museum
AWW... IT'S CLOSED TODAY... TOO BAD.
IT WOULD HAVE BEEN NICE TO TAKE A PEEK.
Free Admittance - Open: 10:00am - Close: 4:00 pm - No Bicycles Allowed
MASTER FUYUKI!
MASTER FUYUKI!!
WHAT ON EARTH IS THIS CONTRAPTION?!
I WONDER...
...COULD IT BE A SECRET POKOPENIAN WEAPON?!
A TRANSPORTABLE FORTRESS?! A ROBOTIC PROTOTYPE?!
HA, HA, HA... I DON'T THINK SO...

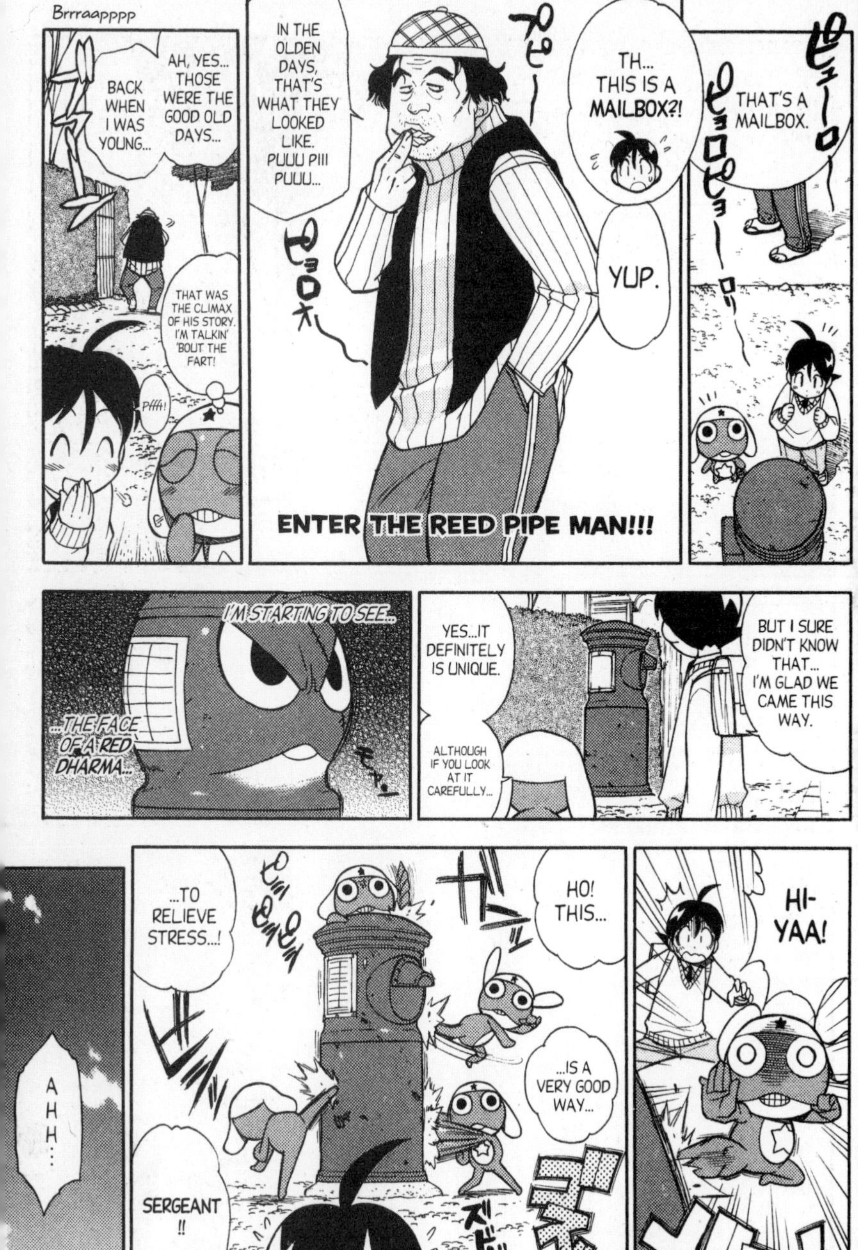
THAT'S A MAILBOX.
TH... THIS IS A MAILBOX?!
YUP.
IN THE OLDEN DAYS, THAT'S WHAT THEY LOOKED LIKE. PUUU PIII PUUU...
ENTER THE REED PIPE MAN!!!
Brrraapppp
AH, YES... THOSE WERE THE GOOD OLD DAYS...
BACK WHEN I WAS YOUNG...
THAT WAS THE CLIMAX OF HIS STORY. I'M TALKIN' 'BOUT THE FART!
PFFF!
BUT I SURE DIDN'T KNOW THAT... I'M GLAD WE CAME THIS WAY.
YES...IT DEFINITELY IS UNIQUE.
ALTHOUGH IF YOU LOOK AT IT CAREFULLY...
I'M STARTING TO SEE...
...THE FACE OF A RED DHARMA...
HI-YAA!
HO! THIS...
...IS A VERY GOOD WAY...
...TO RELIEVE STRESS...!
SERGEANT !!
AHH...

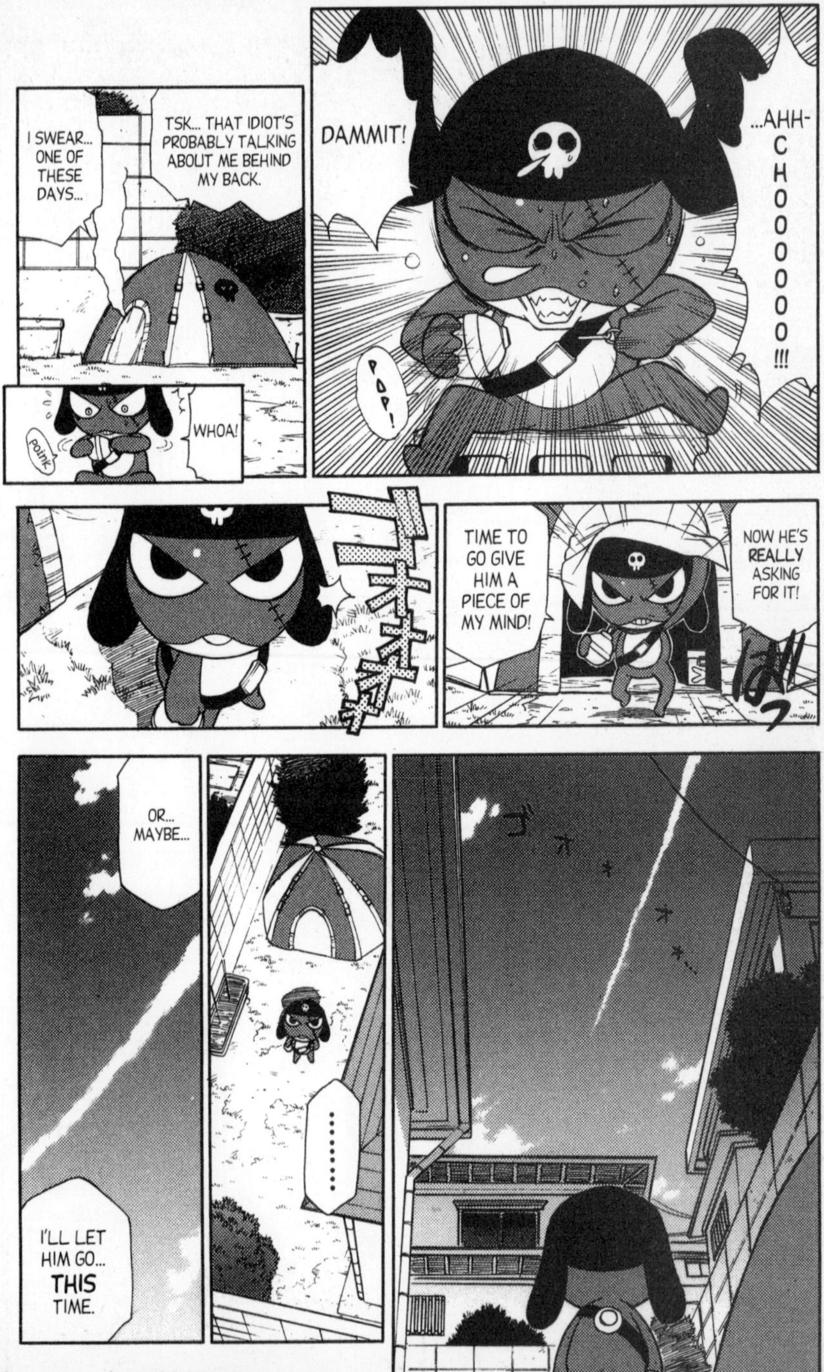
...AHH-CHOOOOOOO!!!
DAMMIT!
POP!
TSK... THAT IDIOT'S PROBABLY TALKING ABOUT ME BEHIND MY BACK.
I SWEAR... ONE OF THESE DAYS...
WHOA!
poink
NOW HE'S REALLY ASKING FOR IT!
TIME TO GO GIVE HIM A PIECE OF MY MIND!
....
OR... MAYBE...
I'LL LET HIM GO... THIS TIME.

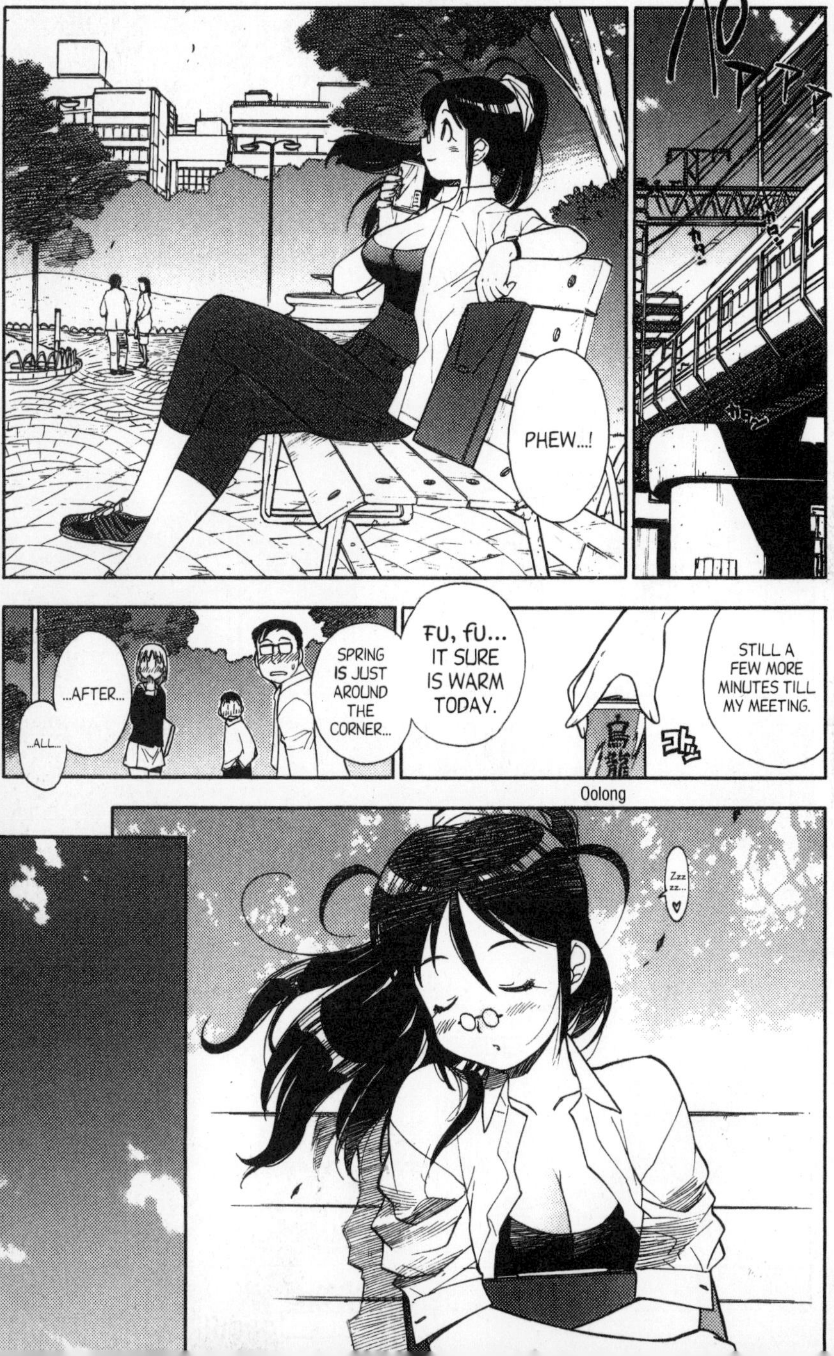
PHEW...!
STILL A FEW MORE MINUTES TILL MY MEETING.
烏龍
FU, FU... IT SURE IS WARM TODAY.
SPRING IS JUST AROUND THE CORNER...
...AFTER...
...ALL...
Oolong
Zzz zz... ♥

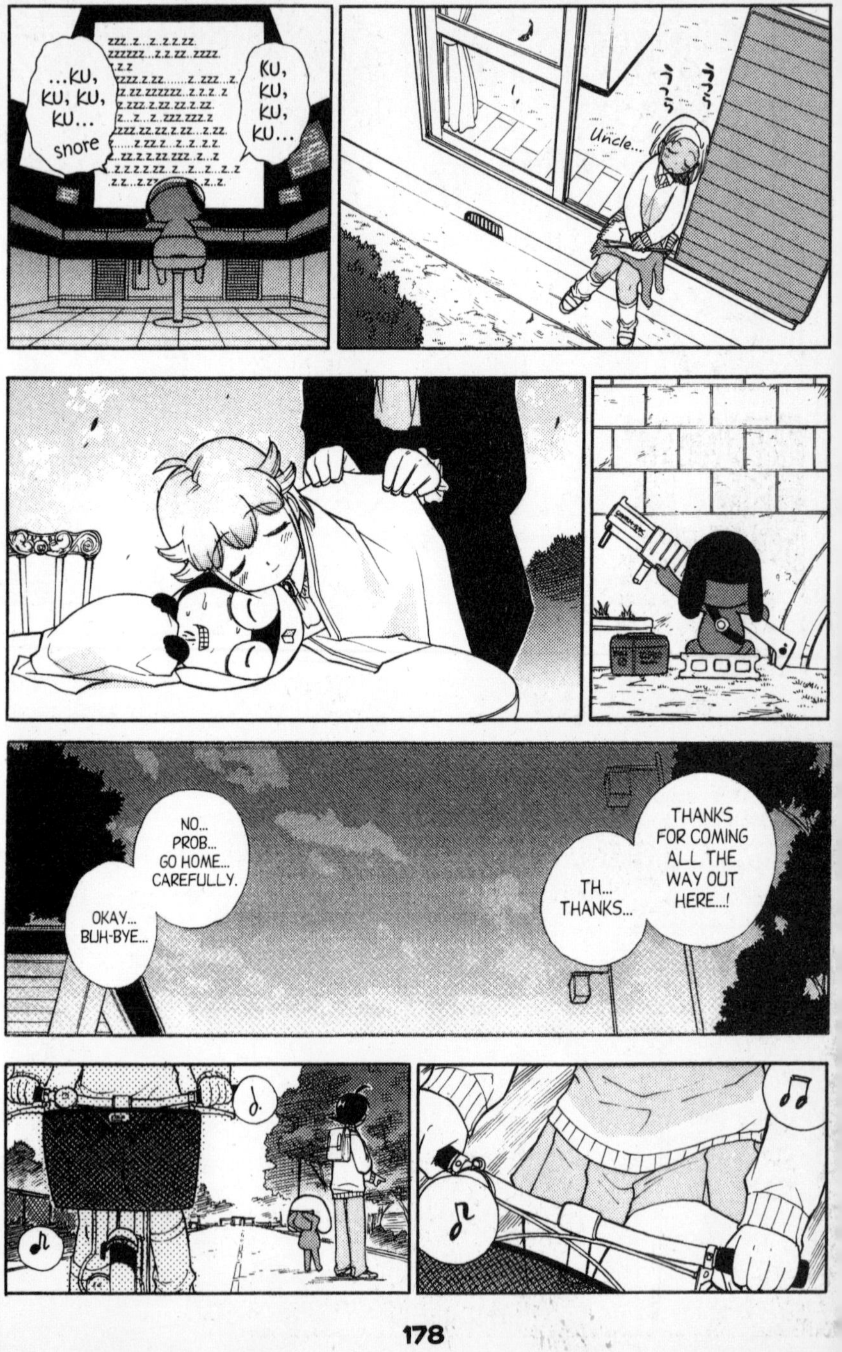
うつら うつら
Uncle...
KU, KU, KU, KU...
...KU, KU, KU, KU... snore
THANKS FOR COMING ALL THE WAY OUT HERE...!
TH... THANKS...
NO... PROB... GO HOME... CAREFULLY.
OKAY... BUH-BYE...

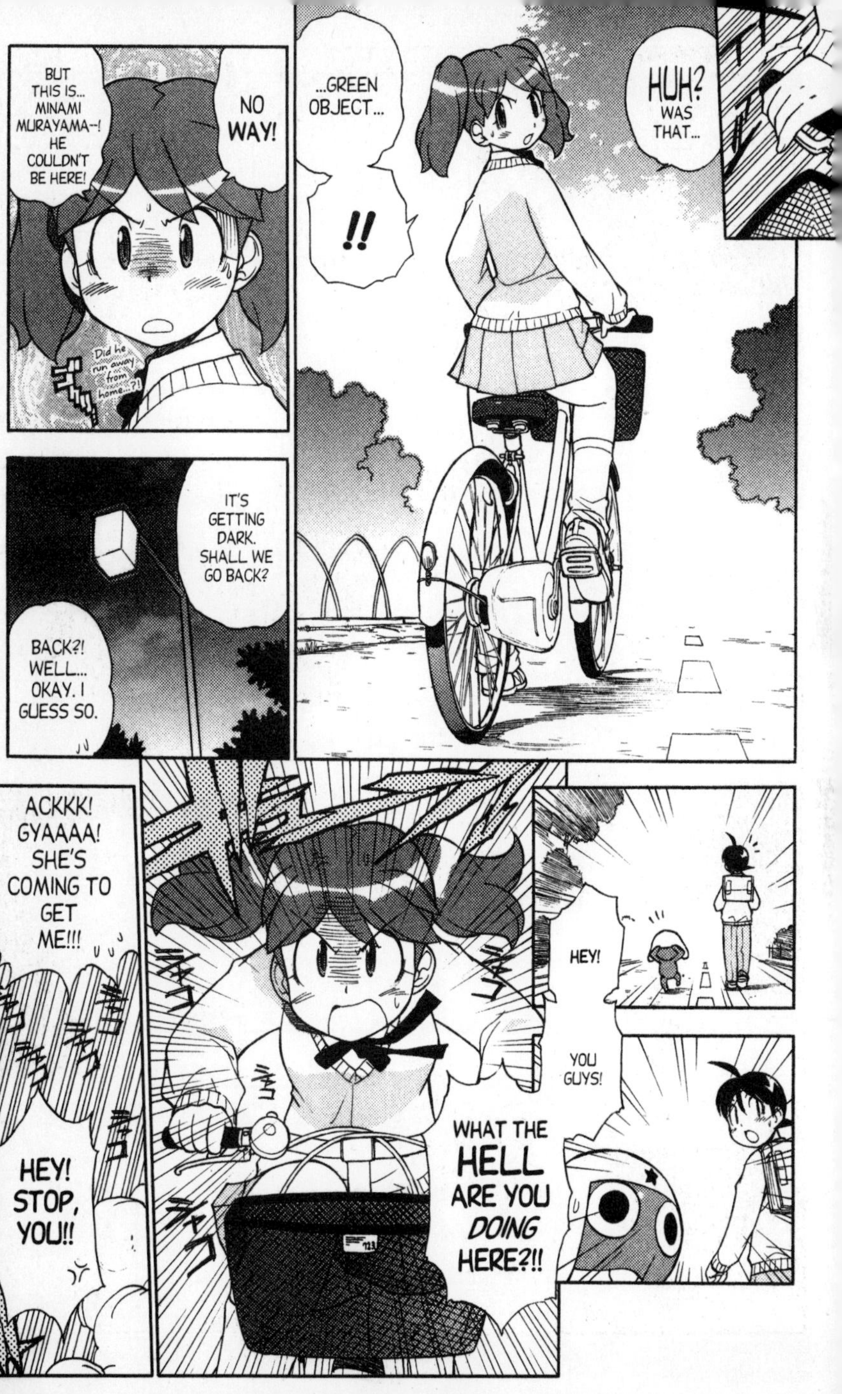
HUH? WAS THAT...
...GREEN OBJECT...
!!
NO WAY!
BUT THIS IS... MINAMI MURAYAMA--! HE COULDN'T BE HERE!
Did he run away from home...?!
IT'S GETTING DARK. SHALL WE GO BACK?
BACK?! WELL... OKAY. I GUESS SO.
HEY!
YOU GUYS!
WHAT THE HELL ARE YOU DOING HERE?!!
ACKKK! GYAAAA! SHE'S COMING TO GET ME!!!
HEY! STOP, YOU!!

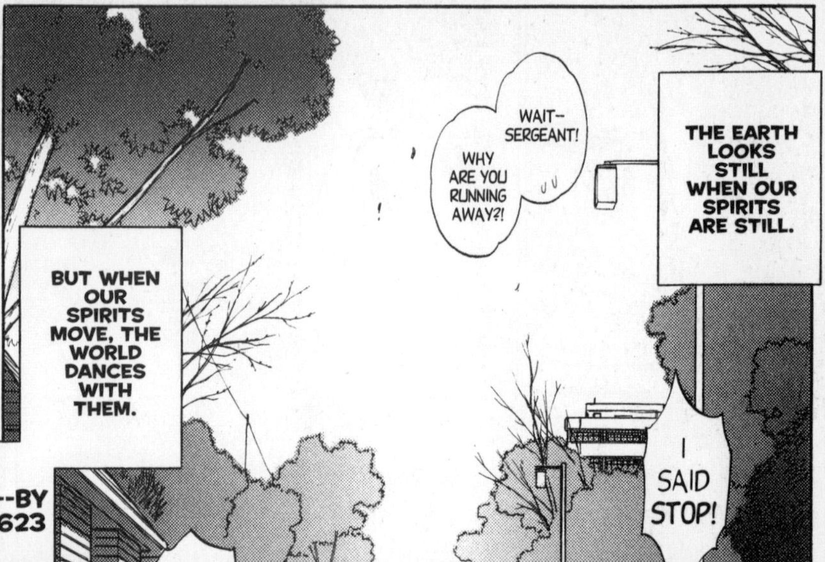
THE EARTH LOOKS STILL WHEN OUR SPIRITS ARE STILL.
WAIT-- SERGEANT!
WHY ARE YOU RUNNING AWAY?!
BUT WHEN OUR SPIRITS MOVE, THE WORLD DANCES WITH THEM.
--BY 623
I SAID STOP!
SHE'S GONNA KILL MEEEE !!
WHAT ARE YOU TALKING ABOUT ?!

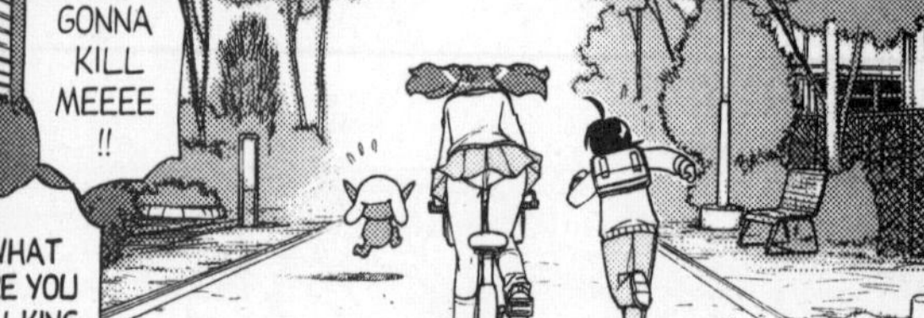

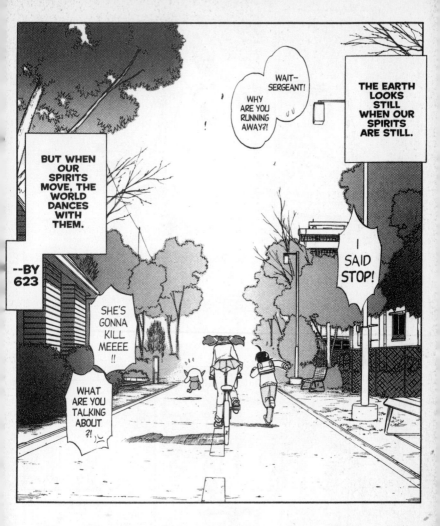

TO BE CONTINUED

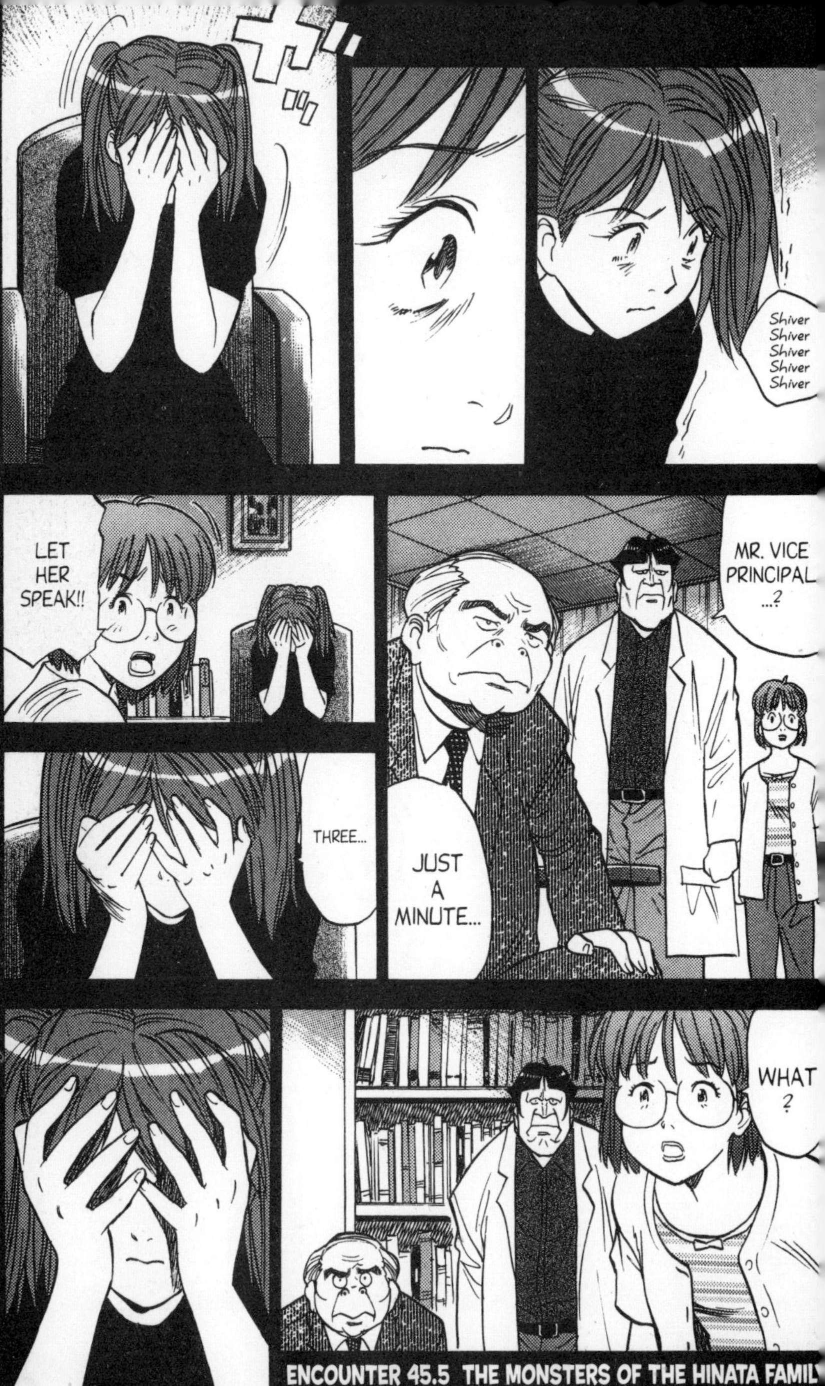
Shiver Shiver Shiver Shiver Shiver
MR. VICE PRINCIPAL ...?
JUST A MINUTE...
LET HER SPEAK!!
THREE...
WHAT?

ENCOUNTER 45.5 THE MONSTERS OF THE HINATA FAMILY

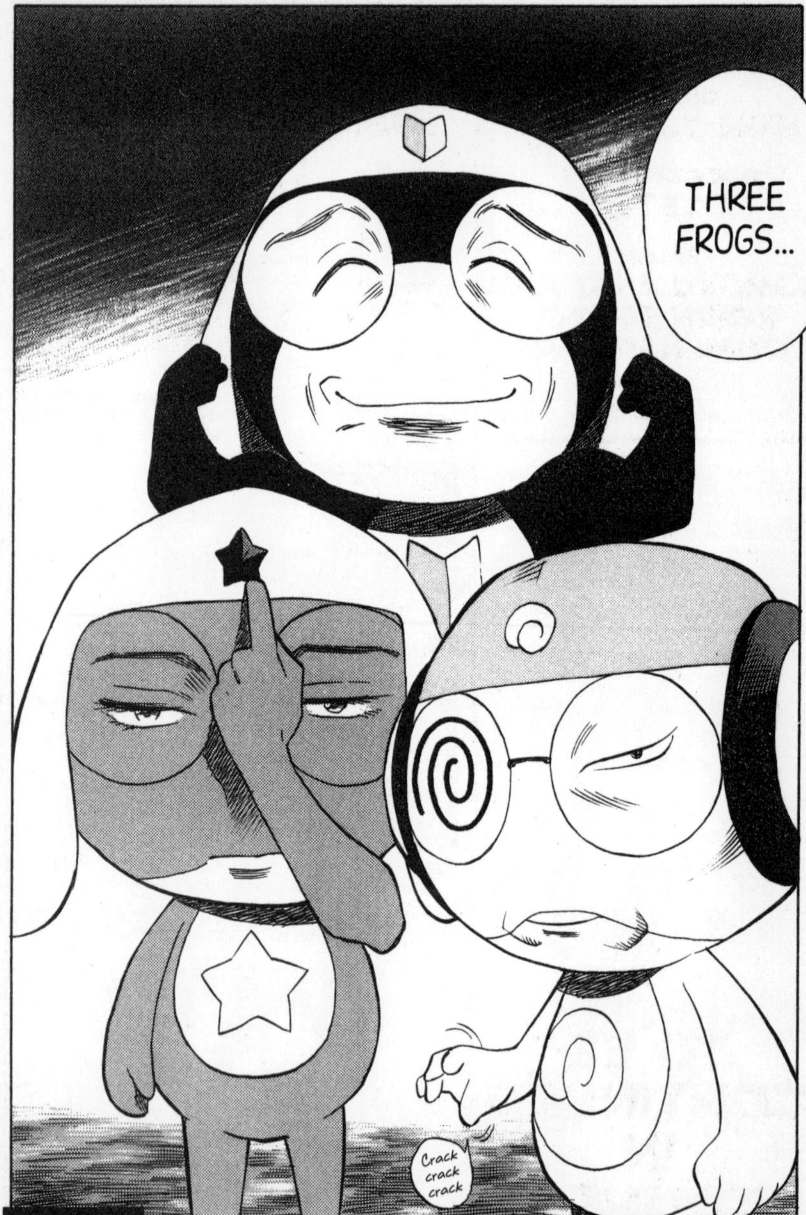
THREE FROGS...
Crack crack crack
TO BE CONTINUED

JAPAN STAFF

CREATOR
MINE YOSHIZAKI

BACKGROUNDS
OYSTER

FINISH
GOMOKU AKATSUKI
ROBIN TOKYO
TONMI NARIHARA

TO BE CONTINUED IN VOLUME 6

GHOST-CHAN WITH RED GOBLIN & BLUE GOBLIN

TOKYOPOP PRESS

LOS ANGELES • TOKYO • LONDON • HAMBURG

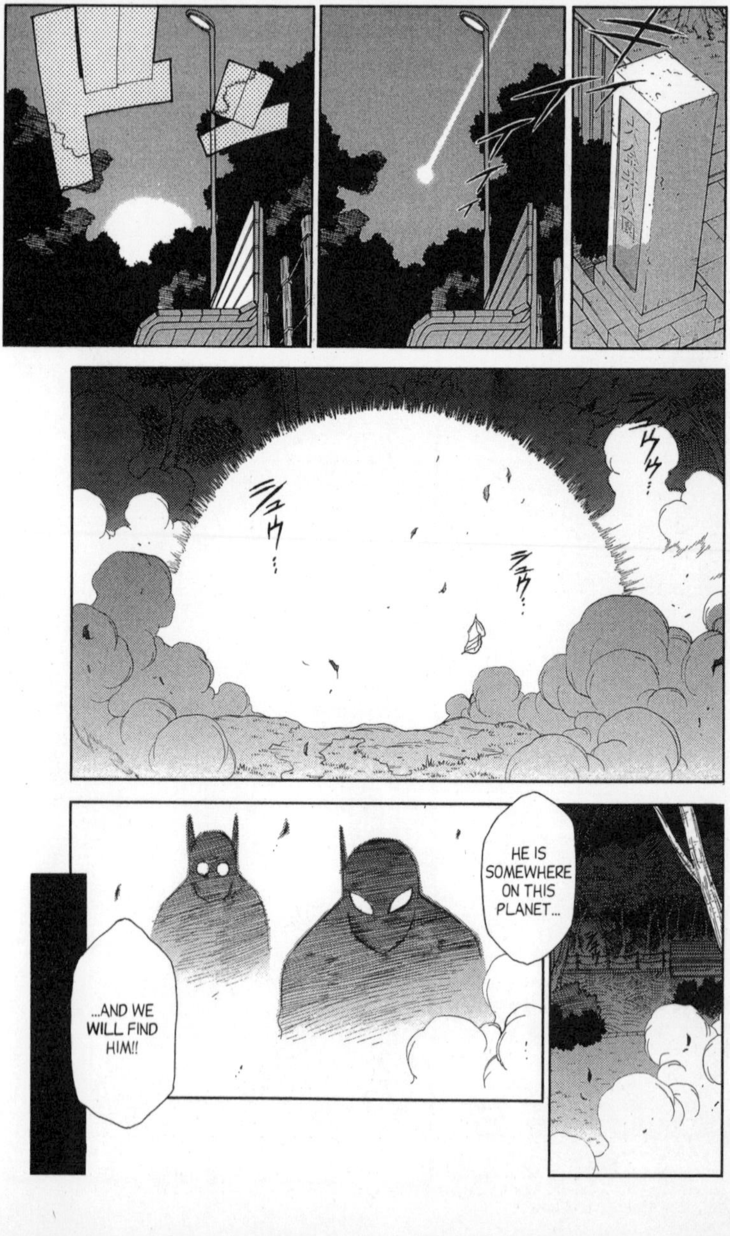

HE IS SOMEWHERE ON THIS PLANET...
...AND WE WILL FIND HIM!!

TOKYOPOP PRESS

LOS ANGELES • TOKYO • LONDON • HAMBURG

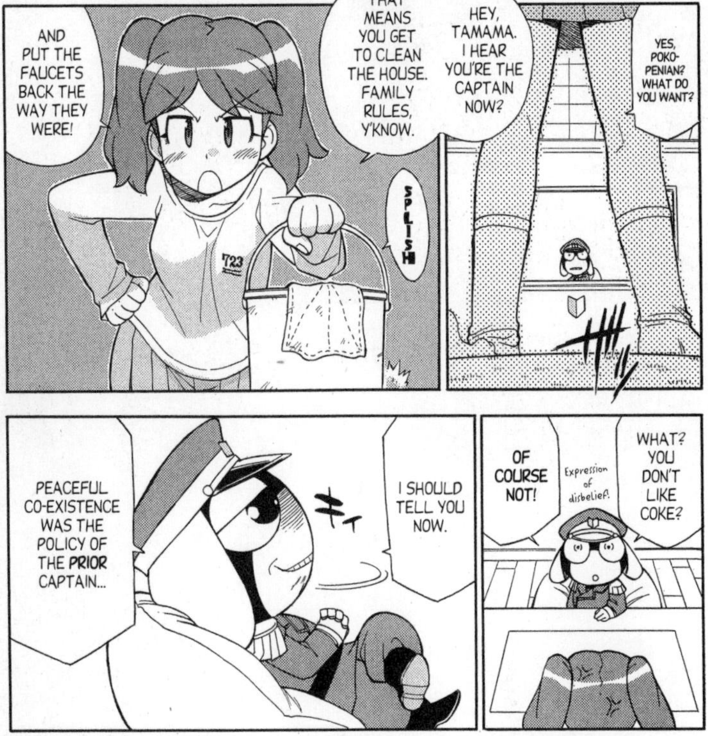
HEY, TAMAMA. I HEAR YOU'RE THE CAPTAIN NOW?
YES, POKO-PENIAN? WHAT DO YOU WANT?
THAT MEANS YOU GET TO CLEAN THE HOUSE. FAMILY RULES, Y'KNOW.
AND PUT THE FAUCETS BACK THE WAY THEY WERE!
SPLISH
WHAT? YOU DON'T LIKE COKE?
Expression of disbelief!
OF COURSE NOT!
I SHOULD TELL YOU NOW.
PEACEFUL CO-EXISTENCE WAS THE POLICY OF THE PRIOR CAPTAIN...

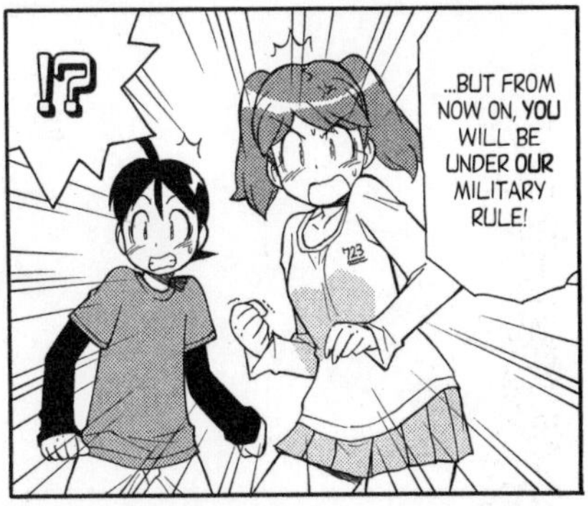
...BUT FROM NOW ON, YOU WILL BE UNDER OUR MILITARY RULE!
!?

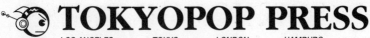

NEXT IN VOLUME 6 OF

SGT FROG

KERORO GUNSO

IN STORES THE MONTH OF JANUARY!

REBEL RIBBIT!

Alien Invasion x2!

It's an intergalactic battle for the planet when Keroro and company come under attack by a mysterious man and his sidekick. Will our fearless froggy fighters be able to hold down their lily pads? Later, an inexplicable order from the higher ups makes Tamama the new leader! The maniacal mutant mutiny continues as someone steals Giroro's trusty belt...leaving him caught with his pants down!

COMIC PARTY™

Behind-the-scenes with artistic dreams and unconventional love at a comic convention

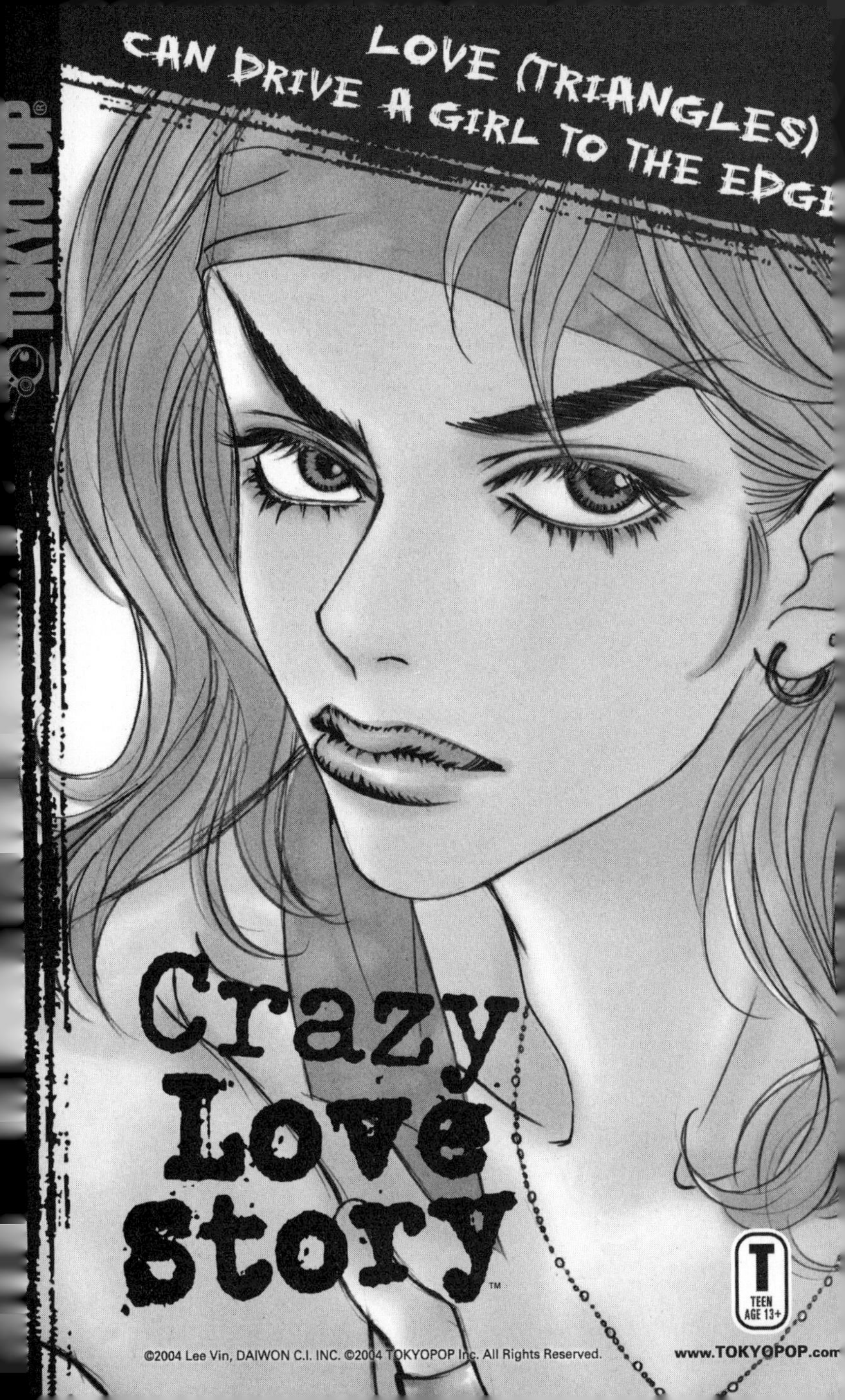
LOVE (TRIANGLES)
CAN DRIVE A GIRL TO THE EDGE
TOKYOPOP
Crazy Love Story™
T TEEN AGE 13+
©2004 Lee Vin, DAIWON C.I. INC. ©2004 TOKYOPOP Inc. All Rights Reserved.
www.TOKYOPOP.com

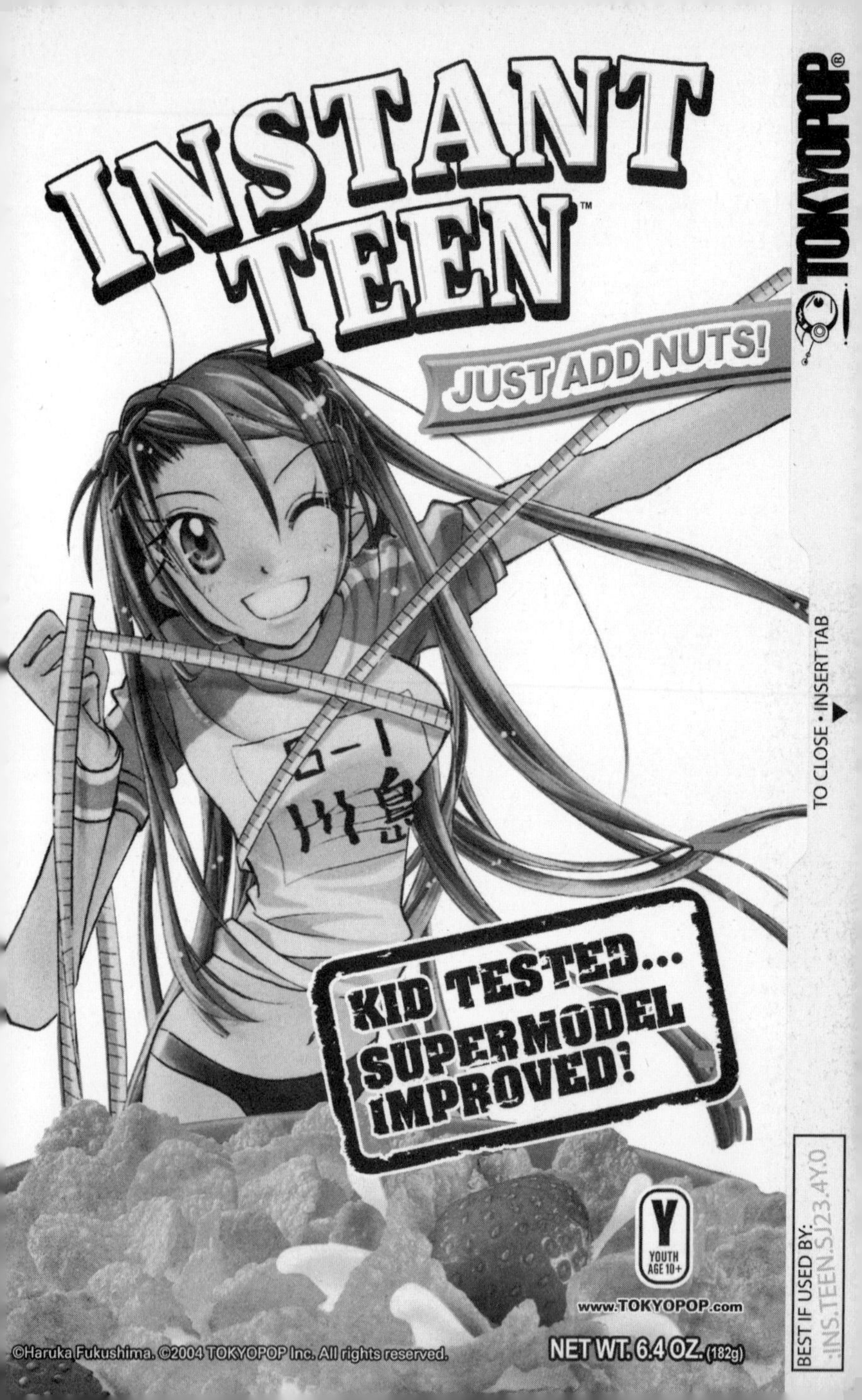
TOKYOPOP®
INSTANT TEEN™
JUST ADD NUTS!
TO CLOSE • INSERT TAB ▼
KID TESTED...
SUPERMODEL
IMPROVED!
Y
YOUTH
AGE 10+
BEST IF USED BY:
INS.TEEN.SJ23.4Y.0
www.TOKYOPOP.com
©Haruka Fukushima. ©2004 TOKYOPOP Inc. All rights reserved.
NET WT. 6.4 OZ. (182g)

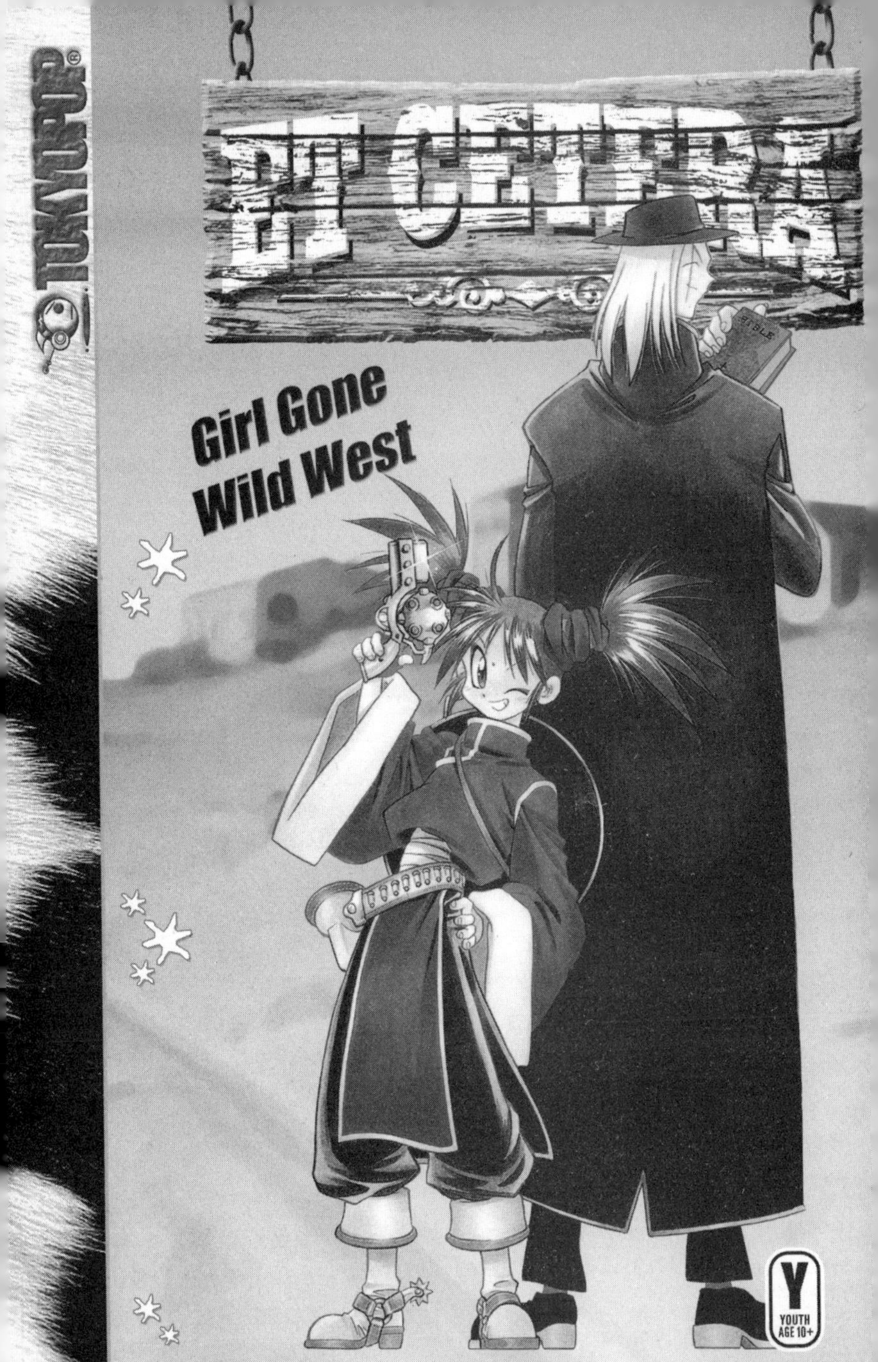
TOKYOPOP®
Girl Gone
Wild West
Y
YOUTH
AGE 10+

ALSO AVAILABLE FROM  TOKYOPOP®

You want it? We got it!
A full range of TOKYOPOP
products are available now at:
www.TOKYOPOP.com/shop

08.20.04T

ALSO AVAILABLE FROM 🔘TOKYOPOP®

MANGA

.HACK//LEGEND OF THE TWILIGHT
@LARGE
ABENOBASHI: MAGICAL SHOPPING ARCADE
A.I. LOVE YOU
AI YORI AOSHI
ALICHINO
ANGELIC LAYER
ARM OF KANNON
BABY BIRTH
BATTLE ROYALE
BATTLE VIXENS
BOYS BE...
BRAIN POWERED
BRIGADOON
B'TX
CANDIDATE FOR GODDESS, THE
CARDCAPTOR SAKURA
CARDCAPTOR SAKURA - MASTER OF THE CLOW
CHOBITS
CHRONICLES OF THE CURSED SWORD
CLAMP SCHOOL DETECTIVES
CLOVER
COMIC PARTY
CONFIDENTIAL CONFESSIONS
CORRECTOR YUI
COWBOY BEBOP
COWBOY BEBOP: SHOOTING STAR
CRAZY LOVE STORY
CRESCENT MOON
CROSS
CULDCEPT
CYBORG 009
D•N•ANGEL
DEARS
DEMON DIARY
DEMON ORORON, THE
DEUS VITAE
DIGIMON
DIGIMON TAMERS
DIGIMON ZERO TWO
DOLL
DRAGON HUNTER
DRAGON KNIGHTS
DRAGON VOICE
DREAM SAGA
DUKLYON: CLAMP SCHOOL DEFENDERS
EERIE QUEERIE!
ERICA SAKURAZAWA: COLLECTED WORKS
ET CETERA
ETERNITY
EVIL'S RETURN
FAERIES' LANDING
FAKE
FLCL
FLOWER OF THE DEEP SLEEP, THE
FORBIDDEN DANCE
FRUITS BASKET

G GUNDAM
GATEKEEPERS
GETBACKERS
GIRL GOT GAME
GRAVITATION
GTO
GUNDAM SEED ASTRAY
GUNDAM WING
GUNDAM WING: BATTLEFIELD OF PACIFISTS
GUNDAM WING: ENDLESS WALTZ
GUNDAM WING: THE LAST OUTPOST (G-UNIT)
HANDS OFF!
HAPPY MANIA
HARLEM BEAT
HYPER RUNE
I.N.V.U.
IMMORTAL RAIN
INITIAL D
INSTANT TEEN: JUST ADD NUTS
ISLAND
JING: KING OF BANDITS
JING: KING OF BANDITS - TWILIGHT TALES
JULINE
KARE KANO
KILL ME, KISS ME
KINDAICHI CASE FILES, THE
KING OF HELL
KODOCHA: SANA'S STAGE
LAMENT OF THE LAMB
LEGAL DRUG
LEGEND OF CHUN HYANG, THE
LES BIJOUX
LOVE HINA
LOVE OR MONEY
LUPIN III
LUPIN III: WORLD'S MOST WANTED
MAGIC KNIGHT RAYEARTH I
MAGIC KNIGHT RAYEARTH II
MAHOROMATIC: AUTOMATIC MAIDEN
MAN OF MANY FACES
MARMALADE BOY
MARS
MARS: HORSE WITH NO NAME
MINK
MIRACLE GIRLS
MIYUKI-CHAN IN WONDERLAND
MODEL
MOURYOU KIDEN: LEGEND OF THE NYMPHS
NECK AND NECK
ONE
ONE I LOVE, THE
PARADISE KISS
PARASYTE
PASSION FRUIT
PEACH GIRL
PEACH GIRL: CHANGE OF HEART
PET SHOP OF HORRORS
PITA-TEN
PLANET LADDER

08.20.04

STOP!

This is the back of the book.
You wouldn't want to spoil a great ending!

This book is printed "manga-style," in the authentic Japanese right-to-left format. Since none of the artwork has been flipped or altered, readers get to experience the story just as the creator intended. You've been asking for it, so TOKYOPOP® delivered: authentic, hot-off-the-press, and far more fun!

DIRECTIONS

If this is your first time reading manga-style, here's a quick guide to help you understand how it works.

It's easy... just start in the top right panel and follow the numbers. Have fun, and look for more 100% authentic manga from TOKYOPOP®!